FROM CORPORATE SOCIAL RESPONSIBILITY TO CORPORATE SOCIAL LIABILITY

This book provides a critical socio-legal study that brings together the latest scholarly advances on corporate social responsibility, and, at the same time, addresses the pressing issue of corporate liability for harmful acts across the supply and production chains.

Corporations have seldom been held responsible and virtually never liable for the acts of their subsidiaries and subcontractors. Actors as different as workers, investors, individual consumers, and shareholder activists claim that corporations should accept greater responsibility for communities and environments affected by their activities.

The book argues that a global value chain's head corporations remain immune to any liability because of the 'economically dependent-legally independent' relationships between core corporations and their periphery suppliers and subcontractors. To tackle this problem, globally, the author acknowledges that 'we' as a society need to reduce the economic dependence as described above – which is far too excessive – by ensuring a level playing field both economically and socially. More concretely, she argues that in order to realise transnational corporate liability, 'we' as lawyers need to find a way (or ways) to establish legally effective relationships between head corporations and their economically dependent entities.

Readers of this book will be able to export the concept of corporate social liability, developed in the context of value chains, and apply it to other contexts involving corporate activities where they need to tackle unrestrained corporate freedom and make global businesses responsible and socially useful.

From Corporate Social Responsibility to Corporate Social Liability

A Socio-Legal Study of Corporate Liability in Global Value Chains

Anna Aseeva

•HART•
OXFORD • LONDON • NEW YORK • NEW DELHI • SYDNEY

HART PUBLISHING

Bloomsbury Publishing Plc

Kemp House, Chawley Park, Cumnor Hill, Oxford, OX2 9PH, UK

1385 Broadway, New York, NY 10018, USA

29 Earlsfort Terrace, Dublin 2, Ireland

HART PUBLISHING, the Hart/Stag logo, BLOOMSBURY and the Diana logo are trademarks of Bloomsbury Publishing Plc

First published in Great Britain 2021

A catalogue record for this book is available from the British Library.

Library of Congress Cataloging-in-Publication data

Names: Aseeva, Anna, author.

Title: From corporate social responsibility to corporate social liability : a socio-legal study of corporate liability in global value chains / Anna Aseeva.

Description: Oxford, UK ; New York, NY : Hart Publishing, an imprint of Bloomsbury Publishing, 2021. | Based on author's thesis (doctoral - Institut d'études politiques de Paris, 2016) issued under title: Global good process standards and world trade law. | Includes bibliographical references and index.

Identifiers: LCCN 2021002345 (print) | LCCN 2021002346 (ebook) | ISBN 9781509930579 (hardback) | ISBN 9781509949144 (paperback) | ISBN 9781509930586 (pdf) | ISBN 9781509930593 (Epub)

Subjects: LCSH: Social responsibility of business—Law and legislation. | Tort liability of corporations. | Tort liability of subsidiary corporations. | Business logistics. | Foreign trade regulation.

Classification: LCC K1329.5 .A974 2021 (print) | LCC K1329.5 (ebook) | DDC 346/.065—dc23

LC record available at https://lccn.loc.gov/2021002345

LC ebook record available at https://lccn.loc.gov/2021002346

ISBN: HB: 978-1-50993-057-9
ePDF: 978-1-50993-058-6
ePub: 978-1-50993-059-3

Typeset by Compuscript Ltd, Shannon

To find out more about our authors and books visit www.hartpublishing.co.uk. Here you will find extracts, author information, details of forthcoming events and the option to sign up for our newsletters.

ACKNOWLEDGEMENTS

Working on my first ever book has been thrilling yet enriching, and I have much to be thankful for. This project began as a PhD thesis at the Sciences Po Law School and was completed during my visiting stay as a Shirley Greenberg International Visiting Scholar at the Faculty of Law-Common Law Section, University of Ottawa.

In between the point of departure and the final destination the project has changed immensely, and my journey of research and writing was supported by La Fondation nationale des sciences politiques (France), Georgetown University Law Center (Washington, DC, the US), National Research University 'Higher School of Economics' (Russia), and the Shirley Greenberg Chair of Women and the Legal Profession at the University of Ottawa (Canada). I am grateful to each of these institutions for their hospitality and support.

I am fortunate to work in an exciting field. Before growing into an engaged legal scholar, I was a trainee at a British leading corporate law firm, worked in commodities trading, then departed towards non-profit to work with corporate social responsibility, and then dealt with sustainable investments at the United Nations in Geneva. Therefore, a more socially useful, responsible, and, indeed, liable global business is not an empty term for me, but a lived experience, a long-term objective, and a life-long vision. This book bears the imprint of many colleagues whose work I admire greatly. For comments, criticism, and support of many kinds, I thank Pascale Cornut St-Pierre, Dimitry Kochenov, Derek McKee, Rafał Mańko, Penelope Simons, and Ada Siqueira.

At Hart Publishing, I owe my deepest thanks to my editor, Roberta Bassi, who managed the manuscript with patience and acumen. I am also deeply indebted to the anonymous reviewers whose useful feedback and comments substantially improved the project. I owe many thanks to the staff at Hart Publishing. This book has also benefited from help from the brilliant and dedicated research assistants Valeria Butyrina and Yulia Dragunova.

Although in all cases the argument of this book is original and thus differs substantially from what has appeared elsewhere in print, small portions of some sections have appeared in my earlier publications. They are the following: 'Global Trade Governance and Informal Voluntary Standards: the Socio-normative Analysis of Legitimacy of the ISO' in A Tutumlu and G Güngör (eds), *Multilateralism in Global Governance. Formal and Informal Institutions* (Oxford, Peter Lang, 2016); '(Un)Sustainable Development(s) in International Economic Law: a Quest for Sustainability' (2018) 10(11) *Sustainability* 4022; 'Développements récents en matière de la protection des droits de l'Homme et de l'environnement dans les chaines globales de valeur', in C Titi (ed), *Droits de l'homme et droit international économique* (Brussels, Bruylant, 2019).

CONTENTS

ABBREVIATIONS AND ACRONYMS

ADR	alternative dispute resolution
ATS	US Alien Tort Statute
B2B	business-to-business
B2C	business-to-consumer
BAP	Best Aquaculture Practice
BCCA	British Columbia Court of Appeal
CAFE	Coffee and Farmer Equity
CASCO	ISO's Committee on Conformity Assessment
CAT	UN Convention against Torture and Other Cruel, Inhuman or Degrading Treatment
CEDAW	Convention on the Elimination of All Forms of Discrimination Against Women
CERD	Committee on the Elimination of Racial Discrimination
CETA	Comprehensive Economic and Trade Agreement
CITES	Convention on International Trade in Endangered Species of Wild Fauna and Flora
COPOLCO	ISO's Committee on Consumer Policy
CSL	corporate social liability
CSP	corporate social performance
CSR	corporate social responsibility
DDHC	Declaration of the Rights of Man and the Citizen 1789
DEFRA	UK Department for Environment, Food and Rural Affairs
DGCCRF	*Direction Générale de la Concurrence, de la Consommation et de la Répression des Fraudes*
ECT	Energy Charter Treaty
ECJ	European Court of Justice

ECOSOC	UN Economic and Social Council
EICC	Electronic Industry Citizenship Coalition
EMAS	Eco-Management and Audit Scheme
EUCMR	EU Conflict Minerals Regulation (Regulation (EU) No 2017/821)
EUNFRD	EU Non-Financial Reporting Directive
EUTR	EU Timber Regulation (Regulation (EU) No 995/2010)
FAO	Food and Agricultural Organisation
FDI	foreign direct investment
FLA	Fair Labor Association
FLEGT	EU Forest Law Enforcement, Governance and Trade Action Plan
FPIC	free, prior and informed consent
FPICON	free, prior and informed consultation
FSC	Forest Stewardship Council
GAL	global administrative law
GAO	General Administrative Order
GAP	Good Agricultural Practices
GATT	General Agreement on Tariffs and Trade
GCC	global commodity chain
GFA	global framework agreement
GRI	Global Reporting Initiative
GSCP	Global Social Compliance Program
GVC	global value chain
HACCP	Hazard Analysis, Critical Control Point
ICJ	International Court of Justice
ICPPED	International Convention for the Protection of All Persons from Enforced Disappearance
ICPRAMW	International Convention on the Protection of the Rights of All Migrant Workers

ICSID	International Centre for Settlement of Investment Disputes
IFA	international framework agreement
IFS	International Food Standard
ILLA	international investment law and arbitration
IMF	International Monetary Fund
ISEAL	International Social and Environmental Accreditation and Labelling
ISO	International Organization for Standardization
ITO	International Trade Organization
MHRDD	mandatory human rights due diligence
MNCs	multinational corporations
MNEs	multinational enterprises
MSC	Marine Stewardship Council
NAPs	National Action Plans on Business and Human Rights
NCP	National Contact Point
NGO	non-governmental organisation
NIE	New Institutional Economics
NIEO	New International Economic Order
NSP	National Service Program
OECD	Organisation for Economic Co-operation and Development
OEEC	Organisation for European Economic Co-operation
OEIGWG	Open-ended Intergovernmental Working Group
OSCJ	Ontario Superior Court of Justice
PCA	Permanent Court of Arbitration
PIEL	Public International Economic Law
PPM	process and production method
PSSA	Private Security Services Abroad
RBI	Swiss Popular Initiative on Responsible Business
RSPO	Roundtable on Sustainable Palm Oil

SCC	Supreme Court of Canada
SEC	Securities and Exchange Commission
SMEs	small- and medium-sized enterprises
SQF	Safe Quality Food
TBHR	Treaty on Business and Human Rights
TCA	transnational company agreement
TNCs	transnational corporations
UKSC	UK Supreme Court
UN	United Nations
UNCITRAL	United Nations Commission on International Trade Law
UNCTAD	United Nations Conference on Trade and Development
UNCTNC	United Nations Commission on Transnational Corporations
UNGC	UN Global Compact
UNGPs	UNHRC's Guiding Principles on Business and Human Rights
UNHRC	UN Human Rights Council
WGTI	Working Group on the Relationship between Trade and Investment
WTO	World Trade Organisation
WWF	World Wide Fund for Nature

TABLE OF CASES

Canada

European Union

International

France

Germany

The Netherlands

Sweden

United Kingdom

United States

TABLE OF LEGISLATION

Australia

European Union

International

France

Germany

Hong Kong

The Netherlands

Russian Federation

Switzerland

United Kingdom

United States

PART I

On the Limits of Law and a Limitless Globalised Market

1

Introduction

I. Meet Corporate Social Liability

Globalisation has overwhelmingly expanded the operating scope of corporations, rendering commonplace cost-saving arrangements such as subcontracting. Today's global economy is shaped by transborder production webs – global value chains (GVCs). In 2019, GVCs accounted for more than two-thirds of the world's economy.[1]

However, to date, virtually limitless corporate power along GVCs bypasses traditional forms of both private law liability and state public control. Indeed, at each distinct attempt to regulate such power through corporate social responsibility (CSR), transparency, due diligence disciplines, and orthodox contract and corporate governance, as well as public international law and human rights channels, law – properly so called – did not seem to work. Arguably, the existing framework of applicable law acted as an enabler of corporate irresponsibility in GVCs, and, indeed, of the massive increase in the number of GVCs themselves. At the same time, the advent and proliferation of GVCs seemed to bring about a structural change to the legal face of the global political economy. Namely, through GVC production and trade, core corporations created a relationship of high economic dependence between them and the periphery firms, and thus introduced a whole system of *economically* dependent but *legally* quite independent entities.

Simultaneously, a general acceptance of the fact that at the end of the day corporations do whatever maximises their profits has resulted in a normalisation of both social irresponsibility and legal impunity of corporations operating transnationally. Throughout this book, I aim to challenge this somewhat fatalistic acceptance.

More precisely, I intend to fill the relevant gaps by adding to the research on and practice of the preventive, anticipatory and proactive ethical obligations of corporations, their transparency and due diligence obligations, which are prescriptive in nature, as well as some proscriptive disciplines such as corporate and contractual liability. The latter disciplines, whilst proscriptive, are mostly toothless in the context of GVCs, as they generally protect corporations from liability for the acts and omissions of their economically dependent entities – typically, subcontractors

[1] World Bank Global Value Chain Development Report 2019 *Technological Innovation, Supply Chain Trade and Workers in a Globalized World* (2019) https://www.worldbank.org/en/topic/trade/publication/global-value-chain-development-report-2019.

and other suppliers. Therefore, I chose the context of GVCs as a litmus test that helps to reveal the true colours of corporate responsibility towards third parties and society at large, hence the 'social' in the term 'corporate social liability'.

A key argument of this book is the following: due to the particular form of GVC production and trade, a chain's head corporations remain immune to any liability because of the 'economically dependent-legally independent' relationships between core corporations and their periphery suppliers and subcontractors. To tackle this problem, globally, 'we' as a society need to reduce the economic dependence as described above – which is far too excessive – by ensuring a level playing field both economically and socially. More concretely, in order to realise transnational corporate liability, 'we' as lawyers need to find a way (or ways) to establish *legally effective relationships* between head corporations and their economically dependent entities. While my ambition in this book is not to propose concrete legislation, as I aim rather at canvassing a roadmap towards such corporate liability, I will of course paint a picture of an emerging legal framework in my conclusions. Readers of this book will be able to export the concept of corporate social liability (CSL), developed in the context of value chains, and apply it to other contexts involving corporate activities where they need to tackle unrestrained corporate freedom and make global businesses responsible and socially useful.

The present book is a critical and contextual study of the 'why' and 'what' of CSL in the context of GVCs. The 'why' question is also followed by a 'how' question, which highlights the complexities inherent in CSL. In this introductory chapter, I set the stage for thinking about CSL. I begin by addressing the questions, 'why CSL?' in section II and 'what does CSL cover?' in section III. I also explain the focus, theory, approach and methods of the present book, as well as its apparent limitations (section IV). In section V, I summarise the structure of the book.

II. Why Corporate Social Liability?

A. Purposes of This Book

Until now, stories of nature, livelihoods, or lives being destroyed by GVC capitalism in countries on the periphery of global production have failed to shock the public anywhere near as much as the story of humans dying from a virus, such as the 2020 coronavirus (Covid-19) pandemic, in the centre of global production. Possibly, if the media provided daily updates (as they did for the number of Covid cases) on the natural habitats destroyed and thousands of people dead or dying along GVCs, this might challenge the status quo. But it is entirely possible that even that level of publicity would fail to generate a response. This leads to one of the biggest issues of our time, which goes beyond legal or even legal-political problems: the normalisation of irresponsibility and impunity for the wrongdoings of corporations who operate transnationally. It is therefore crucial to tell a different story, which, before looking for solutions to the above problem, first addresses its root causes.

Hence, the question 'why CSL?' arose because, until now, corporations had seldom been held accountable – and virtually never legally responsible – for transboundary harm along GVCs that often results from their subsidiaries' and subcontractors' acts or omissions. The wrongs attributable to corporations operating transnationally stretch from armed conflicts and atrocities within and across third world countries, through discrimination and violence against indigenous peoples and local communities in both first and third worlds, to pollution, destruction of the environment, and global climate crisis. For some time, actors as diverse as academics, workers, investors, members of civil society, and individual consumers have argued that corporations should finally take on a fair part of their responsibility for the individuals, communities, and environments affected by the outsourcing of their operations. At the same time, nowadays there seems to be a certain acceptance by society at large that such atrocities are here to stay, thanks to the ever-tightening grip of global capitalism.

The question 'why global value chains?' arose because GVCs epitomise contemporary forms of global capitalism. It is argued that GVCs are essentially marked by a shift from vertically integrated firms to the horizontal contractual arrangements between affiliated entities within a transnational network of enterprises.[2] For more than a century, traditional contract and corporate law constructs of privity, separate legal personality, and limited liability have been reducing the exposure of vertically-integrated corporations to law enforcement action. Today, those constructs make it even more difficult to enforce law against the GVC lead firms because of the horizontal nature of dispersed GVC production. GVCs thus reshape and streamline the whole geoeconomics of – now, globalised – production, thus also marking a legal transformation of transborder business transactions and broader international economic relations. Those dynamics, in turn, introduce multiple governance gaps: not only distributional disparities both in terms of geographic location and social group, but also regulatory ones across and between jurisdictions and regions. Together those gaps constitute, in legal terms, a responsibility deficit *within*, and indeed *of*, GVCs.

As Duncan Kennedy said, in paraphrasing Max Weber, 'interpretation positing gaplessness requires the interpreter to apply in every case, according to their meanings, the legal norms he or she can derive textually, conceptually, or through precedent; it categorically forbids reference to purposes and policies'.[3] While Kennedy addressed particular issues of legal interpretation, and not GVC capitalism, the opposite, *gap-filling*, approach of this book is an inclusion of other relevant

[2] PT Muchlinski, '"Global Bukowina" Examined: Viewing the Multinational Enterprise as a Transnational Law- making Community' in G Teubner (ed), *Global Law Without a State* (London, Dartmouth Publishing Co Ltd, 1997) 79, 81–84.

[3] D Kennedy, 'Legal Formalism' in NJ Smelser and PB Baltes (eds), *Encyclopaedia of the Social and Behavioural Sciences*, vol 13 (Amsterdam, Elsevier, 2001) 8634, 8635.

contexts, looking precisely at the purposes and policies behind applicable – as well as non-applicable – legal norms. As noted above, today we badly need a story that, before looking for the solutions to the problem, will address the root causes of the problem. This book is different from most book-length existing literature on the subject-matter, in that it looks squarely at other, non-legal but nonetheless still relevant contexts to explain the contemporary legal status quo regarding transnational corporate liability. Relevant historico-dogmatic, social, economic, and political accounts all blend together to form what I refer to in this book as 'GVC context'.

Today's transnational 'GVC' norms comprise CSR, corporate, and contractual regimes, as well as transparency, due diligence, and liability legislation. My general idea behind the project for this book is that canvassing everything that happens under the banner of 'corporate social liability' – all that is debated, decided, produced, and dropped – can give us a new understanding of transnational economic governance in more subtle ways, moving beyond either doctrinal and dogmatic deficit or excess.

Where does the term 'CSL' come from? Contrary to corporate accountability, sustainability, CSR, *just* social responsibility and *just* corporate liability, it is not a phrase that is widely – if at all – used, as I coined the term 'corporate social liability' myself. Corporate liability generally covers the extent to which a corporation as a legal person can be held liable for the actions of its managers and employees, including personal injury claims, corporate manslaughter and corporate homicide – thus being a mere employer's responsibility for whatever its employees do, typically by negligence, including numerous exceptions to such liability. The tort of negligence and the tort of breach of statutory duty are the typical venues, and corporations are thus virtually never exposed to broader claims by local communities, environmental groups, and civil society in general. CSR is a set of responsibilities a corporation has towards its stakeholders, including its creditors, its investors, its employees, its community and its environment, and even society at large. However, CSR responsibilities are ethical and not legal. Social responsibility is a predecessor of CSR. It occurred well before the rise and dominance of the corporate form of business organisation and aimed at preventing labour problems, improving workers' basic living conditions and thus boosting the production performance of the factory system emerging in the UK and the US in the mid-1800s.[4] Social responsibility was discretionary and in essence represented mere (corporate) philanthropy. Both sustainability and corporate accountability emerged later than CSR – in the 1990s – but, together with other similar themes of business ethics, such as corporate social performance (CSP), stakeholder theory, and corporate citizenship, constitute ethical rather than legal obligations of corporations.[5] None of the above concepts

[4] A Carroll, 'A History of Corporate Social Responsibility: Concepts and Practices' in A Crane et al (eds), *The Oxford Handbook of Corporate Social Responsibility* (Oxford, Oxford University Press, 2008) 19, 20.

[5] ibid 37.

correctly address the legal responsibility of head corporations with respect to their value chains, thus also covering the acts and omissions of entities economically dependent on corporations within one value chain. Therefore, I argue, introducing CSL is necessary to cover the extent to which head corporations can be held liable for harm, including that which arises out of acts and omissions by their economically dependent entities, towards all stakeholders of their value chains, including their community and their environment, and even society at large.

Indeed, 'delegating', 'subcontracting', 'offshoring' – in a word, 'outsourcing' – seems to have become the institutional vertebrae of contemporary production, market and, indeed, the core of our way of life. In this book, I suggest that starting from the fairly naïve enquiry, 'what is, really, corporate social liability in global value chains?' could help to understand GVC governance as something entirely different: neither innately global nor local, neither essentially public nor private. CSL in GVCs is also, I argue, a set of legal responsibilities of a dominant influencer over transactions in a chain for harm-causing incidents, including negative environmental, social, and economic consequences, as well as obligations to prevent those.

In this book, I seek to critically assess the premises, dynamics, current state of play, and likely future development of the concept and application of corporate social liability. The book first identifies the legal obstacles to CSL. It next explores the theory and policy shifts that are necessary to promote CSL. Finally, it enquires into whether – and, if so, how – CSL could and should be introduced along GVCs. I thus intend to complement the doctrinal (mostly private law) scholarly advances that exist to date.

B. General Outline of the Argument

There is nothing new under the sun. This statement may seem exaggerated, but there is also a good deal of truth to it. The majority of the foundations of the general theoretical framework of this book (ie norms as behavioural imperatives, norms as social facts, norms as subjective perceptions) which led to the development of a socio-legal conception of corporate liability in GVCs were developed – for the most part a century ago – by prominent scholars in law and social sciences. The general theoretical postulate of the socio-legal approach used in this book remains the same: law reflects society.[6] Likewise, the specific doctrinal framework of the book – ie the alternating conceptions of value chains as 'one-off' and 'relational' contracting, as well as the applicable orthodox doctrines, such as tort of negligence, classical and neo-classical contract law, institutional economics premises, and value chains governance studies – have existed for several decades.

[6] Variations on this are possible, such as that law reflects society (and its solidarity) as it is at the present moment (E Durkheim, *The Division of Labor in Society* (New York, Free Press, 1947) 52); or that law is the result of the felt – or constructed – needs of current society (LM Friedman, *The Legal System: A Social Science Perspective* (New York, Russel Sage Foundation, 1975) 5–23).

However, what the general theoretical framework tells me about the specific doctrinal and practical approaches to the subject-matter is that formal orthodox law, as a stable pre-given institution within the actual legal systems of advanced capitalist societies, often remains frozen, while business and economic frameworks advance independently and more rapidly. In the case of this book, the relevant framework evolved into GVCs in the blind spots of most traditional twentieth century approaches to transboundary production and trade, thus creating the so-called governance gaps. The spontaneity of the past century's 'double movement' of business and economic progress, coupled with a freeze of the corresponding legal framework, is at least plainly dubious.

In the twenty-first century, and especially during the last ten years, there has been a sharp increase in litigation, including strategic litigation, aimed at establishing the transnational liability of parent or lead companies' for harms arising from transborder production. Since 2010, national and regional (EU) legislation aimed at regulating offshore production, and specifically GVCs, has also risen. Those developments mark a regulatory move from the traditional private governance and public international (mostly, soft) law approaches to global corporate production towards more local and 'legalistic' approaches to GVC production. Because of the transversal nature of GVCs, it is necessary to emphasise the constantly expanding role of corporations as public actors, as well as the consequences for society at large. In other words, my analysis goes beyond the private law issues of production processes and extends to all GVC actors: businesses, workers, civil society, individual consumers, shareholder activists, local communities, and the environment.

From a more critical perspective, we must ask what the drivers of this recent regulatory shift towards CSL are. The overall socio-legal nature of the present analysis thus lies in a metalevel enquiry of this book: does the emerging discipline of CSL confirm or refute the theory that law reflects society?

III. What does Corporate Social Liability Cover?

A. Manifold Aspects of CSL

As is clear from the previous section, the proposed concept of CSL is not grounded in contract, tort, or even corporate (as the term itself may suggest) law alone. A literal interpretation of the term 'corporate social liability' may thus be more elusive than might first appear. This difficulty may be partially attributed to linguistics. Contrast, for instance, the specific English word 'liability' with the French term 'responsabilité'[7] or the Russian term 'ответственность', which could mean both responsibility and liability.[8] Conversely, the English words 'responsibility'

[7] Note that in French, liability means civil liability (*la responsabilité civile*).

[8] These include both political (ie political accountability) and moral responsibilities, and legal (say, tort or criminal) liability.

and 'liability' have clearer and distinct meanings. Whereas the term 'responsibility' means either to be considerate and responsible for the consequences of one's actions, or to owe a moral duty of care, 'liability' usually refers to the *legal* duties (not necessarily only civil law duties, which is implicit in the French translation of liability) and responsibilities flowing from one's actions.[9]

Yet, the problem is also a consequence of the various ways in which corporate liability, including production liability, is presented in the existing scholarly literature. While much of the previous research has focused on corporate and/or GVC governance mechanisms embedded in contract and (less so) in torts, the fastest growing area of scholarship is the study of foreign direct liability and potential lead firms' transnational 'hybrid' liability for the acts of their subsidiaries and subcontractors. Against this background, I undertake to study and fill the gaps apparent in standard legal-doctrinal approaches to the role of norms in analysing lead firms' liability for harms that occur along their GVCs.

The existing English-language book-length treatment of production-related corporate liability does not always focus on comparative approaches to transnational corporate liability. Nor does it devote enough attention to liability for activities other than production, such as, most typically, services and operations. Taking into account the discussion on the earlier concept and practice of *social responsibility* (section II.A), CSL is first about corporate liability for the effects of production, services, and operations – a responsibility ex post, but also, second, about the corporate responsibility of (re)distribution – a responsibility which is mostly ex ante, such as caring about health and safety in the workplace, training of workers, protecting the environment, and such like. Currently, the focus on normative questions, including the sudden need for an enhanced corporate liability in GVCs, possibly disguised regional and national(istic) protectionism, and distributive justice, is also insufficient. Moreover, in the majority of the existing books, the subject-matter is approached from either private (contract, tort/delict, CSR) *or* international (mostly human rights) perspectives, but virtually never from both perspectives. None of the books acknowledge GVCs as a horizontal continuation of the vertically-integrated and contract-based modern business corporation, and, at the same time, as connectivity norms (and, indeed, a new legal system) of global economic relations.

B. Substantive Scope of the Book

In this book, I initially survey various traditional approaches to the regulation of transborder production, which focus primarily on methods that conceal or remove altogether the issues of GVC production from their local political, environmental, or social contexts (eg voluntary and private self-regulation, soft approaches in various international arrangements, or – most typically – international trade and

[9] This account excludes the doctrine of state responsibility in international law.

investment law). I also provide an overview of relevant orthodox theories underpinning classical contract, tort, and corporate (or company) law that allow the GVC production to pass under the radar of responsibility, let alone liability.

I aim to address the root causes of the problem of blind spots in GVC production. Therefore, a historical and conceptual excursion in the first chapters demonstrates the fundamental rationale of the appearance, growing popularity, and use of voluntary corporate governance schemes in transboundary business relations, as key twentieth-century paradigms change.

By presenting the core elements of the notion of private firms' societal responsibility in a dynamic relationship of development and interdependence, the necessary historical and conceptual overview at the beginning of the book lays down solid groundwork for the remainder of the analysis. It informs us that the world-systems and dependency theories developed in the late 1970s were among the first to theorise an explosion in the number of what we know today as GVCs. An international division of labour, ie the 'international' or 'world' system, favours some countries to the detriment of others and limits the latter's development possibilities. Such disasters as the Rana Plaza collapse are indirect yet empirical proofs of the main postulates of these two theories. Global CSR standards were generally conceived to deal with risks and uncertainties along value chains, including risks occurring in such parts of the world-system as the Rana Plaza garment factory's country, Bangladesh.

I therefore look at the various possibilities, as well as their strengths and weaknesses, for realising corporate liability in GVCs. One option, which is supplemental to a (quasi)judicialisation and an enhanced legalisation of CSL, but no less feasible, is to study behavioural impacts through subjective perception and overall social context. One practical example may be the Bangladesh Accord (Accord on Fire and Building Safety, binding western garment brands and global and local unions). It seeks to affect non-signatories and encourages outsiders to use the information to influence signatories. Having an impact on the behaviour of a lead firm in a GVC could also theoretically change behavioural patterns along the entire chain.

Additionally, drawing on the theoretical model of CSL norms proposed further in this introductory chapter, increasing the hard law character of a commitment through the use of binding language – especially the use of concrete formal sanctions and/or of an obligation of result – might have a deterrent effect, thus inadvertently enforcing a law or a contractual clause ex ante.

I thus use the theoretical accounts of the norm concept to study and explain *how* legal norms governing transborder production should be – and indeed are – construed, thus grounding a normative theory for CSL law on an internal level. 'Internal' is used here with reference to Lawrence Friedman's divide between 'internal/external legal culture'. Friedman contrasts the behaviours and views of those who make the law with the attitudes of the general public towards the law.[10]

[10] The concept of legal culture as used here is mainly concerned with compliance in law. See generally LM Friedman, 'Is there a Modern Legal Culture?' (1994) 7 *Ratio Juris* 117. But see Cotterrell, who says

In the final part of the book I further enquire as to *why* the legal norms of GVC liability are – or should be – construed as they are today in general public debate, thereby explaining the law of CSL from a somewhat external normative angle.

Finally, interdisciplinary approach and methods feature prominently in about a third of the chapters that follow. Since comparative law can serve a variety of purposes, the book initially uses the comparative approach to set the stage, after which normative and behavioural perspectives take the lead. Overall, special emphasis is given to the interdisciplinary dimension, as explained in the following section.

IV. The Book's Approach and Methods

The belief underpinning this book's approach is that the best way to do socio-legal work relevant to the subject matter is by using inductive rather than deductive reasoning. Here, this means studying recent examples of both successful and failed attempts to hold corporations responsible in various fora. I look not only at national and international legal systems but also at some investment (and divestment) possibilities and (de)funding schemes, as well as processes before non-judicial bodies, such as the OECD national contact points. I then try to draw defensible inferences based upon what can be observed about the functioning of law in these episodes. The main source of data used in this book is textual.

A. Comparative Approach

Comparative law approaches will not be ignored. In general, such approaches look at how relevant laws vary across countries and how improvements, based on observed models, may be made. In this sense, this book goes further than a traditional comparative law analysis. Specifically, this book is predominantly (but not exclusively) about the 'what' and the 'why' rather than the 'how' of CSL. Regarding the comparative approach, in this book I privilege the methods traditionally known as 'substantive law and society' – looking at law shaping society and vice versa – in combining the comparative approach with a socio-legal perspective.[11] I then go one step further than substantive socio-legal comparative law, by enquiring *why* this law is applied, which could be called, by analogy, 'normative law and society'. I thus consider placing the 'why' ahead of the 'how', without excluding the latter.

In the corresponding chapters of Parts I, II, and III, I provide a legal-doctrinal systematisation of the recent (see eg Chapter 2) and latest (Chapters 3–5) legal

that an internal/external divide is sociologically ungrounded, since law is part of society: R Cotterrell, 'Is there a Logic of Legal Transplants?' in D Nelken and J Feest (eds), *Adapting Legal Culture* (Oxford, Hart Publishing, 2001) 74.

[11] See eg M Siems, *Comparative Law*, 2nd edn (Cambridge, Cambridge University Press, 2018) 167–78.

debates over the regulation of transboundary production and positive law efforts to tackle the issue. In particular, in relevant orthodox legal doctrine as well as positive law developments, the debate centres primarily on conceptualisations of contract, tort, and product liability, as well as their interpretation and application in practice. I therefore initially try to distil perceptions of 'corporation' as an organisational form, network, or platform for contracts, as well as the intertwined relevant roles of contract and tort in different national settings. Such understandings allow me to further emphasise the dogmatic capital and practical problems relevant for liability beyond the separate corporate personality, limited liability, and corporate veil.

This critically-descriptive study of fragmented production structures aims to investigate GVC governance gaps and simultaneously provide a functionally relevant foundation for further discussion on the public-social governance and regulation of GVCs. At this stage, I therefore privilege the functionalist analysis of comparative law. Notably, my use of the functional approach, focusing on the functions of laws in compared legal systems, requires comparability and underlines not only the differences but also similarities thereof.[12] The functionalist approach is preferred over the universalist one; the latter looks at how laws interact and eventually glances at the possibility of their approximation.[13]

For this introductory legal analysis, I have chosen three primary jurisdictional foci. These are English, French, and United States (US) law. According to basic functionalist understandings, these systems belong to three countries that are socio-economically and politically similar (ie all are democracies and advanced market economies with a relatively present rule of law) which nevertheless have different legal systems (common/civil law divide). On this note, English law and, more recently, US law are said to have influenced all common law jurisdictions today, while French law (together with German law) has done the same with respect to civil law.[14] By addressing these three systems, I thus cover these two legal traditions. Furthermore, US law has adopted some civil law principles, while rejecting certain common law ones. In fact, the US 'adversarial legalism' (ie the fact that law-making, enforcement and dispute settlement rely more often on legal threats and lawsuits, and involve higher pecuniary and non-pecuniary penalties) distinguishes it further from both civil and common law countries.[15] The focus is therefore on not two but, to some extent, three different legal families. Similarity of legal systems makes comparison easier, but differences may provide for richer comparisons and more interesting findings.

[12] See eg U Mattei, *Comparative Law and Economics* (Michigan, University of Michigan Press, 1998); K Zweigert and H Kötz, *An Introduction to Comparative Law*, 3rd edn (Oxford, Oxford University Press, 1998); C Milhaupt and K Pistor, *Law and Capitalism: What Corporate Crises Reveal about Legal Systems and Economic Development around the World* (Chicago, University of Chicago Press, 2008).

[13] For a concise and precise discussion of these approaches in comparative law, see eg Siems (n 11) 31–50.

[14] ibid 51–57 and 231–61.

[15] See generally RA Kagan, *Adversarial Legalism: The American Way of Law* (Cambridge, Harvard University Press, 2003). See also F Easterbrook and D Fischel, *The Economic Structure of Corporate Law* (Cambridge, Harvard University Press, 1996).

Last but not least, another objective reason for the choice of jurisdictions is that the selected countries are a few years ahead of other jurisdictions with regard to law reform projects and/or judicial practice. This is particularly evident in France, with the adoption in 2017 of the French vigilance law.[16] In the UK and the US it is especially – though not exclusively – the relevant litigation that outpaces other countries.[17]

At more advanced stages of the legal systematisation, studies of other selected systems, particular legislation and case law will be added, notably from Canada, the Netherlands, Switzerland, Germany, Australia and some other jurisdictions, as well as at EU and international levels. Here, however, the selection depends on the particular type of governance approach to, and regulation paradigm of, GVCs at a transnational level (for instance, 'transparency' or 'due diligence').

Finally, for the purposes of this book, traditional comparative law has important methodological limitations, be it the functionalist approach, which is prioritised in a few chapters of this book, or the set aside universalist scheme, which consists of identifying commonalities and, ultimately, uniformity of relevant law in compared systems.[18] The case-based solutions of both functionalism and universalism primarily focus on positive law without much reference to non-legal factors or to empirical studies on how problems are actually solved.[19] Therefore, the following explains the overall socio-legal approach of this book, which moves beyond traditional legal comparative methods.

B. Explanation of the Theoretical Framework

Employing a socio-legal approach, I analyse the issue of how governance gaps within the GVC legal infrastructure are shaped and reproduced by historical, social, economic, and political conditions.

In general, a socio-legal approach delves into the character, functioning, and effects of law in the broader context. This means analysing law's relationship to society and the state. In particular, a socio-legal approach I adopt here reconceptualises CSL as a social phenomenon embedded in global economic and socio-political developments, and the social structure of GVCs as more general

[16] Loi n°2017-399 relative au devoir de vigilance des sociétés mères et des entreprises donneuses d'ordre, promulguée le 27 mars 2017, JORF n°0074 du 28 mars 2017, texte n° 1.

[17] Case law on corporate liability in value chains is currently on the rise in both the US and the UK. To quote just a few, see *Doe v Wal-Mart Stores, Inc*, 572 F 3d 677 (9th Cir 2009); *Chandler v Cape plc* [2012] EWCA Civ 525; *Kiobel et al v Royal Dutch Petroleum et al*, Case 10-1491, Supreme Court, 17 April 2013; *Rahaman et al v JC Penney Corporation, Inc et al*, CA No N15C-07-174 MMJ, Del Super Ct 4 May 2016; *Lungowe and Others v Vedanta Resources plc and Konkola Copper Mines plc* [2017] EWCA Civ 1528.

[18] See eg *Common Core of European Private Law*, a project that studies comparative contract, tort, and property law, and is especially interested in uniformity (universalism) of European private law, while also examining contradictions and limitations (functionalism) of the surveyed laws. See www.common-core.org/.

[19] Siems (n 11) 39.

transnational relations and culture of outsourcing. The latter impacts law in a very concrete and important way: it creates endless constellations of the binary relationship 'economic dependence-legal independence'. I use a socio-legal perspective as a lens through which to examine more foundational questions about the context in which today's global economic law is created, implemented, and practised. The social phenomena of law, implicating a wide range of actors and institutions, relate their enquiries to the historical context to reveal how, through creating the global periphery, they reproduce inequality, and thus alienation and dependency.

I also blend a critical analysis of ideological, political, and socio-economic contexts with an examination of the roles of various actors (interests), as well as an assessment of the structural (material) and discursive (ideational) contexts, how they change, and how the specificity of contexts shapes legal meaning. Such a lens, mostly drawing on the sociological and historical institutionalism scholarship of Pierre Bourdieu, helps to reveal the law's 'true colours' and thus complements the purely legal-doctrinal analysis, especially in Parts I and IV of the book.

Regarding the core approach underlying the theoretical premises of the method, I mainly infer the legal theory and concept of CSL from the context, and approach the problem in terms of actors, instruments, and practices. I draw on the work of relevant leading legal sociologists, both classic, such as Pierre Bourdieu and Emile Durkheim, and contemporary, such as Lawrence Lessig and the scholars from the Department of Sociology of Law at Lund University. This is because the latter has the most extensive body of work on the sociology of norms in the context of socio-legal studies.[20]

The method consists of distinguishing between the attributes that underlie the nature of norms – together they form the general delineation of the sociological concept of norms – and other attributes that are characteristic of certain groups of norms – namely, any norm-complex, such as therapy, morals, or religion.[21] One of the advantages of this particular model is its adaptability to different scholarly perspectives: it allows a plurality of perspectives to be combined and integrated.

The model of the concept of norms proposed here can be viewed as a number of attributes. The challenge is to identify which attributes are common for all norm-complexes – and are therefore essential – and which ones separate different

[20] See eg H Hydén, 'Looking at the World through the Lenses of Norms' in K Papendorf et al (eds), *Understanding Law in Society, Developments in Socio-legal Studies* (Münster, LIT Verlag, 2011); H Hydén and M Svensson, 'The Concept of Norms in Sociology of Law' (2008) 53 *Scandinavian Studies in Law* 15; M Svensson and S Larsson, 'Intellectual Property Law Compliance in Europe: Illegal File Sharing and the Role of Social Norms' (2012) 14 *New Media Society* 1147; M Svensson et al, 'The Research Bay – Studying the Global File Sharing Community' in B Gallagher and D Halbert (eds), *IP in Context: Law and Society Perspectives on Intellectual Property* (Cambridge, Cambridge University Press, 2013).

[21] Based on P Nonet, 'For Jurisprudential Sociology' (1976) 10 *Law & Society Review* 525; E Colvin, 'The Sociology of Secondary Rules' (1978) 28 *University of Toronto Law Journal* 196; LA Fallers, *Law without Precedent* (Chicago, University of Chicago Press, 1969). See generally R Cotterrell, *The Sociology of Law: An Introduction*, 2nd edn (Oxford, Butterworths, 1992); B Tamanaha, *A General Jurisprudence of Law and Society* (Oxford, Oxford University Press, 2001).

kinds of norms into categories, and are thus additional attributes.[22] The delineation of a legal norm, therefore, includes its essential attributes, common to all norms, as well as its additional attributes specific to legal norms.[23] This amounts to an elementary categorisation between legal norms and social norms.

Specifying and scrutinising additional norm attributes is, therefore, crucial for the study of what is traditionally presented as a distinction between 'law' and 'non-law' properly so called. The focus is on three clusters: (i) the cognitive context in which the norm is active; (ii) the systemic conditions that apply to the relevant situation; and (iii) the values associated with the imperative (ie an essential norm attribute, relating to an 'ought'). As a result, the analysis is expected to deconstruct norms, that is, their raison d'être and driving forces, as well as a description of the environment from which the norm under scrutiny originates.[24]

In the theoretical framework, I identify and situate the essential attributes deemed common for all norm-complexes. The three different key scholarly perspectives on norms that I use in this book are[25] the 'norm' as: (i) a behavioural imperative, drawing mostly on legal positivism;[26] (ii) a social fact, drawing mostly on sociology and sociology of law;[27] and (iii) a subjective perception, drawing mostly on legal psychology and sociology.[28]

Importantly, such compilation of abstract socio-legal theories of the norm also finds a concrete reflection in the relevant management and business ethics

[22] M Svensson, 'Norms in Law and Society: Towards a Definition of the Socio-Legal Concept of Norms' in M Baier (ed), *Social and Legal Norms* (London, Ashgate Publishing, 2013) 40.

[23] ibid.

[24] Hydén and Svensson (n 20) 24.

[25] A similar theoretical framework of all three elements, slightly re-branded, could be found in Lawrence Lessig's seminal work, L Lessig *Code and Other Laws of Cyberspace* (New York, Basic Books, 1999), see eg 233–40.

[26] See eg H Kelsen, *The Pure Theory of Law*, M Knight tr (Berkeley, University of California Press, 1967); H Kelsen, *General Theory of Law and State* (New York, Russell & Russell, 1961).

[27] E Durkheim, *The Division of Labor in Society* (New York, Free Press, 1947); E Durkheim, *Les règles de la méthode sociologique* (Paris, Flammarion, 1988); E Durkheim, *Les Formes élémentaires de la vie religieuse. Le système totémique en Australie* (Paris, Presses Universitaires de France, 1979); E Durkheim, *The Rules of Sociological Method and Selected Texts on Sociology and its Method* (London, Macmillan Publishers, 1982); M Weber, *The Protestant Ethic and the Spirit of Capitalism* (London, Routledge, 1992); P Bourdieu, *Distinction: A Social Critique of the Judgment of Taste*, R Nice tr (Harvard, Harvard University Press, 1984); HS Becker, *Outsiders: Studies in Sociology of Deviance* (New York, The Free Press, 1963). See also generally R Cotterrell, *Émile Durkheim: Law in a Moral Domain* (Redwood, Stanford University Press, 1999).

[28] LI Petrazycki, *Teoriya Prava i Gosudarstva v Svyazi s Teoriei Nravstvennosti* [*Theory of Law and State in Connection with the Theory of Morality*] (Moscow, Urait, 2018); EV Timoshina (ed), *Petrazycki, Teoriya i Politika Prava. Izbrannie Trudi* [*Petrazycki, Theory and Politics of Law*] (Saint Petersburg, University Publishing Consortium Juridical Book, 2011). See also G Gurvitch, *L'expérience juridique et la philosophie pluraliste du droit* (Paris, Pédone, 1935); G Gurvitch, *Sociology of Law* (New Jersey, Transaction Publishers, 2001); NS Timasheff, *Law and Morality by Leon Petrazicki* (Cambridge, Harvard University Press, 1955), R Banakar, 'The Sociology of Law: From Industrialisation to Globalisation' (2011) University of Westminster School of Law Research Paper No 11-03, 2011 ssrn.com/abstract=1761466; R Banakar, 'Who Needs the Classics? – On the Relevance of Classical Legal Sociology for the Study of Current Social and Legal Problems' in O Hammerslev and MR Madsen (eds), *Retssociologi* (Copenhagen, Hans Reitzels Forlag, 2012).

literature. In particular, S Prakash Sethi proposed a comparable classification of corporate responsibility norms of: (i) social obligation: a proscription regulating corporate behaviour in response to market forces and legal constrains; (ii) social responsibility: a prescription ordering corporations to adapt their behaviour to the prevailing social norms, values, and expectations; and (iii) social responsiveness: a preventive and anticipatory norm requiring corporations to adapt their behaviour to current social needs.[29]

The above echoes not only a narrower legal perspective of Lawrence Friedman's notion of legal culture (outlined earlier in this chapter) but also, and especially, a broader socio-legal perspective based on Emile Durkheim's idea of collective consciousness. His study of the functions of norms of law, religion and morality is extremely useful for resolving ambiguities in the emerging discipline of CSL. The functionalist approach allows for a deeper exploration of the categories and institutions of this new doctrine. Here, I use the Durkheimian theory as a general abstracted theory providing a suitable theoretical tool for analysing the key question of the grounding and justification of CSL. The theory underpinning my concept of the norms of CSL, in line with Durkheim's general approach to law, focuses on the *process* as much as – if not more than – the content. In short, I argue that current norms of liability in GVCs are a form of ritual, expressing beliefs held collectively and shared across state borders, especially in the Global North. In the final part of the book I thus aim to establish the links between the past, the present, and the future of CSL norms viewed through the lens of this theory.

V. Structure of the Book

CSL in global value chains is a 'strange creature'. Thus, it is necessary to explain the scope, aims, approach and methods of the book in some detail. The structure of this book is as follows: the remainder of Part I is an extensive interdisciplinary and contextualised account of the two of three objects of this book – CSR and GVCs. Chapter 2 thus first surveys various post-Second World War attempts to regulate post-colonial globalised capitalist production and trade, primarily focusing on voluntary and private self-regulation. The chapter goes on to analyse the ideational, economic, organisational, social and governance contexts, every time adding to the underlying argument of the book: GVCs, as connectivity norms, create and reproduce countless relationships of *economic* dependence and *legal* independence between the core corporations and the periphery firms.

Allegedly technical discussions about standard content and monitoring conceived CSR as the swords and shields of worldwide GVC capitalism. Those 'voluntary' international standards became the main (and virtually only) regulatory

[29] SP Sethi, 'Dimensions of Corporate Social Performance: An Analytic Framework' (1975) 17 *California Management Review* 58, 62–63.

tools with which to tackle the process of risks occurring in such parts of the global periphery as Bangladesh, where the Rana Plaza disaster occurred, thus creating a 'non-law' sphere of GVC production and other operations.

The remainder of the book addresses its third and main object: CSL. Part II looks at relevant CSR repercussions that also contributed to creating obstacles to controlling corporate behaviour at both national and post-national levels. Chapter 3 offers a historical and comparative analysis of the main national industrial and economic developments, social norms, and legal rules relevant for corporate liability in contractually organised structures of manufacturing and distribution. Chapter 4 surveys pertinent EU and international instruments and initiatives. It demonstrates how the disclosure and due diligence rules have emerged as the mainstream approach to corporate responsibility in GVCs. This approach seems to progressively shape not just new social norms of business behaviour expressed in a 'therapeutic' transparency of corporations, but increasingly legal norms and practices, both local and global.

Part III surveys and analyses all recent legal approaches to CSL in GVCs. Chapter 5 offers a comparative account of relevant national legislation (both in motion and adopted) and litigation aiming to extend corporate responsibility for outsourced production and other operations. Chapter 6 looks at general conditions for founding corporate liability in practice, at specific criteria of differentiation between types of corporate liability within GVCs, and at some concrete possibilities of CSL in GVCs.

Part IV provides an overview of whether a systemic approach to CSL should – and how it could – be adapted and adopted. Chapters 7 and 8 address the recent paradigm shift toward more legalistic approaches to regulating GVC production than the previously prevalent CSR.

The last chapter of Part IV (Chapter 9) and the conclusions of the book offer some normative prospects of CSL. They raise normative questions of whether CSL could be realised, and why and how that should happen. Here, the assessment depends on a particular type of governance and a particular regulatory paradigm. Overall, the analysis concludes that a systemic response to contemporary GVC capitalism's violence in both first and third worlds should comprise, but go beyond, legal and legal-political solutions. Getting rid of economic dependence and inequality, and thus also of global economic periphery, through ensuring a level playing field economically and socially must be our common goal.

2

Setting the Stage: Corporate Responsibility in Context

This chapter introduces the international regime of CSR that developed in the first decades of the post-Second World War era. This regime focused on standard-setting, risk management, private-public alliances, and was essentially voluntary in nature. In order to sketch the history and rationale of the idea and realisation of CSR, I engage with the global post-war endeavours to regulate transboundary business. This historical, conceptual and critical excursion demonstrates the fundamental rationale of the appearance, growing popularity and use of voluntary corporate governance schemes in transboundary economic transactions, as key paradigms change (section I).

Section II of the chapter analyses the ideational context underpinning not only the Washington Consensus' norms of market efficiency and the 'development of underdevelopment' but also the corresponding developments in national contract, tort, and company laws that allowed GVC production and trade to evade any responsibility, let alone liability.

Given the fundamental binary construct 'economic dependence-legal independence' inherent in particular GVC core-periphery relationships, the relevant framework for GVC regulation evolved in the blind spots of most traditional legal approaches to value chains, thus creating so-called governance gaps. Whilst post-colonial international law kept relying on the nation-state to play the necessary role of fostering industrialisation, other international – or, rather, transnational – forces confined newly independent states to the global economic 'periphery'. These forces, which include international commodity markets, the interests of transnational corporations (TNCs), and third-world elites, maintained and enforced the international division of labour captured in the core-periphery dichotomy (Section III). Section IV, in turn, presents an economic and organisational outline of GVC governance. Sections III and IV thus look at value chain governance through the prism of different theories. The general premises and a typology of GVCs and their governance can help us further understand key governance and socio-economic boundaries challenging legal institutions relevant for corporate liability in GVCs.

Behind allegedly technical discussions about standard content and monitoring procedures in GVCs lie issues of access and control, which create the relationship of economic dependence between a core corporation and its subcontractors and suppliers from the periphery. Sections V–VII, therefore, discuss how CSR was generally conceived as part of international standards to deal with the process of production-related risks occurring in such parts of the global periphery as Bangladesh, where the Rana Plaza disaster occurred. Section VIII explores how, since the Rana Plaza construction's collapse, it has become clear that the 'construction' of the regulation of value chains based on CSR does not hold up.

I. The Corporate Responsibility Debate in its Historical Context

In this section, I set the scene by presenting the corporate responsibility debate in a general historical context of international economic relations that emerged after the Second World War. My historical account is roughly divided to 'before' and 'after' the advent of the Washington Consensus.[1] The aim of the first two sections of this chapter is more than a mere intention to give an introductory historical account. In addition to a necessary historical detour, the intention is also to outline how global business and economic governance had been – and still is – a battlefield of clashing views about the essence, role and magnitude of its main instruments governing sustainability topics, including societal responsibility of corporations.

I identified at least two key periods in the relevant debate following the Second World War. In the first phase, there still appeared to be some scope for pluralistic claims regarding such debate (see section A below). However, with the advent of the Washington Consensus into the global political economy, a chilling 'California effect'[2] of the Consensus has standardised, privatised and indeed reduced to corporate voluntary self-regulation virtually any international claim for responsible business behaviour (see section B below).

[1] An agreement between and a set of policy recommendations of the US Department of the Treasury, the International Monetary Fund (IMF), and the World Bank, all of whom are based in Washington, DC, hence the name 'Washington Consensus'. The Washington Consensus insisted that the operation of the free market and a considerable decrease in state involvement were crucial to development in the Global South.

[2] The original term 'California effect' was coined by David Vogel in 1995. Vogel's idea was that export-oriented companies must develop the capabilities to comply with standards in their major export markets. In doing so, they may also lobby governments to adopt similar societal (in the 1990s, mostly environmental) standards domestically: D Vogel, *Trading Up. Consumer and Environmental Regulation in a Global Economy* (Cambridge, Harvard University Press, 1995). What Vogel seems to omit (or take for granted) is that the major export markets are the first-world ones. At the end of the day, access to the rich countries' markets for firms from poorer states has become increasingly dependent on participating in GVCs led by corporations often based in the Global North. Such access is also dependent on the private standards set by those corporations, or hybrid schemes for which those corporations have lobbied at home. The California effect for the regulation of the globalised business could thus be summarised as 'follow our standards, or you will not have access to our markets'. As Peter Muchlinski noted, '[i]n the "global Bukowina" of international business, how far can the interests of MNEs from developed home states create a legal order that refers to their culture and practices, rather than those outside this cultural sphere?': PT Muchlinski, '"Global Bukowina" Examined: Viewing the Multinational Enterprise as a Transnational Law-making Community' in G Teubner (ed), *Global Law Without a State (Studies in Modern Law and Policy)* (Dartmouth, Dartmouth Publishing Co, 1997) 102.

A. Earlier Debate: Still Some Room for Plural Claims

As mentioned above, many of the early direct and indirect attempts to reconcile global corporations and society were multilateral in nature. This was mainly due to a belief in global united efforts, fuelled by a pre-war enthusiasm related to the League of Nations, as well a post-First World War necessity, when international cooperation was not only welcomed, but indispensable.

The League of Nations intergovernmental conference on an international convention on the minimum standards of treatment of foreign investors and investments was held in 1929 in Geneva.[3] It was followed by The Hague conference on the codification of international law, which delved into the responsibility of host states for damages to foreign investors.[4] Both initiatives sought to codify international standards regarding transboundary corporate activities, including their foreign direct investment (FDI). Neither of these had any trace of societal questions (eg formal and concrete obligations of foreign companies investing in capital importing states in case of serious damages, such as obligations to protect natural resources or populations), and considered the interests of no-one but the western capital-exporting states. Neither initiative was met with success.[5]

In 1931, the International Chamber of Commerce in Paris launched a campaign for the creation of an international convention guaranteeing the protection of foreign investments. In 1949 the campaign resulted in a draft code for the 'Fair Treatment of Foreign Investments', which was eventually merged in 1959 with the 1957 draft of the International Convention for the Mutual Protection of Private Property Rights in Foreign Countries.[6] This 'merger' then became the Organisation for Economic Co-operation and Development (OECD) Draft Convention on the Protection of Foreign Property, which finally remained a draft for roughly the same reasons that were the root cause of the failure of the above League of Nations' codification efforts. Those were the bias towards the interests of major capital-exporting states, resulting into a refusal of some OECD (then OEEC) members such as Greece, Portugal, and Turkey to open the draft for signature.[7] The OECD then set about creating a model agreement for investment protection treaties, which – together with other OECD relevant endeavours – is discussed further below.

[3] Questionnaire No 4 adopted by the League of Nations Committee of Experts for the progressive codification of international law, On 'Responsibility of States for damage done in their territories to the person or property of foreigners' in 'Report on International Responsibility' by FV Garcia-Amador, Special Rapporteur on State responsibility, Extract from *the Yearbook of the International Law Commission*, vol II, A/CN.4/96, Annex A, 1956. E-United Nations Treaty Collection, http://legal.un.org/ilc/documentation/english/a_cn4_96.pdf.

[4] See 'Bases of discussion drawn up in 1929 by the Preparatory Committee of the Conference for the Codification of International Law' (The Hague, 1930), in Report by FV Garcia-Amador, ibid Annex B.

[5] PT Muchlinski, *Multinational Enterprises and the Law*, 2nd edn (Oxford, Oxford University Press, 2007) 654.

[6] The latter was the initiative of the German Society to Advance the Protection of Foreign Investments. Muchlinski (n 2) 93.

[7] ibid.

On the trade front, after the Second World War the international community, with a concrete push on behalf of the UK and perhaps especially the US, became more concerned about the many societal issues related to, and magnified by, increasingly global business operations. The main rationale of such concerns was to balance the longer-term objectives of building (or re-building, after the war), through institutional cooperation, an international political and economic equilibrium. This was marked by a particular market economy drive on the one hand, and the instant measures necessary for post-war reconstruction on the other.[8] Specifically, the UK and the US submitted proposals to the UN Economic and Social Council (ECOSOC) regarding the establishment of the International Trade Organization (ITO).[9] The United Nations Conference on Trade and Employment took place in 1946 to consider these proposals. The Conference's Preparatory Committee presented the draft ITO Charter. Further attempts to codify international standards on global business and economic transactions started in 1947, with the drafting of the so-called Havana Charter for a nascent ITO, approved in 1948 at a conference in Havana, Cuba.[10]

The Charter was intended to deal with such socially important topics as labour rights, economic boycotts of all sorts, subsidies, restrictive business practices, natural resources, and commodity agreements.[11] For example, the draft contained an ambitious chapter – Chapter VI – on inter-governmental agreement on trade and investment in energy. It addressed, among other things, such matters as the protection of natural resources from needless exhaustion, and similar developments, tacitly pointing to environmental conservation. Furthermore, Article 7 of the draft Charter contained a far-reaching provision on fair labour norms and principles. The regulation of foreign investments by corporations was proposed through, for example, the draft's Article 12, which stipulated that the host state should control the pre-investment phase conditions, entry and establishment of foreign inward investment.

The Havana Charter was never ratified by the US (generally, due to changes in the US administration and its subsequent withdrawal from the talks, and also, somewhat consequently, due to the inauguration of the Cold War), and the ITO project was abandoned by the international community.[12] For almost five decades, the 1947 General Agreement on Tariffs and Trade (GATT) became virtually the sole multilateral legal basis for international commerce, though most of the societal provisions of the Havana Charter were not included in the GATT 1947.

[8] JE Lockwood and WC Schmeisser, 'Restrictive Business Practices in International Trade' (1946) 11 *Law and Contemporary Problems* 663, 665.

[9] US Department of State, Proposals for Expansion of World Trade and Employment (Washington, Pub 2411, Commercial Policy Series 79, 1945).

[10] Havana Charter for an International Trade Organization, United Nations Conference on Trade and Employment, Final Act and Related Documents, E/CONF.2/78, United Nations publication, Sales No 1948.II.D.4.

[11] C VanGrasstek, *The History and Future of the World Trade Organization* (Geneva, WTO Publications, 2013) 43.

[12] Muchlinski (n 5) 655.

One decisive reason to drop the Charter's societal provisions was the clash of two opposing ideologies of the time. A Keynesian model, favouring active involvement of and policy responses from national governments to stabilise the economy, was progressively unseated by the liberal model until the 1970s, when the latter decisively triumphed over the former.[13] The GATT, being the liberal 'face' of the Havana Charter, anticipated this trend, as the Keynesian part of the Havana Charter, advocating, inter alia, for a stricter regulation of corporate behaviour abroad and for more domestic policy space, was abandoned.

B. A 'California Effect' of the Washington Consensus

On the United Nations (UN) front, one of the main multilateral post-Second World War efforts to collectively hold TNCs socially accountable was through widening, legalising, and formalising state interference in private property rights. The purposes of this included making urban, food and ecological regulation better adopted to specific economic, social and ecological conditions and the varying stages of development in newly decolonised states. That was the rise of the 'New International Economic Order' (NIEO).[14]

In the context of the historic entitlements and reparation of past wrongs based on the notion of distributive justice advanced by the former colonies, starting from the 1950s those countries sought to establish their economic freedom through the UN General Assembly.[15] In this way, between 1952 and 1962 the General Assembly adopted several important resolutions, including one recognising the states' right of permanent sovereignty over their natural resources.[16]

The triumph of those efforts occurred later, in 1973–74, when the international legal principle of nationalisation was recognised, primarily in the framework of Resolution 3171 (XXVIII). This resolution reaffirmed the inalienable rights of permanent sovereignty of states over their natural resources and specified that the

[13] See H Ruiz Fabri, 'Regulating Trade, Investment and Money' in J Crawford and M Koskenniemi (ed), *The Cambridge Companion to International Law* (Cambridge, Cambridge University Press, 2012) 355. See also T Hale et al, *Gridlock. Why Global Cooperation Fails When We Need It Most* (Cambridge, Polity Press, 2013) 139.

[14] See eg UN General Assembly Resolution 3202 (S-VI) 'Programme of Action on the Establishment of a New International Economic Order' (1 May 1974) UN Doc A/RES/S-6/3202. See especially its Parts I, IV and V.

[15] See eg A Newcombe and L Paradell, *Law and Practice of Investment Treaties, Standards of Treatment* (Alphen aan den Rijn, Kluwer Law International, 2009) 25–27; M Sornarajah, *The Pursuit of Nationalized Property* (Leiden, Martinus Nijhoff Publishers, 1986) 120–23. See generally AFM Maniruzzaman, 'State Contracts in Contemporary International Law: Monist versus Dualist Controversies' (2001) 12 *European Journal of International Law* 309, 317.

[16] The principle of permanent state sovereignty over natural resources was established through the UNGA Resolutions 523 (VI) of 12 January 1952; 626 (VII) of 21 December 1952; 1314 (XIII) of 12 December 1958; 1515 (XV) of 15 December 1960; and 1803 (XVII) of 14 December 1962. The term 'permanent sovereignty over natural resources' was mentioned for the first time in UNGA Resolution 626 (VII), which provided for the right of peoples to exploit their natural resources as part of their sovereignty.

exercise of such sovereignty would not be hindered by international law.[17] In the framework laid down by the above resolutions, the former colonies claimed that, once a foreign corporation made its investment in the host state, such investment must be integrally submitted to the municipal law and national tribunals of that state. It would have been surprising if the Global North countries – which at that time were home to the overwhelming part of transnational investors, and thus net exporters of capital – accepted such an interpretation of the principle. Indeed, after 1974 no other General Assembly resolution concerning this matter was adopted, and the NIEO vanished.

Traditionally, there was a gap between developed and developing countries regarding the concentration of TNCs, which today has lessened but still persists. The root cause of the gap is twofold: it stems from the percentage of corporate headquarters in a country, and from the size of the headquartered firms. More specifically, until 1993, the 100 largest corporations making FDI were situated in the Global North, with *zero* such TNCs in the Global South; virtually all TNCs of any size were situated in developed countries.[18] The situation has 'improved' since then: for example, since 2009, around 30% of TNCs have been based in the Global South, with a dozen global corporations among the hundred biggest non-financial firms headquartered in developing countries.[19]

In the 1970s, the discussion on possible abuse of economic power by TNCs continued and intensified in international fora. This led to the establishment, in 1972, of an eminent persons group by the UN Secretary General, at the request of the UN ECOSOC.[20] The Group recognised the limitations faced by host states, particularly the developing ones, in regulating the activities of TNCs.[21]

The Group ultimately recommended the setting up of the United Nations Commission on Transnational Corporations (UNCTNC), as well as launching negotiations on the United Nations Code of Conduct for TNCs.[22] The talks on the

[17] UNGA Res 3171 (17 December 1973) 28th Special Session, GAOR (1973) UN Doc Supp No 30 (A/9030) 52. This was followed by Resolution 3201 (S-VI) entitled 'Declaration on the Establishment of a New International Economic Order'. Moreover, through Resolution 3281 (XXIX), the Assembly adopted the Charter of Economic Rights and Duties of States. In both documents, permanent sovereignty over natural resources has been established as an absolute principle, and (for example, contrary to Resolution 1803 (XVII)) without any counterparty or compromise. The Resolution on the New International Economic Order confirmed the *full* ('*intégrale*' in the French version) permanent sovereignty of the state over its natural resources. See UNGA Res 3201 (1 May 1974) 6th Special Session, GAOR (1974) UN Doc Supp No 1 (A/9559). The Charter of Economic Rights and Duties of States endorsed the principle. It also provided that any dispute shall be settled under the law of the host state, unless a relevant agreement stated otherwise. See UNGA Res 3281 (26 July 1974) 29th Special Session, GAOR (1974) UN Doc Supp No 31 (A/9361). See also Sornarajah (n 15) 122–23.

[18] UNCTAD, (1) World Investment Report 1994: *Transnational Corporations, Employment and the Workforce*; (2) World Investment Report 1996: *Investment, Trade and International Policy Arrangements*; (3) World Investment Report 2002: *Transnational Corporations and Export Competitiveness*; (4) World Investment Report 2009: *Transnational Corporations, Agricultural Production and Development.*

[19] ibid.

[20] WTO, WT/WGTI/W/152, 2.

[21] ibid.

[22] UNCTNC, *Report on the first session 17–28 March 1975*, UN Doc E/5655; E/C.10/6 Economic and Social Council Official Records 59th Session Supplement No 12.

formulation of the Code began in 1977.[23] One of the major bottlenecks in negotiations was the question of whether the Code should expressly refer to 'international law' and thereby to international minimum standards of treatment created and sanctioned by the capital-exporting states; or rather to 'international obligations', that is, only to concrete legal obligations specified in the Code – the option clearly supported by the capital-importing states.[24] The talks over the Code continued through the early 1990s. The draft Code as it evolved could not be adopted because of the strong obligatory stance it began to take (obviously, the emerging economies wanted the Code to be binding, while the major industrialised countries exporting capital preferred it to be voluntary).[25] Some scholars even assert that the Code 'was perceived as a threat to the interests of the [TNCs]' major home states, which supported a greater freedom of investment and greater protection of the contractual and property rights of foreign investors'.[26] Later, there were attempts to modify the subsequent drafts, to bring them more into line with the main capital-exporting countries' interests.[27] The negotiations on the draft Code were finally suspended in 1992, and then abandoned.[28]

What emerged after two decades of intense debates was the regulation of corporate behaviour abroad through *incentives* (and hence the general triumph of the Washington Consensus), as the Code was the victim of attacks from the capital-exporting countries and, primarily, US conservative pressures.[29] Due to the concessions made by the UN to Washington, and the influential US corporate sector and conservative think-tanks such as the Heritage Foundation, the UN reorganised its work on TNCs.[30] Specifically, it first closed down the Centre on Transnational Corporations in 1992, transferring the Programme on Transnational Corporations to the Transnational Corporations and Management Division of the UN Department of Economic and Social Development (1992–1993), and ultimately replaced the Centre by just a division on investment and enterprise within UNCTAD, which exists to this day.[31]

The birth and demise of the draft TNCs Code triggered two major developments. First, to somehow counter the emerging 'threat' of an international binding code of corporate behaviour, after the establishment in 1972 of an UNCTAD eminent persons group and the first talks about the Code, in 1976 the OECD

[23] The first draft of the Code of 1982 can be found in UN Doc E/C.10/1983/S/2, Economic and Social Council Official Records.

[24] See eg Muchlinski (n 5) 661.

[25] For the text of the Draft Code, see UN Doc E/1990/94, 12 June 1990.

[26] Muchlinski (n 2) 95.

[27] See eg the draft of the Code of 1986, UNCTNC, 1986 Series, A No 4 UN Doc ST/CTC/SER.A/4.

[28] For the text, see UN Doc E/1990/94, 12 June 1990.

[29] JW Foster, 'The role of Non-Governmental Organisations and social movements in developing countries' in JJ Kirton and MJ Trebilcock (ed), *Hard Choices, Soft Law. Voluntary Standards in Global Trade, Environment and Social Governance* (Aldergate, Ashgate Publishing Limited, 2004) 204.

[30] ibid.

[31] UNCTAD Division on Investment and Enterprise, https://unctad.org/about/organization/division-investment-and-enterprise.

issued its Guidelines for Multinational Enterprises (OECD Guidelines).[32] The Guidelines contained *recommendations* for responsible business that the adhering governments *encouraged* their domestic firms to *observe* wherever they operated.[33] However, the OECD Guidelines seemed to be too ambitious, were problematic to implement effectively in practice, and were generally vague (though this could have been deliberate). I address this and other relevant OECD instruments in more detail in Parts II and IV of this book.

The second relevant development occurred partly because of the demise of the NIEO and partly because of that of the TNCs Code: the focus of the relevant multilateral action has shifted from the UN to the GATT.[34] With the creation of the World Trade Organization (WTO) in 1995, some relevant debates were held in the framework of the WTO work programme on investment, in particular within the Working Group on the Relationship between Trade and Investment (WGTI).[35] Yet in 1999, the European Communities (EC) started a discussion on investment-related social disciplines and corporate investor behaviour by addressing the matter of codes of conduct or voluntary guidelines.[36] Two main approaches discussed by the WGTI were a government-sanctioned line and a company-driven approach, although both stressed that civil society was playing a driving role.[37] Both approaches were based on voluntary commitments by the investors themselves.

Another document, submitted by a group of certain developing countries, raised important societal concerns within the framework of foreign corporate activities in the Global South, such as respect for the rights of consumers in host states, effective consumer protection, safety and quality of goods and services, adherence by corporations to environmental and safety policies and practices of the host state, steps to protect the environment and to rehabilitate the environment when there is damage caused by the foreign investor, etc.[38] Importantly, the document called for effective multilateral agreements to be concluded, containing legally enforceable rules on corporate behaviour abroad.[39]

The above discussions have, however, gradually moved away from the WTO to bilateral, regional and public-private settings.[40] This was mainly due to the fact

[32] See eg Muchlinski (n 2) 95.

[33] OECD, Guidelines for Multinational Enterprises (2011), and still the latest version: http://mneguidelines.oecd.org/guidelines/.

[34] See eg Muchlinski (n 2) 96.

[35] WTO, 'Trade and Investment', http://www.wto.org/english/tratop_e/invest_e/invest_e.htm.

[36] WTO, Working Group on the Relationship between Trade and Investment 'Communication from the European Community and its Member States, "Where Are We on Foreign Investors' Behaviour?"' WTO Doc WT/WGTI/W/81 (20 September 1999).

[37] ibid.

[38] WTO, Working Group on the Relationship between Trade and Investment 'Communication from China, Cuba, India, Kenya, Pakistan and Zimbabwe, "Investors' and Home Governments' Obligations"' WTO Doc WT/WGTI/W/152 (19 November 2002) 5–6.

[39] ibid 2–3.

[40] See eg Muchlinski (n 2) 94–95.

that foreign investors' behaviour-related talks and settlements within the GATT/WTO met with considerable political opposition. This was especially the case for poorer countries. The latter generally saw the GATT/WTO mandate on foreign corporate investment as essentially 'westernised' and thus a sort of direct threat to the sovereign rights and duty to regulate of the decolonised states.[41] In addition, as mentioned above, most of the emerging economies were seeking some concrete and binding relevant commitments, while developed countries – mindful of, and to some extent driven by, their corporate sector – were advocating corporate behaviour codes and principles that were essentially 'voluntary' in nature and vague in content, even within such multilateral treaty regimes as the GATT/WTO.

To summarise this period, early attempts to integrate societal objectives into global business and economic governance – mainly through multilateral efforts – were rather unsuccessful. Sometimes this was because rich countries saw a highly regulatory position towards TNCs as a real threat to their corporate investors, as in the case of the UN Code of Conduct. Sometimes such efforts failed because the Global South saw relevant developments as 'protectionism with a moral face',[42] for example, in the case of the possibility of an enhanced regulation of foreign investors' behaviour within the GATT/WTO.

Recently, there has been little progress on these issues within public international economic law (PIEL), but not because such issues are considered unimportant. According to some scholars, it was rather that they were not considered appropriate topics, given the limited mandate of PIEL as re-imagined within the neoliberal paradigm.[43] Particularly, in contrast to earlier efforts to regulate transboundary business and economic operations multilaterally through binding instruments, the key players of the transborder economy started dealing with the so-called socially sensitive externalities of the globalised market by directly addressing non-state actors, hence bypassing states.[44]

The above retrospective account illustrates how global business and economic governance has been, and still is, a frontline of different ideologies and conceptual claims regarding the regulation of transboundary business operations. Thanks to it, we can better see how the interpretation of any relevant transnational instrument could be insufficient to assess the influence of – and the use of – norms in law *and* in society, especially if we do not enquire who benefits from that in the

[41] See eg WTO, 'Communication from Bangladesh (on behalf of the LDC Group), Botswana, China, Cuba, Egypt, India, Indonesia, Kenya, Malaysia, Nigeria, Philippines, Tanzania, Uganda, Venezuela, Zambia and Zimbabwe' (2003), WT/GC/W/514 and Corr.1; WT/MIN(03)/W/4 (2003) (a Ministerial document that the WT/GC/W/514, (2003) became after having been formally reissued, with correction).

[42] A phrase used by RM Locke, 'Private efforts to improve global working conditions have failed' (21 May 2013) *Boston Review* http://bostonreview.net/forum/can-global-brands-create-just-supply-chains-richard-locke.

[43] M Koskenniemi and P Leino, 'Fragmentation of International Law? Postmodern Anxieties' (2002) 15 *Leiden Journal of International Law*, 553, 572; A Lang, *World Trade Law after Neoliberalism* (Cambridge, Cambridge University Press, 2011) 10.

[44] See eg UNGC https://www.unglobalcompact.org/.

first place. For instance, such conceptions as 'international minimum standards of treatment', 'voluntary incentivising instruments', 'voluntary consensus-based standards' could act as social norms influencing the application and interpretation of legal norms related to the responsibilities of corporations abroad. In particular, a specific perception, which adjudicators may be somewhat compelled to have, could already be embedded in the metaphors underlying the 'international minimum standards of treatment' and other relevant constructs. These social norms may thus influence the choice of a particular meaning for a given phenomenon. Consequently, the ensuing application of a legal rule or principle, the legal arguments, and the like, would be framed within a given fundamental conception – a social norm – which has already been assumed a priori.

In the context of this chapter, an earlier ontological model which arguably embraced the above conceptions was one of embedded liberalism, with the alleged conceptions of regulatory and sovereign equality, and a general underlying idea of post-war recovery. However, the neoliberalism that was gradually unseating the liberal ontology in the aftermath of the Bretton Woods conference came to dominate the international economic order by the 1970s. De-regulation was one of the main tools of neoliberalism. It aimed to separate politics from the market, and to radically heighten the market freedom of individual market actors, by helping them to grasp and navigate the global web of norms and institutions in order to realise their transboundary business ends. Hence, after the Second World War, and especially from the 1970s onwards, de-regulation, optimisation of conditions for model market citizens to realise their private ends both locally and globally, and overall *market efficiency* as an overarching metaphor, have formed the social norms of the day.

Some commentators allege that the contemporary efficiency of the market is meant to maximise consumer preferences, and is contingent upon the quality and degree of knowledge and information available to individuals about the characteristics of goods and services that matter in terms of satisfying their preferences.[45] According to this account, both voluntary standards and labelling schemes in international trade are obviously the best mechanisms for maximising market efficiency. True, this could rather describe a situation where consumers are individuals belonging to the middle and upper classes of the most economically advanced democracies. Yet, the 'rest' of the world does not seem to have the privilege of seeking only the products that best satisfy their preferences, especially ethical ones. That is to say, today, a considerable part of the 'rest' of the world might well be more concerned with getting any supplies at all.[46]

[45] R Howse, 'Consumer Labelling on Trial at the WTO: Misunderstanding the Behavioural Law and Economics of Consumer Information' in M Cremona et al (eds), *Reflections on the Constitutionalisation of International Economic Law: Liber Amicorum for Ernst-Ulrich Petersmann* (Leiden, Martinus Nijhoff Publishers, 2014) 593.

[46] See eg R Andres Castaneda Aguilar et al, 'September 2019 global poverty update from the World Bank' (24 September 2019) http://blogs.worldbank.org/opendata/september-2019-global-poverty-update-world-bank.

A few other scholars, however, express different opinions regarding the potential for market efficiency that the international voluntary standards, including CSR, are supposed to enhance, as well as the democratic qualities and the overall potential of knowledge and information they embody. Theodore Porter, for example, asserts that various voluntary standards of corporate conduct are most profitable, and hence attractive, to the key decision-makers and beneficiaries of global business operations. The processes that use such instruments can, he argues, be presented as efficient, and therefore as neutral, value-free, impartial, scientific, consistent and transparent: he summarises such qualities as 'objectivity'.[47] Similarly, Kevin Davis et al see the same efficiency and expediency of presenting easily available and ready to use information as most suitable and beneficial not to final consumers, third-world workers, local communities, or the environment, but to the main stakeholders of transboundary commerce.[48] Finally, Peter Muchlinski asserts that '[t]he history of commercial law and regulation rests on the response of the "official" order to discrete business practices'.[49]

To conclude, voluntary and market-based governance increasingly became the dominant regulatory approach of the new ontological foundation of transboundary business transactions and economic relations, promoted by corporations, consumers, investors, and even the UN alike. However, what appears to emerge from such developments is a realisation of arguably societal objectives through the market, and, indeed, *by* the market. This approach has gained overall prominence with the boom of economic globalisation.

II. Ideational Context: The Impact of the Washington Consensus

As outlined in the previous section, since the Second World War most of the multilateral efforts to create legally binding global standards of conduct for TNCs have failed. The legal obstacles to corporate liability occurred mainly in the operations directly or indirectly relating to GVCs, such as the unwillingness of capital-exporting states to mitigate the drive of their corporate investors to go global, including through GVCs.

Since the international efforts of nation-states had largely failed, especially after – and due to – the emergence of the Washington Consensus, the world hence needed

[47] TM Porter, *Trust in Numbers: The Pursuit of Objectivity in Science and Public Life* (Princeton, Princeton University Press, 1995) 84.

[48] 'Reduction in the resources devoted to decision-making: Because indicators simplify information, their use should reduce the burden of processing information in the course of decision-making. In principle therefore, reliance on indicators should reduce the time, money and other resources required to make decisions': KE Davis et al, 'Indicators as a Technology of Global Governance' (2010) *NYU IILJ Working Paper* 2010/2 (Global Administrative Law Series) 6.

[49] Muchlinski (n 2) 101.

a different conceptualisation. The transnational theory of value chains emerged as one such alternative construct.[50] This theory provides a 'holistic view of global industries from two contrasting vantage points: top-down and bottom-up'.[51] The key concept for the top-down perspective is the 'governance' of GVCs, which concentrates on the leading enterprises and the organisation and political economy of global industries.[52] The main idea of the bottom-up view is 'upgrading', focusing on the strategies used by countries, regions and other key public actors of the global economy to maintain or improve their positions therein.[53]

In the context of this book, the top-down construct could actually depict a slightly different but connected phenomenon: namely, the main relevant ideological turn accompanying the global march of the Washington Consensus that assigned certain states and regions to the GVC 'periphery' and 'semi-periphery' (see section A below), while the bottom-up, or 'upgrading', is what could then be associated with the reaction of those countries and regions to the 'California effect' of the Washington Consensus – ie the periphery countries arguably started playing by the rules of the game, that is, 'upgrading' themselves legally and politically in order to participate in the transnational regulatory competition following the new global governance by and through GVCs (see section B below).

A. Relevant Washington Consensus Theories

The legal and institutional side of my top-down perspective (that is, a perspective different from Gereffi et al's 'top-down' theory discussed above) includes several avenues. A few of the top-down approaches that have emerged since the advent of the Washington Consensus can be traced back as far as Ronald Coase's 1937 seminal article, 'The Nature of the Firm'.[54] Coase asserted that a company's choice between producing an input itself or instead buying it on the market, and thus subcontracting it to a third producer, is arguably based upon a consideration of the so-called involved transaction costs – that is, mostly the costs connected to

[50] See generally G Gereffi and M Korzeniewicz (eds), *Commodity Chains and Global Capitalism* (Westport, Connecticut, Praeger, 1994).

[51] G Gereffi, 'Global Value Chains and International Competition' (2011) 56 *The Antitrust Bulletin* 37, 37; G Gereffi, 'A Global Value Chain Perspective on Industrial Policy and Development in Emerging Markets' (2014) 24 *Duke Journal of Comparative and International Law* 433, 440.

[52] See the fertile and enlightening body of work of Gary Gereffi on the subject-matter, eg (1) 'The Organization of Buyer-driven Global Commodity Chains: How US Retailers Shape Overseas Production Networks' (1994) in Gereffi and Korzeniewicz (n 50); (2) 'Global Production Systems and Third World Development' (1995) in B Stallings (ed), *Global Change, Regional Response: The New International Context of Development* (Cambridge, Cambridge University Press, 1995). See also G Gereffi et al, 'The Governance of Global Value Chains' (2005) 12 *Review of International Political Economy* 78.

[53] Gereffi (1) and (2), ibid. For a more critical perspective on such competition, see eg S Strange, 'What Theory? The Theory in Mad Money' (1998) *CSGR Working Paper No 18/98*, 9, https://papers.ssrn.com/sol3/papers.cfm?abstract_id=146958; R Kraakman et al, *The Anatomy of Corporate Law: A Comparative and Functional Approach*, 2nd edn (Oxford, Oxford University Press, 2009) 23–25.

[54] RH Coase, 'The Nature of the Firm' (1937) 4 *Economica* 386.

the purchase contract from the outside producers.[55] Simply put, a company would choose to purchase the inputs or otherwise outsource them only if the costs of doing so are lower than the cost of producing them in situ.

As the transaction costs are determined by the institutional environment in which the company exists, Coase argued that it was this institutional environment that actually governed the scope of production of any particular firm.[56] The New Institutional Economics (NIE) theory, founded by Coase,[57] later also gave rise to the connected approach of Transaction Cost Economics introduced by Oliver Williamson and his associates.[58] Claude Ménard and Mary Shirley describe NIE as a study of the performance of a market economy depending 'upon the formal and informal institutions and modes of organization that facilitate private transactions and cooperative behavior' and focusing 'on how institutions emerge, operate, and evolve, how they shape different arrangements that support production and exchange, as well as how these arrangements act in turn to change the rules of the game'.[59] Notably, NIE intended to unite all social sciences under one dominating paradigm of economics.[60]

Another connected theory also emerged: Law and Economics – a systematic jurisprudential approach to legal analysis. This also drew on Coase's 1937 article, but was conceptually born after the publication of two seminal papers, 'The Problem of Social Cost' by Coase, and 'Some Thoughts on Risk Distribution and the Law of Torts' by Guido Calabresi.[61]

Law and Economics is usually associated with Coase's recognition that the court-made private law rules governing the free market, used by economists to ground their notion of property and contract, also implied the question of externalities.[62] In 1968, this led Canadian economist John Harkness Dales to suggest the introduction of transferable pollution rights to tackle the 'externalities' of rising atmospheric pollution due to global capitalist production.[63] Thus, Coase

[55] ibid, 390–92. See also D Kennedy, 'Law-and-Economics from the Perspective of Critical Legal Studies' in P Newman (ed), *The New Palgrave Dictionary of Economics and the Law* (London, Palgrave Macmillan UK, 1998) 466, 469.

[56] JKM Ohnesorge, 'Developing Development Theory: Law and Development Orthodoxies and the Northeast Asian Experience' (2007) 28 *University of Pennsylvania Journal of International Economic Law* 219, 245; D Danielsen, 'Economic Approaches To Global Regulation: Expanding The International Law And Economics Paradigm' (2011) 10 *Journal of International Business & Law* 28.

[57] RH Coase, 'The New Institutional Economics' (1998) 88 *American Economic Review* 72.

[58] Ohnesorge (n 56) 245.

[59] C Ménard and MM Shelly, 'Introduction' in CM Ménard and MM Shirley (eds), *Handbook of New Institutional Economics* (New York, Springer, 2005) cited in Danielsen (n 56) 27.

[60] 'Modern economics has had a deep influence on thinking in other social sciences, leading to the theoretical integration of all the social sciences under an overarching paradigm': Ohnesorge (n 56) 245.

[61] The origins are usually traced back to Coase's article sharply criticising the 'Pigouvian' tradition. See RH Coase, 'The Problem of Social Cost' (1960) III *Journal of Law and Economics* 1, later elaborated in RH Coase, *The Firm, the Market, and the Law* (Chicago, University of Chicago Press, 1990). See also G Calabresi, 'Some Thoughts on Risk Distribution and the Law of Torts' (1961) 70 *Yale Law Journal* 499.

[62] Kennedy (n 55) 466.

[63] 'If it is feasible to establish a market to implement a policy, no policy-maker can afford to do without one. Unless I am very much mistaken, markets *can* be used to implement any anti-pollution policy that you or I can dream up': JH Dales, *Pollution, Property & Prices: An Essay in Policy-making and Economics* (Northampton, Edward Edgar, 2002) 100.

and Dales were among the first scholars to argue in favour of fixing societal problems through market solutions – in Dales' case, via environmental taxes.[64]

In summary, Law and Economics, Transaction Cost Economics, and NIE could be seen as the primary providers of the intellectual framework for the relevant workings of the Washington Consensus.[65] Following Coase's initial NIE thinking, and responding to the alleged need for systemic reforms in newly decolonised states, and, later, the economies in transition from socialist legal systems, the orthodoxy (typically, the 'golden club' of the OECD states and their most powerful citizens, both corporate and individual) sought to respond to this demand for a legal system 'from bottom to top'.[66]

In the context of this chapter, the key idea of the bottom-up perspective of the GVCs, as described above, is that states and regions strive to 'upgrade' themselves in order to become more competitive for global market shares or simply more attractive for TNCs. Being attractive for the latter means to either make them incorporate or invest in competing countries and regions, or, at least, to convince TNCs to outsource parts of their production to those places. So, starting as early as the 1970s (depending on the region), the bottom-up perspective corresponds to preaching and practising the ideas of the Washington Consensus, as discussed above.

B. Corresponding Legal Developments

The regulatory and general legal competitiveness of countries and regions in the global race for market shares took various forms, such as general openness to, and viable protection of FDI, the speed and simplicity of incorporating a company, the availability and affordability of financing for foreign firms, investor-friendly reforms in corporate law, or else choice of specially-drafted corporate charter provisions versus default provisions.[67]

At the heart of this competition lay private property rights and a vigorous protection thereof. These required national law, both private and public, to provide clear and predictable 'rules of the game' for global private economic actors.[68] This was also in line with a famous maxim of Friedrich Hayek, to stretch the clarity and predictability of the regulatory environment to the full, thus maximising the extent to which private actors can optimally plan and perform their (market) interests and activities.[69]

[64] A Aseeva, 'Intergenerational Climate Justice' in T Cottier et al (eds), *Intergenerational Equity: Environmental and Cultural Concerns* (Boston, BRILL/Nihjoff, 2019) 115, 127.

[65] Ohnesorge (n 56) 247.

[66] CW Gray, 'In Search of Owners: Privatization and Corporate Governance in Transition Economies' (1996) *World Bank Research Observer* 179, 181.

[67] For the latter form, see especially Kraakman et al (n 53) 23.

[68] Ohnesorge (n 56) 247.

[69] FA Hayek, *The Road to Serfdom* (Chicago, University of Chicago Press, 1944) 72.

Regarding private law, clear and secure rules-based contract law facilitating transboundary commerce, as well as other private law constructs to protect and enforce private property rights, have been the focus of the liberal orthodoxy ever since the French Revolution.[70] The novelty of the neoliberal rule of the Washington Consensus was that private property was now also protected by public law, and it was precisely in this realm that NIE and the economics-based critique of public regulation made their greatest impact.[71]

In terms of the particular prism of the top-down and bottom-up governance approaches, governance continued in the same vein as described above. In particular, the fact that norm production came from the 'top' of the global corporate sector, and trickled 'down' to states and their public law systems aimed to ensure that those same states would later not overturn this law.[72] Even – indeed, especially – national constitutional law systems did not escape this fate. To wit, specific Washington Consensus 'top-down' approaches to constitutional law have tried to enhance the neoliberal drift of constitutional law to the extent that the same governments that defined and wrote down the rules of contract and private property rights would not subsequently be able to disregard them.[73] During their formative stages states searched for allies among merchants in order to resist the harsh competition and pressure from the Church, the Empire and the old corporations and joint ventures, thus offering merchants the maximum recognition and protection of the freedom of contract and property rights, including the enshrinement of those in their constitutions.[74]

Now states are being asked to pay the price for those concessions, for today's corporations definitely challenge states' regulatory and law-making monopoly, not to mention the kind of 'corporate economy … [concentrating] capital and people under one command – in other words, the existence of competing, deterritorialized powers, in an ideal position to make the market operate between states, and to limit states' autonomy'.[75]

The administrative law of most countries has also undergone considerable 'upgrading' à la Washington Consensus. The main argument of the neoliberal orthodoxy was again that:

> economic development required a system of administrative law that could tightly constrain government actors within a system of clear rules, which would facilitate freedom of action by private economic actors, as well as reduce opportunities for rent-seeking (which would also be reduced by de-regulation).[76]

[70] JP Robé, 'Multinational Enterprises: the Constitution of a Pluralistic Legal Order' in Teubner (n 2) 45, 59.

[71] Ohnesorge (n 56) 248.

[72] See eg D Schneiderman, 'Constitutional Approaches To Privatization: An Inquiry Into The Magnitude of Neo-liberal Constitutionalism' (2001) 63 *Law and Contemporary Problems* 83, 88–89.

[73] Robé (n 70) 59–61.

[74] ibid 57. See also generally A Salmon, *Les nouveaux empires: Fin de la démocratie?* (Paris, CNRS, 2011).

[75] Robé (n 70).

[76] Ohnesorge (n 56) 248.

On the international law front, PIEL, mainly through international trade and investment treaty-based law systems, lowered several national 'barriers' to the facilitation of transnational production and commerce across the globe. First, through lowering world tariffs, the GATT/WTO system brought about competition between domestic and foreign corporations, which consequently provoked waves of foreign investor-friendly reforms in domestic corporate financing and the investment legislation of most countries.[77] Second, under the contemporary rule of international trade, global labour standards dropped to the lowest point.[78] Last but not least, international investment law enhanced regulatory competition between countries, especially those of the Global South, in order to attract FDI.[79]

This framework, which fully shielded private actors from state and public ones in the name of private property, and the allegedly beneficial role of contract enforcement on economic development, were complemented by strong orthodox claims with respect to several other legal fields. In the context of this book, it is relevant to mention that, based on the doctrine of a separation of ownership and control (including that separate legal persons were not liable for each other's contractual or extracontractual breaches), an 'effective' corporate law was now further protecting shareholders from both managers and society.[80] Moreover, countries, and especially developing ones, had to make their competition law 'effective', so that their markets would be competitive.[81]

To summarise, this section complements the outline of international regulatory approaches that ultimately led to voluntary and private self-regulation (CSR), offered in section A above, by adding the discussion on relevant ideas that informed global governance approaches that removed problems arising from transnational production and trade from the local – and mostly public – law reach.

This arguably voluntary international regime of CSR was thus reinforced by orthodox theories and policies not only in national commercial, contract, tort and corporate law, but also in tax, administrative and even constitutional law. This has allowed GVC production and commerce via contractual relationships to slip somewhat under the radar of any responsibility, let alone liability: the more the entities linked by a value chain were economically dependent, the more they were legally separate. The sphere of 'non-law' of GVCs seems to be even further reinforced by the above regulatory and quasi-constitutional approaches, drawing clear

[77] Kraakman et al (n 53) 29.

[78] See generally K Stone, 'Globalization and the Middle Class' in G de Búrca et al (eds), *Global Governance* (Oxford, Hart Publishing, 2013).

[79] Strange (n 53) 9.

[80] Gray (n 66) 2: 'For small firms this is straightforward. The owners and managers are one and the same. For large firms, however, the likely separation of ownership and management creates the need for monitoring', cited in Ohnesorge (n 56) 249. See also generally B Sjåfjell and M Taylor, 'Clash of Norms: Shareholder Primacy vs Sustainable Corporate Purpose' (2019) 13(3) *International and Comparative Corporate Law Journal* 40.

[81] World Bank, 'World Development Report 1996: From Plan to Market' (1996) 85, 92–93, in Ohnesorge (n 56) 249.

borders in national contexts through minimising the possibility of state intervention through labour, social, environmental, and taxation regulation.

In this book, before thinking about solutions to the problem of corporate irresponsibility in GVCs, I aim to reveal the structures and workings behind the construction of this sphere of 'non-law', indeed of blind spots, of GVC production and commerce. It is, I argue, the finding and revealing of the root causes of this problem that might help to shape solutions to the problem. Therefore, in this Part, a special detour was made to introduce the international vision of corporate responsibility that developed in the first decades of the post-Second World War era, which centred on standard-setting, risk management, private-public alliances, and ultimately became essentially voluntary in nature. This historical excursion demonstrates the fundamental rationale of the appearance and growing popularity and use of voluntary corporate governance schemes in transboundary economic relations, as key paradigms change. By presenting the core elements of the notion of societal (ir)responsibility of corporations in a dynamic relationship of development and interdependence, the historical and conceptual overview above has created a solid foundation for the remaining sections of this chapter.

All in all, post-Second World War *inter*national law focused on the nation-state playing the necessary role of fostering industrialisation for recovery and, later, globalisation. Meanwhile, other international, or rather *trans*national, mechanisms started to consign certain nations to the industrial and production 'periphery'. Those mechanisms were, of course, the interests of western corporations, but also those of their home states, the third-world elites, and international financial and commodity markets, which instead maintained and enforced the international division of labour captured in the core-periphery image.[82] The dependency relationship between the industrial *centre* – the now developed metropolitan states – and the *periphery* – the satellite 'underdeveloped' states – is not simply an essential part of the capitalist system, as noticed by Andre Frank, a founder of dependency theory.[83]

On the flipside of that relationship, formal law as a stable pre-given institution in and between the actual legal systems of advanced capitalist societies often remained relatively static, whereas business and commercial frameworks advanced independently and more rapidly. For the subject matter of this book, the relevant economic framework evolved into GVCs in the blind spots of most of the traditional legal approaches to cross-border business, thus creating the so-called governance gaps.

[82] Ohnesorge (n 56) 242.

[83] AG Frank, 'The Development of Underdevelopment' (September 1966) *Monthly Review* 17; AG Frank, 'The Sociology of Development and the Underdevelopment of Sociology' (1967) *Catalyst* 20. See also T Dos Santos, 'The Structure of Dependence' in KT Fann and DC Hodges (eds), *Readings in US Imperialism* (Boston, Porter Sargent Publishers, 1971) 225.

III. Economic Context: Centre, Semi-Periphery and Periphery of Global Value Chains

In *Historical Capitalism*, Immanuel Wallerstein summarised the distinctiveness of capitalism as a historical social system characterised by the 'widespread commodification of processes – not merely exchange processes, but production processes, distribution processes and investment processes – that had previously been conducted other than via a market'.[84]

The one fundamental concept to grasp, therefore, in the context of the first Part of this book, is undoubtedly that of GVCs. As the transboundary nature of GVCs arguably challenges the realisation of corporate liability, there is an interest in analysing the ways in which GVCs influence business transactions and global economic governance, and how they in turn are governed, if at all. In this context, in order to understand further the transversal challenges of GVC governance, law, and regulation, it is necessary to introduce some general historical premises (see section A below) and the direct ideational predecessors of the concept of GVCs (see section B below).

A. General Premises of Global Value Chains

Since the beginning of the industrial revolution, firms have used production networks as a means to reduce uncertainty, manage reputation, enhance market reach, control quality, and fuel innovation.[85] Given that for-profit companies typically avoid directly designing and openly implementing standardised regulation for the entire supply chain, the first standardisation organisations, such as the International Organization for Standardization (ISO), epitomised a joint effort by key stakeholders of transborder production and commerce to reduce risk and uncertainty throughout production networks.[86]

A basic definition of a value chain, or, more precisely, commodity chain, given in 1986 is a 'network of labour and production processes whose end result is a finished commodity'.[87] The OECD complemented this definition 30 years later, in its guidelines for mineral supply chains, with the following understanding:

> [t]he process of bringing a raw mineral to the consumer market involves multiple actors and generally includes the extraction, transport, handling, trading, processing, smelting,

[84] I Wallerstein, *Historical Capitalism* (London, Verso, 1983) 15.

[85] P Aerni, 'Do Private Standards Encourage or Hinder Innovation?' (2013) 18 *NCCR Trade Working Paper* 2–4.

[86] B Frydman, 'Prendre les standards et les indicateurs au sérieux' (2013) 4 *Working Papers du Centre Perelman de Philosophie du Droit* 8–11, 13; P Hatto for the European Commission, 'Standards and Standardisation. A Practical Guide for Researchers' (2010) https://ec.europa.eu/research/industrial_technologies/pdf/practical-standardisation-guide-for-researchers_en.pdf, 5.

[87] T Hopkins and I Wallerstein, 'Commodity Chains in the World Economy Prior to 1800' (1986) 10 *Review* 157, 159.

> refining and alloying, manufacturing and sale of end product. The term supply chain refers to the system of all the activities, organisations, actors, technology, information, resources and services involved in moving the mineral from the extraction site downstream to its incorporation in the final product for end consumers.[88]

B. Ideational Predecessors of the Global Value Chains Approach

The world-system and dependency theories that appeared in the late 1970s were some of the first to theorise an unprecedented increase in what we know today as GVCs. The world-system theory was developed by Immanuel Wallerstein,[89] later joined by Terrence Hopkins in their joint commodity-chain research, while the dependency school was typically associated with Raúl Prebisch, Andre Gunder Frank, and their followers.[90]

In their 1977 research agenda-setting article on commodity chains, Hopkins and Wallerstein presented their world-system approach.[91] The two scholars sought to offer an understanding of capitalism's *territorial* scope, which would radically differ from the standard paradigm of globalisation, presenting the global economy's development as a progressive process whereby national markets 'naturally' evolve towards expanded foreign trade geared to an international market:[92]

> Let us conceive of something we shall call, for want of a better conventional term, 'commodity chains'. What we mean by such chains is the following: take an ultimate consumable item and trace back the set of inputs that culminated in this item – the prior transformations, the raw materials, the transportation mechanisms, the labor input into each of the material processes, the food inputs into the labor. This linked set of processes we call a commodity chain.[93]

In 1986, the productive commodity-chain duo of Hopkins-Wallerstein offered a refined definition of commodity chains, in an article analysing trade and capital flows in the global economy prior to 1800.[94] They also introduced the

[88] OECD, *2016 Due Diligence Guidance for Responsible Supply Chains of Minerals from Conflict-Affected and High-Risk Areas* (2016) http://www.oecd.org/daf/inv/mne/OECD-Due-Diligence-Guidance-Minerals-Edition3.pdf, 14.

[89] I Wallerstein, 'The Rise and Future Demise of the World Capitalist System: Concepts for Comparative Analysis' (1974) 16 *Comparative Studies in Society and History* 387.

[90] See eg Frank (n 83). See also S Newton, 'The Dialectics of Law and Development' in DM Trubek and A Santos (eds), *The New Law and Economic Development: A Critical Appraisal* (Oxford, Hart Publishing, 2006) 174, 182–87.

[91] T Hopkins and I Wallerstein, 'Patterns of Development of the Modern World-System' (1977) 1 *Review* 111.

[92] For a concise and precise historical and conceptual recap of this theory and its underlying rationale, see generally J Bair, 'Global Capitalism and Commodity Chains: Looking Back, Going Forward' (2005) 9 *Competition and Change* 153.

[93] Hopkins and Wallerstein (n 91) 128.

[94] T Hopkins and I Wallerstein, 'Commodity Chains in the World Economy Prior to 1800' (1986) 10(1) *Review* 157, 159, cited in Bair (n 92).

core-periphery distinction that was further explained and complemented in 1986 by Giovanni Arrighi and Jessica Drangel, positing that core-periphery divide 'is meant to designate the unequal distributions of rewards among the various activities that constitute the single overarching division of labor defining and bounding the world economy. All these activities are assumed to be integrated in commodity chains'.[95] The first ever book on commodity chains was edited by Gary Gereffi and Miguel Korzeniewicz in 1994.[96]

Notably, Gereffi and Korzeniewicz's stream of commodity chain research (that later became the 'GCC' – *global* commodity chains – approach) essentially focused on the question of how participation in supply chains can facilitate industrial 'upgrading' for developing country exporters.[97] Thus, the GCC's essential focus was on inter-firm networks connecting manufacturers, suppliers and subcontractors of a business line to each other, and ultimately to global markets.[98] World-system scholarship, on the other hand, rather concentrated on how commodity chains structure, streamline, and reproduce a stratified and hierarchical *world system*.[99] Furthermore, the world-system camp saw commodity chains not only as platforms for activities that aimed to add value to a raw material, thus making it into a product, but also as webs connecting productive actions with the social reproduction of human labour power as a critical input into this process:[100] '[i]f the ultimate consumable were, say, clothing, the chain would include the manufacture of the cloth, the yarn, etc., the cultivation of the cotton, as well as the reproduction of the labor forces involved in these productive activities'.[101]

But both GCC and the world-system school ultimately agree that the commodity chain is a useful concept for thinking about the international division of labour that is characteristic of capitalist production.[102]

Though there are differences between the world-system school of thought and dependency theory, the two can be said to share their basic views.[103] However, the following are seen differently by the two groups:

(i) the temporal and spatial scope of globalisation; and
(ii) the objectives of commodity chain analysis.[104]

At the same time, both assign different countries to categories such as 'core-periphery or 'centre-periphery' or else 'dominant/dependent', based upon their wealth and power, as well as industrial development.[105]

[95] G Arrighi and J Drangel, 'The Stratification of the World-economy' (1986) 10 *Review* 9, 16, cited in Bair (n 92).
[96] Gereffi and Korzeniewicz (n 50).
[97] See generally section II.A above.
[98] Bair (n 92) 156.
[99] Bair (n 92) 155.
[100] ibid.
[101] Hopkins and Wallerstein (n 91) 128.
[102] Bair (n 92) 155.
[103] Ohnesorge (n 56) 241.
[104] See eg Bair (n 92) Table 1.
[105] Ohnesorge (n 56) 241.

The concept of centre and periphery per se was first introduced in the 1950s by the economist of the structuralist school Raúl Prebisch (also the first Secretary-General of the UNCTAD). Prebisch exposed the structural inequalities and flaws of the Ricardian comparative advantage theory, which consigned certain nations to the 'periphery' of globalised capitalist production.[106] This was followed by more social sciences-adapted theories of social networks, with a centre-periphery structure in international relations by Roger Nemeth and David Smith,[107] and, of course, the above world-system and dependency schools. On the whole, according to the research surveyed here, the advanced industrialised states make up the core, whereas poor countries make up the periphery, and the 'semi-periphery' is situated somewhere in between.[108]

In the actual *global* value chains, the lead firms are very often from the western 'centre' of the capitalist production, and the value chain goes via 'semi-periphery' (such as, for instance, Hungary, Moldova, Romania, Slovakia and some other Central- and Eastern-European countries) down to 'periphery' (Bangladesh, Brazil, China, Haiti, India, Vietnam).[109] Generally, TNCs tend to relocate frequently, arguably especially when they can achieve significant production-related cost savings in countries with sufficiently low labour, social, health and environmental standards. There is considerable evidence that, since the 1980s, diversified TNCs have developed global strategies to not only move production between locations in order to exploit differentials in such cost-related disparities between countries of the global capitalist periphery, but also to relocate it repeatedly as these cost differentials change.[110] For example, since the 1980s, many textile and apparel-related firms moved from Brazil to Haiti, then from Haiti to Cambodia, Mexico and Bangladesh, then from there to China, and when they were faced with the prospect of rising labour costs, some moved to Vietnam.[111]

Arguably, in constantly relocating their production along GVCs, corporations are therefore the key global actors who *actually* assign certain nations to the periphery and semi-periphery (and, sometimes, from semi-periphery to periphery and back again). This assertion is, however, relevant for only certain industries, in which labour costs constitute a large proportion of total costs, such as textile, that would certainly move to take advantage of lower societal standards in different

[106] R Prebisch, 'Le développement économique de l'Amérique latine et ses principaux problèmes' (1962) New-York: United Nations, reprinted in *Economic Bulletin for Latin America* (7 February 1962) 1–22. See also AN Agarwala and SP Singh (eds), *The Economics of Underdevelopment* (Bombay, Oxford University Press, Indian Branch, 1958).

[107] JN Nemeth and DA Smith, 'International Trade and World-System Structure: A Multiple Network Analysis' (1985) 8 *Review (Fernand Braudel Center) Quantitative Studies of the World-System* 517.

[108] Ohnesorge (n 56) 241.

[109] See UNCTAD, (1) World Investment Report 1994: *Transnational Corporations, Employment and the Workforce*; (2) World Investment Report 1996: *Investment, Trade and International Policy Arrangements*; (3) World Investment Report 2002: *Transnational Corporations and Export Competitiveness*; (4) World Investment Report 2009: *Transnational Corporations, Agricultural Production and Development.*

[110] Stone (n 78) 4.

[111] ibid.

countries. But the pattern is often more complex for those business lines in which labour and related costs are not a large proportion of total costs, such as building services or health chains, which are thus less likely to relocate than those that are labour-intensive.[112] This book's key focus is plainly on labour-intensive GVC production.

There are even more complicated examples in cases when geopolitics and opposing ideologies intermingle with the clear economic cost-benefit analysis of production cost differentials. To wit, during Cold War, Central Europe was simultaneously the eastern periphery of the capitalist world-system and the western periphery of the Soviet bloc. In the aftermath of Cold War, following the transition, it became 'a unique amalgamation of postcolonialism (vis-à-vis the former Soviet power) and neo-colonialism (vis-à-vis the West)', thus creating something of a *double peripherality*.[113]

The overall GVC capitalist international (as per dependency theory), or world (as per world-system), system of international division of labour hence favours some nations to the detriment of others and limits the development possibilities of the subordinate economies.[114] The Rana Plaza disaster is thus an indirect yet undisputable proof of the main postulates of these theories.[115]

Global CSR standards were generally conceived to deal with the processing of production-related risks, including the risk of such events as the Rana Plaza catastrophe. The first standardisation organisations and associations were thus created as private non-profit organisations whose business was the provision of standard-related services and insurances.[116] As such, key players in value chains typically seek to ensure that all actors in the value chain follow the same standards that guarantee uniformity, simplification, modularisation and interchangeability, thus creating production and economic dependence.

IV. Organisational Context: Global Value Chain Governance

Following on from the discussion on conceptual and normative predecessors of GVCs in the previous section, it is important to specify a practical difference

[112] ibid 5.

[113] R Mańko et al, 'Law and Critique in Central Europe: Laying the Cornerstone' in R Mańko et al (eds), *Law and Critique in Central Europe: Questioning the Past, Resisting the Present* (Oxford, Counterpress, 2016) 1, 3. See also R Mańko, 'Being Central European, or Some Reflections on Law, Double Peripherality and the Political in Times of Transformation' in T Gábriš and J Sombati (eds), *Central and Eastern Europe as a Double Periphery?* (Berlin, Peter Lang, 2020) 17.

[114] ibid.

[115] For details of this incident, see further section VIII.B below.

[116] Frydman (n 86) 13; see also generally J Yates and CN Murphy, 'Coordinating International Standards: The Formation of the ISO' (2007) *MIT Sloan Research Paper* No 4638-07.

between value chains and supply chains.[117] While in the latter, competition between firms is primarily based on price and less so on quality (of either product or production process), in the former companies add value through transforming commodities into products of certain quality. In GVCs, corporations therefore produce, accumulate, distribute, and exchange *value*. These processes, in turn, depend on the way a value chain is governed.

Gereffi et al developed a theory of value chain governance and established five types of such governance. The main criteria for appreciation of the five types were: (i) the degree of complexity of information and knowledge transfer; (ii) the extent to which these transfers can be codified; and (iii) the ability of actual and potential suppliers to comply with the requirements.[118]

The first type in this taxonomy is *market-based* and is characterised by the small size of the final clientele that rely on bigger and more competent suppliers in a value chain that is based on relatively easy and 'codifiable' transactions.[119] Learning by imitation and from spillovers allows these small firms to capture knowledge for adaptive change.[120] Arguably, market-based GVC governance is somehow close to supply chains governance, the latter being about making processes efficient. The second kind of governance is termed *modular chains* – chains with highly codified links and transactions. Here it is the suppliers that are dependent on the customers, as the former must respond to the latter's specifications and learn how to produce components and modules in accordance with highly-specified technical standards.[121] In this type of governance, adherence to standards and delivering on time is part of the learning process.[122] The third type is a *network*. Transactions in such GVCs are not easily codified as they heavily rely on tacit knowledge.[123] Cooperation is mainly based on longer-term mutual trust and characterised by social and/or spatial proximity.[124] In the absence of fully codified standards, mutual assurances and commitments, as well as reputation, play a key role.[125] Where the competence gap between the lead firm and suppliers is large, a network-type chain can quickly become part of a larger *captive* chain (the fourth type) with a dominant lead firm making up for the lack of ability to codify transactions with increased control through hierarchical structures and vertical integration.[126]

[117] J Hughes, 'What Value Creation Will Look Like in the Future' *Harvard Business Review* (17 May 2013) https://hbr.org/2013/05/what-value-creation-will-look-like-in-the-future.

[118] Gereffi et al (n 52).

[119] J Humphrey and H Schmitz, 'Governance in Global Value Chains' (2001) 32 *IDS Bulletin* 19.

[120] ibid.

[121] C Pietrobelli and R Rabellotti, 'Global Value Chains Meet Innovation Systems: Are There Learning Opportunities for Developing Countries?' (2011) 39 *World Development* 1261.

[122] ibid.

[123] P Aerni, 'Do Private Standards Encourage or Hinder Innovation?' (2013) 18 *NCCR Trade Working Paper* 9–10.

[124] ibid.

[125] M Sako and S Helper, 'Determinants of Trust in Supplier Relations: Evidence from the Automotive Industry in Japan and the United States' (1998) 34 *Journal of Economic Behavior and Organization* 387.

[126] Aerni (n 123) 9.

The fifth type is an alternative to vertical integration: lead firms of an industry get together to develop common standards or, at least, benchmarks, for their particular business and to assume responsibility for all their actions and transactions. This happens when the biggest competitors of an industry decide that it makes more sense to cooperate than to compete at the basic level with an elementary added-value, as at a more advanced level this would improve the overall market.[127] They hence create an industry-wide regulation and even contribute to the shape of the applicable law that emerges.[128] The ability to control or at least influence the nature and scope of commercial obligations is an aspect of market power, and, traditionally, the most common commercial market- or industry-wide obligations are those that have been influenced by the leading firms of a business line.[129] However, this ability to determine or at least influence the nature and scope of commercial obligations of all actors of a GVC is also arguably a form of de facto legal control – the control that the head companies have over their business partners in GVCs and sometimes beyond.

The three last types of the way GVCs are governed, and especially the fifth one, are the most relevant for the present analysis. Notably, given that today's global assemblers and retailers are profit-oriented firms, and as such are not only unable but very often unwilling to assume their direct influence on standard-setting for the entire value chain, they make use of their standard-setting power to transfer responsibility to actors further down the value chain.[130] They often do so through private non-profit organisations that provide third-party accreditation and certification to suppliers wishing to gain access to the global market.[131] Global standard-setting bodies such as the ISO, naturally, provide such services.

V. Social Context: CSR Standards for and within Global Value Chains

The socialisation between firms in a value chain takes place through contracts, mostly ad hoc, but also – and increasingly – through information about accreditation, certification, and other means of compliance. This compliance obviously comprises CSR standards and may be directed at various types of entities. Those standards that are mainly directed to business and industry are called 'business-to-business' (B2B).[132] Today they include voluntary consensus standards set by

[127] D Vogel, 'The Private Regulation of Global Corporate Conduct. Achievements and Limitations' (2010) 49 *Business & Society* 77.

[128] Muchlinski (n 2) 80.

[129] ibid.

[130] Aerni (n 123) 5.

[131] ibid.

[132] A Kudryavtsev, 'Private Standardization and International Trade in Goods: Any WTO Law Implications for Domestic Regulation?' *Society of International Economic Law Working Paper* (2012) http://dx.doi.org/10.2139/ssrn.2082022, 12. See also generally GH Stanton, 'Private (Commercial) Standards

industry bodies or coalitions of firms, proprietary standards set by corporations, and third-party standards set by independent standard-setting bodies and other non-governmental organisations (NGOs).[133]

In addition to these B2B standards, corporations, especially in retail business, increasingly use their own particular 'business-to-consumer' (B2C) standards that are mainly directed at final consumers. They are used to inform consumers that the products so-labelled are addressing consumers' ethical and societal concerns to the greatest extent possible.[134] However, since retail firms may also be the final consumers of products, big firms are not excluded from the application of B2C standards.[135] For example, private B2C standards may come on top of B2B standards that are jointly set up by a coalition of corporations to guarantee the safety and sustainability of products, processes and production methods in GVCs, especially in food networks.[136]

These are the variations at the receiving end of international private standards. At the providing end of such standards, distinctions and differences also take place across the concepts and over time. Even inside the ISO itself – the world biggest standardisation entity – norm-production could be divided into at least three different phases, generating different types of norms:[137]

1 scientific standards: 1947–1980s: these standards cover only purely technical issues, such as industrial metrology, etc that are usually common in any country;
2 quality standards: the 1980s-early 1990s: these standards relate to management by objectives/quality management, with a never-ending search for improvement and rational decision-making. The cornerstone of this phase is the notion of responsibility for quality;
3 process- or management-based standards: starting from the 1990s onwards: this stage concerns a standardisation of corporate behaviour and production process. What is crucial now is no longer, or at least not only, the customer's satisfaction with quality (and therefore the producer's responsibility for low quality) but also, perhaps especially, the image of the producer, built and perceived through the degree of goodness and rightness of its production

and the SPS Agreement' (24 September 2007) *Remarks at The Round Table on The Role of Standards in International Food Trade*, The Cosmos Club, Washington, DC; GH Stanton, 'Food Safety-related Private Standards: The WTO Perspective' in A Marx et al (eds), *Private Standards and Global Governance. Economic, Legal, and Political Perspectives* (Northampton, Edward Elgar, 2012) 235; Humphrey and Schmitz (n 119); S Henson and J Humphrey, 'The Impacts of Private Food Safety Standards on the Food Chain and on Public Standard-setting processes' FAO/ WHO Report (2009) http://www.fao.org/docrep/016/ap236e/ap236e.pdf.

[133] Aerni (n 123) 4.

[134] Kudryavtsev (n 132) 11–13; see generally Henson and Humphrey (n 132).

[135] Aerni (n 123) 3–5; Henson and Humphrey (n 132).

[136] Aerni (n 123).

[137] Based on A Aseeva 'Global Trade Governance and Informal Voluntary Standards: The Socio-Normative Analysis of Legitimacy of the ISO' in A Tutumlu and G Gungor (eds), *Multilateralism in Global Governance: Formal and Informal Institutions* (Oxford, Peter Lang, 2016) 71, 74.

processes, brand management, and thus the consumer's ethical satisfaction with that image. In this phase, it is all about process quality (as opposed to product quality).

As mentioned in section IV above, in management terms, the difference between supply chains and value chains is that in the former companies compete on price and thus concentrate on the efficiency of the process of production, whereas in value chains, firms compete on value. GVC production therefore needs consumers much more than supply chain production does: consumers who buy certain products, not necessarily and not always because of their low price, but because those products correspond to their values and thus bring them aesthetic, ethical, or similar satisfaction – through the brand reputation, among other things.[138] The use of the corresponding ISO standards of the third generation and similar standards and labelling schemes is hence crucial for GVC head firms in their business and governance strategies for the whole chain.

As scientific progress does not stand still, so the standards accompanying it change too. Typical international CSR standards correspond in some degree to the 'last-generation' international standards, that is, the third type of the three generations of international private standards presented above in the example of the ISO.

VI. The Advent of International Standards

In this section, I offer an account of the fundamental rationale of the appearance and growing global popularity and use of private regulation and standards in transboundary business operations.

A. Voluntary Standards: Who Needs Them and Why?

While voluntary standards can be created by anyone, having them used and recognised in practice is a far more difficult task. For instance, in the 1990s, Microsoft managed this very successfully with MS DOS and Windows, whereas, essentially until the late 2000s Apple had much less success with its Mac/OS; and CPM, a popular operating system in the early 1980s, is hardly heard of by anyone today.[139] All of these standards were created by or for individual companies, which then used them to distinguish themselves in an effort to gain market share.[140]

[138] Hughes (n 117).

[139] International Institute for Sustainable Development (IISD) reports: (1) *Global Green Standards, ISO 14000 and Sustainable Development* (1996); (2) *ISO Social Responsibility Standardization* (2004a); and (3) *Issue Briefing Note: Stakeholder Engagement, ISO and Corporate Social Responsibility* (2004b).

[140] ibid.

Things are different when the lead firms make use of their position at the top of the hierarchy or, simply, their power to coordinate a GVC without having to assume responsibility for all its actions and transactions. For that purpose, they may make use of voluntary standards and similar corporate governance schemes as strategic business tools. Through different standards schemes, corporations gain and control market access, coordinate operations according to their preferences, provide product and production process quality and safety assurance, and even enhance their reputation in the eyes of the consumer and society at large. The last of these could be done by complementing their brands with niche premium products that respond to societal concerns expressed by consumer advocacy groups,[141] or else states, NGOs, and international organisations. It seems to be an alternative to vertical integration in some GVCs, as well as to the situation where firms adopt their own codes of conduct. For 'targeted' firms, an industry-wide regulation may make sense, strategically speaking. More specifically, because adopting higher societal standards can raise a firm's production costs, corporations try to compel their competitors to adopt similar standards, thus levelling the playing field.[142] As noted in previous sections, this could especially happen when big competitors in an industry or a business line decide that, rather than competing with one another through constantly searching for lower cost differentials than those of their competitors, they should standardise their corporate governance, as at a more advanced level this would improve the overall market.

When a larger base of public concerns, such as labour rights, consumer protection, public health, or the environment is involved, such 'sustainability' standards are most often outsourced to global standardising bodies in order for corporations or coalitions of firms to avoid a direct and individual responsibility for the creation of standards that are both global and collective. They are thus more usually prepared and adopted through a broader consensus process governed by stricter guidelines and regulations[143] in order to exhibit a certain deliberation, inclusiveness, and other corollaries of legitimacy for the process of the private standard-setting. Standards of this nature could especially be developed by accredited bodies that provide process assurances, such as the ISO, thus acting as professional facilitators of a consensual process.[144] These types of standards are usually developed 'by *industry experts* with a little push from *accountants* and *marketers*. Industry associations and private sector standards developers often provide the forum' (emphasis added).[145]

The advent of such international voluntary standards is mainly associated, at least in the Global North, with a rapid growth in the concentration of very large wholesalers and retailers. For instance, until very recently, the European food

[141] See eg T Reardon et al, 'Rural Nonfarm Income in Developing Countries' in *The State of Food and Agriculture* (Rome, United Nations Food and Agriculture Organization, 1998).

[142] Vogel (n 127) 77–78. See also IISD reports 1996 and 2004a (n 139).

[143] See IISD reports 1996 and 2004b (n 139).

[144] ibid.

[145] IISD report 1996 (n 139).

sector counted numerous mid-size intermediaries and a plethora of very small retailers.[146] Today, a handful of large supermarkets have consolidated power over the food value chain, and increasingly bypass any intermediary to source directly from domestic and foreign suppliers alike.[147]

The primary entities imposing purely private standards within GVCs are most often the wholesalers such as supermarkets and hypermarkets, eg Tesco, Walmart, Lidl, Carrefour, etc. For example, as relevant international trade surveys indicate, the major retailers and suppliers in the US and the EU impose private standards throughout their value chains.[148] All types of businesses seem to be impacted by such standards, including small-, medium- and large-scale enterprises.[149] Private standards used and imposed down the value chain by such global food and wholesale giants as Heinz, McDonalds, Aldi, Edeka/Netto, Carrefour, Lidl, Metro, Norma, Plus, Rewe, Tegut, Tengelman, Marks and Spencer, and Metro Cash and Carry are also mentioned.[150] The most cited standards and codes in the responses to surveys regarding food and safety are GLOBALGAP, Hazard Analysis, Critical Control Point (HACCP), and Safe Quality Food (SQF), as well as various ISO standards.[151]

B. A Facilitative Role of GVC Governance 'Gaps'

Along with this concentration of market and purchasing power, as well as a marked reduction in the number of players – and, particularly, smaller competitors – has come a shift in consumer expectations.[152] Taste, freshness, price and quality of food, availability or affordability of fuel are no longer enough for consumers from the most advanced economies. Today they also want the goods and services they consume to reflect their progressive values – social, ethical, environmental.[153]

One response of governments to the above developments was to shift the health, safety, environmental, food quality and like controls from the testing of final retail products to the much lauded, more holistic farm-to-fork or stable-to-table approach.[154] This attempt to bring the regulation of GVCs to the realm of

[146] Stanton (n 132) 1.

[147] ibid.

[148] WTO, Committee on Sanitary and Phytosanitary Measures 'Effects of SPS-Related Private Standards' Descriptive Report – Note by the Secretariat, WTO Doc.NO. WTO G/SPS/GEN/932 10, 13.

[149] ibid 11–14.

[150] ibid 10, 13.

[151] ibid 11.

[152] See eg Stanton (n 132) 1–3.

[153] See eg Alessandra Arcuri, who discusses such a trend of 'value-based labelling' against the background of Polanyi's 'human economy': A Arcuri, 'The TBT Agreement and Private Standards' in T Epps and MJ Trebilcock (eds), *Research Handbook on the WTO and Technical Barriers to Trade* (Northampton, Edward Edgar, 2013) 485, 488.

[154] See eg P Aerni, 'Do Private Standards Encourage or Hinder Innovation?' (2013) 18 *NCCR Trade Working Paper* 12–13.

public law and policy has ultimately pushed the lead firms of value chains to put in place risk management, certification, labelling, and similar systems that ensure safety at all stages of a value chain – from the upstream level to final retail sale.[155]

It is thus important to sketch how and why, since the 1990s and especially for the last two decades, an important proliferation of the societal legislative, regulatory and litigation framework took place, in particular across the Global North.[156] National, regional, and global instruments, of both a soft and a hard law nature, applying to labour, the environment, health, and safety have tightened up and represent increasingly stricter requirements for gradually targeted issues.[157] Litigation aiming to expand the scope of corporate societal obligations and liability for harms arising from cross-border production and commerce is also on the rise.[158]

Acknowledging that many private standards fill the governance gaps and, at times, that governments allocate the social costs of transboundary production without any democratic delegation to do so, not to mention the very questionable fairness of such re-allocation, is one thing. But it is important to stress that the very evolution of relevant public law and regulation has significantly contributed to the advent and proliferation of private and hybrid schemes as a response to a growing public pressure to ensure that private firms meet those increasingly stringent regulatory requirements. Notably, as described in previous sections, these initial public regulations were often themselves an outcome of active lobbying and at times pressure by the most powerful domestic industrial and corporate lobbies of the most advanced economies.[159]

In other words, today's *private* corporate self-regulation as well as *global* CSR standards produced by public (eg the UN) and private (eg ISO) norm-setters alike are mostly the direct result of *public* and often *local* hard laws, the latter themselves being an outcome of previous lobbying of the same *global* and *private* actors.

Take the example of the introduction of the strict liability and due diligence requirements in the UK Food Safety Act 1990.[160] It bound food businesses all along the supply chain to be able to prove that they did their best to ensure that their products complied with food safety requirements, by being 'of the nature, substance and quality demanded' and correctly so described (or labelled).[161] It also held food businesses liable for the safety and quality of the food supplied to customers.[162]

[155] ibid.

[156] ibid 13.

[157] I discuss several such instruments below, starting in Chapter 3.

[158] See eg Chapter 5, section II and Chapter 7, sections I–III below.

[159] H Schepel, *The Constitution of Private Governance: Product Standards in the Regulation of Integrated Markets* (Oxford, Hart Publishing, 2005): for Europe see 38 ff, and for the US see 77 ff.

[160] UK Food Safety Act 1990 (c 16); The Food Safety Act 1990 (Amendment) Regulations 2004, SI 2004/2990. See also S Henson and J Northern, 'Economic Determinants of Food Safety Controls in the Supply of Retailer Own Branded Products in the UK' (1998) 14 *Agribusiness* 113; Henson and Humphrey (n 132); Stanton (n 132) 2–3.

[161] UK Food Safety Act 1990, ibid.

[162] ibid.

One important impact on the production and distribution of food products was that a food business operator at every next stage of production and/or distribution was from now on deprived from employing a 'warranty defence' based on assurance from its supplier that the provided product was safe.[163] In order to be exempted from such strict liability obligation, a business had to exercise due diligence prior to performing its work on the product in question.[164]

The above developments have had quite far-reaching consequences, first in the UK, and later throughout the world. In order to provide this proof of due diligence, the food industry had to immediately set up a system of standards to increase the control and monitoring of supply chains. At first, this created a certain amount of confusion and conflict, as well as lack of accreditation and monitoring mechanisms, because each operator would set its own standards.[165] Later in the 1990s, the codes of good practice and other private voluntary standards, such as Good Agricultural Practices (GAP) schemes, and a protocol of good hygiene practices (which later became the British Retailer Consortium Global Standard) helped to standardise and simplify the overall control of producers.[166] Over the years, the use of private regulation by the food industry increased dramatically in the UK and globally, and it now plays a major role in global food value chains.[167]

Some scholars define the body of private standards dealing with the social, safety and environmental impacts of transboundary business operations as 'civil regulation'.[168] The 'civil' seems to point here to the public demand for regulating the transboundary production and supply, as well as the distribution of social costs, and is supposed to be addressed to and especially *influenced* by the citizen-consumer,[169] or maybe by society at large. Those who do not comply with such so-called civil regulation would thus typically face civil (or 'social') sanctions, such as communal or market penalties rather than formal legal sanctions.[170]

The consumer-led, or 'civil' part of the scope of private standards is most often based on, and streamlined through, labelling schemes. Take the Max Havelaar story, for example. The Max Havelaar scheme emerged as a response to the absence of restrictive legislation that would name and blame bad labour practices outside the Dutch jurisdiction that were resulting in the production of goods that were

[163] ibid.
[164] ibid.
[165] S Henson and J Humphrey, 'Private Standards in Global Agri-food Chains' in Marx et al (n 132) 101, 105.
[166] Stanton (n 132) 2–3.
[167] ibid.
[168] 'Civil regulations employ private, non-state, or market-based regulatory frameworks to govern multinational firms and global supply networks. A defining feature of civil regulations is that their legitimacy, governance, and implementation is not rooted in public authority. Typically operating beside or around the state rather than through it, civil regulations are based on "soft law" or private law rather than legally enforceable standards: Violators typically face social or market penalties rather than legal sanctions': Vogel (n 127) 86–87. See also Arcuri (n 153) 487–89.
[169] Arcuri (n 153) 488.
[170] Vogel (n 142) 68–87.

imported into the Netherlands. The Max Havelaar scheme has actually filled that regulatory gap.[171] It was only later that national binding hard law has been created, for example the new Dutch Child Labour Due Diligence Law (2019).

Finally, and importantly, there are 'meta-regulation' standards.[172] They set the rules on how to produce and manage private and hybrid standards. First of all, the difference between standards and schemes of standards (or standardisation schemes) should be emphasised. Standards schemes include and introduce a series of pre-requisite programmes to comply with control points before being able to apply a standard.[173] That is, such programmes are not part of standards themselves, but a series of preconditions.[174]

In food safety, for instance, those pre-requisites are defined as 'the basic conditions and activities that are necessary to maintain an hygienic environment suitable for the production of safe food'.[175] Notably, the standards schemes are more flexible than the standards themselves, because they could include additional items of concern when public laws and regulations change, or even sometimes when consumers' tastes and habits change. Those added items are additional because they are not main drivers of a scheme, ie not the raison d'être or the core of the scheme. For example, based on article L.641-1 of French *Code rural*, the French Label Rouge Scheme's main standard attests that food or non-food and unprocessed agricultural products have specific characteristics establishing a superior level of taste quality, resulting especially from their specific production conditions,[176] while it can additionally include such preconditions to use the scheme as environmental impact or workers' welfare at firms seeking to apply their standard to relevant products.[177]

Another form of meta-regulation is the establishment of procedural and substantive guidance for standard-setting and implementation.[178] For example, the ISO's Committee on conformity assessment (CASCO) itself develops standards and addresses issues related to conformity assessment. In fact, ISO per se does not participate in the certification, inspection, testing, and the like of firms, but offers ready-to-use standards for such activities.[179]

A meta-regulation of a similar kind is the one that is handled by global non-government consortiums focused on sectoral standards, related to sustainability

[171] See World Fair Trade Organization (WFTO), 'History of Fairtrade' https://wfto.com/about-us/history-wfto/history-fair-trade#:~:text=It%20all%20started%20in%20the,in%201958%20in%20the%20USA. See also Ecolectia, 'Max Havelaar: How a fictional story becomes a reality' https://ecolectia.com/en/news/detail/max-havelaar-how-a-fictional-story-becomes-a-reality.html.

[172] Arcuri (n 153) 495–96.

[173] Henson and Humphrey (n 165) 108–109.

[174] ibid.

[175] K Swoffer, 'GFSI and the Relationship with Codex' (2009) *Presentation made at CIES international Food Safety Conference*, Paris, slide 2.

[176] Label Rouge, 'Label Rouge' http://www.labelrouge.fr/.

[177] Henson and Humphrey (n 165) 101.

[178] Arcuri (n 153) 495–96.

[179] ISO, *Conformity assessment*, see above.

concerns. One of the most prominent examples in the area is the International Social and Environmental Accreditation and Labelling (ISEAL) Alliance, which is the global membership association for sustainability standards.[180] The ISEAL Code of Good Practice for Setting Social and Environmental Standards defines effective standard-setting on procedural and substantive levels, thereby arguably increasing the credibility of the final products – the standards.[181] Notably, ISEAL's Code was referenced and used by a variety of national and international public institutions including the UK Department for Environment, Food and Rural Affairs, Food and Agricultural Organisation (FAO), the World Bank, the UNCTAD and the World Wide Fund for Nature (WWF).[182]

VII. The Many Shades of Voluntary Standards and Corporate Self-Regulation

A general illustration of voluntary standards at the global level is governance practices by which global infrastructures such as GVCs are managed, or which develop in a situation where the conflict of fundamental interests of different social groups must be dealt with.[183] Regarding a possible taxonomy of such activities, they are today extremely diverse and are operated by a wide range of entities and through various arrangements. Virtually the only features they have in common appear to be an arguably voluntary and consensual nature; allegedly technical, as opposed to legal, scope; and, consequently, an absence of any legal validity or formal binding force.

Research often classifies relevant standards by theme,[184] such as social and environmental standards (eg FSC,[185] MSC,[186] ISO 14000 series,[187] Carbon Trust,[188] Blue Angel,[189] Nordic Swan,[190] GSCP,[191] and many others), food standards

[180] ISEAL, 'About us' http://www.isealalliance.org/about-iseal.

[181] Arcuri (n 153) 495–96. See also ISEAL, 'Our work' https://www.isealalliance.org/get-involved/resources/iseal-codes-good-practice.

[182] ISEAL, ibid.

[183] See eg A von Bogdandy et al, 'Developing the Publicness of Public International Law: Towards a Legal Framework for Global Governance Activities' (2008) 9 *German Law Journal* 1375, 1385.

[184] See generally A Marx et al, 'Introduction: Private Standards and Global Governance' in Marx et al (n 132); F Van Waarden, 'Governing Global Commons: The Public-Private Protection of Fish and Forests' in Marx et al, *Private Standards* (n 132); A Marx et al, 'Private Standards in Forestry: Assessing the Legitimacy and Effectiveness of the Forest Stewardship Council' in Marx et al, *Private Standards* (n 132); GH Stanton, 'Food Safety-related Private Standards: The WTO Perspective' in Marx et al, *Private Standards* (n 132); B Holvoet and B Muys, 'Sustainable Forest Management Worldwide: a Comparative Assessment of Standards' (2004) 6 *International Forestry Review* 99.

[185] FSC, 'FSC' https://ic.fsc.org/.

[186] MSC, 'MSC' http://www.msc.org/.

[187] ISO, 'ISO 14000' https://www.iso.org/iso-14001-environmental-management.html.

[188] Carbontrust, 'Carbon Trust' http://www.carbontrust.com/.

[189] Blue Angel, 'Products' http://www.blauer-engel.de/en/.

[190] Nordic Ecolabel, 'Nordic Ecolabel' http://www.nordic-ecolabel.org.

[191] Global Social Compliance Program, 'GSC' http://supply-chain.unglobalcompact.org/site/article/126.

(eg Codex Alimentarius,[192] ISO 22000 series, IFS,[193] SQF,[194] BAP,[195]), or human rights and CSR standards (eg ISO 26000 series,[196] Max Havelaar,[197] now actually part of Fairtrade[198]). Some authors instead classify such standards depending on their design and governing structure.[199] For example, a guarantee for consumers through labelling schemes visible on products (eg the US 'Dolphins safe label'[200] or the label 'Swedish Seal'[201]) would differ under such classification from the B2B mechanisms that could still inform customers if they are other businesses, but are not directly designed to inform final – individual – consumers (eg GLOBAL GAP[202]).

Focusing specifically on the types of actors, Michael Cardwell and Fiona Smith offer a spectrum of relevant standards and standardising bodies as follows:[203]

- global actors' outputs, such as the World Bank and its Doing Business Index,[204] Codex Alimentarius,[205] or GLOBAL GAP,[206] and more hybrid entities, such as the ISO;[207]
- regional arrangements, such as the EU biofuel feedstock certification;[208]

[192] Codex Alimentarius 'Codex Alimentarius Commission' http://www.fao.org/fao-who-codexalimentarius/committees/cac/about/en/.

[193] International Food Standard, 'Certification' http://www.ifs-certification.com/index.php/en.

[194] Safe Quality Food, 'Services' http://www.intertek.com/food/services/sqf/.

[195] GAA Alliance, 'Best Aquaculture Practice' https://www.lr.org/en/gaa-bap/.

[196] ISO, 'ISO 26000' https://www.iso.org/iso-26000-social-responsibility.html.

[197] WFTO (n 171).

[198] Fair Trade, 'Fair Trade' http://www.fairtrade.net/.

[199] Generally, J Wouters et al, 'Private Standards, Global Governance and International Trade: The Case of Global Food Safety Governance' in Marx et al (n 184).

[200] US Government, 'USDC Dolphins Safe Label' https://www.federalregister.gov/documents/2013/04/05/2013-07990/enhanced-document-requirements-to-support-use-of-the-dolphin-safe-label-on-tuna-products.

[201] Swedish Government, 'Swedish Seal Label' https://www.svensktsigill.se/. In English, see https://www.klimatmarkningen.se/in-english.

[202] GLOBAL GAP, 'About Us' https://www.globalgap.org/uk_en/who-we-are/about-us/.

[203] M Cardwell and F Smith, 'Contemporary Problems of Climate Change and the TBT Agreement: Moving Beyond Eco-labelling' in T Epps and MJ Treblicock (eds), *Research Handbook on the WTO and Technical Barriers to Trade* (Northampton, Edward Edgar, 2013) 391, 397–400, 414–15.

[204] World Bank, 'Doing Business Index' https://doingbusiness.org/.

[205] Codex Alimentarius (n 192).

[206] GLOBAL GAP (n 202).

[207] ISO, 'ISO' https://www.iso.org/home.html.

[208] Notably, such supranational/regional schemes, especially the EU ones, may derive from EU soft or even hard law, such as the Regulation on EU Ecolabelling. See Regulation (EC) No 1980/2000 of the European Parliament and of the Council of 17 July 2000 on a revised Community eco-label award scheme, OJ L 237, 21 September 2000, 1. See also EU Renewable Energy Directive: Council Regulation (EC) 2009/28/EC, OJ L 140, 5 June 2009, 16. However, these instruments merely 'call', 'encourage' or 'motivate' countries to meet goals or make policy reforms: eg 'encourage the development of multilateral and bilateral agreements and voluntary international or national schemes that set standards for the production of sustainable biofuels and bioliquids, and that certify that the production of biofuels and bioliquids meets those standards': EU Renewable Energy Directive, ibid, Preamble, 79.

- outputs by national public actors, such as German 'Blue Angel' or Scandinavian 'Nordic Swan' eco-labels;[209] and
- outputs by private actors, such as the Marks & Spencer carbon labelling scheme, for example.[210]

Under the last rubric, firms could be self-certified, thus constituting a self-declaration by the standard-setter or by the standard-implementer (second-party certification).[211] Another type of standards scheme under this rubric is a third-party certification through, most typically, a conformity assessment done by a third party: notably, the ISO-developed guidelines for both the operation of standards and for auditing by certifiers.[212]

The seminal 'governance triangle' of Kenneth Abbott and Duncan Snidal is of course crucial for classifying international standards, including private standards in GVCs.[213] The scheme is quite in unison with the preceding classification focused on types of actors setting the standards. Indeed, the above triangle mainly focuses on the norm-givers, that is, standard-setters, although, Abbott and Snidal's taxonomy is at once broader, as it comprises the largest spectrum possible for standard-setting groups of actors such as states, private firms and civil society (thus covering the whole potential regulatory space); and deeper, as it distinguishes seven zones of action, illustrating situations when one (Zones 1–3), two (Zones 4–6), or three (Zone 7) groups set standards.[214]

In their studies, Spenser Henson and John Humphrey focus specifically on food chains,[215] but their distinction between standards could be applicable to standards in other types of GVCs. While they classify standards by norm-producers just as many other authors cited above, Henson and Humphrey also offer a valuable distinction between two groups of private standards regarding their level of requirements.[216] The first kind is the so-called baseline type of standards, which sets a minimum standard: a minimum threshold below which a producer or distributor of goods could not actually go, otherwise, they will be de facto penalised by being denied access to a given market. In contrast, the second type is the 'high-level' standard, which, while still being optional, sets a maximum threshold. The baseline standard would thus represent an incentive for producers to improve the quality of their products, as well as their brand image. The high-level standards are, however, likely to introduce an additional motivation, and, if applied,

[209] 'Blue Angel' and 'Nordic Swan' labels (nn 189, 190).

[210] Marks & Spencer, 'Marks & Spencer carbon labelling scheme' https://corporate.marksandspencer.com/sustainability.

[211] Henson and Humphrey (n 165) 100–101.

[212] ISO, 'What is conformity assessment?' https://www.iso.org/conformity-assessment.html.

[213] KW Abbott and D Snidal, 'Strengthening International Regulation through Transnational New Governance: Overcoming the Orchestration Deficit' (2009) 42 *Vanderbilt Journal of Transnational Law* 501, 513.

[214] ibid 501–519.

[215] See Henson and Humphrey (n 132).

[216] Henson and Humphrey (n 165) 101–103.

a possibility for producers and suppliers to gain and maintain access to richer markets.

Grethen Stanton identifies relevant standards as generally addressing consumer interests in many categories. Such standards can cover food safety, environment, social or labour conditions, corporate responsibility, the carbon footprint of products, and their associated 'food miles'; they can range from individual retailer labels (eg Tesco Nature's Choice[217]) to collective national and international schemes such as GLOBAL GAP, a coalition between the major global retailers; and they may cover just one or all stages from farm to processing to distribution.[218]

As discussed in previous sections, different researchers delved into what private voluntary standards in transborder commercial transactions represented in terms of the interface between business organisations and public policies and society.[219] Those standards today comprise voluntary consensus standards set by industry or consortiums of firms; third-party standards set by independent standard-setting bodies and other non-governmental associations; and proprietary standards set by individual companies. They comprise both B2B and B2C schemes, as in practice the application of standards to these two categories very often intermingles. The objective of those schemes is arguably to signal to customers down the value chain, but also and increasingly to both home and host governments, watchdogs, civil society – and society at large – that the products or services marked by such standards are addressing their sustainability concerns to the greatest extent possible, thus becoming important tools of *reputation* management.

Notably, the OECD divides relevant standards into private and public standards, although the line separating them is not always well defined.[220] As already emphasised in section VI above, in many instances, standards eventually sanctioned by governments and based on public law have their origins in private industry and corporate production. These government policies and regulations, in conjunction with the input, process and performance standards for products, in fact significantly influence how private markets function and develop.

From the perspective of economic theory, the distinction between public and private standards in a functional context depends more on *whose interests* are taken into account when a standard is set and enforced.[221] Regarding a state-sanctioned standard based on a public policy, it is assumed that the interests of all actors in

[217] Tesco, 'Tesco Nature's Choice' http://midkentgrowers.co.uk/tesco-standard/.

[218] Stanton (n 132).

[219] Henson and Humphrey (n 165) 101–103; Stanton (n 132).

[220] This paragraph is based on OECD, Activity F of the programme of work 2005–2006 *The Impacts of Private Voluntary Standards on Market Access*, 'Interaction of public and private standards in the food chain', Document AGR/CA/APM(2006)21/FINAL, 5–6; see also Table 1 'Classification of food standards': (i) Standards by measurement; (ii) Standards by definition; (iii) Standards for products Standards for processes;(iv) Standards on design; (v) Standards on performance; (vi) Public standards; (vii) Private standards; (viii) Mandatory standards; (ix) Voluntary standards. See also T Becker, 'The Economics of Food Quality Standards' Workshop paper presented to Second Interdisciplinary Workshop on Standardisation Research Hamburg (24–27 May 1999).

[221] Based on OECD, ibid.

a given economy – producers and consumers alike, as well as the society at large (externalities) – are taken into consideration when a standard is set by the government. Conversely, private standards are assumed to primarily take account of the profits and interests of firms or other such private entities. They are likely to reflect the interests of consumers, but only to the extent that such interests correspond to those of the entity that created the standard, and are reflected in the price. Standards can also be set by NGOs, thus forming yet another category of private standards. NGOs tend to be non-profit oriented and do not always pursue the same objectives as governments in standard setting. However, NGOs do not necessarily pursue the objectives of consumers or other concerned communities either, but primarily those of their main donors.

The ISO's Committee on Consumer Policy (COPOLCO), while addressing the standards within its realm, offers a compendious taxonomy as follows:

- inter-governmental initiatives;
- governmental legislative initiatives;
- investor-driven initiatives;
- initiatives from recognised standards bodies;
- multi-jurisdictional initiatives from non-recognised standards bodies;
- domestic voluntary initiatives.[222]

UNCTAD's 2011 typology of sources of the compliance mechanisms of selected international standards relevant for international production and development (mainly sorted by source of standard) is as follows:

- intergovernmental organisations' standards, such as UN Global Compact; OECD Guidelines; ILO Tripartite Declaration;
- multistakeholder/NGOs standards: eg ISO14000; MSC; FSC; FLA RSPO; SA8000; 4C Assoc; ISO 26000; GRI; and
- company/industry association standards: eg CAFE Practices, Leather Working Group; BSCI; International Council of Toy Industries; EICC; Pharmaceutical Industry Principles for Responsible Supply Chain Management.[223]

To summarise the above accounts, actors in both the supply and demand sides of global voluntary standard-setting and the rationale of their practices complement each other. But sometimes they could also overlap and mirror each other, as in the case of the tightening up of national and international laws and regulations in socially imperative sectors.

[222] ISO, 'Report to ISO COPOLCO on Desirability and Feasibility of ISO CSR Standards' (2002) Final report https://www.iso.org/files/live/sites/isoorg/files/archive/pdf/en/sr_ims_5-2002.pdf.

[223] UNCTAD, *World Investment Report 2011: Non-Equity Modes of International Production and Development*, 115, Table III.4.

VIII. The Rise and Fall of CSR

In this section, I offer a general discussion of an unprecedented profusion of international private and hybrid standards relating to CSR in global economic governance in the second half of the twentieth century, and especially since the 1980s, as well as the overall drive to globalisation and technical innovation of the late twentieth century (Section A). I then turn to a concrete vantage point, the Rana Plaza catastrophe, which could be said to be a boundary dividing the 'before' and the 'after' of corporate social responsibility in global value chains (Section B).

A. Globalisation, Technical Innovation and the Rise of Global Private Regulation

In the previous sections of this chapter I have demonstrated that regulatory processes in socially imperative sectors go hand-in-hand with the scientific progress. This brings to any area marked by technical innovation an increase of labour division, introduction of trademarks, labelling and certification, risk and safety standards, and other corollaries of scientific progress; the economic globalisation only enhances such processes.[224] It seems to be reciprocal, as through the standardisation of distinct and otherwise often incompatible products, the private standard-setters also participate in the processes of globalisation.[225]

Regulation is needed when there is risk and thus something to keep safe. Intuitively, this would be a regulation by democratically elected actors, such as state and other *public* actors. At the same time, such public goods as the environment, for example, are today recognised as typical global public goods.[226] Indeed, as there is a *global* interdependency regarding climate change, the loss of biodiversity, or human rights abuses in GVCs, global governance and regulatory cooperation are said to be necessary on a global scale.[227]

As established in the previous sections of this chapter, traditional governance methods relying on public law, including public international law, are increasingly complemented, and, indeed, unseated by private and hybrid initiatives and corresponding transnational arrangements, with all the consequent questions that typically arise: eg accountability and responsibility, as well as the actual societal effectiveness of such initiatives and arrangements.

As early as in 1977, the corporate code of conduct, known as the first of the two Sullivan Principles' codes was developed to compel TNCs operating in apartheid South Africa to oppose the regime by putting economic pressure on the

[224] Hale et al (n 13) 131.

[225] Arcuri (n 153) 485.

[226] See various contributions to S Cogolati and J Wouters (eds), *The Commons and a New Global Governance* (Cheltenham, Edward Elgar, 2018).

[227] See Marx et al (n 132) 1; Van Waarden (n 184) 15–16.

country's government through divestment, as well as by promoting social justice through ensuring workers' and labour unions rights for the Black population of the country.[228] It was ultimately adopted by more than 125 corporations as the first ever voluntary CSR code.[229]

While US (and some Dutch) corporations started using corporate self-regulation on a regular basis in the early 1990s, the current UK and French understanding of CSR emerged only towards the early 2000s.[230] For example, in the early 1990s Levi Strauss introduced in its GVCs strict ethical standards applying to the 'terms of engagement' that its subcontractors along the value chain had to respect in order to obtain a contract from the company.[231] In 1993, the global jeans producer even withdrew from production in Myanmar and investment in China.[232]

On the dark side of the dawn of transnational CSR, some corporations went so far as to attempt to influence the laws of the foreign state hosting those firms. A pioneer in this feat, the ambitious 1992 Caterpillar Code of Worldwide Business Conduct and Operating Principles aimed to 'offer recommendations to governments concerning legislation and regulation' and to 'selectively analyse and take positions on *issues* which affect the company …', without, however, promising to respect laws of host countries.[233]

A necessary historical, ideational and conceptual detour in the previous sections of this chapter (especially sections I–III) has shown that the existing public national and international arrangements fail to appropriately handle the global societal challenges resulting from trade liberalisation and the globalisation of production. An operational, and above all, accurate and fair allocation of the social costs of transnational production and distribution is one such challenge. It is nowadays often asserted that private and hybrid mechanisms succeed where governments seem to fail.[234] However, it is also regularly claimed that such global governance through private standards impedes transboundary trade flows,[235] and even more so the development of poorer countries.[236]

[228] The second code was adopted in 1999 as a more general global CSR code beyond the target of the already abolished apartheid regime of South Africa. See generally A Gwendolyn 'The Global Sullivan Principles' in N Cohen (ed), *Green Business: An A-to-Z Guide*, vol 5 (Thousand Oaks, Sage Publications, 2011) 1.

[229] Muchlinski (n 2) 84.

[230] University of Amsterdam and KPMG Global Sustainability Services, *KPMG International Survey of Corporate Responsibility Reporting 2005* (2005) http://www.theiafm.org/publications/243_International_Survey_Corporate_Responsibility_2005.pdf. But compare with a later KPMG's report: KPMG International Cooperative, *The KPMG Survey of Corporate Responsibility Reporting 2017* (2017) https://assets.kpmg/content/dam/kpmg/xx/pdf/2017/10/kpmg-survey-of-corporate-responsibility-reporting-2017.pdf.

[231] Muchlinski (n 2) 84.

[232] ibid.

[233] ibid 90.

[234] Arcuri (n 153) 486.

[235] ibid.

[236] See section III.B above.

As outlined in section VII above, many authors distinguish between the individual firm standards, as well as hybrid national, regional, international standards schemes, and so on, by categorising them mainly on the basis of the *source* of a standard – namely, by actors who created the standard.[237] However, and more in line with the preferred methodology of this book, I would rather focus on the individual consumers, third-world workers, the environment, and society at large who are on the receiving end of the standards, and the real-world effects on them, rather than on the upstream sources of the standard-setting. For example, as I previously argued, an ability of head corporations to determine – or at least influence – the nature and scope of commercial obligations of all actors of a GVC by setting standards for the whole chain is arguably a form of de facto legal control.

What could – and should – lawyers do about the controversial normative force of such standards, and especially their adverse actual effects on the actors of GVC production as well as on third parties?

The existing legal scholarship has addressed these questions from a number of angles. One such strand has studied voluntary standards established by hybrid global and regional organisations, as outlined in previous sections. This angle attracted much attention in the past.[238] However, it appears that these past academic debates did not consider many purely private regulatory instruments, or some ethical and fairness standards.[239] To date, only a few book-length studies have paid attention to private regulation, including fairness and ethical standards, in GVCs.[240]

Another thread of the debate considers the various approaches to law and norms per se in a globalised world. More 'black-letter' legal scholars view private regulatory instruments as social – or, more often, *non-legal* – norms since, they argue, law properly so called is restricted to the rules stemming from classically legitimate – ie legally valid – sources of law.[241] Classical liberal and neoliberal

[237] See the many authors cited in section VII on a general classification of global standards. See also for example C Wolff and M Scannell, 'Implication of Private Standards in International Trade of Animals and Animal Products' (2008) in *Proceedings of OIE 76th General Session of the Informal Committee*, 2–3 and Table 1.

[238] Today some scholars continue studying transnational sustainability standards from this angle. See eg P Paiement, *Transnational Sustainability Laws* (Cambridge, Cambridge University Press, 2017).

[239] But see generally C Glinski, 'Bridging the Gap: the Legal Potential of Private Regulation' in O Dilling et al (eds), *Responsible Business: Self-governance and Law in Transnational Economic Transactions* (Oxford, Hart Publishing, 2008) 41; A Beckers, *Enforcing Corporate Social Responsibility Codes: on Global Self-regulation and National Private Law* (Oxford, Hart Publishing, 2015).

[240] But see generally A Rühmkorf, *Corporate Social Responsibility, Private Law and Global Supply Chains* (Cheltenham, Edward Elgar, 2015); L Vytopil, *Contractual Control in the Supply Chain. On Corporate Social Responsibility, Codes of Conduct and (Avoiding) Liability* (The Hague, Eleven International Publishing, 2015); V Ulfbeck et al (eds), *Corporate Social Responsibility in Supply Chains: Contract and Tort – Interplay and Overlap* (Abingdon, Routledge, 2019).

[241] See relevant debates of different schools of thought in eg Aseeva (n 137) 73–76. See also generally L Boisson de Chazournes, 'Standards, régulation internationale et organisations internationales' in B Frydman and A Van Waeyenberge (eds), *Gouverner par les standards et les indicateurs: de Hume aux rankings* (Brussels, Bruylant, 2014) 69; JF Riffard, 'La mutation de la norme: l'avènement d'un droit nivelé? Ou retour sur quelques aspects de l'unification et la globalisation des droits' in N Martial-Braz et al (eds), *Les mutations de la norme* (Paris, Economica, 2011) 93.

lawyers, especially in the field of international arbitration, often have private law-oriented ideas of self-organisation, or else governance by professional customs and standards, such as, most typically, the ideas on the *lex mercatoria*.[242] They thus plead in favour of recognising hybrid and purely private regulation as legal norms, and hence as legitimate and valid.

Other scholarly strands, often called progressive, such as global legal pluralism, global constitutionalism, or else the pragmatic approach to law, also tend to recognise private regulation as law. Relevant discussions and analyses thus far include a systems approach addressing the fragmentation of international law, proliferation of various legal systems, and regulatory powers and implications beyond states[243] and global[244] – as well as transnational[245] legal pluralism; the neighbouring normative pluralism;[246] global constitutionalism approaching the plurality of global governance manifestations from a constitutionalist perspective,[247] and global administrative law (GAL) doing so from an administrative law viewpoint;[248]

[242] See eg A Kassis, *Théorie Générale des usages du commerce : Droit comparé, contrats et arbitrage internationaux, lex mercatoria* (Paris, Librarie Générale de droit et de jurisprudence, 1984); B Goldman, 'The Applicable Law: General Principles of Law – the Lex Mercatoria' in JDM Lew (ed), *Contemporary Problems in International Arbitration* (London, The Eastern Press, 1987) 113–25; ME Basile et al (eds), *Lex Mercatoria and Legal Pluralism: A Late Thirteenth Century Treaties and Its Aftermath* (Cambridge, Ames Foundation, 1998); KP Berger, *The Creeping Codification of the New Lex Mercatoria*, 2nd edn (Zuidpoolsingel, Kluwer Law International, 2010). For critiques, See eg G Teubner, '"Global Bukowina": Legal Pluralism in World Society' in Teubner (n 2) 3, 9–11; see generally HJ Mertens, 'Lex Mercatoria: A Self-appying Beyond National Law?' in Teubner (n 2) 31.

[243] See generally A Fischer-Lescano and G Teubner, 'Regime Collisions: The Vain Search for Legal Unity in the Fragmentation of Global Law' (2004) 25 *Michigan Journal of International Law* 999; Teubner (n 2).

[244] Teubner (n 2).

[245] P Zumbansen, 'Transnational Leal Pluralism' (2010) 1 *Transnational Legal Theory* 141; R Cotterrell, 'Spectres of Transnationalism: Changing Terrains of Sociology of Law' (2009) 36 *Journal of Law and Society* 481; R Cotterrell, 'What is Transnational Law?' (2012) 37 *Law & Social Inquiry* 500; R Cotterrell, 'Rethinking "Embeddedness": Law, Economy, Community' (2013) 40 *Journal of Law and Society* 49.

[246] WL Twining, *Globalisation & Legal Theory* (Cambridge, Cambridge University Press, 2000); WL Twining, 'A Post-Westphalian Conception of Law' (2003) 37 *Law and Society Review* 199; WL Twining, 'Diffusion of Law: a Global Perspective' (2004) 49 *Journal of Legal Pluralism* 1; WL Twining, 'Social Science and Diffusion of Law' (2005) 32 *Journal of Law & Society* 203; WL Twining, 'Legal Pluralism and Normative Pluralism: A Global Perspective', 20 *Duke Journal of Comparative and International Law* 472.

[247] DZ Cass, 'The "Constitutionalization" of International Trade Law: Judicial Norm-Generation as the Engine of Constitutional Development in International Trade' (2001) 12 *European Journal of International Law* 39; JL Dunoff, 'Why Constitutionalism Now? Text, Context and the Historical Contingency of Ideas' (2005) 1 *Journal of International Law & International Relations* 191; JL Dunoff and JP Trachtman (eds), *Ruling the World? Constitutionalism, International Law, and Global Governance* (Cambridge, Cambridge University Press, 2009); AM Slaughter and W Burke-White, 'An International Constitutional Moment' (2002) 43 *Harvard International Law Journal* 1; Cremona et al (n 45).

[248] S Cassese, 'Global Standards for National Administrative Procedure' (2005) 68 *Law and Contemporary Problems* 109; S Cassese, 'Administrative Law Without the State? The Challenge of Global Regulation' (2005) 37 *NYU Journal of International Law and Politics* 663; DC Esty, 'Good Governance at the Supranational Scale: Globalizing Administrative Law' (2006) 115 *Yale Law Journal* 1490; C Harlow, 'Global Administrative Law: The Quest for Principles and Values' (2006) 17(1) *European Journal of International Law* 187; B Kingsbury et al, 'The Emergence of Global Administrative Law'(2005) 68 *Law & Contemporary Problems* 15; N Krisch and B Kingsbury, 'Introduction: Global Governance and Global Administrative Law in the International Legal Order' (2006) 17 *European Journal of International Law* 1; L Boisson de Chazournes et al (eds), 'Symposium on Global Administrative Law in the Operations of International Organizations' (2009) 6 *International Organizations Law Review* 315.

the so-called managerial theory, studying matters of compliance and efficiency in global governance;[249] and the network scholarship especially highlighting and analysing the transnational networks of different actors other than states and their regulatory powers and implications.[250]

The approach of this book is different; it looks at practices of private governance and regulation in GVCs by the upstream actors – corporations – and their effects on potential and actual receivers of those norms, as well as on third parties adversely affected by such regulation. Relevant governance and regulation is thus ultimately addressed from a socio-legal perspective, as well as from a mix of private and public law viewpoints.

To date, one of the few works on enhanced corporate responsibility in such a context is Anna Beckers' 2015 monograph.[251] However, while asserting that the CSR codes involve genuine legal obligations, and using socio-legal and comparative methodologies, Beckers ultimately emphasises the private role and private obligations of corporations. Beckers proposes to enforce CSR codes through private – mostly commercial and contract – and essentially domestic law. The remainder of this book, however, demonstrates that, while CSR could be more closely linked to commercial and contract law, the concept of corporate social liability that I propose also embraces tort law, human rights, labour law, and even customary international law.

Second, and perhaps as a consequence, in this book I seek to put more emphasis on the constantly growing role of corporations as *public* actors and the effects of such a role on the global public, including the remote periphery of 'technical' and 'voluntary' GVC norm-setting. In other words, I claim that the analysis should go beyond production processes and relating contractual and commercial law obligations, and extend to the *actors* of GVC production, services, and operations: shareholders, investors, businesses, indigenous peoples, local communities, individual consumers, and the environment.

Overall, in contrast to existing hard-law approaches often centred on the private role of companies and private law, I seek to offer an interdisciplinary perspective on the multilevel socio-legal spaces yielding responsibility in global value chains. Furthermore, following the Rana Plaza disaster, several regulatory,

[249] A Chayes and AH Chayes, 'On Compliance' (1993) 47 *International Organization* 175; A Chayes and AH Chayes, *The New Sovereignty: Compliance with International Regulatory Agreements* (Cambridge, Harvard University Press, 1995). See also LB Edelman et al, 'Diversity Rhetoric and the Managerialization of Law' (2001) 106 *American Journal of Sociology* 1589; R Fisher, *Improving Compliance with International Law* (Charlottesville, University Press of Virginia, 1981); AT Guzman, 'A Compliance-Based Theory of International Law' (2002) 90 *California Law Review* 1826.

[250] J Braithwaite, *Regulatory Capitalism. How it Works, Ideas for Making it Work Better* (Cheltenham, Edward Elgar, 2008); J Braithwaite et al, 'Can Regulation and Governance Make a Difference?'(2007) 1 *Regulation & Governance* 1; J Braithwaite and P Drahos, *Global Business Regulation* (Cambridge, Cambridge University Press, 2000); C Harlow and R Rawlings, 'Promoting Accountability in Multilevel Governance: A Network Approach' (2007) 13 *European Law Journal* 542; AM Slaughter, *A New World Order* (Princeton, Princeton University Press, 2004).

[251] Beckers (n 239).

legislative, adjudicatory, and activist developments have happened during the last two to three years and many more will take place in the next few years. Until now, the analysis has delved into the relevant topics surrounding two of the three objects of the book: CSR and GVCs. The time has come to turn to the third and main object of the book: CSL.

B. The Collapse of the Rana Plaza Garment Factory's Structure: The Collapse of the CSR Regulatory Structure?

On 24 April 2013, a five-storey commercial building, *Rana Plaza* in Savar, an industrial suburb of Dhaka, Bangladesh, collapsed and killed almost 1,200 people, while over 2,500 were gravely injured.[252] It is considered to be one of the biggest structure catastrophes and the deadliest garment-factory catastrophe in history.[253] The disaster has led to two major legal developments. The first involved class action lawsuits in torts, claiming billions in damages, brought in the US and in Canada. These were brought by representatives of Rana Plaza victims against major US and Canadian retailers (and the related social auditor in case of the Canadian giant Loblaws), since the retailers had indirectly sourced clothing through factories in Rana Plaza, while the auditor – inaccurately – certified that the garment factory's workplace safety was satisfactory.[254] The second development took place in 2013, when a group of deputies of the French Parliament started working, together with French civil society and a handful of NGOs, on a Bill on the duty of care of corporations over their value chains.[255]

The first line of actions failed completely. In May 2016 and July 2017, the legal claims were dismissed by the Superior Court of Delaware and by the Ontario Superior Court, respectively.[256] This development demonstrates that tortious GVC liability alone is currently not the most prominent avenue for litigation. In particular, the common law doctrine of negligence, which theoretically implies an indirect duty of care – the duty of care of companies towards the employees of their subcontractors – was not successfully applied in the two litigations. The second development materialised in February 2017 when a new French law on the corporate duty of care (or vigilance) came into force. The law introduces liability of

[252] S Mollah and W Bin Habib, 'It crumbles like a pack of cards' *The Daily Star* (25 April 2013) https://www.thedailystar.net/news/like-a-pack-of-cards-it-crumbles; J Burk, 'Rana Plaza: one year on from the Bangladesh factory disaster' *The Guardian* (19 April 2014) https://www.theguardian.com/world/2014/apr/19/rana-plaza-bangladesh-one-year-on.

[253] Burk, ibid.

[254] *Abdur Rahaman v JC Penny Corp Inc, et al* [2016] CA No N15C-07-174 (Super Ct Del) [*Rahaman*]; *Das v George Weston Ltd* [2017] ONSC 4129 [*Das*].

[255] Amnesty International, 'Entreprises : Il était une fois une loi' (2017) *Amnesty France* https://www.amnesty.fr/responsabilite-des-entreprises/actualites/entreprises-il-etait-une-fois-une-loi.

[256] *Rahaman*; *Das* (n 254).

parent companies for harm caused by their subsidiaries – chiefly, to the employees of subsidiaries.[257]

The law represents one of the few but growing number of legislative acts on corporate liability (arguably) across the entire value chain. Whether this French law will become an effective national legislative model for transnational value chain liability, and thus sustain the premises of the concept of CSL as delimited in the introduction to this book, remains to be seen. This 'French model' is only one piece in a collection of approaches slowly but surely emerging in first-world jurisdictions to deal with issues of GVC liability for breaches of obligations generally known as CSR.[258] Moreover, on the regional, transnational, and international fronts, there are, for instance, the EU Directive on Non-Financial Disclosure, the EU Conflict Minerals Regulation, the Bangladesh Accord on Fire and Building Safety, and the draft UN Treaty on Business and Human Rights.[259]

As demonstrated throughout this part of the book, economic power aside, another way by which leading corporations maintain their top position in GVCs has to do with the power to streamline standards and contractual requirements into the production processes all along a value chain. Indeed, dominant firms of a GVC shape the functional division of labour and entry conditions along the whole chain. Today, lead corporations (or the biggest companies) in a value chain usually subcontract some stages of the production abroad. That is, the production of their goods and services is organised by coordinating the activities of different companies whose operations together constitute a GVC. In accordance with the essential argument of this book, this results into the already familiar binary relationship 'economically dependent-legally independent' between head corporations and other actors of a GVC.

For example, Primark, the global clothing retailer headquartered in Ireland, used to buy garments from the Rana Plaza factory.[260] Apple computers and phones are designed in California but most are assembled in China by firms which are not part of the Apple group. From the perspective of corporate law, some of these firms are independent from the company at the top of the chain and are arguably independent suppliers, often located in another country. Other parts of the chain belong to the same corporate group as the coordinating company, but are separate legal persons, ie subsidiaries of the coordinating parent. When workers, consumers, or a part of the community (such as people exposed to the pollution caused by a factory) become victims of the activities of one part of such a GVC, the question arises whether liability claims should be directed against the coordinating

[257] Loi n°2017-399 relative au devoir de vigilance des sociétés mères et des entreprises donneuses d'ordre, promulguée le 27 mars 2017, JORF n°0074 du 28 mars 2017, texte n° 1 (Fr).

[258] I analyse relevant national legislative developments in Chapter 5 below.

[259] See eg Chapters 6, 7 and 8 below.

[260] 'Bangladesh Building Collapse: Factory "Supplied High Street Fashion Retailers"' *Huffington Post* (24 April 2013) https://www.huffingtonpost.co.uk/2013/04/24/bangladesh-building-collapse_n_3147634.html.

company, or rather against the different firms that are involved in the value chain and directly related to a given harm.

In the case of Rana Plaza, cracks in the building had been reported the day before the disaster, but managers still required that workers come back to work on the day of the collapse.[261] After the collapse, people often blamed the management, the main factory owner, Sohel Rana, engineers who designed the building, the local administration, or the government.[262] However, the management decision to send workers back into the cracked Rana Plaza building on 24 April 2013 was also due to the pressure to complete orders, to meet extremely sharp production deadlines, no matter what.[263]

Such sharp deadlines today are usually preferred by the *final buyers* – mostly, global clothing brands from rich countries – because of the culprit global demand for cheap clothing, which dictates quick changes of designs, referred to as *fast fashion*. Such demand for fast fashion arguably encourages minimal oversight of the garment factories' working conditions by the final buyers situated at the top of apparel GVCs. First-world head firms, who introduce and/or adjust sharp production deadlines and similar requirements – say, product characteristics – for third-world suppliers thus force them to breach legal standards, such as workplace safety, environmental or human rights norms, in order to deliver the ordered quantities on time. Thus, even if the management of Rana Plaza may be directly responsible for sending the workers back to the collapsing building, the main responsibility should be on those who compelled the suppliers to breach the law.

As demonstrated in sections III–VI of this chapter, it is the first firm or a coordinating company, often based in a rich country, that actually has the decision-making power with respect to what will be produced where, and why. Foreign subcontractors in remote areas are rather delegated the task of execution – typically, part production or assembly. This adds to my argument –which runs through the whole book – that lead corporations should be held liable for harm-causing activity across their entire value chain, including for that of its economically dependent entities, and not only 'softly' responsible through existing CSR schemes.

The firms that are part of value chains are of course subject to binding statutory rules on issues such as minimum workers' rights or product safety. Moreover, CSR, as a form of corporate self-regulation governing responsibility of corporations towards people, communities and environments concerned by their operations is still in vogue these days. On the research front, there is a large and burgeoning literature on corporate accountability,[264] CSR codes and domestic private law,[265]

[261] ibid.

[262] Mollah and Bin Habib (n 252); Burk (n 252).

[263] RD Wolff, 'Economic Development and Rana Plaza' *Monthly Review* (16 May 2013) https://mronline.org/2013/05/16/wolff160513-html/; C Long, 'After Rana Plaza' *Jacobin* (16 June 2014).

[264] See eg D McBarnet et al (eds), *The New Corporate Accountability. Corporate Social Responsibility and the Law* (Cambridge, Cambridge University Press, 2007).

[265] Beckers (n 239).

business and human rights,[266] the interface of consumer law, market regulation and ethical consumption,[267] and, recently, even CSR in GVCs.[268]

What is missing, however, is a critical socio-legal analysis that would bring together – but go beyond – the whole range of the latest substantial scholarly advances on CSR, and, at the same time, address the pressing practical and conceptual issues of corporate liability for harmful acts across GVCs. Some scholarship has already started a legal-doctrinal analysis of corporate *liability* in GVCs.[269] In this book, I aim to complement this literature, but also, and especially, to answer a normative enquiry about the extent to which it is feasible and desirable to realise first firms' liability in GVCs, and how this can be brought about, if at all. The analysis in the chapters that follow therefore complements these doctrinal (mostly, of private law) scholarly advances.

Concluding Remarks on Part I

In the aftermath of the Second World War, while colonialism was formally over and the newly decolonised states had started to claim their resource sovereignty, a post-colonial capitalism in the first world gradually assigned the third world to the capitalist production periphery. Once the NIEO vanished, in addition to enduring mining and crops exports, the newly created global capitalist periphery was confined to manufacturing.

The workings of capitalist market efficiency brought competition in what had become a world-system. Market efficiency and competition, as the new social norms of this system, triggered a peculiar development in global post-colonial capitalism: the core's corporations started to outsource less value-intense stages of manufacturing, by relocating most of the intense industry stages to the former colonies. One of the initial reasons was that the first-world corporations saw increasing competitive advantages to the much lower labour and collateral costs in the former colonies. (Notably, as I discuss further below, market competition and its incentives for first-world corporations put more pressure on corporate

[266] M Karavias, *Corporate Obligations under International Law* (Oxford, Oxford University Press, 2013); S Deva and D Bilchitz (eds), *Human Rights Obligations of Business: Beyond the Corporate Responsibility to Respect?* (Cambridge, Cambridge University Press, 2013); J Nolan and D Baumann-Pauly (eds), *Business and Human Rights: From Principles to Practice* (Abingdon, Routledge, 2016); N Bernaz, *Business and Human Rights. History, Law and Policy – Bridging the Accountability Gap* (Abingdon, Routledge, 2017); various contributions to the *Business and Human Rights Journal* (2015–2020).

[267] D Leczykiewicz and S Weatherill (eds), *The Images of the Consumer in EU Law: Legislation, Free Movement and Competition Law* (Oxford, Hart Publishing, 2016).

[268] Rühmkorf (n 240); Ulfbeck et al (n 240).

[269] Vytopil (n 240); P Rott and V Ulfbeck, 'Supply Chain Liability of Multinational Corporations?' (2015) 23(3) *European Review of Private Law* 415; P Verbruggen, 'Private Regulatory Standards in Commercial Contracts: Questions of Compliance' in R Brownsword et al (eds), *Contract and Regulation: A Handbook on New Methods of Law Making in Private Law* (Cheltenham, Edward Elgar, 2017).

managers to meet their responsibilities towards corporate shareholders by reducing their responsibilities to virtually one key quantitative indicator – value.)

Concurrently, market efficiency had introduced among the third-world elites, representing the nascent local capitalism, a fierce competition for deals and contracts with the first-world primary capitalists or their local subsidiaries and suppliers. Rana Plaza's owners and management were typical periphery capitalists, ensuring that the contracts that they fought for so intensely were duly executed and the supplies delivered to the final core's buyers, no matter what.

Those drastic conditions, based on de-humanised 'social' norms of market efficiency, competition, and – ultimately – outsourcing, that characterise our current society are often punctuated by such disasters as the Rana Plaza collapse. The latter also seems to punctuate CSR as a means of regulating post-colonial globalised production. Meanwhile, the periphery remains dependent not only on exports to the centre, but now also on the latter's manufacturing and distribution networks – GVCs. As per a key argument of this book, GVC head corporations remain immune from any liability because of a binary relationship that is 'economically dependent-legally independent', between the core's corporations and their periphery suppliers and subcontractors, created thanks to GVCs. While the global economic dependence could be reduced and – hopefully – eradicated through levelling the playing field economically and socially, the legal dependence could and should be revealed by lawyers. In this book, I seek to found precisely such a legally effective relationship.

Since I argue that voluntary and non-binding – thus unenforceable – CSR is not appropriate to regulate GVCs, there is a pressing need to answer the following questions: Is an enhanced corporate liability in GVCs possible through compulsory binding mechanisms of CSL? And if so, is it more efficient, enforceable, and fair? I answer those questions in Parts II and III, and Part IV, respectively.

PART II

The Shortcomings of Corporate Responsibility and Obstacles to Corporate Liability

Nowadays, lawyers working in and with existing business corporations, and also architects of newly created ones elsewhere in the world, employ and acknowledge the limited liability concept as a fundamental one. Its fundamentality, though, is often taken for granted, somewhat akin to an axiom. However, as with any legal concept, this basic legal concept and all the constructs that it involves, such as separate corporate personality and the corporate veil, are socially constructed. The construct of limited liability, influenced by the patterns of corporate ownership in most industrialised western societies, nowadays continuously shapes, influences, and even justifies capitalist production all over the world – far beyond the West, in advanced and emerging economies alike.

The origin and history of corporations in international law, covering the Dutch East and West India Companies, corporate colonisation and plunder, and the like, also ultimately explain classical corporate legal constructs, including separate legal personality and limited liability. An account of the colonial origins of corporations' construction in international law is, however, beyond the scope of this book. The first chapter of this part (Chapter 3) looks at selected *national* legal doctrines and social and political contexts that influenced, directed, and determined the appearance and evolution of the patterns of corporate ownership and the ensuing (limited) liability that we see across western jurisdictions and that directly or indirectly affect the formation of liability in GVCs today.

The doctrine of limited liability has not changed so far; what has changed is the way in which capitalist production and trade are organised today, namely through GVCs, thus limiting corporate liability even further. Until the last decade, the interests of first-world corporations have directly or indirectly influenced and promoted GVC governance through the economic dependence of the actors in a GVC on the head firm, private self-regulation, as well as international non-binding instruments introducing soft transparency obligations, such as the United Nations Guiding Principles on Business and Human Rights (UNGPs) and the OECD Guidelines. The last ten years have also witnessed the rise of regional initiatives proclaimed as 'binding', especially in EU law. Their actual nature is, however, essentially the same as that of the above international instruments, for they carry the reporting obligations that induce a 'therapeutic disclosure',[1] particularly because they rely virtually only on reputational sanctions and broader social expectations. Chapter 4 addresses those international and European instruments.

[1] See eg SM Bainbridge, *Corporate Governance after the Scandals and the Financial Crisis* (Oxford, Oxford University Press, 2012) 34.

3

National Law: Shades of Publicness in Private Regulation

As the rather straightforward structure of this chapter indicates, it addresses the relevant workings of private societal regulation in corporate (section I), tort and contract (section II), and commercial (section III) law. The overarching idea of this chapter is the functional construct of 'corporation', the importance of which for the present analysis extends far beyond corporate law. The corporate form per se is crucial for the study of corporate liability in value chains because one of its main purposes, by its very nature, is to cut the variable costs of business organisation.

I. Corporate Law

According to a key argument of this book, GVC's head corporations remain immune from any liability mostly because of the 'economically dependent-legally independent' relationships between core corporations and their periphery suppliers and subcontractors. Even though this relationship is quite specific to the context of GVCs, as shown in Part I above, the limited liability construct also plays an important role in it. I therefore begin this chapter with an historico-dogmatic analysis of this and related constructs.

The historical reasons explaining classical corporate legal form, including separate legal personality and limited liability, and comprehensive, in-depth multidisciplinary analysis of the origins and concept of the corporation have been narrated elsewhere.[1] There is thus no need to repeat such descriptions here. This section explores only the structures and functions of corporate (or company) law that are relevant to CSL. More precisely, it is about the patterns of corporate law across jurisdictions that are directly or indirectly relevant for corporate liability for harms arising from outsourced production and other operations.

[1] To quote just a few, see eg S Soederberg, *Corporate Power and Ownership in Contemporary Capitalism* (Abingdon-on-Thames, Routledge, 2009); G Baars and A Spicer (eds), *The Corporation, A Critical, Multi-Disciplinary Handbook* (Cambridge, Cambridge University Press, 2017); G Baars, *The Corporation, Law and Capitalism: A Radical Perspective on the Role of Law in the Global Political Economy* (Boston, BRILL-Nijhoff, 2019); D Lustig, *Veiled Power: International Law and the Private Business Corporation, 1886–1981* (Oxford, Oxford University Press, 2020).

The construction of corporate law in a given jurisdiction generally builds on that country's conception of corporate ownership. The latter depends on the country's industrial enterprise and broader micro- and macro-economic patterns, which in turn depend on the forms and nature of control in its society.[2] Hence, as is common in this book, I deal with two analytic levels at once. At an internal, legal-doctrinal level, this section looks at relevant constructs of corporate law, governance, and responsibility as direct consequences of corporate ownership in different jurisdictions (see section B below). At an external, socio-legal level, the section explores the shaping of those relevant corporate law constructs across national boundaries (see section A below).

A. The Influence of Patterns of Industrial Enterprise on Corporate Ownership

Since the evolution of the large integrated business corporation in the late nineteenth century, the two general approaches to corporate ownership have been the shareholder and stakeholder models.[3] The shareholder conception views the corporation as the private property of its *share*holders – that is, the owners of the shares of that corporation.[4] In this construct, the primary function of the corporation as well as the preoccupation of its managers is to advance those owners' interests, which are, principally, to maximise their financial returns.[5] The literature usually labels it as either the property model (conceiving of the corporation as the property of shareholders) or the contract model (because autonomous shareholders freely contract in it).[6]

The stakeholder model views the corporation as a social institution, comprising, and therefore also serving interests of, a wider group of its *stake*holders – that is, all parties who deal with the firm, such as creditors, investors, employees, customers,

[2] JC Coffee Jr, 'The Rise of Dispersed Ownership: The Roles of Law and the State in the Separation of Ownership and Control' (2001) 111 *Yale Law Journal* 1, 1. See generally RK Morck (ed), *A History of Corporate Governance around the World: Family Business Groups to Professional Managers*, National Bureau of Economic Research Conference Report (Chicago, Chicago University Press, 2005).

[3] JD Bauman, *Corporations, Law and Policy: Materials and Problems*, American Casebook, 7th edn (Eagan, West Academic Publishing, 2009) 34–35; R La Porta et al, 'Corporate Ownership Around the World' (1998) 54 *Journal of Finance* 471, 491–96.

[4] La Porta et al (n 3).

[5] See eg SM Bainbridge, 'Director Primacy in Corporate Takeovers: Preliminary Reflections' (2002) 55 *Stanford Law Review* 791, 794; R Kraakman et al, *The Anatomy of Corporate Law: A Comparative and Functional Approach*, 2nd edn (Oxford, Oxford University Press, 2009) 28.

[6] 'The relationships among the participants in a corporation are, to an important degree, contractual. The principal contract that binds them is the corporation's charter (or 'articles of association' or 'constitution', as it is termed in some jurisdictions). The charter sets out the basic terms of the relationship among the firm's shareholders, and between the shareholders and the firm's directors and other managers': in Kraakman et al, ibid 17. See also Bauman (n 3) 34; see generally A Berle and GC Means, *Modern Corporation and Private Property* (New York, Harcourt, Brace & World, 1968).

etc. Here, the corporation's primary purpose is to make sure that corporate transactions are beneficial not just to the stockholders, but to all its participants.[7]

Some legal researchers note that, since the second half of the nineteenth century, the view that corporations may serve a broader purpose of promoting general social welfare was influential.[8] However, some management historians specify that 'in the late 1800s a charter of incorporation was a favor bestowed only on those businesses that were *socially useful*. But, by the end of the [US] Civil War, charters were available under any business pretext, and were nearly impossible to revoke' (emphasis added).[9] From either perspective, it is not the autonomous will of property owners that grants a corporation its legal personality and limited liability, as it would be under the shareholder model, but state institutions.[10] I therefore argue that the corporation is also charged with certain public goals. This construct is often called the social entity conception, the institutionalist conception, or the managerialist conception.[11]

Both views, however, are still 'internal' in the sense of the constituencies they address. Unlike the shareholder approach, the stakeholder model does care about general social welfare and corporations' public purposes. Yet, despite being more inclusive, it still primarily addresses participants *in* a corporation. However, the global and transborder nature of GVCs often implicates remote actors and environments who, despite not dealing with a corporation in any meaningful way, are still adversely affected by corporate activities. Therefore, there is a need for a more 'external' approach to corporations' purposes and accountability, at least in the context of GVCs, to supplement the aforementioned models. This approach would extend to all impacted parties, including natural or man-made environments (which are not necessarily regarded as actors in most orthodox legal approaches).

There already exist some perspectives in this vein. One of them focuses on 'an emerging third way'. It argues that the UK embodies this third path, oscillating between the shareholder and the stakeholder models and blending certain features of the two.[12] I analyse further in this section whether such a path is truly different, and – if it is – to what extent. In addition, a more external view on the overall nature of the corporation leads to general questions of its accountability and, it follows, liability: Is the corporation contractual in nature or is it responsible to the state apparatuses that created it? That is, is its nature private, or does it imply

[7] Kraakman et al (n 5) 28.

[8] Bauman (n 3) 34. See generally JW Hurst, *The Legitimacy of the Business Corporation in the Law of the United States 1780–1970* (Charlottesville, The University Press of Virginia, 1970).

[9] Archie Carrol, citing Daniel Wren, in A Carroll, 'A History of Corporate Social Responsibility: Concepts and Practices' in A Crane et al (eds), *The Oxford Handbook of Corporate Social Responsibility* (Oxford, Oxford University Press, 2008) 19, 21.

[10] Bauman (n 3) 34.

[11] ibid.

[12] See generally CA Williams and JM Conley, 'An Emerging Third Way – The Erosion of the Anglo-American Shareholder Value Construct' (2005) 38 *Cornell International Law Journal* 493.

any public ends, and should it strive to maximise the welfare of its shareholders, stakeholders, or society as a whole?[13]

As highlighted above, the power balance typical for any given society influences, to varying degrees, the rationale of how corporate ownership is constructed therein, the process of the construction of corporate ownership, and hence also this construction itself. The model of corporate ownership, in turn, determines to some extent the nature of the corporation and the structure of corporate rights and obligations in that country.[14]

Regarding the formation and distribution of share ownership in continental Europe, firms conventionally have a controlling shareholder.[15] In France, it is typically the state.[16] In contrast, in Germany the controlling shareholder is usually an influential corporate group, while in Italy it is generally an influential family or an individual.[17] A more concentrated corporate ownership in continental Europe partially resulted from specific patterns of industry and production development.[18] To wit, a controlling shareholder is usually thought to be in a better position to commit to workers, which in turn may facilitate positive labour relations – notably union relationships, which are especially characteristic of France.[19] A more subtle rationale for such a facilitation of labour relations, however, is that it boosts productivity with the aim to motivate employees to use existing technologies, rather than to claim new ones.[20] Under this historical premise of industrial enterprise in France (and in most of continental Europe), non-shareholder constituencies, especially direct stakeholders such as workers, are traditionally said to have more voice in corporate governance and accountability. It is reasonable to expect, however,

[13] See recent developments in France on the *PACTE* Bill, discussed further in this chapter. See also Bauman (n 3) 75.

[14] See eg Kraakman et al (n 5) 31.

[15] France, Ministry for the Economy and Finance, Government Shareholdings Agency, 'The French State as Shareholder' (2012) https://www.economie.gouv.fr/files/directions_services/agence-participations-etat/Documents/Rapports-de-l-Etat-actionnaire/2012/2012_Report_on_the_Government_as_a_shareholder.pdf. It is projected that the traditional position in some jurisdictions, notably Germany, is starting to change towards more dispersed shareholdings: see generally D Wojcik, 'Change in the German Model of Corporate Governance: Evidence from Blockholdings 1997–2001' (2003) 35 *Environment and Planning A: Economy and Space* 1431; S Thomsen, 'Convergence of Corporate Governance during the Stock Market Bubble: Towards Anglo-American or European Standards?' in A Grandori (ed), *Corporate Governance and Firm Organization: Microfoundations and Structural Forms* (Oxford, Oxford University Press, 2004) 297, 306–12, cited in Kraakman et al (n 5) 31 and fn 85.

[16] France, Ministry for the Economy and Finance ibid.

[17] Kraakman et al (n 5) 30.

[18] See generally W Carlin and C Mayer, 'Finance, Investment and Growth' (2003) 69 *Journal of Financial Economics* 191; B Eichengreen, *The European Economy since 1945: Coordinated Capitalism and Beyond,* The Princeton Economic History of the Western World (Princeton, Princeton University Press, 2006) 23.

[19] France, Ministry for the Economy and Finance (n 15).

[20] SM Jacoby, 'Corporate Governance in Comparative Perspective: Prospects for Convergence' (2001) *SSRN Electronic Journal* http://dx.doi.org/10.2139/ssrn.285949; PA Hall and D Soskice (eds), *Varieties of Capitalism: The Institutional Foundations of Comparative Advantage* (Oxford, Oxford University Press, 2001).

that the *nature* of such accountability would vary from country to country even within continental Europe.

The US is characterised by quite the opposite pattern of share ownership formation. A mix of populist political context and a drive to create and support the myriad of new businesses created a favourable climate for policies mitigating state, institutional, or family control of industry and production patterns. This has, to a substantial degree, influenced the fragmented nature of shareholding in the US.[21] In turn, as a result of the country's shareholding patterns, the majority of publicly-traded firms have a dispersed share ownership, which means that the affiliated group of shareholders, let alone a single shareholder, cannot control a corporation in the manner of a French majority shareholder, for example.[22]

This Anglo-American approach to corporate ownership saw the risks of failure and losses of shareholders as inherent because, unlike banks and other lenders, they had no financial security.[23] The fear of losing it all historically led to increasing reluctance from businessmen to set up new business ventures, fearing loss of personal property through repossession to pay off debts owed in situations where business endeavours failed.[24] In order to avoid such events faced by business starters, a legal principle was enacted, stating that the liability of shareholders and directors be 'limited, meaning that investors – the shareholders – are liable for only a portion of the amount, and personally not liable for all debts and acts of the company'.[25] Furthermore, a company must be legally assessed separately, thus making companies entities with a separate legal personality.[26] However, initially conceived for the protection of business starters,[27] the construct of corporate personality with limited liability created a loophole for many shareholders to evade paying back large sums of credits.[28] Today it also creates loopholes for many companies that are far from business starters to avoid liability, including in GVCs.

[21] See eg H Hansmann and R Kraakman, 'The End of History for Corporate Law' (2001) 89 *Georgetown Law Journal* 439, 449–58. For a less optimistic and/or more critical, post-*Enron* era view on convergence, the allocation of power between shareholders and labour, and the predominance of the US shareholder-centric view of the corporation, see M O'Connor, 'Labor's Role in the American Corporate Governance Structure' (2000) 22 *Comparative Labor Law & Policy Journal* 97, 123–26. See also CG Holderness, 'The Myth of Diffuse Ownership in the United States' (2009) 22 *The Review of Financial Studies* 1377.

[22] See generally Holderness (n 21); MJ Roe, *Strong Managers, Weak Owners: The Political Roots of American Corporate Finance* (Princeton, Princeton University Press, 1994).

[23] See generally R Kolb, *Lessons from the Financial Crisis: Causes, Consequences, and Our Economic Future* (Hoboken, NJ, Wiley, 2010).

[24] B Sjåfjell and M Taylor, 'Clash of Norms: Shareholder Primacy vs. Sustainable Corporate Purpose' (2019) 13(3) *International and Comparative Corporate Law Journal* 40, 45–46.

[25] ibid 46.

[26] ibid.

[27] See eg the landmark case of UK company law giving an orthodox view of separate legal personality: *Salomon v A Salomon & Co Ltd* [1897] AC 22.

[28] C Amsler et al, 'Thoughts of Some British Economists on Early Limited Liability and Corporate Legislation' (1981) 13(4) *History of Political Economy* 774, 776–80.

The types of entities by or through which shares are held in the US differ from those in Europe and tend to change over time.[29] More specifically, today individual investors still directly own a large proportion of shares. However, two types of institutional investors – employer-established pension funds and mutual funds – now hold the majority of shareholdings. At the same time, rarely is a sufficiently large share of a given company's stock held by one type of fund, investor, or individual to allow them to exert substantial control.[30]

It is often argued that the UK's patterns of industrial enterprise, and thereby of formation and distribution of corporate ownership as well, lie somewhere between the US model and the continental European one.[31] On the one hand, the UK shares with the US its stockholder approach, since a majority of publicly-traded UK companies have a dispersed share ownership.[32] On the other hand, in contrast to the US, the types of entities by or through which a large fraction of corporate stock is held in the UK are institutional investors (especially insurance companies and pension funds, although the figures for both types of institutional investors are progressively in decline since 2010).[33]

Recent years have also seen the rise of new types of institutional investors. First, private equity firms are (typically) non-public firms holding, at least temporarily, complete ownership of acquired formerly public companies with the aim of entirely restructuring them.[34] Second, hedge funds are relatively unregulated collective investment funds holding substantial shares in individual firms and sometimes seeking to control those firms, while exercising highly speculative investment strategies.[35] Both types focus on short-term, often high-risk, profits instead of caring about a longer-term sustainability of institutional investments,

[29] See eg P Muchlinski, *Multinational Enterprises and the Law*, 2nd edn (Oxford, Oxford University Press, 2007) 8–18. See generally Berle and Means (n 6); Hurst (n 8).

[30] US Board of Governors of the Federal Reserve System, 'Financial Accounts of the United States. Flow of Funds, Balance Sheets, and Integrated Macroeconomic Accounts' Third Quarter 2019, Release of 12 December 2019 https://www.federalreserve.gov/releases/z1/.

[31] See generally Williams and Conley (n 12).

[32] Kraakman et al (n 5) 30.

[33] UK Office for National Statistics, 'Ownership of UK quoted shares: 2018', 14 January 2020 (the latest available, so far).

[34] See generally S Thomsen, 'Should Private Equity Be Regulated?' (2009) 10(1) *European Business Organization Law Review* 97; J Payne, 'Private Equity and Its Regulation in Europe' (2011) 12(4) *European Business Organization Law Review* 559.

[35] Some regulators have actually been and remained more concerned about the limits of activities of hedge funds than others. The German regulator, for instance, has tightened significantly the relevant regulation, when in the 2000s hedge fund activity was directed towards taking over the Deutsche Boerse. Especially after the 2008 recession, hedge funds are increasingly regulated in Europe, particularly through the EU's AIFMD and EMIR legislation. And in fact, even in the US and the UK, the two hedge fund countries *par excellence*, the activity of managing assets for another (including a fund) has always been a regulated activity. Thus, New York and Mayfair-based hedge funds have always been quite inside the regulatory net, though the funds themselves are mostly established offshore. In addition, the EU primary legislation, the Markets in Financial Instruments Regulation (MiFIR in force from July 2014) and the Markets in Financial Instruments Directive (MiFID II in force from January 2017), as well as the secondary implementing measures from the European Securities and Markets Authority (ESMA), are in force and still bound the UK before the Brexit implementation was entirely

such as security of pensions. They thus clearly underline the preference of their utmost objective as per the shareholder model: maximising value through financial returns to their shareholders.

B. The Influence of Models of Corporate Ownership on Corporate Law, Governance and Responsibility

Having analysed the repercussions of patterns of industrial enterprise on corporate ownership across selected jurisdictions, in this section I investigate the influence of shareholding characteristics on corporate law and governance. The US sphere of corporate ownership and corporate law is often juxtaposed with that of continental Europe. In general, the latter is characterised as the 'outsider' model, while the former is labelled 'insider'.[36] This means that in the corporate governance of the shareholder system, in the US, only 'insiders' – typically, stockholders and corporate managers – are involved, while the stakeholder system model, in Europe, extends to a wider group of 'outsiders' – at its narrowest, all those who participate in an enterprise, and at its broadest, non-shareholder constituencies and society as a whole. The inhabitants of these different spheres of corporate ownership not only have distinct corporate governance structures but also different visions and practices of corporate goals and accountability.[37]

In France, the Vigilance – or Corporate Duty of Care – law is the most relevant law regarding the resonance of patterns of industrial enterprise on direct *stake*holders' and wider non-shareholder constituencies' actual participation and influence in corporate governance and accountability.[38] It also defines the nature of such accountability as being liability and foresees sanctions.

Under the French Vigilance law, the duty of care lies on 'parent and instructing companies'.[39] Based on national legislation, in order to determine a company's influence, one needs to know, among other things, the nature of the shareholdings and the number of employees.[40] The nature of shareholdings is hence an essential prerequisite for identifying the direct and indirect subsidiaries of a given firm. Therefore, the responsibility of companies, or groups of companies,

completed: Thomson Reuters, White Paper 'Regulatory Implications for Hedge Funds: What Does this Mean for Your Personal Liability?' (2019) https://legal.thomsonreuters.com/en/insights/white-papers/regulatory-implications-hedge-funds-what-does-mean-your-personal-liability. See also generally M Kahan and EB Rock, 'Hedge Funds in Corporate Governance and Corporate Control' (2007) 155 *University of Pennsylvania Law Review* 1021; A Riviere, 'The Future of Hedge Fund Regulation: A Comparative Approach: United States, United Kingdom, France, Italy, and Germany' (2011) 10 *Richmond Journal of Global Law & Business* 263.

[36] See generally Williams and Conley (n 12).

[37] ibid.

[38] eg Chapter 5, section I and Chapter 7, sections I–III below.

[39] '*Des sociétés mères et des entreprises donneuses d'ordre*' in French.

[40] Pursuant to the provisions of art L. 225-102-4, I of the French Commercial Code [*Code de commerce*].

is commensurate to their control or, more precisely, *influence* – ie the influence of the head company (as opposed to just a larger entity's influence over its commercial partners). This identification of subsidiaries is, in turn, crucial for counting employees and determining whether a given company is liable under the Vigilance law. Here, it is this notion of control that must be considered in determining the scope of the law, especially as it pertains to direct and indirect subsidiaries based on the nature of shareholdings.[41] However, it is French commercial law that governs this type of company regulation. I address relevant commercial law questions in section III.C below, while the various CSL aspects of the French Vigilance law will be discussed in great detail in different chapters of Parts III and IV of the book.

On the French civil law front, certain changes to corporate liability and overall corporate purpose and duties were proposed in the 2018 framework of the draft Bill, PACTE. Notable were the proposed modifications to articles 1832 and 1833 of the French Civil Code, defining the responsibilities of companies.[42] As of 16 May 2019, the French Constitutional Council has censured 24 provisions under this legislative proposal; however, it validated the one pertaining to companies' social duty (*l'objet social de l'entrepise*).[43] These modifications, though, are minimal and insufficient. In particular, regarding corporate liability, instead of lifting the responsibility of companies to society and the environment to actual legal liability, the project modestly proposed that companies 'take into account' the social and environmental impacts of their activities.[44] At face value, the final version of the *loi PACTE* appears to fall squarely within the scope of the insider – or US – model of corporate governance and responsibility rather than the French – allegedly outsider – model.

Regarding transparency, both France and the UK require their institutional investors – typically, pension funds – to disclose the scope and the degree of inclusion of environmental, social, and ethical variables in their investment portfolios.[45] Additionally, until recently, the UK was under the same institutional pressures currently present in the US in far more mitigated forms.[46] Thus, the UK was driven to adopt a 'third way'[47] or, at least, to distance itself from the US shareholder approach in favour of the European stakeholder model.

[41] One of the arguments to support this position is the parallel that can be drawn with companies exempt from the duty of care obligations, which are 'subsidiaries or companies controlled' by 'the company which controls them, under article L. 233-3': art L. 225-102-4, I, para. 2 C. Com.

[42] See *La proposition du gouvernement de compléter l'article 1833 du Code civil, la Commission spéciale à l'Assemblée nationale le projet de loi PACTE (Plan d'action pour la croissance et le développement de l'entreprise)*, 25 September 2018.

[43] Consitutional Council, *La décision n° 2019-781 DC du 16 mai 2019* – Communiqué de presse Loi relative à la croissance et la transformation des entreprises.

[44] 'La société est gérée dans son intérêt social et en prenant en considération les enjeux sociaux et environnementaux de son activité' : *La proposition du gouvernement* (2018).

[45] Bauman (n 3) 88.

[46] These would typically include EU consumer protection, health, safety, and environment supranational policies, for instance, as well as more recent EU CSR policies.

[47] See generally Williams and Conley (n 12).

For instance, despite some hesitations due to high levels of uncertainty regarding the effects of compulsory reporting of the environmental and social risk of corporate activities, in the early 2000s the UK adopted relevant regulation in the field.[48] However, starting from the mid-2000s, the UK progressively distanced itself from enhanced corporate accountability. The UK backslid, for example, in terms of compulsory sustainability reporting. In 2006, as part of its national sustainability strategy the UK government repealed its prior compulsory reporting policy at least for the big firms. It justified its decision by the policy's potential to stifle innovation and to damage the competitiveness of British-based companies listed on the London Stock Exchange.[49] The ultimate decision to allow firms to report voluntarily is more in line with the traditional approach to business regulation in the UK, which is much closer to the US model of stockholder ownership and corresponding corporate law, governance, and accountability models. In addition, the consequences of Brexit are hardly likely to bring the UK in the near future closer to continental Europe's stakeholder approach and relevant corporate governance.

One of the mainstream hard law tools that governs corporate responsibility in the UK today is the Companies Act 2006. It lays down the board of directors' right to determine the best interests of the company, while still being bound to balance the interests of other stakeholders participating in an enterprise.[50] This model underlines companies' and – especially – directors' discretion as to corporate governance and responsibility.[51]

In the US – home to the shareholder model of, and insider approach to, corporate governance – legislation tries to fill these governance gaps from a variety of legal perspectives, all of which implicate GVCs. For example, tort law, through the Alien Tort Statute, is supposed to hold US firms accountable for their alleged complicity in fundamental rights abuses by the governments of states where these corporations do business.[52] Criminal law, mainly through the Foreign Corrupt Practices Act, prohibits firms and agents from using bribery to advance their interests abroad.[53] Additionally, US Customs regulations ban imports produced using forced or child labour.[54] Notably, the US Dodd-Frank Act of 2010, a response to the 2008 financial crisis, made some incremental changes to the 'governance solution', focusing on board independence and shareholder power.[55]

[48] O Delbard, 'CSR Legislation in France and the European Regulatory Paradox: An Analysis of EU CSR Policy and Sustainability Reporting Practice' (2008) 8 *Corporate Governance International Journal of Business in Society* 397, 399, 403.

[49] ibid 399.

[50] Companies Act 2006, s 172(1) (UK).

[51] See generally A Rühmkorf, *Corporate Social Responsibility, Private Law and Global Supply Chains* (Cheltenham, Edward Elgar, 2015).

[52] Alien Tort Statute (28 USC § 1350; ATS).

[53] Foreign Corrupt Practices Act of 1977 (FCPA) (15 USC § 78dd-1, ff). See also C van Dam, 'Tort Law and Human Rights: Brothers in Arms on the Role of Tort Law in the Area of Business and Human Rights' (2011) 2 *Journal of European Tort Law* 221, 225–27.

[54] US Customs and Border Protection, 'Basic Importing and Exporting' (4 March 2020) https://www.cbp.gov/trade/basic-import-export.

[55] See Chapter 5, section I below.

To close this section, two concluding remarks are in order. In general, relevant constructs of corporate law clearly reflect the corporate interests dominating in a jurisdiction: (i) in the past, at a particularly significant moment in the formation of the structure of corporate ownership, representing here a sort of stock; and (ii) in dynamic workings of corporate investment, financing, and management, the forms and nature of which change over time, thus being in flux. These dominant corporate interests, in turn, both inform and affect the overriding economic, political, and institutional forces at play impacting the corporate (or company) law of a given jurisdiction. As established above, in France such a dominant force is typically the state; in the UK it is institutional investment funds and banks; and in the US it is institutional investment funds and corporate managers.

Accordingly, concerning the form and nature of corporate responsibility in GVCs, in France (and in most continental Europe), the forms of compulsory reporting of corporations for environmental and social risks of corporate activities along their value chains, as well as their liability, which may even be backed by sanctions, gain the legislative terrain. In contrast, in the UK, following a brief period of increasingly stringent regulation of corporate activities in early 2000s, the country is making its corporate responsibility and reporting rules more lax, aligning with the US model, where most of the pertinent corporate law approaches are voluntary. However, the US tries to tackle these governance gaps through criminal law, customs regulation, and tort law.

II. Tort Law and Contract Law

As observed in section I above, the relations among the participants in a corporation are generally contractual. This starts with the corporation's founding charter, which binds all of its participants. The charter sets out and governs the basic relations among the firm's shareholders, directors, and other managers, as well as, implicitly, its employees, creditors, and customers.[56]

Kraakman et al note:

> In the [...] literature, a firm is often characterized as a 'nexus of contracts'. As commonly used, this description is ambiguous. It is often invoked simply to emphasize that most of the important relationships within a firm – including, in particular, those among the firm's owners, managers, and employees – are essentially contractual in character, and hence based on consent, rather than involving some form of extracontractual command-and-control authority. This is an important insight, but it does not distinguish firms from other networks of contractual relationships. It is perhaps more accurate to describe a firm as a 'nexus *for* contracts', in the sense that a firm serves, fundamentally, as the common counterparty in numerous contracts with suppliers, employees, and customers, coordinating the actions of these multiple persons through exercise of its contractual rights.[57]

[56] Kraakman et al (n 5) 18.
[57] ibid 6.

In other words, through their very organisational form, corporations act as single contracting entities distinct from the various individuals who own, manage, or work for them. In so doing, corporations streamline the shared engagements of these individuals in joint projects.[58] In this sense, a corporate organisational form is surely based on contracts and is governed by contract law. Yet, it expands far beyond contractual relationships, acting as the key link in a chain of contracts, thus becoming a platform for contracts and further joint projects governed by corporate, tort, and commercial law and more.[59]

It is, therefore, impossible to talk about corporate accountability limited solely to that of managers toward shareholders. For instance, corporate operational activities such as control between higher and lower levels of management in transnational divisions, contractual relations between different affiliates of an enterprise, intra-firm codes of behaviour, and especially industry- or GVC-wide codes of conduct all go beyond the limited liability doctrine.[60] The last category of activities (setting GVC-wide codes of conduct) is especially relevant for this book because it can be taken into account when courts determine liability in tort (typically, the extent of a duty of care in tort) or in contract (especially, the consumer contract).[61]

It is traditionally accepted that the doctrine of limited liability in corporate studies only means limited liability in contract. Particularly, corporations are liable only toward creditors who have contractual claims on the firm – that is, broadly, all persons who may have contractual claims on the corporation, such as customers, suppliers, and employees.[62] Limited liability in contract is effectively distinct from limited liability in tort – the latter meaning liability to persons who are limited, that is, who cannot adjust the terms on which they extend credit to the firm, such as third parties adversely affected by corporate misconduct.[63] The basic difference remains in the nature of duties: breach of contract involves a breach of a duty allegedly voluntarily assumed by the party who agreed to that contract exclusively with the other contracting party(ies), whereas a tort is a breach of a duty fixed by the state and owed to society at large.

[58] PT Muchlinski, '"Global Bukowina" Examined: Viewing the Multinational Enterprise as a Transnational Law- making Community' in G Teubner (ed), *Global Law Without a State (Studies in Modern Law and Policy)* (Dartmouth, Dartmouth Publishing Co, 1997) 81–84. See also generally H Hansmann and R Kraakman, 'The Essential Role of Organizational Law' (2000) 110 *Yale Law Journal* 387.

[59] AE Tenbrunsel et al, 'Building Houses on Rocks: The Role of the Ethical Infrastructure in Organizations' (2003) 16(3) *Social Justice Research* 285, 287–302.

[60] Muchlinski (n 58) 81–82. See also generally PA French, 'The Corporation as a Moral Person' (1979) 16(3) *American Philosophical Quarterly* 207; LK Trevino and KA Nelson, *Managing Business Ethics* (New York, John Wiley & Sons, 2010).

[61] Muchlinski (n 58) 84.

[62] V Ulfbeck and A Ehlers, 'Tort Law, Corporate Groups and Supply Chain Liability for Workers' Injuries: The Concept of Vicarious Liability' (2016) 13 *European Company Law* 167, 168. See also Kraakman et al (n 5) 10; generally P Rott and V Ulfbeck, 'Supply Chain Liability of Multinational Corporations?' (2015) 23 *European Review of Private Law* 415.

[63] See section I.A above.

Paradoxically, the opposite is also possible: in certain situations, firms may be liable in tort to creditors and in contract to third parties. The examples of such tortious liability include customer product claims or claims based on companies' CSR codes as a minimum threshold defined by the practice of a certain fraction of the community of peers, spurring the duty of due diligence and requiring that damages must be foreseeable and thus avoidable. Cases of exceptions of contractual liability to third parties could be founded on so-called sustainability clauses in transnational contracts. These examples are all addressed in the following subsections.

My aim here is to present a fair description of relevant aspects of both contract law and tort law followed by a subsequent critical analysis of the interface of corporate creditors, liability, and CSR norms with that of adversely affected third parties.

A. Direct and Indirect Creditors

i. Contract Law

At the interface of contract law and a particular branch of consumer protection law lies the construct of contractual promises. The latter is relevant to this analysis both in terms of the past and present shortcomings of CSR and of present obstacles to, and prospects of, CSL. For example, a value of a consumer good produced or assembled in different parts of the globe through a value chain – such as a smartphone – often includes some form of sustainability labelling or statement of good corporate governance. These public statements of sustainability of a product and/or the process of its production may be seen as contractual or at least pre-contractual promises. Indeed, they assert certain characteristics, promising specific qualities of a final good to the customer. For example, eco-labels can contain references to process and production methods (PPMs), since a product's environmental features may relate to its origin and means of production, as well as its use and disposal.

PPMs can be divided into two categories: product-related PPMs; and non-product-related PPMs. When analysing codes of conduct as parts of contracts, the example of eco-labels can illustrate both types of PPMs. ISO 14020 (an environmental labelling standard),[64] for instance, is likely to be deemed a potential PPM. In this case it could incentivise certain producers (especially exporters) to introduce a label stating, for example, that no chemically synthesised fertilisers were used during the growing process – say, of wheat. Hence, buyers would assume that such wheat, as well as products made with the wheat, are pesticide-free, unlike other wheat and wheat products that carry *no such label*. One apparent problem is that not all food products or commodities used for final food products that do *not* carry a 'pesticide-free' label are necessarily grown with help of pesticides. Rather,

[64] ISO, 'ISO 14020: 2000' https://www.iso.org/obp/ui#iso:std:iso:14020:ed-2:v1:en.

not all producers can afford an expensive labelling scheme – especially third-world producers. Furthermore, such requirements, which focus primarily on the process by which the commodity is grown, may affect the final product itself. For example, the nutritional quality of the final wheat product – say, bread – may change as a consequence of modifying the production process of the wheat itself.[65] This would be a product-related PPM because such PPMs affect the physical characteristics of the final product.

Based on the same ISO 14020 scheme, however, a label claiming that a good – say, paper – was made from recycled materials, thereby enabling consumers to make informed choices about its ethical value and environmental impact, is a non-product-related PPM. Indeed, such a label does not affect the physical characteristics of the final product. In both cases, the application of the ISO 14020 scheme requires such labels to be environmentally relevant, specific, and verifiable. However, in terms of contract law, a published, or otherwise publicised, label, standard, or code of corporate self-regulation may be seen as a promise to buyers that, as per the above examples, wheat, wheat products, or paper are ethically sound and environmentally friendly products.

A promise, in turn, creates legitimate expectations, and the principle of protection of trust could overcome legal and judicial formalism in contract law and litigation.[66] Namely, the trusting party derives legitimate expectations from the promises of the partners with whom it interacts, including those involving labelling, corporate codes, customs and professional standards, and even advertising.[67] In sales transactions, an agreement often occurs at the moment of, or shortly after, purchase (under French law, for example, it is generally after seven days).[68] Consumers are thereby shielded by contract law through the mechanism of protection of their legitimate expectations.

Returning to the paradigmatic smartphone example, smartphones are often purchased remotely (typically, online). Such a purchase constitutes the consumer's tacit consent to a sales contract. Especially relevant here is the element of contracts of adhesion. Such a contract involves tacit, and often unwanted, consent on behalf of the consumer, particularly when it comes to the 'beginners' of online purchasing.[69] Indeed, the simple click of mouse allows the buyer to consent to the proposed contract on a commercial website. Conversely, the conventional method

[65] Food and Agricultural Organization of the United Nations (FAO), *Food Safety and Quality as Affected by Organic Farming*, paras 39–43 (22nd FAO Regional Conference for Europe, Porto, 24–28 July, 2000).

[66] See eg M Herberg, 'Global Legal Pluralism and Interlegality. Environmental Self-Regulation in Multinational Enterprises as Global Law-Making' in O Dilling et al (eds), *Responsible Business: Self-Governance and Law in Transnational Economic Transactions* (Oxford, Hart Publishing, 2008) 35.

[67] ibid.

[68] Art L.121-16 C. Com.

[69] JL Baudouin, *Les obligations* (Cowansville, Yvon Blais, 1989) 109: 'Dans le contrat d'adhésion, celui qui désire contracter doit donc accepter automatiquement toutes les clauses et conditions de la convention, puisqu'elles sont unilatéralement fixées par le sollicitant. Il est impossible de parler ici de véritable liberté contractuelle'.

of expressing consent to be bound by a legal agreement is the signature of a duly authorised person.[70]

Even when the contract is a written agreement, the fact of requiring a handwritten signature may create various delays. This would make the conclusion of a legally binding agreement lengthy and burdensome. It might even render it overdue and thus inadmissible, at least from the black-letter perspective of contract law. This signature is nevertheless necessary when a contract is a prerequisite for the transfer of the material concerned. It is for this reason that the global smartphone market, and the IT industry more generally, nowadays use peculiar contractual forms, such as 'click-wrap' purchase agreements[71] and, especially, 'shrink-wrap' agreements[72] to avoid the need for written signatures. In both cases, the contract in question is similar to distance contracts. Although 'click-wrap' and 'shrink-wrap' contracts are common in most jurisdictions, there is virtually no case law addressing their enforceability.[73] Especially because the 'shrink-wrap' contract is not subject to any verbal or written agreement, its enforceability – including that relating to the legitimate CSR expectations of consumers – may potentially pose problems in some jurisdictions.

The legal principles governing the enforceability of unsigned agreements vary according to national laws. In the US, for example, the Seventh Circuit Court considered that 'shrink-wrap' agreements are enforceable only if: (i) the packaging clearly indicates to the buyer that the good (a software, in that case) is licenced; (ii) the buyer is, or can easily become, fully aware of the conditions of the licence; and (iii) the buyer has the option to reject the contract by returning the software, and obtain a refund.[74] Under the French Consumer Code, a contract is considered concluded only when a clear and precise offer is accepted without reservation.[75] However, this offer-acceptance condition may be deemed unfulfilled if the buyer only becomes aware of the 'shrink-wrap' contract's provisions once the transaction is completed.[76] Article L.121-16 of the Consumer Code provides for a period of seven clear days; therefore, consent is formulated only at the conclusion of these seven days.

[70] ibid.

[71] For instance, in the FAO's Standard Material Transfer Agreement, in the so-called 'click-wrap' contracts consumers (or 'beneficiaries') accept the terms and conditions posted online only after having read them. They then express their consent by entering typical words indicating the acceptance or by clicking on a specified icon, or, more recently, by checking a dedicated box (icon click or box click): FAO, *Standard Material Transfer Agreement* (2004) 2, 8, 12.

[72] The 'shrink-wrap' agreements are typical for software commerce. The contract is provided with the very packaging of the software; the user does not sign a contract, but these contracts are often included in a transparent package, sealed and delivered with the software. However, a dedicated notice on the package informs that the user agrees to respect the clauses of the agreement by opening the package: ibid 2, 8.

[73] See eg MW de Hoon and V Mak, 'Consumer Empowerment Strategies – A Rights-Oriented Approach versus a Needs-Oriented Approach' (2011) 19 *Zeitschrift für Europäisches Privatrecht* 518, available as Tilburg Law School Research Paper No 018/2011, see 7–10; A Beckers, *Enforcing Corporate Social Responsibility Codes: on Global Self-regulation and National Private Law* (Oxford, Hart Publishing, 2015) generally Ch 5.

[74] See eg *ProCDInc v Zeidenberg*, 86 F 3d 1447 (Seventh Circ 1996); *Hill v Gateway*, 105 F 3d 1147 (Seventh Circ 1997).

[75] Art L.121-16 C. com.

[76] ibid.

In the nineteenth century, Oliver Wendell Holmes saw contracts not only as agreements based on the free choice of promissors to either keep their promises or pay damages to the promisees but also, and especially, as tools for the allocation of risk.[77] However, twenty-first century courts in most national legal systems remain rather reluctant to recognise that value statements in CSR could also be contractual.[78] In the UK, for instance, the avenues for consumers to successfully enforce the doctrine of legal misrepresentation – ie to seek a remedy against a company's violations of its promises on the basis of the company's misrepresentation to adhere to CSR guidelines – are quite uncertain. UK courts consider buyers' lawsuits uniquely on the basis of whether the consumer's purchase is inherently defective.[79] Most consumers' claims are hence restricted to clear material defects – a characteristic, which is unlikely to apply to the ethical rightness of a product. As a result of similar restrictions globally – in both wealthy and less wealthy countries – beyond boycotts, individual consumers are limited in their ability to enforce corporate governance acts before national courts.

Another impediment to effectively enforcing consumer contract for breaches of CSR-related promises is that, even if accepted, such claims would most probably lead to limited compensation. Full compensation is, in principle, unavailable due to various barriers to the recovery of damages – both notional limits, such as non-pecuniary loss or remoteness, and practical ones, such as the costs of litigation.[80] England's full compensation approach, which recognises and emphasises a so-called consumer surplus (a value in excess of the 'objective' market value of losses) in consumer litigation is an exception to the rule.[81] Yet, even in England, it is rare that full expectation damages are awarded in practice.[82]

At the EU level, however, the Consumer Rights Directive as well as its national implementations include within the product conformity assessment the totality of the characteristics that determine the value of a product.[83] This normally comprises CSR-based corporate promises and all related corporate governance statements.[84] In so doing, European law – at the interface of sales and consumer rights – enables the retailers', the producers', and producer's representatives' statements about both

[77] OW Holmes, 'The Path of the Law' (1897) 10 *Harvard Law Review* 457, 462.

[78] C Glinski, 'Bridging the Gap: the Legal Potential of Private Regulation' in Dilling et al (n 66) 41, 45; generally, Beckers (n 73).

[79] See generally Rühmkorf (n 51).

[80] A Eisenberg, 'Actual and Virtual Specific Performance' (2005) 93 *California Law Review* 975, 998.

[81] *Ruxley Electronics v Forsyth* [1996] AC 344.

[82] R Kreitner, 'Multiplicity in Contract Remedies' in N Cohen and E McKendrick (eds), *Comparative Remedies for Breach of Contract* (Oxford, Hart Publishing, 2005) 27–28.

[83] Directive of the European Parliament and of the Council 2011/83/EU of 25 October 2011 on consumer rights, amending Council Directive 93/13/EEC and Directive 1999/44/EC of the European Parliament and of the Council and repealing Council Directive 85/577/EEC and Directive 97/7/EC of the European Parliament and of the Council Text with EEA relevance [2011], OJ L 304/64.

[84] This includes conformity with public statements, including labelling, on the qualities determining the value of a good and made about by the retailer, as well as the producer and/or producer's representatives: Directive of the European Parliament and of the Council 1999/44/EC of 25 May 1999 on certain aspects of the sale of consumer goods and associated guarantees [1999] OJ L 171/12, art 2(2)(d).

product- and non-product-related PPMs to have the value of a legal statement – that is, a contractual promise – rather than that of a mere communication between sellers and consumers.[85]

Notably, the former EU Unfair Contract Terms Directive specified that unfair terms used in a consumer agreement by a sales operator (producer, supplier, retailer, etc) are null and void and do not bind the final consumer, and it is essential to 'remove unfair terms' from such contracts 'in order to facilitate the establishment of the internal market and to safeguard the citizen in his role as consumer when acquiring goods and services under contracts which are governed by the laws of Member States other than his own'.[86] Today, the new Consumer Rights Directive, which consolidated existing EU consumer directives (namely, the Sale of Consumer Goods and Guarantees, Unfair Contract Terms, Distance Selling, and Doorstep Selling), takes up these consumer contract law disciplines.[87]

In this regard, the research suggests that consumers who have incurred additional costs resulting from purchases clearly encouraged by CSR assurances may use those as the basis for class action lawsuits against corporations, aimed at inducing corporate liability and deterring future deviance.[88] In the UK, for instance, similar legal alternatives exist in the context of post-2014 amendments to the UK's Consumer Protection from Unfair Trading Regulations 2008[89] as a means for consumers to hold corporations liable for CSR breaches.[90] However, while the amendments confirm that a buyer's single purchase from a company is a contract, the resulting claim can be easily remedied by a simple refunded return. The amendments, therefore, do not have the effect of influencing corporate conduct unless massive class action claims take place.[91]

ii. Tort Law

Under tort law, minimum standards of care could be established based on CSR statements. If so, their breach would involve tort liability. These would be based on measures recognised as necessary as well as common practices of producers, assemblers, etc.[92] Notably, the corporate codes of self-governance by some companies could evolve into a global minimum threshold as defined by the practice of only a certain fraction of the community. It would then extend to those producers and other actors in production and retail who never expressly adhered to them.

[85] Glinski (n 78) 45.

[86] Council Directive 93/13/EEC of 5 April 1993 on unfair terms in consumer contracts [1993] OJ L 95/29, the Preamble and art 1.

[87] Directive 2011/83/EU.

[88] See generally Rühmkorf (n 51).

[89] SI 2008/1277, as amended by SI 2014/870.

[90] S Deakin et al, *Markesinis and Deakin's Tort Law*, 7th edn (Oxford, Oxford University Press, 2013) 541 ff; generally Rühmkorf (n 51).

[91] ibid.

[92] Glinski (n 78) 50.

Here, we observe the workings of the tort law obligation of due diligence, requiring that damages must be foreseeable and thus avoidable.[93]

It could thus be said that every 'CSR minimum standard' arises from the typical practices and measures taken to prevent damage of a subset of the community of business operators in a given GVC or, speaking about national law, of firms working in the same line of business or industry. A presumption of negligence could arise if an actor does not comply with these minimum standards.[94]

A different situation may be observed in the context of GVC production in the Global South, where subsidiaries of multinational corporations often compete with local operators in the same line of business.[95] Corporations that relocate a part of their business to countries with weaker safety and environmental regulations, cheaper labour, and so forth, already appear to seek lower minimum CSR standards. So too do domestic businesses who often operate under even lower levels of labour, safety, and other sustainability standards.[96] For instance, many corporations moved their businesses, in part or entirely, from Brazil to Haiti and then from Haiti to Bangladesh when they faced rising labour – hence production – costs in each country.[97] Evidently, this is not illustrative of all corporations; businesses for which labour costs form a small share of their total production costs are less likely to move than labour-intensive ones. But, there exist myriad other attractive cost differentials for mobile global businesses, such as disparate health and safety regulations, poor environmental laws, tax breaks, low or no capital requirements, and exchange rate fluctuations.

It must be asked how the relevant category of operators that establishes the 'golden sample CSR' standard of care, upon which a tort liability for negligence may be founded, is selected. In the aforementioned situations of corporate cost differentials – or, a corporate cost 'shopping' in the context of operations in poor countries – it is argued that other standards must be taken into account, such as technological know-how and access to advanced technologies, financial capacity, as well as management abilities, including environmental management.[98]

B. Adversely Affected Third Parties

i. *Contract Law*

Some scholars argue that inserting so-called sustainability clauses into contracts would probably compel companies to respect their CSR and other sustainability

[93] ibid.
[94] See eg *Ward v The Ritz Hotel (London)* [1992] PIQR 315.
[95] Glinski (n 78) 51.
[96] See eg CK Prahalad and YL Doz, *The Multinational Mission: Balancing Local Demands and Global Vision* (New York, Free Press, 1987) 102.
[97] K Stone, 'Globalization and the Middle Class' in G de Burca et al (eds), *Critical Legal Perspectives on Global Governance* (Oxford, Hart Publishing, 2013).
[98] Glinski (n 78) 51.

commitments. Positive obligations and reporting, which could also be monitored and signalled by civil society and other social actors, would effect such change.[99] Sustainability clauses are 'provisions in business contracts that cover social and environmental issues, which are not directly connected to the subject-matter of the specific contract'.[100] In other words, these clauses do not specify the physical quality of the finished product (ie product quality). Rather, they prescribe how the parties should generally behave when conducting business, including PPM-related issues, such as the process of production quality, brand and reputation management, ethical behaviour, and other ethical matters.[101] Typically, though, they appear to be too general and vague to be enforced in national courts under contract law or meet any other condition of formal enforcement.[102]

In general, the enforceability of contractual undertakings is closely linked to parties' relationship to the rules and liabilities of their own drafting. This means that the standard, dispositive rules of both tort law and contract law can be overruled by private ordering so long as it does not infringe mandatory public policy rules. These default rules can thus be seen as 'public' in relation to the parties' own private rules. The rules governing the use of 'public' contract law and private ordering – ie the requirements of entering into an agreement – can, nevertheless, differ greatly between jurisdictions, leading to different kinds of pressures. For instance, formal contractual pledges are stricter under English law than under French law, thus allowing French judges remain within the 'box' of black-letter contract law, whereas English courts are often compelled to expand the use of tort law in 'special agreements' situations.[103] As such, in some cases, English tort law exclusively governs what appear to be clear contractual, liability agreements.[104]

Ultimately, the basic difference between tort law and contract law is the nature of the respective duties. The former relates to breaches of a duty fixed in tort by the applicable state law and owed to society at large. Conversely, the latter concerns breaches of a duty supposedly voluntarily assumed by parties to a contract who agreed to it exclusively between themselves under contract law. Situations involving a firm's tort liability to creditors and contract liability to third parties are nevertheless also possible. Examples include customer product claims or claims based on companies' minimum threshold CSR codes as defined by the practices of a subset of the relevant community, inducing the duty of due diligence and requiring that damages must be foreseeable and thus avoidable. Otherwise, a duty of care could be invoked by complainants; I discuss this and related options below.

[99] K Peterkova Mitkidis, 'Sustainability Clauses in International Supply Chain Contracts: Regulation, Enforceability and Effects of Ethical Requirements' (2014) *Nordic Journal of Commercial Law* 1, 12–20. See also generally K Peterkova Mitkidis, *Sustainability Clauses in International Business Contracts* (The Hague, Eleven Publishing, 2015).

[100] Peterkova Mitkidis (n 99) 5.

[101] ibid.

[102] Generally Peterkova Mitkidis (n 99).

[103] Baudouin (n 69) 99–113. See generally B Markesinis, 'An Expanding Tort Law – The Price of a Rigid Contract Law' (1987) 103 *Law Quarterly Review* 354.

[104] See section II.B.ii below.

ii. Tort Law

The tort law duty of care doctrine usually produces binding effects on third parties, thus advancing objective standards of care and precaution.[105] In the UK, for instance, the general elements of the duty of care are: damage, foreseeability, causation between a damage and a duty, and the duty of care per se.[106] Until the 2000s, a three-stage test was used to determine a general duty of care in English common law. Elements of the test were gradually developed in earlier paradigmatic rulings, such as *Donoghue v Stevenson*, *Anns v Merton London Borough Council*, and *Murphy v Brentwood District Council*.[107] Its three key conditions were definitively laid down in the *Caparo v Dickman* judgment.[108] The elements are: (i) a damage which is foreseeable; (ii) a relationship between the party owing the duty and the party to whom it is owed, characterised by the law as one of proximity, or neighbourhood; and (iii) a general situation which leads the court to deem it fair, just, and reasonable that the law should impose a duty of a given scope upon one party for the benefit of the other.[109] The claim in the *Caparo* case was that the concerned financiers had a general duty of care towards any shareholder interested in increasing its share of the company – basically, to a broader public. The claim eventually failed before the House of Lords.[110]

The three-stage test to establish a general duty of care is not without its flaws. Critically, it does not establish how judges should proceed in determining the incidence of a duty of care or when exactly such a duty arises.[111] To remedy these difficulties, a new – 'incremental' or five-stage – approach was recently developed in English common law. There are several variations of the stages of this method, but a comprehensive test includes at least the following elements: (i) an existing and actually followed precedent for the situation being considered as the one when possible duty of care is owed; (ii) an analogous precedent that can be extended to recognise *or* deny a duty of care in the case at hand; and if denied, the three-stage test then applies.[112]

The special duty of care and forms of corresponding liability relevant for this book are liability for negligent misstatement and some other special types of negligence and liability, such as product liability in value chains, employer liability, and vicarious liability. The product liability issue features prominently in such

[105] Generally DJ Ibbetson, *An Historical Introduction to the Law of Obligations* (Oxford, Oxford University Press, 1999) Ch 9.

[106] Deakin et al (n 90) 102–107.

[107] The facts of the cases are not relevant for this discussion. For full rulings, see *Donoghue v Stevenson* [1932] AC 562; *Anns v Merton London Borough Council* [1978] AC 728; *Murphy v Brentwood District Council* [1991] 1 AC 398.

[108] *Caparo Industries plc v Dickman* [1990] 2 AC 605.

[109] ibid 617.

[110] Generally, *Caparo v Dickman* ibid.

[111] K Horsey and E Rackley, *Tort Law* (Oxford, Oxford University Press, 2009) 67–68.

[112] ibid, 70–71. For case law, see eg *Customs and Excise Commissioners v Barclays Bank plc* [2006] UKHL 28, paras 7, 14, 25.

judgments as *Hedley Byrne v Heller* and *Junior Books*.[113] In both cases, a special duty of care arises from a special relationship tantamount to an agreement. The latter occurs when one party reasonably entrusts itself to the expertise and care of the other, which renders indeterminate the exact nature of their special relationship: '[o]nce it is accepted that tort recognises liability for careless words as well as careless behaviour there is a clear need for a control device to deal with the threat of *indeterminate* [...] liability'.[114] Different theoretical avenues for, and practical cases of, tortious liability for such 'careless words' and 'careless behaviour' may arise in different CSR-related situations and will be discussed further in this section.

Notably, the *Caparo* test has recently been challenged in the 2011 UK Court of Appeal's *Chandler* decision, establishing the duty of care of a parent company to its subsidiary's worker suffering from harms related to production.[115] Regarding employers' liability, injured employees have two avenues to assert their rights in common law: claiming social security or invoking the tort system.[116] The latter is rooted in statutes and common law, which can be subdivided into employers' direct liability (personal non-delegable duties) and indirect or vicarious liability (generally through one employee's tort committed against another).[117] Vicarious liability is a slightly more complex concept and does not exist in some civil law jurisdictions (see eg para 831 of the German Civil Code).[118] Different rules apply to direct and indirect liability, but these are outside the scope of this section, which aims to outline the obstacles to CSL and corresponding mainstream approaches in relevant jurisdictions. I analyse specific problems and opportunities of production and vicarious liability further in the chapters addressing national CSL litigation with relevance to tortious liability (Chapters 5–7).

Remarkably, most of the above situations giving rise to a duty of care have one feature in common: they plainly involve theoretically overlapping and concurrent duties governed by obligations in either tort or contract.[119] There are, however, pertinent constructs in tort obligations that are clearly separate from those in contract law. One such construct is the safe harbour concept. Under this concept, a vague default standard, such as 'recklessness' is combined with specification of the outcomes for those factual scenarios that are foreseeably most likely to arise.[120] Safe harbours arguably reduce the uncertainty created by simply employing a vague standard, combining the virtues of vague standards and precise rules, and

[113] *Hedley Byrne & Co Ltd v Heller & Partners Ltd* [1964] AC 465; *Junior Books Ltd v Veitchi Co Ltd* [1983] 1 AC 520.

[114] Deakin et al (n 90) 543.

[115] *Chandler v Cape plc* [2012] EWCA Civ 525.

[116] Deakin et al (n 90) 542.

[117] C Elliott and F Quinn, *Tort Law*, 7th edn (Essex, Pearson, 2009) 141–43.

[118] Deakin et al (n 90) 543.

[119] For a detailed discussion of those, see eg Deakin et al (n 90) 168–73.

[120] A Stumpff Morrison, 'Case Law, Systematic Law, and a Very Modest Suggestion' (2013) 35(2) *Statute Law Review* 159, 159–180.

thus allowing the legislator to prescribe with certainty the advance outcome for specific foreseeable cases, and to leave to the adjudicators to decide the cases that remain.[121]

Under this concept, CSR pledges and other sustainability labels and standards could constitute either 'careless words' or 'careless behaviour', or even both. At least two different situations are discussed in the relevant literature.[122] Imagine some damage was caused. In the first situation, the tortfeasor did, or was presumed to have done, their due diligence. The second situation is the converse. In the first case, the tortfeasor would be found not liable because of their presumed due diligence. They would thus be seen to respect the relevant CSR or sustainability standard. In the second case, the presumed absence of due diligence – and hence negligence – constitutes a breach of the standard in question.[123]

Any private regulation relating to the safe harbour principle could thus directly apply to remote actors adversely affected by corporate activities, including natural or built environments. However, the environment is not necessarily regarded as an actor in traditional legal approaches; rather, it is traditionally seen as falling within the realm of public policy. Notably, due diligence in tort law is not an obligation of result, but of conduct. In addition, the CSR guidelines, and similar norms adopted either unilaterally or through common corporate practice, may lack the legitimacy and legal validity to constitute substantive law on account of the lack of safeguards to ensure that they reflect the public interest, or their substantial correctness.[124]

However, the use of private corporate regulation in tort law, namely as a safe harbour in due diligence procedures to prevent the damage or otherwise compensate, may be hazardous in several ways. On the one hand, to prevent damages, the standard of due diligence is substantively correct regarding damage minimisation, which could be defined by experts in the field.[125] On the other hand, assessing the allocation of damages necessitates a comprehensive and inclusive representation of various interests, also including the interests of third-world workers, indigenous peoples, local communities, and the environment.[126]

In conclusion, if one seeks to enforce legitimate expectations in the GVC context – especially third-party expectations resulting from words and behaviours likely to be deemed 'careless' in tort and contract law – one must first determine whether or not a lead firm's CSR statement shapes those expectations.

[121] P Swire, 'Safe Harbors and a Proposal to Improve the Community Reinvestment Act' (1993) 79 *Virginia Law Review* 349.

[122] Glinski (n 78) 57–59.

[123] ibid 57.

[124] See generally A Aseeva, 'Global Trade Governance and Informal Voluntary Standards: The Socio-Normative Analysis of Legitimacy of the ISO' in A Tutumlu and G Gungor (eds), *Multilateralism in Global Governance: Formal and Informal Institutions* (Oxford, Peter Lang, 2016).

[125] Glinski (n 78) 59.

[126] A Aseeva and KL Yip, 'Stakes and Prospects of the Right to Free, Prior & Informed Consent in "One Belt One Road" Projects in the Framework of Transnational Investment Law and Arbitration' in J Chaisse and J Górski (eds), *The Belt and Road Initiative. Law, Economics, and Politics* (Leiden, BRILL-Nijhoff, 2018) 523, 523–27.

Some research asserts, at least regarding consumer rights, that whether CSR and self-regulation have 'the effect of shaping consumer expectations is a question of fact'.[127] That is, while making a corporate code known to peers (traders, retailers, producers, etc) is expected to make it most efficient, rendering it *public* through extensive advertising makes it known to a broader community of end-users – typically, consumers, but also society at large.[128] Shaping but not meeting those legitimate expectations may thus amount to an unlawful intentional or negligent violation of codified norms in both tort and contract law. In the context of GVCs, I partially discuss this option and related avenues in my analysis of the *Vedanta* litigation in later chapters, for example Chapters 5–7.

More generally, today's relevant debate concerns certain situations when obligations under both tort and contract law may be seen as being of a *public*, or at least *private-public*, nature. Evidently, the immediate dilemmas to resolve are: the appropriate legal framing of the problem; the criteria for determining the publicness of such obligations, often stemming from the nature of the agreement and the relationship between allegedly purely private parties; the nature of agreements falling under such an allegedly public realm; and related practices that could be deemed legally-effective. I consider most of the prospects of potential solutions to these obstacles to corporate liability in Parts III and IV of this book, addressing, respectively, the new forms of governance approaches to corporate liability in GVCs and CSL per se.

III. Commercial Law

A key challenge to which this book aims to respond is to found a legally-relevant relationship between the 'economically dependent-legally independent' GVC head corporations and their periphery suppliers and subcontractors. In this regard, commercial law, including *lex mercatoria* and other commercial customs and standards, plays a certain role in both the upstream of CSL – voluntary private regulation originally involving no legal obligations – and its downstream – obligations leading to liability. When determining the latter, the notion of *influence* – ie the influence of leading firms over their commercial partners – is key. For voluntary private regulation, the power of dominating companies to shape the core of commercial laws through business practices is especially relevant.[129] Regarding such de facto domination through business practices, '[t]he question in such cases is whether the practice concerned should be accepted as *legally effective* …' (emphasis added).[130]

[127] Glinski (n 78) 49.
[128] ibid.
[129] See eg Muchlinski (n 58) 85–90.
[130] ibid 85.

In the context of this book, just as in the above reflections on tort law and contract law, the main means of considering relevant private regulation would thus be the general terms and analogous legal expressions referring to CSR and similar sustainability norms and production processes. Those expressions may serve as a stepping stone between relevant law-on-the-books, that is, legislation and other hard law rules on corporate conduct and judicial practice on the subject matter.

The standards and conditions for concretising such general terms vary across different jurisdictions depending on whether a more normative or more empirical method is used.[131] An empirical method, partially employed in previous sections, analyses the relevant general terms based on stable and repeated interactions between business and trade counterparts, including final consumers. It comprises the observations of guidelines, labelling, corporate codes, business practices, customs, professional standards, and even advertisement. The particularity of a normative method, added in this section to the above empirical analysis, lies in an observation of the exercise of oversight or any other form of general normative control by a legal system – most typically, a national one – with the help of general ethical and fairness standards.[132]

Unlike in previous sections of this chapter, here I primarily focus on the normative side. From this perspective, one interesting aspect relates to unfair commercial and collateral practices, embracing the principles of bona fide, fairness, good morals, and good practices. In this regard, an important instrument in the EU is the EC Directive on Unfair Commercial Practices.[133] Additionally, today, the previously discussed EU Consumer Rights Directive has consolidated existing EU consumer directives, including the Sale of consumer goods and guarantees, Distance selling, and Doorstep selling.[134]

Another aspect is the issue with final goods, details, or commodities produced in deviation from elementary thresholds of good practices, public policy, and public morals. Here, the possible proscriptions of commercial law would actually echo those of the relevant public international law disciplines – for example, international trade and investment law. A standard set of such limitations, usually protecting public morals, the environment, and human, animal, or plant life or health is similar to the list of article XX GATT provisions,[135] today partially or totally replicated in different international investment treaties and mega-regional

[131] See eg Glinski (n 78) 53.

[132] ibid.

[133] Directive 2005/29/EC of the European Parliament and of the Council of 11 May 2005 concerning unfair business-to-consumer commercial practices in the internal market and amending Council Directive 84/450/EEC, Directives 97/7/EC, 98/27/EC and 2002/65/EC of the European Parliament and of the Council and Regulation (EC) No 2006/2004 of the European Parliament and of the Council. Text with EEA relevance [2005], OJ L 149/22.

[134] Directive 2011/83/EU.

[135] See eg Chapter 2, section I above.

agreements: for instance, in article 28(3) CETA and many other international trade and investment instruments.[136]

Regarding the European market – and principally corporations based in the EU – there is some consensus on the minimum threshold of such good morals and practices. This is particularly evident in public international law instruments, such as bilateral and multilateral trade and investment agreements (as noted above, WTO agreements or CETA are typical examples of these) or due diligence in commercial law – for example, in the EU Timber Regulation and EU Conflict Minerals Regulation. Due diligence in EU law is addressed in more detail in Chapter 4.

Some avenues for corporate liability in commercial law could also be considered from the perspective of unfair competition practices. That is, protecting the competition itself as a public good in a rule of law system, as well as the consumers and competitors in a given market or sector, could be one such avenue.[137] For example, some appealing prospects lie at the interface of contract law, consumer law, and regulation of market behaviour. It is argued that CSR policies themselves could be defined in contract terms. That is, companies' CSR self-regulation can be seen as unilateral contractual promises that create legal effects towards outsiders, including consumers.[138] Other approaches look to the attribution of liability in the 'economic unity' of the parent and the subsidiary theory established in the doctrine of entity in competition law.[139] In EU law, it is especially featured at the interface of regulation, consumer law, and competition law.[140]

Different constructs of competition law could also apply jointly with tort law elements. First, just as in the case of tort law and the minimum standard of due diligence, in competition law, a relevant 'sample' group should be established in order to examine its applicable customs, codes, and practices. Classically, such a group would include the majority of operators in a particular industry or geographically delimited market.[141]

Second, a standard of fairness for commercial practices among competitors should be based on the 'sample' group's consensus position regarding a particular

[136] Comprehensive Economic and Trade Agreement (CETA) between Canada and the European Union and its Member-States. Signed 30 October 2016, entered into force 21 September, 2017. See also arts 14 and 24 of Reciprocal Investment Promotion and Protection Agreement between the Government of the Kingdom of Morocco and the Government of the Federal Republic of Nigeria (signed 3 December 2016, not yet in force); arts 8, 9, 10 and 14, Draft Pan-African Investment Code, UNECA (2017) https://repository.uneca.org/handle/10855/23009.

[137] Glinski (n 78) 55-57.

[138] See generally Dilling et al (n 66); Beckers (n 73).

[139] eg R Hilty and F Henning-Bodewig (eds), *Corporate Social Responsibility – Verbindliche Standards des Wettbewerbsrechts?* (Cham, Springer, 2014).

[140] See generally D Leczykiewicz and S Weatherill (eds), *The Images of the Consumer in EU Law: Legislation, Free Movement and Competition Law* (Oxford, Hart Publishing, 2016).

[141] See generally V Ulfbeck, 'Vicarious Liability in Groups of Companies and in Supply Chains – Is Competition Law Leading the Way?' (December 5, 2019) *CEVIA Working Paper Series*, Issue 4/2019 http://dx.doi.org/10.2139/ssrn.3498997.

societal issue and related codes and practices.[142] For instance, a code or norm of private regulation should be adopted or accepted by a substantial number and variety of the 'sample' group of operators in a given market.[143] Third, because of the considerable governance and normative disparities between jurisdictions of the Global North and South – or, in the context of this book, between the core, semi-periphery, and periphery of GVCs[144] – the containment mechanism for 'deliberately taking advantage' should be based on the 'sample' group's consensus on the unfairness of that activity.[145] Such a consensus, it is argued, should be reached between corporations from both the Global North and South.[146] Fourth, higher ethical and fairness standards, even when based on common consensus, should not distort the public good of fair market competition, as is the case, for instance, in EU law.[147]

Nevertheless, it could be argued – and often is, by competition lawyers themselves – that the above ethical and fairness standards relevant for good corporate societal practices relate in fact to production, and hence to the pre-competition stages of business. And since they take place before the actual competition on the market occurs, they should instead fall within the realm of public law.[148]

To summarise, the potential of such a consensus on minimum ethical and fairness standards that are to have normative repercussions on producers – and ultimately, on consumers – seems to be realistic only in cases of transboundary corporate practices that grossly violate relevant common minimum standards.[149]

Some such common ethical and fairness thresholds, as well as environmental and human rights due diligence ones, exist at the supranational and international levels. In the next chapter, I discuss their form, substance, strengths, and weaknesses.

[142] Glinski (n 78) 55.

[143] ibid.

[144] See Chapter 2, section III above.

[145] See section II above, speaking about corporate operations' cost differentials 'shopping' in and even between the jurisdictions of the Global South attractive for mobile global businesses.

[146] Glinski (n 78) 55.

[147] For EU law, the paradigmatic examples of the ECJ decisions in this vein are the so-called Laval-quartet (the Laval/Viking/Ruffert/Luxemburg judgments). They concerned EU commercial law more generally and not competition law in particular. But the general message of the ECJ in these four cases is quite clear: market and economic integration (including fair competition) come first; fairness standards and social rights – second. See Case C-341/05, *Laval un Partneri Ltd v Svenska Byggnadsarbetareförbundet and Others* [2007] IRLR 160; Case C-438/05, *International Transport Workers' Federation and Finnish Seamen's Union v Viking Line ABP and OÜ Viking Line Eesti* [2007] ECR I-10779; Case C-346/06, *Dirk Rüffert v Land Niedersachsen*, [2008] ECR I-1989.

[148] Glinski (n 78) 55.

[149] See generally Beckers (n 73).

4

Post-national Law: Mandatory Disclosure, Environmental and Human Rights Due Diligence, and Supply Chain Liability

I. Supranational Law

In Chapter 3, in section I, I discussed the effects of industrial enterprise patterns on corporate ownership and the subsequent influence of shareholding characteristics on corporate governance and, ultimately, on corporate liability. Specifically, the (continental) 'European way' of corporate ownership, law, and governance was contrasted with the Anglo-American sphere. The former is the 'outsider' model, while the latter is the 'insider' one. This means that the shareholder system, especially predominant in the Anglo-American world, accounts for only 'insiders' in corporate governance, such as stockholders and corporate managers. Inversely, the continental European stakeholder system makes efforts to extend to a broader group of 'outsiders' – namely, all those who participate in an enterprise, including non-shareholder constituencies and society as a whole. Those who belonged to these two different spheres of corporate ownership, I argued, not only had distinct corporate governance structures but, consequently, different approaches to corporate goals and accountability as well. In this section, I look at the related accomplishments within the European sphere of corporate governance and regulation.

Supranational efforts to govern and regulate corporations across jurisdictions during the last twenty years feature prominently in the EU's endeavours to further the integration of its common market.[1] Roughly, those efforts take two different – and largely opposing – paths: regulatory competition and harmonisation.[2] The former refers to the situation that arises between individual EU Member States when they impose their national corporate law on companies incorporated in other Member States but operating locally. This path primarily concerns EU rules

[1] R Kraakman et al, *The Anatomy of Corporate Law: A Comparative and Functional Approach*, 2nd edn (Oxford, Oxford University Press, 2009) 30.

[2] ibid.

infringing on the freedom of incorporation,[3] and is thus outside the scope of my analysis in this section. Conversely, the harmonisation efforts to coordinate the regulation of corporations across EU jurisdictions include the recent enactment of mandatory disclosure rules (see section A below) and mandatory due diligence rules (see section B below).

A. The EU Directive on Non-Financial Disclosure

The 2014 EU Non-Financial Reporting Directive (EUNFRD) is one of the most prominent supranational instruments regulating companies' activities across EU jurisdictions and, by extension, in third countries. Its scope of application ranges from human rights and environmental protection to anti-corruption regulation.[4] Under the EUNFRD, as of 2018, large entities based in the EU must disclose information about their operations regarding environmental and human rights due diligence and related matters.[5]

This directive is a key example of a shift in EU law away from corporate governance through legal rules applying to internal corporate structure as a means of providing corporate accountability and protecting stakeholders and third parties, towards regulation through external monitoring by interested stakeholders, including investors, consumers, and civil society. Its aim is to evaluate the non-financial performance of big firms and to encourage them to develop a responsible approach to business.[6]

The scope of the EUNFRD's non-financial disclosure requirements includes so-called public interest entities and is determined by reference to their balance sheet total, net turnover, and, most importantly, the threshold of employing more than 500 persons.[7] This covers approximately 6,000 large EU undertakings.[8] These large public interest companies must publish reports detailing their policies regarding environmental protection, social and employee matters, respect for human rights, anti-corruption and bribery issues, and diversity on company boards.[9]

[3] The paradigmatic ECJ decisions on the freedom of incorporation include Case C-212/97, *Centros Ltd v Erhvervs-og Selskabssyrelsen* [1999] ECR I-1459; Case C-208/00, *Uberseering BV v Nordic Construction Company Baumanagement GmbH* (NCC) [2002] ECR I-9919; Case C-210/06, *Cartesio Oktato es Szolgaltato bt* [2008] ECR I-9641.

[4] Directive 2014/95/EU of the European Parliament and of the Council of 22 October 2014 amending Directive 2013/34/EU as regards disclosure of non-financial and diversity information by certain large undertakings and groups [2014] OJ L 330/1.

[5] European Commission, *Non-Financial Reporting* https://ec.europa.eu/info/business-economy-euro/company-reporting-and-auditing/company-reporting/non-financial-reporting_en.

[6] ibid.

[7] Directive 2014/95/EU, art 1(1).

[8] European Commission (n 5).

[9] Directive 2014/95/EU, art 1(1) and (2).

The EUNFRD does not require companies to respect a particular form or standard of reporting. Covered entities can choose to disclose relevant information in their reports using national, European, or international guidelines. The directive gives as examples, among others, the EU EMAS and its national implementation schemes and the ISO 26000, both of which were discussed in Part I of this book. The Directive also mentions the UN Global Compact and the OECD Guidelines for Multinational Enterprises, which are addressed in the next sections of this chapter.[10]

Notably, entities subject to the EUNFRD must report the risks of harm stemming not only from their own activities, but also from those relating to their operations, products, services, and business relationships, including their value chains.[11] At the same time, there are no legal obligations incumbent on them to do so – they must simply provide a clear and reasoned explanation for not pursuing such reporting.[12]

All in all, the main strength of the EUNFRD is that it introduces a minimum standard of corporate social goals regarding the conduct of large EU firms, especially in the countries of the Global South. The directive attains its goals primarily through corporate transparency via non-financial reporting. Its major limit, in the context of this book, is that its penalties for corporate misconduct are only reputational sanctions and not legal ones. Most of the EUNFRD measures thus represent a 'healing' disclosure, meant to very softly influence behaviour of the covered companies.

B. Recent EU Law on the Sustainability of Imported Commodities: The Examples of Timber and Conflict Minerals Regulations

i. *The EU Timber Regulation*

The EU Timber Regulation (EUTR) has been in force since 3 March 2013. It is part of the national legal systems of all EU Member States.[13] Illegal logging threatens forests and biodiversity and undermines sustainable forest management and development, as it contributes to desertification and soil erosion and can exacerbate extreme weather events and flooding.[14] The commercial viability of operators acting in accordance with applicable legislation is thus crucial. The regulation

[10] Directive 2014/95/EU, Preamble, at 9.
[11] ibid art 19a(1)(d) and Preamble, para 8.
[12] ibid art 19a(1).
[13] Regulation (EU) No 995/2010 of the European Parliament and of the Council of 20 October 2010 laying down the obligations of operators who place timber and timber products on the market. Text with EEA relevance [2010] OJ L 295/23.
[14] European Commission, *Environment: New timber regulation comes into force* (Press release of 1 March 2013) https://ec.europa.eu/commission/presscorner/detail/en/IP_13_175.

applies to both domestically produced and imported timber and timber products and covers the whole wood trade value chain, 'from paper and pulp to solid wood and flooring'.[15] Products made from recycled materials are not included.

The prohibition on placing illegally harvested timber or timber products on the EU market means that operators should verify, either themselves or through an existing certification system, the legality of the imported timber.[16] This implies that the timber or timber products they place on the market should not contain timber that is illegally harvested as per the relevant legal framework of its country of origin.[17]

The EUTR lays down operators' mandatory due diligence obligations in the timber sector,[18] as well as the obligation of traceability along their entire supply chain. That is, traders should be able to identify both the purchase and sales ends of their business, of each transaction they performed. They must also keep that information for at least five years and provide it to competent authorities upon request.[19]

ii. The EU Conflict Minerals Regulation

Similarly to the EUTR, a new EU Regulation for global supply chains of certain minerals lays down mandatory due diligence obligations. It is even more relevant for the present analysis than the EUTR because of its legal and geographic scope. This legislation, in force since 17 May 2017 and known as the EU Conflict Minerals Regulation (EUCMR), applies to trade in four minerals – tin, tantalum, tungsten (and their ores), and gold – obtained in areas of armed conflict or through forced labour.[20]

The EUCMR is the European counterpart of US conflict minerals legislation, namely, the Dodd-Frank Act (specifically, section 1502 of the Dodd-Frank Wall Street Reform and Consumer Protection Act of 2010) that covers the same four minerals.[21] The EU regulation is based to a greater extent on pre-existing UN OHCHR[22] and OECD[23] relevant guidelines. With this Regulation, the EU aims to

[15] ibid.

[16] Regulation 995/2010, arts 4(1) and 5.

[17] ibid art 2(g).

[18] ibid art 4(2).

[19] ibid art 4(2).

[20] Regulation (EU) No 2017/821 of the European Parliament and of The Council of 17 May 2017 laying down supply chain due diligence obligations for Union importers of tin, tantalum and tungsten, their ores, and gold originating from conflict-affected and high-risk areas. Text with EEA relevance [2017] OJ L 130/1.

[21] European Commission, DG Trade, *Combatting Conflict Minerals* (7 March 2019) http://ec.europa.eu/trade/policy/in-focus/conflict-minerals-regulation/index_en.htm.

[22] UN Office of the High Commissioner for Human Rights (OHCHR), Guiding Principles on Business and Human Rights: Implementing the United Nations 'Protect, Respect and Remedy' Framework, HR/PUB/11/04 (2011).

[23] OECD, *OECD Due Diligence Guidance for Responsible Supply Chains of Minerals from Conflict-Affected and High-Risk Areas*, 3rd edn (2016).

go beyond such guidelines and impose clear liability on EU importers and operators of the supply chains of the four minerals.

The Regulation aims to prevent conflict minerals from being imported to the EU, and in particular to prevent EU smelters and refineries from using them. To that end, it is designed to ensure the transparency and security of importers' supplies, as well as of smelters, and refineries sourcing from conflict or high-risk areas. To achieve these objectives, the EUCMR requires that covered minerals must be imported into the EU from 'responsible sources'.[24]

Since it is difficult for customers at the end of a supply chain to know whether a product they have purchased is in any way financing or benefiting from violence, hostility, human rights violations, or other crimes in third countries, the EUCMR aims to fill this gap. It should be noted, however, that there is no trace of a liability clause requiring that for the covered breaches, the legislator – in this case, a Member State – adopt effective, dissuasive, and proportionate sanctions against operators in breach. In case of a violation by a covered operator, the Commission explains that a Member State will: (i) require that operator to remedy the problem within a certain timeframe; and (ii) monitor appropriately to ensure that the operator does so.[25] Each Member State will have its own competent authority in charge of the enforcement of the EUCMR. For example, in April 2020 Germany adopted the law on mineral raw materials due diligence within the framework of the EUCMR.[26]

Thus, an overall emphasis of the EUCMR is on compliance and not sanctions, and EU Member States are free to impose the penalties they deem appropriate. National laws on the tort of negligence and tortious liability hence theoretically apply to violations that constitute unlawful acts towards third parties. However, it should be noted that the application of liability in tort will depend on each jurisdiction.

Finally, EUCMR Article 17(2) states that on or after 1 January 2023, and every three years thereafter, the Commission must review the operation and effectiveness of this regulation. This review makes it possible to assess *in situ* the relevance and effectiveness of the implementation of the covered due diligence mechanisms. It also enables the Commission to take, if necessary, additional mandatory measures to ensure that the single EU market has sufficient influence on the GVCs of the relevant minerals.[27] That is, upon such a review, in case of persistent non-compliance with the obligations of the EUCMR, the Commission may order Member States to impose firm and concrete sanctions.

[24] Regulation 2017/821, art 1(1).

[25] European Commission (n 21).

[26] Gesetz zur Durchführung der Verordnung (EU) 2017/821 des Europäischen Parlaments und des Rates vom 17. Mai 2017 zur Festlegung von Pflichten zur Erfüllung der Sorgfaltspflichten in der Lieferkette für Unionseinführer von Zinn, Tantal, Wolfram, deren Erzen und Gold aus Konflikt- und Hochrisikogebieten sowie zur Änderung des Bundesberggesetzes, aus Nr 21 vom 06.05.2020, Seite 864.

[27] Regulation 2017/821, art 17(2).

To summarise this section on supranational law with CSL relevance, if CSL gradually increases in normative force, I submit that mandatory disclosure disciplines would be just the first stage of CSL norms. Following this logic, the second stage would be mandatory due diligence disciplines, followed by the third stage – liability laws. Parts III and IV of this book are largely dedicated to this third stage of CSL: national and transnational laws and regulations, establishing liability for the non-respect of due diligence obligations. In the next and final section of this chapter, I address the second phase of CSL norms at the international level – that is, various international mandatory disclosure instruments that are aspiring to be mandatory due diligence rules, but do not seem to achieve their aim.

II. International Law

Contrary to the surveyed EU law on responsible business conduct, which is formally mandatory (albeit its actual and potential normative force and effectiveness are very limited, as demonstrated in Chapter 8 below), similar norms at the international level are typically soft.

There are two main sets of soft law instruments that are relevant for non-financial disclosure, due diligence and an overall liability in GVCs. First, the UN Human Rights Council's Guiding Principles on Business and Human Rights (UNGPs) embody the first global attempt to achieve corporate liability under voluntary guidelines (see section A below). Second, various relevant OECD Guidelines represent allegedly more detailed and concrete attempts by way, among others, of tackling targeted industrial sectors and corresponding types of GVCs (see section B below).

A. UN Guiding Principles on Business and Human Rights: Forward to the Past of CSR?

The UNGPs were developed by the Special Representative of the Secretary-General (SRSG) Professor John Ruggie and comprise 31 principles.[28] They represent the first joint effort to codify, at the global level, the prevention of and responsibility for adverse impacts on human rights resulting from transboundary business activities.[29] On 16 June 2011, the UN Human Rights Council (UNHRC)

[28] UN Human Rights Council, Human Rights and Transnational Corporations and Other Business Enterprises, A/HRC/Res 17/4 (16 June 2011), endorsing 'Guiding Principles on Business and Human Rights: Implementing the United Nations "Protect, Respect and Remedy" Framework', A/HRC/17/31 (21 March 2011).

[29] S Lagoutte, 'The UN Guiding Principles on Business and Human Rights. A Confusing "Smart Mix" of Soft and Hard International Human Rights Law' in S Lagoutte and JC Gammeltoft-Hansen (eds), *Tracing the Roles of Soft Law in Human Rights* (Oxford, Oxford University Press, 2016) 244.

unanimously endorsed the UNGPs, making them the first global initiative seeking to provide some clarity on corporations' human rights responsibilities to be endorsed by the UN.[30]

As one of the experts in the field, Surya Deva, put it:

> [t]he [UN]GPs did not come to the centre stage out of the blue. They are part of a long on-going process to formulate the human rights responsibilities of companies at international level.[31]

Indeed, looking at the history of the attempts to create global legal standards of conduct of TNCs,[32] the principles represent an effort to revive the UN's combat fought from the late 1950s to early 1990s, with the regulation of TNCs on the agenda of the NIEO and then of the UNCTNC.[33] After a total failure to create legally binding instruments to regulate the conduct of TNCs and a decade-long break, the UN came up with this much softer approach.

On the one hand, the UN Global Compact (UNGC), an initiative of the late UN Secretary General, Kofi Annan – commonly known for his liberal attitude – was launched in 2000.[34] The UNGC comprises ten principles in the areas of human rights, labour, environment, and anti-corruption. However, overall it is so diplomatic in nature that is not worth analysing further here, in a chapter discussing legalistic obstacles to, and avenues for corporate *liability*. On the other hand, in 1998, the UN Sub-commission on the Promotion and Protection of Human Rights established a five-member Working Group on the Working Methods and Activities of Transnational Corporations.[35]

Furthermore, in 2003, the Sub-Commission made a proposal to adopt Norms on the Human Rights Responsibilities of Transnational Corporations and Other Business Enterprises (Draft UN Norms).[36] That effort, however, shared the fate of the NIEO and the draft UNCTNC Code, largely for the same reasons – that is, the reluctance of both global business and the home states of that business to support the initiative. In addition, according to Olivier De Schutter, it was due to a 'certain naïveté in transposing to corporations norms designed to be addressed to states'.[37]

The UNGPs lay down recommendations addressing states' *duty* as well as the corporate *responsibility* to protect human rights in transnational business. The first peculiar feature here is that the duty – and hence, main liability – is placed on states rather than on companies. The duty to protect is enshrined in the first (principles 1–10)

[30] S Deva, 'Guiding Principles on Business and Human Rights: Implications for Companies' (2012) 9(2) *European Company Law* 101.

[31] ibid 102.

[32] See Chapter 2.

[33] See Chapter 2, section I.B.

[34] UN, UN Global Compact https://www.unglobalcompact.org/what-is-gc/mission/principles.

[35] Deva (n 30) 102.

[36] O De Schutter, 'Towards a New Treaty on Business and Human Rights' (2016) 1 *Business and Human Rights Journal* 41, 43.

[37] ibid.

and third (principles 25–27 and 31) pillars of the UNGPs framework.[38] The second pillar establishes the corporate responsibility to protect human rights.[39]

As was made clear above, the UNGPs are an attempt to achieve consensus under a set of *voluntary* guidelines. There are advantages and disadvantages to this and other associated features. A prominent point of progress is that the UNGPs favour policy coherence. That is, the goal of coherently encouraging TNCs to take into account their responsibility to respect human rights and act accordingly, rather than circumventing such responsibility, is at the heart of the UNGPs.[40] This requirement for coherence means that both vertical and horizontal policy coherence must be ensured. The latter calls on states to create and support, at both national and sub-national levels, dedicated agencies to shape and monitor responsible business practices.[41] The former (vertical policy coherence) requires states to create regulatory, legal, and policy frameworks to realise their international human rights law obligations.[42] Such National Action Plans on Business and Human Rights (NAPs) are political tools that are likely to trigger cooperation among dedicated government agencies, as well as between national and sub-national authorities and private companies, thus promoting both vertical and horizontal policy coherence.[43]

Notably, the UNGPs contain human rights due diligence obligations. However, while principles 17, 18, and 21 establish obligations for companies to implement due diligence throughout their value chains, unlike the aforementioned recent EU law, they are not mandatory (eg firms *should carry out* human rights due diligence[44]). Thus, these requirements merely form part of CSR.[45] The UNGPs also include due diligence obligations applying to state-owned enterprises (principle 4) but, due to their subject-matter, they are outside the scope of this analysis.

There remain different limits in scope and substance between the principles. As outlined above, their main subjects are states. However, the UNGPs – particularly, principle 2 – seem to lower states' extraterritorial duty to protect human rights, especially their 'duty […] to control the corporations they are in a position to influence, wherever such corporations operate'.[46] This problem has rightly

[38] UNGPs, principles 3–12, 22–30 and 33–35.
[39] ibid 13–26.
[40] De Schutter (n 36) 56.
[41] ibid.
[42] ibid.
[43] UNGPs, principle 8.
[44] UNGPs, principle 17.
[45] Some research is of a different opinion though, distinguishing between the adverse effects on human rights directly due to the operations of a firm (making companies liable to provide effective remedies, and hence allegedly constituting obligations of result), and the activities of third parties (no liability and no obligations of result). See J Bonnitcha and R McCorquodale, 'The Concept of "Due Diligence" in the UN Guiding Principles on Business and Human Rights' (2017) 28 *European Journal of International Law* 899. But see JG Ruggie and JF Sherman, III 'The Concept of 'Due Diligence' in the UN Guiding Principles on Business and Human Rights: Reply to Professors Bonnitcha and McCorquodale' (2017) 28 *European Journal of International Law* 921.
[46] De Schutter (n 36) 45.

triggered a proposed solution as part of the UN Binding Treaty on Business and Human Rights, currently being negotiated. Instead of emphasising corporate responsibility, the new proposal focuses on establishing contractual relationships with suppliers, sub-contractors, or franchisees of the concerned lead company.[47]

Ultimately, it can be argued that some of the purported flaws of the UNGPs are in fact advantages, as they have triggered debate on a new Treaty on Business and Human Rights (TBHR).[48] I analyse that debate, as well as the latest draft TBHR, in Part IV of the book. Moreover, the UNGPs are also said to have influenced the 2011 amendment of the OECD Guidelines for Multinational Enterprises, which included a new chapter dedicated to human rights.[49] In the next section I therefore address environmental and human rights due diligence and supply chain liability in the OECD framework.

B. OECD Guidelines for Multinational Enterprises and Various Due Diligence Guidance

i. OECD Guidelines for Multinational Enterprises

The rise and fall of the NIEO and of the draft UNCTNC Code triggered two major developments in the global attempts to regulate TNCs.[50] On the one hand, with both the NIEO and the draft Code gradually disappearing, the focus of relevant multilateral efforts slowly but surely shifted from the UN to the GATT.[51] On the other hand, to counter the emerging 'threat' of an international binding code on TNCs, the OECD issued its Guidelines for Multilateral Enterprises.[52] The guidelines contain *recommendations* for responsible business that the adhering governments *encourage* their domestic firms to *observe* wherever they operate.[53]

It could be argued that the creation of the Guidelines is rooted in a particular concern of capital-exporting countries. Namely, the dynamics of such developments as the NIEO and the activities of such entities as the UNCTNC represented an assault on (traditionally) first-world FDI and its main vehicle – corporations. I suggest that, to counter these dynamics, the major capital-exporting states, led by the US, apparently decided to adopt a 'counter-policy instrument'. I elaborate on this assertion below.

[47] ibid 53–54.

[48] D Bilchitz, 'The Necessity for a Business and Human Rights Treaty' (2016) 1(2) *Business and Human Rights Journal* 203, 227.

[49] OECD, *Guidelines for Multinational Enterprises*, the 2011 update, the latest so far, http://mneguidelines.oecd.org/guidelines/, ch IV.

[50] See Chapter 2, section II above.

[51] ibid.

[52] ibid.

[53] OECD (n 49).

Such a 'counter-policy instrument' aimed to influence 'external' – and parallel – international developments, such as UNCTNC Code talks to abandon a highly regulatory stance. It also sought to meet some 'internal' (ie originating from among the 'club' of FDI exporters) demands for greater restraint of TNCs[54] – although, understandably, through a voluntary incentivising instrument, hence the soft form of 'guidelines'.

The OECD Guidelines were originally adopted in 1976 and have since been reviewed on several occasions (in 1979, 1982, 1984, 1991, 2000, and for the last time in 2011).[55] The Guidelines are an annex to the OECD Declaration on International Investment and Multinational Enterprises.[56] They provide a set of principles and standards for responsible business conduct for TNCs operating in or from countries adhering to the Declaration.[57] The Guidelines, being recommendatory in nature, clearly constitute soft law.

The OECD Investment Committee (the Committee) is the highest body supervising the functioning of the Guidelines. A Working Party on Responsible Business Conduct (the Working Party) was established in 2013 as a subsidiary body of the Committee, to assist it in implementing the Guidelines.[58] The Committee and its Working Party encourage the implementation of the Guidelines among adherents, 'strive' to co-operate with non-adherents who may have a special interest in the Guidelines, and promote responsible business conduct worldwide in accordance with the Guidelines to create a level playing field.[59]

The OECD Guidelines are supported by an implementation mechanism of National Contact Points (NCPs). These are entities that each adhering country must set up to promote and implement the Guidelines at the national level.[60] The NCPs assist TNCs and their stakeholders with all enquiries and matters related to the Guidelines in that state, including investigating complaints and providing a mediation and conciliation platform for resolving conflicts that may arise.[61] Notably, not only the business community, but also labour unions and NGOs make up the stakeholder community per the Guidelines.[62]

A general flaw of the OECD Guidelines is that some of their goals have proved problematic to implement effectively in practice – hence the difficulties with their implementation procedures,[63] as well as somewhat vague wording in the matters

[54] PT Muchlinski, *Multinational Enterprises and the Law*, 2nd edn (Oxford, Oxford University Press, 2007) 659.

[55] OECD (n 49).

[56] OECD, *Declaration on International Investment and Multinational Enterprises*, the 2011 update, the latest so far, http://mneguidelines.oecd.org/guidelines/.

[57] OECD (n 49).

[58] OECD, *On-Line Guide to OECD Intergovernmental Activity*, https://oecdgroups.oecd.org/.

[59] OECD (n 49) part II.II.

[60] ibid Preamble.

[61] ibid Preamble and part II.I.1.

[62] ibid part II.I.1.

[63] See eg R Blanpain, 'Multinational Enterprises and Codes of Conduct, The OECD Guidelines for MNEs in Perspective' in R Blanplain (ed), *Comparative Labour Law and Industrial Relations in*

of corporate responsibilities.[64] Fundamentally, to use a recurring term from this book, the Guidelines seem to have very little CSL *normative force* – precisely, they represent mere transparency requirements.

ii. OECD Due Diligence Guidance

With the aim of furthering practical support for TNCs in implementing its Guidelines, the OECD created a series of due diligence guidance documents. Together with the FAO, it produced the OECD-FAO Guidance for Responsible Agricultural Supply Chains. On its own, the OECD created the following: the Due Diligence Guidance for Responsible Supply Chains of Minerals from Conflict-Affected and High-Risk Areas, 2016; the Practical Actions for Companies to Identify and Address the Worst Forms Of Child Labour in Mineral Supply Chains; the Due Diligence Guidance for Meaningful Stakeholder Engagement in the Extractive Sector, 2017; the Due Diligence Guidance for Responsible Supply Chains in the Garment and Footwear Sector, 2017; the paper on Responsible Business Conduct for Institutional Investors, 2017; and the Due Diligence Guidance for Multinational Enterprises, 2018.

The Due Diligence Guidance for Multinational Enterprises offers practical support to enterprises on the implementation of the OECD Guidelines, by providing plain language explanations of its due diligence recommendations and associated provisions.[65] The recommendations aim to clarify to enterprises how to avoid and address adverse impacts on work conditions, as well as human rights, the environment, bribery, consumer policy and corporate governance that may be associated with their operations, supply chains and other business relationships. The Guidance includes explanations, tips and illustrative examples of due diligence additional to the OECD Guidelines.

The OECD-FAO Guidance for Responsible Agricultural Supply Chains assists any company operating throughout the entire agricultural supply chain to comply with existing responsible business conduct frameworks and to observe related legal instruments.[66] It encourages businesses to address pertinent risks and undertake risk mitigation and risk-based due diligence in the agricultural sector by identifying risks and proposing structural risk mitigation measures with regard to several areas, such as human rights, food security and nutrition, health and safety, etc.

Industrialized Market Economies (Alphen aan den Rijn, Kluwer Law International, 2004); LJ Cernic, 'Corporate Responsibility for Human Rights: A Critical Analysis of the OECD Guidelines for Multinational Enterprises' (2008) 3 *Hanse Law Review*; LJ Cernic, 'The 2011 Update of the OECD Guidelines for Multinational Enterprises' (2012) 16 *American Society of International Law Insights*; O De Schutter, 'Transnational Corporations and Human Rights' (2005) *Global Law Working Paper* 01/05.

[64] See OECD (n 49).

[65] OECD (2018) http://mneguidelines.oecd.org/due-diligence-guidance-for-responsible-business-conduct.htm.

[66] OECD (2015) http://mneguidelines.oecd.org/OECD-FAO-Guidance.pdf.

The renewed 2016 edition of the Due Diligence Guidance for Responsible Supply Chains of Minerals from Conflict-Affected and High-Risk Areas creates a framework for due diligence in supply chains of all mineral resources from conflict-affected or high-risk areas.[67] It allows enterprises to identify and manage pertinent risks across the entire spectrum of mineral supply chains in order to avoid contributing to conflicts, whilst aiming to promote responsible business engagement in conflict-involved or post-conflict states. As well as proposing the due diligence framework and risk mitigation measures, the document provides a model policy, with a set of structured principles for mineral supply chain management in addition to specific recommendations regarding tin, tantalum, tungsten and gold supply chain due diligence, reflecting its particularities.[68]

The Practical Actions for Companies to Identify and Address the Worst Forms of Child Labour in Mineral Supply Chains document intends to clarify existing recommendations on identifying and dealing with the risks relating to the worst forms of child labour in the mineral supply chains enshrined in the 2016 OECD Due Diligence Guidance.[69] It formulates five stages in due diligence process throughout all steps of mineral supply chains, and provides an overview of the international legal framework and applicable legal instruments on the subject matter.[70] However, the document is limited to mere explanation of existing standards and does not establish any new recommendations shaping the OECD 2016 Due Diligence Guidance as a primary source on the issue.

The 2017 Due Diligence Guidance for Meaningful Stakeholder Engagement in the Extractive Sector provides industry operators with a framework to identify and mitigate risks related to relevant stakeholder engagement across the full life-cycle of an extractive project.[71] It also covers specificities of particular types of stakeholders, such as indigenous peoples, women, workers and trade unions, and tailors recommendations appropriately. Nevertheless, it does not go into the nitty-gritty of conducting stakeholder engagement activities but limits itself to identifying and managing related risks to avoid the grave effects of extractive activities.

The 2017 Due Diligence Guidance for Responsible Supply Chains in the Garment and Footwear Sector guides enterprises operating in the garment and footwear sector on the elaboration of responsible corporate policies, development of collaborative and risk-based due diligence and enabling remediation in relation to human rights, labour and environmental impacts.[72] The OECD says that for the purposes of the guidance, due diligence should be ongoing, proactive and reactive, applying with flexibility and not just ticking the boxes.[73] However, the

[67] OECD (2016) https://mneguidelines.oecd.org/mining.htm.
[68] ibid.
[69] OECD (2016) https://mneguidelines.oecd.org/child-labour-risks-in-the-minerals-supply-chain.htm.
[70] ibid.
[71] OECD (2017) http://www.oecd.org/daf/inv/mne/stakeholder-engagement-extractive-industries.htm.
[72] OECD (2017) http://mneguidelines.oecd.org/responsible-supply-chains-textile-garment-sector.htm.
[73] ibid.

effectiveness of the document is limited due to the fact that major garment and textile producers, such as Bangladesh and Cambodia, are not OECD members.

The 2017 paper on Responsible Business Conduct for Institutional Investors is created to assist institutional investors to implement due diligence recommendations throughout the investment value chain in order to identify and avoid risks connected to human rights, environment and working conditions.[74] The document specifies actions that asset managers and asset owners may perform under each phase of the due diligence process. It also includes reflection on existing practices, challenges and regulations that are likely to affect due diligence approaches. The paper, however, does not indicate approaches for the entities that facilitate investment (eg market research providers or investment banks).

Concluding Remarks on Part II

In the second half of the twentieth century, the interests of first-world corporations have promoted the global fragmentation of production and division of labour captured in the core-periphery dynamic. This also partially explains why, until recently, a particular GVC production was governed either by international non-binding instruments, such as the UNGPs and the OECD Guidelines, or by the orthodox private means, including traditional national private law. Thanks to GVCs, the core's corporations started outsourcing less value-intense stages of production, such as parts manufacturing, to the periphery. Orthodox – essentially western – corporate and contract law, in turn, presented a means of limiting corporate liability for harms and other issues arising from transboundary production. Thus materialised the main riddle of GVC production and trade, which has also became a fundamental issue of the contemporary global political economy: GVC head corporations avoid virtually any liability, because of the 'economically dependent – legally independent' relationships between the core's corporations and their periphery suppliers and subcontractors.

Today, powerful corporations are increasingly created and domiciled outside the Global North. The Global North-Global South geo-political and socio-economic distinction per se is gradually becoming blurred. Hence today, we can fairly speak about *just* corporations and not necessary *transnational* corporations. At the very least, those corporations, transnational or not, come today from the four corners of the earth. However, such constructs as limited liability are but one proof among many of a westernised 'minimalist' corporate and contractually-focused approach to corporate liability for outsourced production that today is eagerly embraced and implemented by corporate lawyers and the architects of newly created corporations all over the world.

[74] OECD (2017) https://mneguidelines.oecd.org/rbc-financial-sector.htm.

The idea of separate corporate personality leading to limited corporate liability is therefore at once a powerful lesson and the vehicle of corporate non-responsibility in GVCs. Its continual re-examination in national and global settings is fascinating. The forms and nature of social control in a given country influence the broader micro- and macro-economic patterns in that jurisdiction, as well as – more narrowly – its industrial enterprise. Those, in turn, determine that country's context of corporate ownership and hence not only the particular construction of national corporate law, but also the country's overall legal approaches to corporate liability, including transnational liability. These factors ultimately determine today's different national approaches to the regulation of transboundary business transactions.

The story that started in the most industrialised western jurisdictions with the emergence of corporate ownership and separate corporate personality approaches nowadays continues, always hand-in-hand with capitalist production. The separate corporate personality doctrine has not yet changed. Rather, what has changed is how the capitalist production is organised today: namely, through GVCs. And, based on, and shielded by the old orthodox doctrines, today's corporations are, to say the least, unenthusiastic at the prospect of disturbing the GVC equation 'economically dependent – legally independent' by exposing their control or even substantive influence over other parts of GVCs. A clearer determination of the duties and responsibilities of the dominant influencers over transactions within GVCs is thus an arduous feat.

During the latest decade, the number of both national legislation and lawsuits aiming to enhance head companies' duties of care – and, more recently, transnational liability – has expanded dramatically, with varying degrees of success. One clear trend is in establishing both a statutory duty and a common law duty of care through the tort of negligence. This necessitates a distancing from black-letter contract and corporate law principles, such as privity and separate corporate personality and a move towards using more relevant tort law principles. Therefore, in the next part of this book, I address those and other more recent domestic approaches to CSL in an international comparison, as well as examining the challenges and opportunities they introduce.

PART III

Corporate Liability in Theory and Practice: Recent Approaches and an Introduction to Corporate Social Liability

As established in Part I, the impact of the GVCs as a contemporary emanation of the corporate form of production on today's global political economy reaches far beyond mere transboundary commercial fabrication and distribution. At the same time, as demonstrated throughout Part II, the traditional functional construct of the corporation and one of its main purposes – to cut the variable costs of business organisation through its very form – nowadays go beyond corporate law. Today they extend to national and post-national legal, economic and political systems, and assign different participants – from regions to states to individuals – to the global centre or the periphery both in terms of geographic location and social class. It is thus difficult to overestimate the role of corporations and big firms in GVCs. Things are not so clear cut, however, when it comes to developing a stricter determination of the duties and responsibilities of the dominant influencers over transactions within GVCs.

Through the detailed historical and doctrinal accounts in Parts I and II respectively, I showed that traditional norms regulating transboundary production and trade have their foundations in public international law and private regulation. The first two parts of the book equally revealed the countless shortcomings – normative, doctrinal, and practical – of these two approaches to GVC governance. The latest decade has seen an unprecedented increase in both national binding legislation and lawsuits aiming to enhance head companies' duty of care, and, more recently, transnational liability (Chapter 5).

Notwithstanding the recent global drive towards both national hard laws and litigation targeting the negligent behaviour of lead firms and their poor governance of their offshored operations, in practice most of these actions ultimately fail. Above all, contemporary corporations are more than reluctant to expose their control or even substantive influence in GVCs. This is precisely because disclosing such a lead role might not only impede their reputation but may also – in particular – involve enhanced legal obligations and even liability. In this regard, one key issue is the extent to which 'influence' means 'control', and how the two merge into a larger power play perspective. In Chapter 6 I thus look at general conditions for establishing influence, control, or power, and, hence founding corporate liability in practice. In that chapter, I consider specific criteria of differentiation between types of corporate liability within GVCs, as well as some concrete possibilities of CSL in value chains.

5

Corporate Liability in International Comparison

In Chapter 4 it was established that corporate social liability could be positively correlated with an increase in the normative force of relevant norms. This line of argumentation also includes a presumption that normative force, and hence also CSL itself, gradually increases with the transition from mandatory disclosure disciplines to mandatory due diligence disciplines, and from the latter to liability disciplines. More precisely, by 'liability disciplines' I mean normative sets which clarify the liability of the head corporation, and the consequences thereon if there is negligence, and ultimately non-compliance, of this corporation or its controlled and economically dependent entities, with triple obligations of disclosure, due diligence, and duty of care.

In Part II above, I additionally underlined various national and post-national limits to such liability disciplines. However, these limits could also be seen as mere subordinate stages of the normative force of CSL, hence also *steps to* CSL. As outlined above, these include various mandatory disclosure norms (eg the EUNFRD; the UNGPs) and mandatory due diligence laws and regulations (eg the EUTR and EUCMR; the French Vigilance law; the Dutch Child labour due diligence law).[1] The last two sets of norms, the French and the Dutch laws, could also arguably be part of the ultimate degree of CSL – the disciplines establishing the consequences of liability in case of non-compliance with the obligations of disclosure, due diligence, and duty of care.

In short, the previous part of this book determined that, while the norms of stage one (mandatory disclosure) and stage two (mandatory due diligence) of CSL could be found across different jurisdictions in both national and post-national law, that is, at supranational (EU) and international (public international law) levels, an ultimate stage of CSL (liability disciplines per se), however, to date seems to exist only in few jurisdictions. I discuss these in section I of this chapter.

In section II, in order to shed light on the relationship between corporate societal (non-financial) disclosure and due diligence (steps one and two of CSL), and liability (step three), I focus on relevant legal claims against companies within the framework of the societal disclosure, due diligence and, ultimately, liability

[1] This Dutch law is fully referenced and described further in this subsection.

regarding adverse societal impacts. To date, virtually all relevant litigation has occurred before national courts. However, all those cases have a transnational character and importance.

I. Legislative Landscape

In the UK, the legislative drift of corporate governance and related responsibilities started in the 1990s. The UK's first Code of Corporate Governance was, however, voluntary in nature and laid down a rather lax, typical CSR, set of norms.[2] Its list of best practices did not imply any concrete compliance obligations for the covered firms, but just an obligation to explain non-compliant behaviour.[3] A voluntary regulation approach persisted in the UK (and in fact elsewhere in the EU) throughout the 2000s, with the UK Bribery Act 2010 marking a departure from that model.

The Bribery Act 2010, statutory in nature, introduced a new type of offence.[4] The offence is said to be committed by commercial organisations carrying out on a business, or part of a business, in the UK if they fail to prevent persons associated with them, including employees, agents and subsidiaries, as well as contractors performing services for the covered organisations, from bribing another person on the organisation's behalf. The Act outlines the potential situations which can be considered as an offence. The failure of the covered firms to prevent bribery or corruption would lead to strict corporate liability and a requirement to pay a fine. However, if a firm put in place adequate procedures designed to prevent people associated with it from undertaking bribery or corruption, that might constitute a defence against the violation, and, hence, against criminal liability.

Another piece of the UK corporate liability legislation, the Modern Slavery Act 2015, requires any commercial organisation carrying out business in the UK with a total annual turnover of more than £36 million to prepare annual statements disclosing measures they have taken to identify slavery and human trafficking in supply chains; alternatively they should release a statement that such measures are not being taken.[5] The statement should include a description of the organisation's structure, business model and supply chain relationships, information on its policies related to slavery and human trafficking, details of due diligence regarding its supply chains, the areas at highest risk of violations and their means of managing such risk, such as any training that is available to staff. Failure to comply with this obligation impels the Secretary of State to apply to the High Court for an injunction against the wrongful organisation. Not complying with the injunction would result in an unlimited fine.

[2] Report of the Committee on the Financial Aspects of Corporate Governance (Cadbury Report), Committee on the Financial Aspects of Corporate Governance 1992 (UK).

[3] ibid, para 1.10.

[4] Bribery Act 2010 (c 23) (UK).

[5] Modern Slavery Act 2015 (c 30) (UK), s 54(4)(a).

While the two above Acts represent expedient tools of due diligence, they do not amount to liability disciplines in the sense of the three steps to CSL outlined in the introduction to this part. Primarily, the 2010 Act makes clear that satisfactory conduct (ample paperwork and procedures) to prevent bribery is a guarantee against criminal liability and hence fines. In contrast, the 2015 Act does mention fines but does not specify the type of liability. Second, neither Act represents obligations of result, but only of conduct; and, moreover, while the 2010 Act lays down mandatory due diligence obligations, the 2015 Act in fact requires only a disclosure of information on due diligence. That is to say, even though disclosure contributes to the general policy goal of targeting slavery, the obligation to disclose is not matched by the imposition of a duty of care or legal liability in the case of non-compliance. Therefore, the Modern Slavery Act 2015 corresponds only to the first degree of CSL (mandatory disclosure), while the Bribery Act corresponds to the second one (mandatory due diligence).

Australia and New South Wales also have Modern Slavery Acts. The Australian (Federal) Act applies to firms based or operating in Australia, with an annual consolidated income of more than AUD 100 million.[6] The Act in New South Wales covers organisations with employees in New South Wales and a total annual turnover starting at AUD 50 million; at the date of writing, this Act is not yet in force.[7]

Both Acts require the covered entities to provide annual statements on their supply chain regarding the risks of modern slavery and the actions they have taken to address those risks. The New South Wales Act is restricted to firms' direct suppliers, while the Federal Act applies to further entities owned or controlled by the first company. At the same time, the latter does not penalise a failure to provide a modern slavery statement or the lodging of an incomplete statement, while the former issues sanctions in the form of fines for non-compliance. Under the Act in New South Wales, a modern slavery statement may outline the organisation's structure and its supply chains, modern slavery due diligence processes and steps taken to reduce the risk of modern slavery in its supply chain. The Act specifies a fine amounting to AUD 1.1 million for non-compliance with obligations to prepare and publish the said statement and for providing false or misleading information about it, as well as criminal penalties – two years of imprisonment. Under the Federal Act, however, the relevant Australian authority may publish information about any failure to comply with the obligation in the Modern Slavery Statements Register or elsewhere. Thus, both instruments have followed a scheme similar to the UK Modern Slavery Act 2015. Both Acts hence belong to mandatory disclosure disciplines.

In the US, the California Transparency Act imposes an obligation on retail sellers and manufacturers that are doing business in California and have annual worldwide gross receipts of more than US$ 100 million to disclose information

[6] Modern Slavery Act (No 153) 2018 (Cth).
[7] Modern Slavery Act (No 30) 2018 (NSW).

concerning the efforts they undertake to eradicate human trafficking and slavery within their direct supply chains.[8] The Act covers five areas:

(i) verification of product supply chains;
(ii) audits of suppliers;
(iii) certification of the compliance of materials incorporated into the products with domestic laws on slavery and human trafficking of the producers;
(iv) internal accountability for employees and contractors; and
(v) training for company employees and management with direct responsibility for supply chain management.

The disclosure is to be posted on the company's website with an accessible link to all related documents or, if the company does not have a website, it should be provided through written disclosures upon consumers' requests. An exclusive remedy for the violation of the obligation would be an action for injunctive relief brought by the Attorney General. However, while, like the UK, Australia, and New South Wales' modern slavery Acts, California's Act only obliges the covered firms to make the required disclosures, it does not check whether those companies do anything concrete to ensure that their value chains are free from any manifestation of modern slavery. Thus, this is a typical mandatory disclosure law in that, in fact it goes no further than a compulsory disclosure of relevant information. In terms of scope, it is also quite limited as it covers only direct supply chain and direct suppliers of the concerned entities.

The US Dodd-Frank Act, in particular section 1502 imposes additional disclosure obligations on companies using tin, tantalum, tungsten, and gold, regarding the origin of these materials.[9] The aim of this provision is to avoid mineral trading exacerbating the conflict in the Democratic Republic of the Congo. Companies have to pass the three-step requirement process: (i) determination of whether the issuer is subject to section 1502; (ii) whether the mineral(s) in question originated in the stipulated countries; and (iii) subsequent supply chain due diligence. Afterwards, firms have to report the findings on supply chain due diligence, third party verification, and in certain circumstances private sector audits in their annual Securities and Exchange Commission (SEC) filings,[10] reports and websites. In addition, if a non-SEC filing company supplies to a SEC filing company, the latter is required to conduct due diligence on its supply chains. Nevertheless, section 1502 contains only a disclosure requirement and does not represent a ban or introduce a penalty for the use of conflict minerals. Where the requirement is not fulfilled, it will lead to liability for fraudulent or false reporting. The Act thus arguably falls within the first step to CSL – mandatory disclosure disciplines – because its obligations are

[8] California Transparency in Supply Chains Act 2010 (USA), s 1714.43(a)(1).
[9] Dodd–Frank Wall Street Reform and Consumer Protection Act 2010 (USA), s 1502(b)(p)(1)(a).
[10] Filings to the US Securities and Exchange Commission.

not backed by sanctions beyond the obligation to justify false statements or general non-compliance. In addition, in 2017 the SEC suspended enforcement of the Act, which is still unenforceable at the time of writing. In particular, companies still have to perform due diligence, but are under no obligation to publicly state that their products are 'conflict-free'.

The French law on a duty of care for parent, instructing and buying companies (French Vigilance law) requires covered French companies and corporate groups to ensure that serious violations of human rights and fundamental freedoms, as well serious environmental damage, do not occur in their value chains.[11] The law applies to firms employing at least 5,000 persons in France or at least 10,000 employees worldwide, including the workers of their subsidiaries. To this end, the law requires the covered actors to make a vigilance plan to prevent and detect violations of those rights and freedoms in France and abroad by their subsidiaries, subcontractors and suppliers with whom they maintain an established business relationship, to the extent that these activities are related to the relationship. Failure to comply with the Vigilance law may result in fines of up to €10 million. Where the violation causes damage, the size of the fine may be tripled, ie up to €30 million. Notably, the law does not envisage fines for harmed individuals under torts rubric for reparation of damages caused by a violation of the law. The law lays down delictual liability and, coupled with the above, is thus part of the third degree of CSL, namely, liability disciplines.

Switzerland recently introduced a whole range of significant laws and proposals. First, the 2013 Swiss Federal Act on Private Security Services Abroad (PSSA) prohibits Swiss private security services from participating in hostilities abroad or providing services which are part of serious human rights breaches.[12] In addition, the Act obliges Swiss private security services to report to relevant authorities on their activities abroad along with necessary documents in order to prevent those services from contributing to human rights violations in other countries. Violation of statutory prohibitions might lead to a custodial sentence for the persons carrying out the prohibited activities. However, where an offence is committed through negligence, the Act prescribes only a fine. Non-cooperation, in the form of refusal to provide relevant information, to allow the examination of documents, or to grant access to premises, would also result in fines. On the one hand, the Act is thus arguably part of liability disciplines. On the other hand, it is very partially relevant to GVC production.

Unlike the above Act, the Swiss Popular Initiative on Responsible Business (RBI) is directly relevant to GVC production. It proposes to impose an obligation on Swiss companies (excluding low-risk small- and medium-sized enterprises

[11] Loi n° 2017-399 relative au devoir de vigilance des sociétés mères et des entreprises donneuses d'ordre, promulguée le 27 mars 2017, JORF n° 0074 du 28 mars 2017, texte n° 1.

[12] Federal Act on Private Security Services provided Abroad (PSSA) (Switzerland) of 27 September 2013.

(SMEs)) to carry out mandatory due diligence in the sphere of the protection of human rights and the environment.[13] In terms of scope and nature, RBI is nothing less than a proposal for the partial revision of the Swiss Constitution aiming to introduce disciplines on responsible business, and Swiss citizens will have to decide whether to adopt or reject such a revision.[14] According to the Initiative, the covered firms should identify risks affecting human rights and the environment, and take measures to prevent the potential and imminent, or cease current, internationally-recognised human rights and environmental abuses. They also have to report publicly about the measures taken. These obligations apply to companies' supply chains and all their business relationships, including any entities they own or control at home or abroad (ie both subsidiaries and economically controlled entities). Naturally, if the RBI is confirmed by the Swiss popular vote (public referendum), it will become part of the ultimate stage of CSL, that is, liability disciplines. The Initiative is set for public referendum in November 2020. There is also a parliamentary counter-proposal to the above Initiative.[15] The proposal affects Swiss companies with a balance sheet of CHF 40 million, sales of CHF 80 million or at least 500 full-time employees. The proposal also covers companies with activities entailing a high risk of human rights violations or damaging the environment in Switzerland or abroad. Like the Initiative, it provides for due diligence and risk management obligations for companies in the sphere of protection of human rights and environment relevant to their areas of activity, including abroad. Unlike the Initiative, it does not provide for any formal sanctions. Although under the proposal, Swiss parent companies may be held liable for their foreign legally controlled subsidiaries, if damage occurs to life and limb or property as a result of violation of relevant international norms that have been ratified by Switzerland. That is to say, while due diligence obligations of first companies extend to other business relationships, such as, typically, suppliers, liability does not. The counter-proposal therefore potentially is part of obligatory due diligence disciplines.

Note that on 18 December 2019 the Swiss Council of States (a chamber of the Swiss Parliament) voted against this due diligence counter-proposal and instead adopted a proposal encouraged by the Government (mostly right-wing and conservative parties), limited to reporting and issue-specific (child labour, conflict

[13] L'initiative populaire 'Entreprises responsables – pour protéger l'être humain et l'environnement' (2017) www.admin.ch/opc/fr/federal-gazette/2017/5999.pdf.

[14] For a thorough overview and analysis, see N Bueno, 'The Swiss Popular Initiative on Responsible Business. From Responsibility to Liability' in LFH Enneking et al (eds), *Accountability and International Business Operations: Providing Justice for Corporate Violations of Human Rights and Environmental Standards* (Abingdon-on-Thames, Routledge, 2020).

[15] Proposal by the Legal Affairs Committee of the Swiss National Council. Responsible Business Initiative: indirect counter-proposal www.bhrinlaw.org/180508-swiss-parliament-counter-proposal_unofficial_en-translation_updated.pdf.

minerals) due diligence without liability rules.[16] It was eventually approved by both chambers of the Parliament, the National Council (by a narrow majority) and the Council of States on 8/9 June 2020.[17] So, if the RBI is dismissed by the Swiss population in November 2020, the counter-proposal adopted by the Parliament would enter into force as a new Swiss law.

Last but definitely not least, the new Dutch Child labour due diligence law (or Child Labor Duty of Care Act) intends to prevent the importation into the Netherlands of goods and services produced using child labour.[18] It establishes the responsibility of Dutch and foreign companies, delivering goods or services to the Netherlands at least twice a year, to assess whether child labour contributed to these goods and services, and provide an action plan if there is a reasonable presumption that children were involved. Failure to submit a statement of due diligence in covered entities' full supply chain entails a fine. Any natural or legal person with sufficient evidence may file a complaint to the relevant regulatory authority on the basis that children were exploited. If the regulator finds that the firm in question failed to exercise due diligence, the company receives binding instructions. Non-compliance with these instructions may result in a fine and, if the company has already been previously fined twice, may even lead to the imprisonment of the responsible director. In comparison with French Vigilance law, the Dutch law arguably applies to the whole value chain and not only to the entities with which the first company maintains an established business relationship – basically, subsidiaries and tier-one and direct suppliers and subcontractors. This law is definitely part of liability disciplines, at least in theory. I offer a comparative analysis of the questions of actual application and overall effectiveness of the above Dutch and French laws in Part IV of the book (Chapter 7).

To summarise the findings on relevant legislation landscape, the table below compares domestic instruments on corporate liability in light of their different degrees of normative force. Note that for each Act, the table indicates the highest possible degree of CSL, even if in most cases, logically, the legislation also covers previous stages. For example, the French Vigilance law contains CSR, mandatory disclosure and due diligence obligations; however, since it also extends to a strict liability stage, it is presented as making part of the highest step of CSL disciplines.

[16] https://www.business-humanrights.org/en/latest-news/swiss-due-diligence-initiative-set-for-public-referendum-as-parliament-only-opts-for-reporting-centred-proposal/.

[17] https://www.business-humanrights.org/en/latest-news/swiss-parliament-adopts-reporting-focused-proposal/.

[18] Law of 24 October 2019 on the introduction of a duty of care to prevent the delivery of goods and services that have been produced with the help of child labor (Child Labor Duty of Care Act) https://zoek.officielebekendmakingen.nl/stb-2019-401.html.

Table 5.1

Instrument	**Zero level: CSR disciplines**	**Level 1: Mandatory disclosure disciplines**	**Level 2: Mandatory due diligence disciplines**	**Level 3: Liability disciplines**
UK Code of Corporate Governance, 1992	x			
UK Bribery Act 2010			x	
UK Modern Slavery Act 2015		x		
California Transparency in Supply Chains Act, 2010		x		
US Dodd-Frank Act, s 1502, 2010		x		
French Vigilance Law, 2017				x
Swiss Popular Initiative on Responsible Business, 2017				x
Swiss 'Stronger' Parliamentary Counter-Proposal to Responsible Business Initiative, 2018			x	
Swiss 'Weaker' Parliamentary Counter-Proposal to Responsible Business Initiative, 2019		x		
Dutch Child Labour Due Diligence Law, 2019				x
NSW Modern Slavery Act (No 30) 2018		x		
Australia's Modern Slavery Act (No 153) 2018 (Cth)		x		

II. Litigation Landscape

In the above legislative landscape discussion, I presented and arranged instruments by country, covering the primary jurisdictions selected for comparison in this book (UK, US, France), and then adding the most recent legislative developments from other countries. In the following overview of the most relevant cases, I cover specific issues one after another, thus not necessarily organising cases by primary selected jurisdictions and other countries.

The ruling in the UK case *Chandler v Cape* is usually seen as the decision in which, for the first time, a court found that, in certain circumstances, a parent company might be held liable for the health and safety of its subsidiary's employees.[19] It therefore deserves particular attention. The plaintiff David Chandler had been working for the Cape plc subsidiary between 1959 and 1962.[20] In 2007, he developed asbestosis due to exposure to asbestos during the aforementioned period of employment.[21] It was not covered by the subsidiary's insurance policy, chiefly because the subsidiary had no insurance policy to indemnify against claims for damages for asbestosis.[22] In addition, by the time of the claim, the subsidiary no longer existed, so Chandler brought a claim against the parent company, Cape plc, alleging that it owed him (and subsequently breached) a duty of care.[23] The parent company denied that it owed a duty of care to Chandler, on the basis that Chandler was not its direct employee but was an employee of its subsidiary company.[24]

The court ultimately held that Cape plc owed a duty of care to Chandler as it was responsible for the injuries of its subsidiary's employees, because it knew or ought to have known that the subsidiary would rely on its parent company using that superior knowledge for the employees' protection.[25] Specifically, the judges used the *Caparo* test and established that the parent had actual knowledge of the subsidiary employees' working conditions, and the asbestos risk was obvious. As it had also employed special scientific and medical officers to be responsible for health and safety issues, it had, in the circumstances, retained responsibility for ensuring that its own employees, and those of its subsidiaries, were not harmed by asbestos.[26]

The *Chandler* case is important because a parent company was for the first time recognised liable for harms to its subsidiary's employees without proving that the parent was substantively intervening in the concerned policies of the subsidiary. Particularly, the parent company's practice of intervening in the trading operations of the subsidiary was enough for purposes of establishing tort liability.[27] However, while this case concerns a regular supply relationship, it deals with domestic activities and thus is not a typical supply-chain transnational liability dispute focusing on subcontracting.

[19] *Chandler v Cape plc* [2012] EWCA Civ 525.
[20] ibid paras 4.1–4.2.
[21] ibid para 5.1.
[22] ibid para 6.1.
[23] ibid para 7.1.
[24] ibid.
[25] ibid para 80.
[26] ibid para 75.1.
[27] ibid para 80.

Although not a claim of negligence in subcontracting inside a regular supply relationship, the *Kiobel* case is one of the lead claims in transnational corporate liability.[28] The question in this case was about the extraterritoriality of the US Alien Tort Statute (ATS) application.[29] Namely, a putative class action was filed by a group of Nigerian citizens who were victims of violations of the law of nations by the Nigerian Government, which had been allegedly supported by Royal Dutch Petroleum (Shell) and its local subsidiary. The claims were dismissed by federal courts. The US Supreme Court was asked whether and under what circumstances courts may recognise a cause of action under the ATS for violations of the law of nations that occur within the territory of another sovereign state. The Supreme Court held explicitly that the ATS did not apply extraterritorially for violations of the law of nations outside of the US territory, unless there was a clear indication otherwise, as it would violate the presumption against extraterritoriality.[30]

Another series of claims were brought by Nigerian citizens against Shell at home – in the Netherlands – in 2015. This *Shell* litigation is of vital importance on many counts. The final decisions in the three cases[31] recognised that the Dutch courts had international jurisdiction to hear claims against Shell and its Nigerian subsidiary even if the damage occurred outside the Netherlands, and the court ordered Shell to produce relevant documents.[32] Moreover, the Court of Appeals in The Hague also allowed an NGO, Milieudefensie, acting as a co-applicant in all three cases, to inspect relevant Shell documents about the maintenance of particular pipelines, in order to substantiate plaintiffs' claims.[33]

To summarise, four Nigerian citizens brought claims for compensation against Royal Dutch Shell and its Nigerian subsidiary in The Hague. The claims concerned the oil spills from pipelines of the subsidiary that occurred in the Niger Delta in 2005 and 2006. The plaintiffs alleged that Shell was liable for (consequential) damages and had to remedy the soil and water pollution as well as making promises and taking further actions to prevent new leakages and environmental damages.

The Court dismissed Shell's defences, including the lack of jurisdiction claim. It found that the Dutch courts had international jurisdiction to hear these claims against Shell and its Nigerian subsidiary outside of the state where the damage occurred, a move which potentially opened the floodgates to seise Dutch courts for compensation for environmental damage against any Dutch corporation.

In the *Arica Victims v Boliden Mineral* case, initiated in 2013, Arica Victims KB, a company representing 707 Chileans, appeared before the county court of Skellefteå, Sweden, against a Swedish mining company, Boliden Mineral.[34]

[28] *Kiobel et al v Royal Dutch Petroleum et al*, Case 10-1491, Supreme Court, 17 April 2013.

[29] See Chapter 3 of this book, in particular section I.

[30] *Kiobel* (n 28) paras 116, 125, 133.

[31] *Dutch Shell Nigeria cases*: Court of Appeal, The Hague, 17 December 2015, ECLI:NL:GHDHA:2015:3586-7-8 (Oguru-Efanga/Shell), (Dooh/Shell), (Shell/Akpan).

[32] ibid.

[33] ibid.

[34] Skellefteå Tingsrätt [TR] [Skellefteå District Court] 2018-02-07 T 1012–13 (Swedish).

Between 1984 and 1985, Boliden Mineral had sold toxic waste from its arsenic plant in Sweden to a Chilean company that was supposed to handle the waste. However that firm went bankrupt and dumped the waste in the Polygono area of Arica, Chile.[35] Since the 1990s, the community there has suffered from serious diseases, including cancer, miscarriages, skin conditions and breathing problems, due to excessive levels of arsenic in the local residents' blood.[36] The plaintiffs argued that Boliden acted negligently when it deliberately outsourced operations to a clearly incapable actor, which then caused damage to others, as there was evidence that the defendant knew that the waste would pose a significant health threat.[37] Boliden denied the claims in their entirety.

The legal question here was thus whether a company could be held liable for health and environmental damage even after the tort happened. In 2018, the District Court in Skellefteå decided that Chilean law applied, and that adequate causation between the injuries of Chilean victims and the waste was not shown, thus dismissing the plaintiffs' torts and compensation claims.[38] The plaintiffs appealed the decision and in March 2019 the Upper Norrland Court of Appeal ruled on the matter.[39] Unlike the District Court, it held that Swedish tort law should apply instead. This was the law of the place in which a wrong had been committed, because in its view the Swedish mining company's alleged negligence had its centre in Sweden and not in Chile.[40] According to Swedish law, claims for damages expire after ten years, and the court thus found the claim time-barred and dismissed it.

The *Nevsun* row is an outstanding example of an action of foreign nationals for damages against a Canadian transnational mining corporation for the acts of its subsidiary abroad.[41] The suit was initiated in November 2014 in the British Columbia courts by three Eritrean nationals, refugees in Canada, who launched a representative proceeding against Nevsun Resources Ltd, a Vancouver-based mining company.[42] The former workers sued Nevsun for complicity in violent, cruel, inhuman and degrading treatment at Bisha Mine, owned and operated by the Bisha Mine Share Company (BMSC)[43] where Nevsun held an indirect majority

[35] Given the language of the decision, the review of the case is provided in L Hallberg and T Pöpke, 'Liability for Damages Due to Export of Toxic Waste: Final Ruling' (2019) *International Law Office* https://www.internationallawoffice.com/Newsletters/Environment-Climate-Change/Sweden/Advokatfirman-Lindahl/Liability-for-damages-due-to-export-of-toxic-waste-final-ruling?utm_source=ILO+Newsletter&utm_medium=email&utm_content=Newsletter+2019-07-15&utm_campaign=Environment+%26+Climate+Change+Newsletter&redir=1.

[36] Boliden lawsuit (re Chile), *Business and Human Rights Resource Centre* https://www.business-humanrights.org/en/latest-news/boliden-lawsuit-re-chile/.

[37] ibid.

[38] ibid.

[39] Hallberg and Pöpke (n 35).

[40] ibid.

[41] *Nevsun Resources Ltd v Araya* 2020 SCC 5 [*Nevsun*].

[42] *Araya v Nevsun Resources Ltd* 2016 BCSC 1856 [*Araya*], para 42.

[43] *Araya* (n 42) para 33.

of a 60 per cent interest, the other 40 per cent being held by the national mining company, an arm of the Eritrean government.[44] Notably, in 2018 the Chinese mining group Zijin acquired Nevsun for €1.2 billion.[45]

BMSC subcontracted the construction of the Bisha Mine to the Engineering, Procurement and Construction Manager (EPCM), and the EPCM then further outsourced to other subcontractors owned by members of the Eritrean military.[46] The respondents (applicants in the initial suit) claimed that the subcontractors forced Eritreans conscripted into the country's National Service Program (NSP) to provide their labour at the mine in inhuman and degrading conditions, and under the constant threat of physical punishment, torture and imprisonment.[47] In addition to basing their claim in tort law, the respondents partially based their claim on the customary international law prohibitions against forced labour, slavery, cruel, inhuman or degrading treatment, and crimes against humanity,[48] on the basis that existing torts such as assault, battery, unlawful confinement and unjust enrichment did not adequately reflect the harm they allegedly suffered.[49] They also sought damages on behalf of all Eritreans that had been forced to provide their labour at that mine from September 2008.[50] Their claims were based on violations of peremptory norms of customary international law, namely prohibition of forced labour, slavery, cruel, inhuman or degrading treatment, and crimes against humanity.[51]

In its appeal to the Supreme Court of Canada (SCC), Nevsun argued in part that the court should strike out the portion of the respondents' claim based on customary international law, on the basis that, even if the prohibitions against torture, slavery and forced labour were part of the law of Canada, they did not on their own create a cause of action. Rather, the respondents' claims would require the development of new torts and this was a task for the legislator, not the judiciary.[52]

On 28 February 2020, the SCC released its long-awaited decision on Nevsun's appeal against the lower courts' rulings: to the extent that customary international law norms have been adopted into Canadian law, they bind Nevsun as a Canadian corporation.[53] In a 5-4 landmark judgment, the majority of the SCC recognised Canada's international human rights obligation to provide an effective remedy[54] and ruled that 'it was not plain and obvious' that Canadian courts cannot develop

[44] *Nevsun* (n 41) para 7.
[45] J Poole and L Millan Lombrana, 'Nevsun Finds a White Knight in Zijin With $1.41 Billion Deal', *Bloomberg* (5 September 2018) https://www.bloomberg.com/news/articles/2018-09-05/zijin-mining-to-buy-nevsun-resources-for-1-41-billion-in-cash.
[46] *Araya* (n 42) para 26.
[47] *Araya v Nevsun Resources Ltd*, 2017 BCCA 401, [Appeal], paras 3–4.
[48] *Araya* (n 47) para 2.
[49] *Araya v Nevsun*, Respondents' Factum, BCCA, CA44025, para 146.
[50] *Araya* (n 49) para 48.
[51] *Araya* (n 49) para 2.
[52] *Araya v Nevsun*, Appellant's Factum, SCC File Number 37919, para 61.
[53] *Nevsun* (n 41) para 132.
[54] *Nevsun* (n 41) para 119.

a civil remedy in domestic law for corporate violations of customary international law norms' that are part of the law of Canada.[55] Moreover, this could be done either through the development of new torts or through a direct remedy for violations of customary international law.[56]

The SCC held that the civil lawsuit could go forward. A lower court's judge will have to decide, at the British Columbia Supreme Court in September 2021, whether Nevsun breached customary international law and, if so, how such harm should be remedied.[57] This decision opens the door for more cases to be brought in Canadian courts for violations of human rights or failure to engage with environmental due diligence against Canadian extractive corporations operating transnationally.

Another such 'Canadian' case that is crucial for this discussion, *Garcia v Tahoe Resources*, also arose out of a claim for damages. The damages in question were caused by private security personnel employed at a mine in Guatemala, who shot and injured the participants of the protest outside the mine.[58] Those victims constituted plaintiffs who contended that the shooting was planned, while Tahoe Resources, a Canadian company who owned and controlled the mine through its subsidiaries, had thus de facto authorised the use of force by the security personnel of the mine in order to prevent a possible interference by protestors with the operation of the mine. Regarding the substance of the case, the main legal issues at stake were the doctrine of separate legal personality, and thus questions of the corporate veil and limited parent's liability. In the initial decision, the chambers judge declined jurisdiction under *forum non conveniens*, concluding that the plaintiffs could obtain a fair trial in Guatemala.[59]

On appeal, the British Columbia Court of Appeal (BCCA) overturned this decision, finding that the chambers judge had applied an incorrect test concerning the risk of unfairness in the foreign jurisdiction. The BCCA found that, instead of assessing whether foreign courts were *capable of providing the justice*, the court should establish whether *the real risk of unfair process* existed in Guatemala.[60] Otherwise, upon the BCCA's judgment, the civil law suit would remain a potentiality. The new evidence concerning the criminal proceeding was admitted because it was deemed likely to have affected the outcome of the chambers judge's decision. However, at the time of writing, according to the decision on the appeal, there was doubt as to whether the proceedings would go forward in a timely manner or even happen at all.[61] From the viewpoint of the actual possibility of such claims being judged at the home country of the head firm, the aforementioned SCC *Nevsun* decision has clearly increased the chances of the *Garcia* lawsuit now proceeding in

[55] *Nevsun* (n 41) para 122.
[56] *Nevsun* (n 41) paras 127–28.
[57] *Nevsun* (n 41) para 131.
[58] *Garcia v Tahoe Resources Inc*, 2017 BCCA 39.
[59] ibid para 1.
[60] ibid paras 128–131.
[61] ibid Summary and para 132.

Canada as the place of central management, instead of Guatemala – a mere place where the subsidiary's operations took place.

Choc v Hudbay is yet another case brought against a Canadian mining company for the actions of its subsidiaries, thus also fully involving questions of piercing the corporate veil and disregarding the rules of separate legal personality.[62] Indigenous Mayan Q'eqchi' people from El Estor, Guatemala brought three related actions against Hudbay Inc, a Canadian mining company headquartered in Toronto, and its wholly-controlled subsidiaries operating mining projects in Guatemala.[63] The claims concerned the Fenix mining project, a proposed open-cast nickel mining operation, in eastern Guatemala by Compañía Guatemalteca de Níquel (CGN), which was a wholly controlled Guatemalan subsidiary until August 2011.[64]

The claimants were part of El Estor's Mayan Q'eqchi' community and argued that the concession was on their ancestral land and had been granted to Hudbay without their consent or even without adequately consulting the Q'eqchi' community.[65]

The claimants brought three related accusations against Hudbay, CGN and HMI (another subsidiary) stating that Fenix security personnel were controlled and supervised by Hudbay, and that they had committed human rights violations, including shootings, murder, and gang rape.[66] The defendants brought three preliminary motions seeking to dismiss the case on the basis that no cause of action existed, that one of the claims was limitation statute-barred and that the Ontario courts had no jurisdiction over the claim against CGN.[67] The Ontario Superior Court of Justice (OSCJ) dismissed the defendant's motion to strike out the plaintiff's actions as well as the motion to bar the claims based on limitation statute. The OSCJ identified three types of situations when the corporate veil can be lifted and an undertaking cannot claim separate legal personality: (i) when there is a statutory or contractual requirement to do so; (ii) when the parent company completely controls the subsidiary and merely uses it as a shield for a fraudulent conduct; or (iii) when the subsidiary acts as an agent of the parent.[68] The OSCJ upheld the final condition.

Notably, while the respondents raised the question of jurisdiction, they did so as a secondary, fallback position. However, precisely because of this strategy, the judge ultimately decided that she did not have to address this question.[69] At the time of writing, the *Choc* litigation is still ongoing, as both sides are still trying to position themselves for an eventual trial.[70]

[62] *Choc v Hudbay Inc* 2013, ONSC 1414.

[63] ibid para 4.

[64] ibid para 8.

[65] Business & Human Rights Resource Centre https://www.business-humanrights.org/en/latest-news/hudbay-minerals-lawsuits-re-guatemala/.

[66] *Choc* (n 62) paras 4–6.

[67] *Choc*, para 1.

[68] For similar reasoning, see eg V Ulfbeck and A Ehlers, 'Tort Law, Corporate Groups and Supply Chain Liability for Workers' Injuries: The Concept of Vicarious Liability' (2016) 13 *European Company Law* 167; V Ulfbeck, 'Vicarious Liability in Groups of Companies and in Supply Chains – Is Competition Law Leading the Way?' (5 December 2019) *CEVIA Working Paper Series*, Issue 4.

[69] *Choc* (n 62) para 86.

[70] Business & Human Rights Resource Centre (n 65).

Similar to the current results of the *Garcia* litigation, at this stage the decision in *Choc* is illustrative, as it recognises the home jurisdiction of a corporation as predominant. And just as in the case of *Garcia*, based on the acts of the subsidiary as those of an agent of the parent, it lifts the corporate veil and disregards separate legal personality. Last but not least, a likely future development of the *Choc* row has obviously gained new impetus since the 2020 *Nevsun* ruling opened Canadian courts for claims of violations of human rights against Canadian extractive corporations operating transnationally.

Together with the landmark *Nevsun* decision, the 2019 UK Supreme Court's (UKSC) judgment in another mining-related case, *Vedanta*, contributes to the doctrine of CSL, including for failure to engage with social and environmental due diligence. The ruling provides that a mining company owes a duty of care to those affected by the actions of its subsidiaries in other jurisdictions.[71] To summarise the original claim, approximately 1,826 Zambian citizens initiated proceedings in the UK against a UK parent company, Vedanta, and its subsidiary Konkola Copper Mines plc (KCM), incorporated in Zambia, stating that toxic emissions from the Nchanga copper mine, owned by KCM, polluted watercourses, damaging health and farming activities of local population.[72] It is worth noting that the UK Supreme Court, while eventually ruling on jurisdiction only,[73] still delved into the factors establishing the parent's duty of care to those affected by its subsidiary's actions. Therefore, while the current *Vedanta* ruling is only about jurisdiction, it offers crucial elements for future assessment of liability and damages.

On the basis of decisions of the 2016 High Court and the 2017 Court of Appeal, the UKSC concluded that a parent would owe such a duty if, in addition to (and somehow aside of) four indicia given in the *Chandler* decision, it was the author of corporate policies with direct relevance for the claim at hand.[74]

Specifically, the UKSC determined that Vedanta owed a duty of care to the original complainants (local population) because it had:

(i) made public a sustainability report, including clear oversight over its affiliates;
(ii) made public statements about maintaining the standards of sustainability (health, safety and environmental) control over the activities of its subsidiaries, and in particular over KCM's operations and compliance with its sustainability standards; and
(iii) implemented those standards by training, monitoring and enforcement regarding KCM.[75]

[71] The UK Court of Appeal judgment is *Lungowe and Others v Vedanta Resources plc and Konkola Copper Mines plc* [2017] EWCA Civ 1528 [*Lungowe*]. The UK Supreme Court decision is *Vedanta Resources plc and Another (Appellants) v Lungowe and Others (Respondents)* [2019] UKSC 20 [*Vedanta*].
[72] *Vedanta* (n 71) para 1.
[73] ibid para 3.
[74] ibid paras 49, 55.
[75] ibid para 61.

Regarding the jurisdictional issues, the decisive argument in denying Vedanta Resources and KCM's assertions about *forum non conveniens* and an abuse of EU law (namely, the Brussels Recast Regulation (Regulation (EU) 1215/2012 on Jurisdiction and the Recognition and Enforcement of Judgments in Civil and Commercial Matters))[76] was that even though England was not 'the proper place in which to bring the claim', the English courts should have jurisdiction over the claim because otherwise the claimants would not be able to obtain substantial justice in Zambia.[77] Notably, a parallel can be drawn with the approach of the Ontario judges in *Garcia*, who dismissed a *forum non conveniens* corporate defendants' motion on the grounds that the forum of the country where torts occurred was not one that guaranteed substantial justice.

In substance, the court dismissed the argument that the negligence claim against Vedanta raised a novel and controversial legal issue, as the liability of parent companies related to the activities of their subsidiaries was not seen as a distinct category of negligence by the court.[78]

Overall, together with the *Nevsun* ruling, the *Vedanta* judgment seems to be the most significant breakthrough in terms of heightened CSL for transnational operations, especially in comparison with the related decisions on duty of care due to the third parties in *Arica* and *Walmart*. However, contrary to the *Nevsun* and *Vedanta* cases, *Arica* concerned a relationship outside regular supply chain dealings, ie subcontracting the management of hazardous sludge to an actor who could foreseeably not handle it, while *Walmart* was about supply chain liability for harm to the first company's subcontractor's workers, not for harm to third parties affected by the actions of the head firm's subsidiary.

Another case, *Jabir v KiK*, concerned human rights abuses committed by German companies abroad.[79] It arose from a claim for damages brought by four Pakistani nationals against a German retailer, KiK Textilien und Non-Food GmbH (KiK), for personal injuries and death from fire at the Karachi factory of KIK's supplier, Ali Enterprises (Ali).[80] Notably, this German – so, a non-common law – case involved the *Caparo* criteria, a test from the English common law of negligence. Thus, drawing on the approach in *Caparo*, the applicants argued that there existed a duty of care based on: (i) close integration of Ali into KiK's supply chain; (ii) contractual agreements creating promises of a safe work environment; and

[76] ibid paras 16–18 and 23.

[77] *Lungowe* (n 71) paras 160–68; *Vedanta* (n 71) paras 70–72, 87.

[78] *Vedanta* (n 71) paras 49–51, 54.

[79] *Mohamed Jabir et al v KiK Textilien und Non-Food GmbH*, Case No 7 O 95/15.

[80] Due to the language of the original judgment, I rely on the case overview from Professor Geer Van Calster: GV Calster, 'Jabir and others v. KiK Textilien und Non-Food GmbH. German court kicks supply chain CSR litigation into the long grass. Questions on Statutes of limitation under Rome II left out in the open' *GAVC Law* (2019) https://gavclaw.com/2019/02/27/jabir-and-others-v-kik-textilien-und-non-food-gmbh-german-court-kicks-supply-chain-csr-litigation-into-the-long-grass-questions-on-statutes-of-limitation-under-rome-ii-left-out-in-the-open/.

(iii) sufficient likely influence over supplier to enforce the safety standards.[81] According to the claimants, KiK hence could have foreseen the harms suffered by the victims, and moreover, sufficient proximity existed between the claimants and KiK and a duty of care should thus be assigned to KiK. Notably, the German adjudicator granted legal aid to the claimant to cover legal fees. Following a negotiation facilitated by the ILO, in 2016, KiK agreed to compensate the victims.[82]

In January 2019, the Regional Court (*Landgericht*) of Dortmund held that, pursuant to the Rome II Regulation, Pakistani tort law applied as the law of the place in which torts occurred, because it viewed the KiK's alleged negligence as having its centre in Pakistan.[83] The Dortmund Court thus saw the claim as a time-barred one based on the statute of limitations. Regarding the decision on jurisdiction, the *KiK* ruling is the opposite of the judges' conclusion in *Vedanta*, discussed above, stating that the English courts should have jurisdiction over the claim because otherwise the victims would not be able to obtain substantial justice in the country of the law of the place in which torts occurred. Since in both *Vedanta* and *KiK* the essential *forum non conveniens* questions did not depend on the legal tradition – common or civil law jurisdiction – I suggest that the judges in *Vedanta* simply exercised more judicial assertiveness than those in *KiK*. The same could be said about the decision on jurisdiction in the *Garcia* and *Choc* cases discussed earlier. I discuss the particular construct of judicial assertiveness in detail in the next part of the book (Chapter 7, for example).

Doe v Wal-Mart Stores Inc[84] is the best known case to date on foreign direct supply chain liability for subcontracting – namely, a buyer's liability for gaps in its value chain governance. Because both the district and the appeals courts rejected the claims, in this overview there is no need to scrutinise the decisions in meticulous detail. To sum up, the Walmart suppliers were located in, among others, Bangladesh, China, Indonesia, Nicaragua, and Swaziland. The workers of suppliers from these countries initiated a suit against Walmart in California. Here, the factual situation and the applicants' motion were similar to those of *Vedanta*. In particular, the key argument was that Walmart had failed to enforce its corporate governance code, which required suppliers to respect general and specific local laws, as well as applicable safety-related standards. Walmart's allegedly unlawful

[81] L Nowak et al, 'Supply chain liability under the law of negligence: What does Jabir and Others v KiK Textilien und Non-Food GmbH mean for European companies with supply chains in the sub-continent and other common law countries?' (2018) www.hlregulation.com/2018/12/10/supply-chain-liability-under-the-law-of-negligence-what-does-jabir-and-others-v-kik-textilien-und-non-food-gmbh-mean-for-european-companies-with-supply-chains-in-the-sub-continent-and-other-common-la/.

[82] ibid.

[83] L Nowak et al, 'Jabir and others v KiK Textilien und Non-Food GmbH – Dortmund court dismisses lawsuit' (2019) https://www.hlregulation.com/2019/01/11/jabir-and-others-v-kik-textilien-und-non-food-gmbh-dortmund-court-dismisses-lawsuit/.

[84] *Jane Doe I et al v Wal-Mart Stores Inc*, Federal Civil Lawsuit, Cal Cent Dis Ct, CA No 2:05-cv-07307 [California Central District Court judgment]; *Jane Doe I et al v Wal-Mart Stores, Inc*, US Ct of Appeals, 9th Circ, CA No 08-55706 2:05-cv-07307-AG OPINION [the Appeals Court judgment].

conduct thus allowed several breaches of labour law, safety requirements, and human rights, such as discrimination and physical abuse, lack of safety-related equipment, and excessive work hours and denial of a basic social package. Unlike in the *Vedanta* litigation, though, the *Wal-Mart* courts rejected the claims in their entirety.

Rahaman and *Das* are the two 'Rana Plaza' cases. The former was filed and decided in the US, in Delaware, while the latter was in Ontario, Canada, by the Superior Court of that province, both in the wake of the aforementioned collapse of the Rana Plaza garment factory. The first case was initiated by the representative of a deceased garment factory worker and another injured worker bringing the lawsuit as a class action on behalf of other injured workers against JC Penney Corporation, Inc, The Children's Place, Inc, and Wal-Mart Stores, Inc.[85] The plaintiffs introduced claims for negligence and wrongful death, alleging that the defendants acted negligently in failing to ensure safe and healthy working conditions for garment factory employees at Rana Plaza.[86]

The Delaware Superior Court dismissed the lawsuit. It ruled that, because the respondents were not the applicants' direct employers, the concerned companies should not be held directly responsible for what went on in their supply chains.[87] As the respondents were not the plaintiffs' direct employers they hence did not owe a duty of care to them.[88] The three-tier test for establishing negligence (a duty of care due by the defendant to the applicant; if such a duty was due, whether it was breached; and if such a duty was breached, was there harm done to the applicant due to this breach) thus fell short at the first tier.

In the *Das* case, a class action was brought by citizens of Bangladesh against Canada's largest retailer, Loblaws, and its direct suppliers, such as George Weston Ltd and others, as well as Bureau Veritas, a France-based global consulting services firm that Loblaws had hired to conduct social audits of factories in Bangladesh.[89] I address the relevant parts of the judgment in more detail in the next chapter. Here, it is important to highlight the fact that the claimants submitted that Loblaws failed to protect the safety of workers in Rana Plaza producing clothes mostly for the brands, owned by Loblaws and employed by manufacturers to whom some work of Loblaw's direct suppliers was outsourced.[90]

The court rejected the claim, failing to find a direct link between Loblaws and the workers, or to find direct control over these workers by Loblaws.[91] Ontario Superior

[85] *Rahaman et al v JC Penney Corporation, Inc et al*, CA No N15C-07-174 MMJ, Del Super Ct 4 May 2016.

[86] ibid para 3.

[87] ibid paras 19 and 27–28.

[88] ibid para 28.

[89] *Das v George Weston Ltd*, 2017 ONSC 4129.

[90] ibid paras 3–4.

[91] ibid see, eg para 450.

Court's Judge Perell also came to the conclusion that auditing the structural integrity of Loblaws' suppliers' facilities was outside the mandate of Bureau Veritas.[92]

In the two above cases, key relevant issues regarding the duty of care were the *peculiar risk* doctrine (a limited responsibility of head firms to monitor relevant peculiar risks throughout their supply chain) and the *substantial relationship* issue. Regarding the latter more specifically, the question at stake was the duty of the defendants (buyers) to protect the claimants (indirect supplier's workers) from a foreseeable risk of harm caused by third parties (indirect suppliers), thus making it a question of a general 'GVC' duty of care. In both cases, such a legally effective relationship was not established and thus the duty of care was – unfortunately for the purposes of realising CSL – denied, leaving open the question of a possibility of a general 'GVC' duty of care.

In France, a recent litigation addressed the questions of parent liability for the harm caused to employees of a subsidiary. In the 2013 *Areva* litigation, the French nuclear giant Areva won an appeal against the family of a diseased worker from one of its uranium mines in Niger, who died of lung cancer.[93] Serge Venel died in 2009, after having worked for six years in the early 1980s in a uranium mine in Akokan, presented by Areva as the largest underground uranium mine in the world. His cancer was caused by inhaling uranium dust and cobalt, according to a medical certificate, and was recognised as a professional disease by social security.[94]

The Paris Court of Appeals held that Areva, the holder of the mining deposit concession, could not be held responsible as an employer.[95] Only the Nigerian company Cominak, which was running the site and with which Venel had signed his employment contract, could possibly be attacked. The Court decided that, in terms of private law, namely corporate ownership, Cominak could not be considered a subsidiary of Areva, as the latter was shareholder of only 34 per cent of the shares in Cominak.[96] Here we clearly see a factual situation which is comparable to the above UK *Chandler* case, but with very different legal consequences, approach and ultimate decision.

I submit that the *Areva* judges' final verdict was affected not only by the corporate ownership structure, plainly representing a 'minimalist' contractual approach to the parent company's liability, but also by the transnational nature of the claim. At the same time, the *Areva* judges could have examined other criteria to explore the actual influence and control of the parent, generally navigating under the banner 'legally-effective bonds'. Such bonds could be both those considered in the

[92] ibid paras 54–57, 59.

[93] Cour d'Appel de Paris, Arrêt du 24 octobre 2013, no 12/05650 [*Areva*].

[94] *Le Figaro*, 'Areva gagne contre un salarié au Niger' (25 October 2013) https://www.lefigaro.fr/flash-eco/2013/10/25/97002-20131025FILWWW00382-areva-gagne-un-proces-contre-un-salarie.php.

[95] *Areva* (n 93).

[96] ibid.

Chandler case, and those related to control factors, such as the exchange of letters and emails, the parent company's practice of intervening in the trading operations, and the issue of who was giving orders to whom in general. In 2013, under existing French law, it seems that a lot depended on judicial assertiveness and the will of French judges to behave with that assertiveness. It could have been expected that after hardening the relevant French legislation, things would change.

In January 2018 the very first complaint under the Vigilance law was filed by two NGOs with the Tribunal de Grande Instance in Paris, alleging misleading commercial practices against the parent company Samsung and its French subsidiary, Samsung Electronics France.[97] According to two NGOs, Sherpa and Peuples solidaires, there was blatant evidence of a number of violations registered in Chinese, Korean, and Vietnamese Samsung production factories, such as the involvement of workers under the age of 16, extended working weeks (72 hours), use of hazardous health products, etc.[98] The two NGOs wrote a report documenting those working conditions.[99] In terms of the head firm's failure to enforce its code of conduct, which required suppliers to respect work-related local laws and specific standards, the situation here is similar to that in the *Walmart* case. However, unlike the latter's factual background, which favoured the defendant's arguments of lack of corporate ownership bonds, the Chinese, Korean, and Vietnamese Samsung production factories were Samsung's direct suppliers. At the same time, the fact that Samsung allegedly failed to correctly monitor the respect and application of its CSR code along its value chain, and, especially, by its immediate business partners, is reminiscent of the facts of the *Vedanta* case.

The complaint filed in 2015 concerned serious gaps between the group's ethical pledges in its corporate governance codes, including official communication and actual working conditions observed at the concerned factories.[100] Based on the Vigilance law, the NGOs argued that such working conditions were in full contradiction of the official CSR, ethical and reputation commitments of the Samsung group, compliance with which the latter also rigorously requested from its suppliers.[101] The gaps were identified between those pledges and the reality on the shop floor observed and documented by the NGOs. However, in March 2018, the Bobigny public prosecutor closed the case.[102]

[97] E Jarry and M Rosemain, 'Plainte contre Samsung en France pour pratiques trompeuses' Reuters (2018) https://fr.reuters.com/article/topNews/idFRKBN1F00HT-OFRTP.

[98] ibid.

[99] Sherpa (25 June 2018) https://www.asso-sherpa.org/samsung-sherpa-actionaid-france-deposent-plainte-constitution-de-partie-civile-contre-leader-mondial-smartphone.

[100] ibid.

[101] ibid.

[102] ibid.

In June 2018, the two NGOs filed a civil party lawsuit to the Paris court following the closing of the preliminary investigation by the Bobigny prosecutor. They submitted that evidence of working conditions at the concerned Samsung factories highlighted serious diseases developed by workers and that this justified the request for instruction by an investigating magistrate.[103] After mediation procedures, in November 2018 Samsung accepted that it had exposed its South Korean factory workers to toxic chemicals and agreed to compensate each employee for damages from work-related diseases.[104] On 17 April 2019, a Paris investigating magistrate charged Samsung Electronic France for misleading advertising.[105] The litigation is still ongoing.

Note that following the Rana Plaza disaster, a very similar lawsuit had already been filed in April 2014 by the two above NGOs together with Collectif Ethique sur l'étiquette in Lille, France against the supermarket Auchan. The main argument that the organisations used was about misleading advertisements regarding the conditions in which its clothing was produced.[106] Notably, while Auchan has denied placing any order at the Rana Plaza and said it was the victim of 'concealed subcontracting', labels from Auchan's 'In Extenso' line of clothes were found in the ruins of the Rana Plaza factory in April 2013.[107] Consequently, the plaintiffs highlighted the fact that the company had made public statements regarding its commitment to societal standards in its value chain. In January 2015, the prosecutor's office in Lille dismissed the case.[108] In terms of the arguments and laws invoked by the NGOs, the *Auchan* case is quite similar to the above *Samsung* litigation, however, the complaint was filed before the Vigilance law was adopted in France, and was thus dismissed.

The table below outlines the claims discussed in this section, ordered by type of plaintiff. Note that at the time of writing, the two last types of complaints, namely those initiated by consumers and by investors, had not properly occurred in a particular GVC context. However, I expect such claims to start in near future, as they are already possible under the current French Vigilance law, and are likely to become prominent after the Dutch due diligence law has entered into force.

[103] Business & Human Rights Resource Centre, 'Samsung Lawsuit' https://www.business-humanrights.org/en/latest-news/samsung-lawsuit-re-misleading-advertising-labour-rights-abuses/.

[104] ibid.

[105] ibid.

[106] Sherpa (27 May 2014) https://www.asso-sherpa.org/effondrement-du-rana-plaza-ouverture-dune-enquete-preliminaire-suite-la-plainte-deposee-auchan.

[107] ibid.

[108] Business & Human Rights Resource Centre, https://www.business-humanrights.org/fr/derni%C3%A8res-actualit%C3%A9s/r%C3%A9sum%C3%A9-du-proc%C3%A8s-auchan-usine-textile-au-bangladesh/.

Table 5.2

Type of claimant/ Year of ruling	**Employees' claims**	**Local population's claims**	**Civil society's claims**	**Consumers' claims**	**Investors' claims**
Doe v Wal-Mart Stores, Inc, 2009	x				
Chandler v Cape, 2012	x				
Kiobel et al v Royal Dutch Petroleum et al, 2013	x				
Choc v Hudbay, 2013, ongoing	x				
Venel v Areva, 2013	x				
Auchan/ Rana Plaza claim, 2014			x		
Dutch Shell Nigeria cases, 2015		x	x		
Araya v Nevsun Resources Ltd, 2016, and *Nevsun* SCC appeal 2020	x	x			
Rahaman et al v JC Penney Corpn, Inc et al, 2016	x				
Das v George Weston Ltd, 2017	x				
Garcia v Tahoe Resources Inc, 2017		x			
Sherpa and *Peuples solidaires v Samsung*, 2018, ongoing			x		
Arica Victims v Boliden Minerals, 2019		x			
Lungowe and Others v Vedanta, 2019		x			
Jabir v KiK, 2019	x				

In conclusion of this chapter, a comparative survey of recent legislation (both forthcoming and already in force) on transnational corporate liability has revealed a general legislative drive to regulate corporations' offshore activities extraterritorially. While, among those measures that are in force, transparency measures prevail in the current configuration, a roughly equal share of those measures focus on either obligatory due diligence or delictual and/or criminal liability.

The highlighted norms are meant to support the primary aims of that legislative drift to remove and avoid environmental and human rights abuses, poor labour and health conditions, and the like, in GVCs and generally in offshore operations. However, regarding all surveyed disciplines, the mandatory disclosure cluster and – to a lesser extent – obligatory due diligence and stricter liability norms, carry obligations of conduct but virtually none of them carries obligations of result, such as, for example, issuing a ban or introducing penalties where primary resources, parts or commodities are produced unlawfully. Most of these measures rather offer a sort of 'therapeutic disclosure', meant to gently influence corporate behaviour through 'social shaming'.[109]

Some of the measures, such as French Vigilance law, go slightly further by introducing enhanced due diligence obligations as well as a duty of care, but they usually do not go beyond obligations of conduct and general incentives for compliance. French Vigilance law is part of the rubric of 'liability disciplines'. I thus discuss it in more detail, together with other disciplines of this rubric, in further sections of this and the next part.

Regarding the litigation landscape, as the first few claims show, at the beginning of the drive to CSL, workers were the only applicants claiming a parent company's duty of care. However, as more recent litigation developments show, today not only employees, but also local populations and civil society are claiming that corporations should accept greater responsibility for individuals, communities and environments affected by their offshore operations. Now the turn has also come for individual consumers and shareholder activists to litigate.

Against several failures and all odds, in many ways *Vedanta* and *Nevsun* are two landmark rulings that will surely be referred to by future decisions in the field of foreign direct liability of corporations for societal abuses and even for 'mere' failures of governance in their value chains. The *Nevsun* judgment especially opens the door for more cases to be brought in Canadian courts for violations of human rights or failure to engage with environmental due diligence against Canadian extractive corporations operating transnationally. Future developments in the *Choc* case also deserve close attention.

On a darker note, neither the *Vedanta* nor the *Nevsun* ruling, encouraging more submissions to the jurisdiction of the head firms' home state courts, will prevent corporate defendants from challenging the validity of the decision in the enforcement stages. This may affect access to a remedy for victims of such governance gaps and abuses. Moreover, while it is realistic to hope for transnational liability of lead firms' dealings within direct and/or regular supply relationships in *supply*

[109] See eg SM Bainbridge, *Corporate Governance After the Scandals and the Financial Crisis* (Oxford, Oxford University Press, 2012) 34.

chains (for example, in cases concerning resources or hazardous waste such as *Dutch Shell*, *Garcia*, *Vedanta*, *Nevsun* and *Choc*), the overall dismissal of claims of liability for subcontractors outside the first tier in a *value* chain and the questions relating to the duty of reasonable care in tort law, leave most of the relevant questions unanswered. Moreover, it remains to be seen which position will be taken in this regard by the courts outside the common law systems.

6

Analysis of Avenues for Corporate Social Liability in Global Value Chains

As demonstrated in the preceding analysis, it is quite complicated to define the duties and responsibilities of the dominant influencers, express or tacit, over transactions within GVCs beyond first-tier suppliers and direct affiliates. Nowadays, when GVCs are often organised on the basis of ad hoc subcontracting, negotiated through brokers and similar one-off transactions, it could become even more difficult.

The survey of relevant litigation in Chapter 5 reveals that one of the key issues in defining transnational corporate liability is to determine to what extent 'influence' is 'control'. This is especially true in the claims about tort of negligence and health, environmental and human rights abuses in value chains. A possible way to answer this question would be to approach the relevant obligations and ensuing liability as commensurate with the size of a company and influence over specific practices. Immediate challenges for this avenue of enquiry, however, include: (i) demonstrating or proving such influence; (ii) how exactly such influence could be demonstrated, ie the criteria for such demonstration; and (iii) when it is and is not practical to establish such influence (see section I below).

The advanced criteria of differentiation between various types of pertinent obligations and ensuing liability within GVCs could be: (i) the existence and scope of the legally effective practices or other bonds between the dominant influencer and other actors within a chain; and (ii) the effects of such legally-effective bonds (see section II below).

Ultimately, drawing on the theoretical model for the delineation of CSL norms from the introductory chapter, the practices of creation and streamlining of shorter-term agreements, longer-term governance, and a GVC-wide regulation through standards could all be seen as legally effective, thus proving an overall influence over a value chain. However, I suggest that it is conceivable to approach corporate liability as commensurate with the size of a company, as well as its influence over specific practices in a GVC through its: (i) *shorter-term* contractual and commercial arrangements with other links of the chain; (ii) *longer-term* chain-wide planning and hence governance thereof; and/or (iii) *overall* chain-wide standard-setting and further streamlining of such standards, creating ties of control or, at the very least, a substantial economic dependence (see section III below).

I. Common Criteria for Founding Liability: An Overview

A. Lead, Influence or Control? The Many Shades of Power Over a Value Chain

Muchlinski discerns three general kinds of behaviour and influence of TNCs that affect markets and law transnationally, and which hypothetically could exert control, thus implying corporate duties and liability:

(i) control by the headquarters, or management just above, of affiliates, including financial control;
(ii) the influence through contractual relations between parties who deal with the firm within a value chain; and
(iii) firm- or corporate group-wide CSR guidelines for all affiliates in an enterprise or even an industry.[1]

The second and especially the third avenues are relevant in the context of this book, since the very organisation of GVCs implies a package of allocated rights and duties along the chain, while internal regulation of corporate behaviour – typically through firm-wide CSR codes – is to be respected by all managers and employees.[2] Industry-wide codes have even more far-reaching effects, as they could be used when determining liability in contract – typically, the consumer contract – as well as liability in tort when delimiting the scope of a duty of care.[3]

The above assertion about the link between the size and power of a firm and its GVC-wide obligations has its theoretical underpinnings in the literature in the field that is over 20 years old, which notoriously says that 'the more powerful is [an enterprise] [...] the more likely it is to generate [norms] [...], and, at the highest level of influence, to persuade courts and legislators to give official legal sanction to those [norms] ...'[4] It could thus be argued that the more influential the private actors – such as corporations – are, the more they will impact not only on a value chain, but also on law and norms at national and transnational levels. Hence, they will receive more rights within the legal systems where they operate, including traditional international law. Indeed, as early as the mid-twentieth century, progressive legal scholarship asserted that corporations, to the extent that they deal directly with (foreign) states, can also be the subjects of international law, including being subject to obligations stemming from this law.[5]

[1] PT Muchlinski, '"Global Bukowina" Examined: Viewing the Multinational Enterprise as a Transnational Law-making Community' in G Teubner (ed), *Global Law Without a State (Studies in Modern Law and Policy)* (Dartmouth, Dartmouth Publishing Co, 1997) 79, 80–81.

[2] ibid 83.

[3] ibid 84.

[4] ibid 80.

[5] W Friedman, *The Changing Structure of International Law* (London, Stevens and Sons, 1964) 222–30; W Jenks, 'Multinational Entities and the Law of Nations' in W Friedman (ed), *Transnational Law in a Changing Society. Essays in Honor of Philip C Jessup* (New York, Columbia University Press, 1972) 70, 71–73.

In the twenty-first century, though, those theories still receive little practical confirmation. For instance, within the realm of foreign investment law and arbitration, this line of jurisprudence has only started since 2016.[6] Namely, in the 2016 *Urbaser* decision, the International Centre for Settlement of Investment Disputes (ICSID) arbitral tribunal ruled that, since corporations were the rights-holders under international investment agreements, they were equally subjects of international law and thus also bore obligations in international law, including international human rights law obligations to adversely affected third parties.[7] In this arbitral award, which has already become paradigmatic, the tribunal rejected the claimant's view that, as a non-state actor, it was not bound by human rights obligations.[8] The *Urbaser* arbitrators have also ruled that CSR was 'a standard of crucial importance for companies operating in the field of international commerce'.[9] I will come back to the *Urbaser* case in relevant discussion in Part IV of this book.

Regarding obligations within the private law realm, a duty of care could, for instance, arise in new situations if there are enough 'policy reasons' for it to do so. Especially in the English common law system, it rather depends on judges as to whether they would take into account a broader context rather than only the strict legal framework for establishing a duty in new circumstances.[10]

At the same time, earlier I presumed that the size of a company and its consequent influence over specific practices could be among the main factors for establishing liability.

B. Size Matters (or Does it?)

A set of characteristic conditions for establishing liability linked to the size of a firm could be best founded by the disciplines that bind fewer actors, such as the biggest firms. First, they clearly underline a link between entities' size and their strict liability (eg French Vigilance law).

Second, the very notion of determining the responsibility of these biggest companies or groups of companies is tied to the notion of influence. Such laws typically underline the influence of the head company or simply that of a bigger

[6] As I argued elsewhere. See eg A Aseeva, '(Un)Sustainable Development(s) in International Economic Law: a Quest for Sustainability' (2018) 10(11) *Sustainability* 4022, 4030–31; A Aseeva and KL Yip, 'Stakes and Prospects of the Right to Free, Prior & Informed Consent in "One Belt One Road" Projects in the Context of Transnational Investment Law and Arbitration' in J Chaisse and J Górski (eds), *The Belt and Road Initiative. Law, Economics, and Politics* (Leiden, Brill-Nijhoff, 2018) 523, 550–53.

[7] *Urbaser SA and Consorcio de Aguas Bilbao Bizkaia, Bilbao Biskaia Ur Partzuergoa v The Argentine Republic* [Urbaser]; Award, 8 December 2016, ICSID Case No ARB/07/26, para 1155.

[8] ibid para 1194.

[9] ibid para 1195.

[10] I discuss these avenues of enquiry in greater detail in Chapter 7.

entity over their business partners. In the French example, the responsibility of vigilance is on 'parent and instructing companies'.[11] Pursuant to the French Commercial Code:

> any company that employs, for a period of two consecutive financial years, at least five thousand employees itself and in its direct or indirect subsidiaries whose registered office is located within French territory, or at least ten thousand employees itself and in its direct or indirect subsidiaries whose registered office is located within French territory or abroad, shall establish and implement a vigilance plan in an effective manner.[12]

Hence, there are at least three criteria for this concrete model of GVC liability based on the size of a company to determine the level of influence: (i) the corporate form required to fall within the scope of the law; (ii) the nature of the shareholdings; and (iii) the number of employees. Under such a model, the second criterion, namely the nature of the shareholdings, is also a stepping stone necessary for, and linking, the first and the third criteria. In other words, the first step in determining whether a company is covered by the law in question is to identify its corporate form.

The second step is to identify the lead firm's direct and indirect subsidiaries.[13] This identification of subsidiaries is therefore an essential prerequisite to then counting employees (the third step). Here, the notion of control is one which should be taken into account in determining the scope of the law, and especially the second criterion – that of determining the subsidiaries through defining the nature of shareholdings.[14] Under the French Vigilance law, for instance, one of the arguments in favour of this position is the comparison with companies exempt from obligations which are 'subsidiaries or companies controlled' by 'the company which controls them, under article L. 233-3'.[15]

As follows from Chapter 4, both the UNGPs and the OECD Guidelines encourage an extensive interpretation of the notion of control.[16] Regarding in particular French Vigilance law, it is argued that the notion of control should be interpreted 'in the widest possible manner, at least within the meaning of article L. 233-3 of the [French] Commercial Code which is usually used, in order to satisfy the objectives of the legislation'.[17]

Regarding the third point mentioned in the introduction to this chapter, of when it is and is not practical to establish such influence, we should first establish

[11] '*Des sociétés mères et des entreprises donneuses d'ordre*' in French.

[12] French Commercial Code, art L.225-102-4(I) (author's translation).

[13] French Commercial Code, art L.233-16(II).

[14] ibid.

[15] eg French Commercial Code, art L.225-102-4(I)(2).

[16] eg UN Human Rights Council, Human Rights and Transnational Corporations and Other Business Enterprises (16 June 2011) A/HRC/Res 17/4, endorsing 'Guiding Principles on Business and Human Rights: Implementing the United Nations "Protect, Respect and Remedy" Framework' (21 March 2011) A/HRC/17/31 [UNGPs] principle 14, which relates to the notion of a company regardless of its ownership and structure.

[17] See C Hannoun, *Le devoir de vigilance des sociétés mères et entreprises donneuses d'ordre après la loi du 27 mars 2017* (Paris, Dalloz, 2017) 813.

what is the most important aspect for all stakeholders (including local population, civil society and the environment) related to a particular enterprise in a concrete situation. It needs to be decided whether to focus on calling one particular big firm to liability in a given situation, albeit with the strictest sanctions possible (and available), or whether it is better to establish a less coercive type of CSL but which is, however, applicable to either a larger number of economic actors, or even to all types of actors, including non-economic ones, such as standard-setting and/or certifying organisations or social auditors, for example.

To be fair, of all the categories of corporate liability disciplines surveyed in Chapter 5 (see Table 5.1), only the most lax ones (namely, CSR disciplines, such as the UK Code of Corporate Governance of 1992) would cover the broadest scope of actors of GVCs. Mandatory disclosure disciplines, such as the US Dodd-Frank Act (or, at the European level, the EUNFRD), are often less coercive or even of a soft-law nature, and also have the potential to apply to a large number of participants in GVCs. In this way, the stricter the type of GVC liability disciplines is, the fewer actors it will cover. Thus, mandatory due diligence disciplines (eg the EUCMR) will cover fewer actors and situations, and proper liability laws, such as the French Vigilance law – will cover even fewer of those. This observation, however, does not represent a strict rule, as, for example, the Dutch Due diligence law represents the strictest CSL discipline – liability – but covers any company that sells its products on the Dutch market at least twice a year.

To sum up, the size of a company and its consequent influence over specific practices would be a defendable set of main factors for establishing liability. This adaption could, however, easily be criticised for not going far beyond the status quo. As the size of multinationals is frequently referred to as a purported reason for liability and influence over a specific practice, it has already been established in several tort law systems as giving rise to liability.[18] Hence, a *via media* for establishing liability in GVCs would be to draw both on the size having an impact on the influence of the head firm over other business partners (corporate and commercial law avenues) and on its influence over specific practices through contractual relationship and governance (contract law and tort law ones).

C. Are We Contracting or Having a Relationship, or Both?

Contrary to an earlier avenue of enquiry, which suggested that GVCs tend to be organised on the basis of one-off agreements, the opposite hypothesis has its merits. My main presumption in this section is therefore that GVCs could otherwise be characterised by long- or medium-term relational agreements. Indeed,

[18] Liability in common law is generally founded in control theories, whereas in civil law it is identifiable through contract theories. However, recently in civil law jurisdictions, such as France, law has looked at control when identifying parent and instructing companies and their subsequent responsibility is thus based on the French law of civil liability: French Civil Code, arts 1240 and 1241.

'in the twenty-first century, where the corporate form dominates, [...] a company represents the greatest relational contract of them all'.[19]

One of the enquiries in this section is thus whether 'influence' – and, even more so, 'control' – could stem from a relational obligation? For instance, the NIE school has a particular view on contractual relations.[20] It draws a line between anonymous ad hoc transactions (supported by the doctrine of discrete contract law as well as those of neoclassical contract law and Law and Economics) and ongoing transactions forming a long-term relationship.[21] Ian Macneil's relational contract theory, a socio-legal counterpart to the NIE, effectively fills the gaps in contract law between one-off market contracting and full vertical integration.[22]

Moreover, both the NIE and relational contract theory see contract not only as a market construct but also, and especially, as long-term planning.[23] As per Oliver Williamson, the parties to commercial transactions (including those of GVCs) are never fully integrated but instead remain separate entities, though they have contractual relations extending beyond one-off deals and evolving into governance – or 'relational contracting'.[24] An influence of a lead firm in such a relational contracting could thus be established based precisely on the long-term relationship and planning.

Yet a key analytical limitation to the above lines of argument, and especially to contract as longer-term planning, is 'the bounded rationality of contractors[:] [l]ong-term contracts must inevitably suffer from gaps, and become "obsolescing bargains"'.[25] That is to say, while this theory challenges the discrete contract approach and provides a compelling case for long-term contractual relations materialising into governance, it is quite unclear how the authors of this theory have foreseen the modelling of these matters.[26]

A more practical avenue emerging from the above is that the contractual relations between affiliated entities within a transnational network of an enterprise could, in principle, establish liability. Namely, such obligations as the one to protect supplier employees could actually stem from the kind of control implied by the contractual relations between affiliated entities within the transnational network of the enterprise,[27] as well as from intra-enterprise codes of corporate behaviour.

[19] J Morgan, *Contract Law Minimalism. A Formalist Restatement of Commercial Contract Law* (Cambridge, Cambridge University Press, 2013) 65.

[20] RH Coase, 'The New Institutional Economics' (1998) 88 *American Economic Review* 72.

[21] Morgan (n 19) 62.

[22] See generally IR Macneil, 'The Many Futures of Contract' (1974) 47 *Southern California Law Review* 691.

[23] IR Macneil, 'Relational Contract: What We Do and Do Not Know' [1985], reprinted in D Campbell (ed), cited in Morgan (n 19) 65 and fn 17.

[24] See generally O Williamson, *The Economic Institutions of Capitalism* (New York, Free Press, 1985).

[25] Morgan (n 19) 62.

[26] ibid 64.

[27] Muchlinski (n 1) 81–84.

Yet real-life empirics also suggest that, first, contemporary corporations are more than reluctant to expose their control or even substantive influence in GVCs.[28] Indeed, disclosing such a lead role may not only impede their reputation, but also involve enhanced obligations and liability.[29] A more conceptual doubt regarding the above view of GVCs is precisely the extent to which one can see them as contractual networks of the enterprise.

One argument for making a case for the above is that nowadays corporations expand far beyond contractual relationships of all sorts, acting as a key link in a chain of contracts, and thus themselves act as a platform for contracts and further joint projects governed by corporate, tort and commercial law and more.[30] In other words, through its very organisational form, a corporation acts as a single contracting entity distinct from the various individuals who own, manage or work for it.[31] In so doing, corporations streamline the shared engagements of these individuals in joint projects.[32]

Furthermore, some researchers argue that, through merely deciding on whether production is subcontracted and, if so, to whom, a lead firm is already making some elementary planning for the whole value chain,[33] thus also exercising basic governance and hence influence. With such influence should come duties and liability.

However, in the *Walmart* judgment,[34] contrary to the above presumptions, a US appeals court established neither a negligent retention of control and supervision nor a negligent undertaking.[35] Hence, the lack of sufficiently considerable control and the lack of any undertaking to protect the employees were the deciding arguments for founding an absence of a tort duty on Walmart to protect supplier employees.[36]

It will be recalled that in the *Chandler* case,[37] the UK Court of Appeal found that tort law may impose liability on a parent company on behalf of its subsidiary for the health and safety of the subsidiary's workers.[38] In scrutinising the

[28] J Salminen, 'From Product Liability to Production Liability: Modelling a Response to the Liability Deficit of Global Value Chains on Historical Transformations of Production' (2019) 23 *Competition and Change* 420, 427–29.

[29] Various judgments concerning transnational liability surveyed in Chapter 5 clearly show the reluctance of TNCs to demonstrate any control sufficient for founding their liability.

[30] AE Tenbrunsel et al, 'Building Houses on Rocks: The Role of the Ethical Infrastructure in Organizations' (2003) 16 *Social Justice Research* 285, 287–302.

[31] See Chapter 3, section I.A. See also generally H Hansmann and R Kraakman, 'The Essential Role of Organizational Law' (2000) 110 *Yale Law Journal* 387.

[32] Muchlinski (n 1) 81–84.

[33] J Salminen and M Rajavuori, 'Transnational Sustainability Laws and the Regulation of Global Value Chains: Comparison and a Framework for Analysis' (2019) 26(5) *Maastricht Journal of European and Comparative Law* 602, 608.

[34] *Doe v Wal-Mart Stores, Inc*, 572 F3d 677 (9th Cir 2009).

[35] ibid paras 8–12.

[36] ibid.

[37] *Chandler v Cape plc* [2012] EWCA Civ 525.

[38] ibid para 80.

relationship between the parent and the subsidiary, the *Chandler* judges determined four conditions for liability, including requirements of control. Notably, the court established that it was unnecessary to prove that the parent company was substantively intervening in the concerned policies of the subsidiary. The judges found that in order to establish the criterion drawing on foreseeability,[39] it was enough to demonstrate that 'the parent has a practice of intervening in the trading operations of the subsidiary, for example production and funding issues'.[40]

The *Walmart* case was transnational in nature because it concerned a GVC liability, though no such liability was in the end determined in that case. The *Chandler* judgment, in contrast, established very relevant elements for founding a practice of intervening that would also help to determine control, but concerned a domestic, not a transnational, enterprise. The question is how to apply, if at all, those findings to a case of a transnational harm through subcontracting, outsourcing or buying from other suppliers within a GVC and hence imply a CSL due to third parties? Following the cases surveyed in Chapter 5, listed in Table 5.2, it could be fairly said that, to date, virtually the only successful case to shed light on the issues of transnational liability and transnational duty of care owed by a parent company to third parties, is the *Dutch Shell* litigation. The *Vedanta* and *Nevsun* rulings are other such precedents, but the relationships they concern and avenues they offer are more complex. I discuss them in more detail in Part IV of this book.

To summarise, the doctrinal accounts and case law considered in this section show that it is necessary to prove that a given lead firm is indeed a central GVC influencer; and infer conditions for founding a liability of the value chain influencer not only for its own acts, but also – and, indeed, especially – for the acts of others, for both its direct subsidiaries and subcontractors, and other business partners.

II. Further Criteria for Founding Liability: Various Relevant Practices

A. Legally Effective Practices

Throughout Chapter 3 I established that, while black-letter corporate law, particularly as per the shareholder model, could still perceive corporations as mere legal fictions with the sole aim of enhancing the pecuniary economic interests of their shareholders,[41] corporations arguably possess some agency, which makes them the

[39] '… (4) the parent knew or ought to have foreseen that the subsidiary or its employees would rely on its using that superior knowledge for the employees' protection': ibid.

[40] ibid.

[41] R La Porta et al, 'Corporate Ownership Around the World' (1998) 54 *Journal of Finance* 471, 491–96; JD Bauman, 'Corporations, Law and Policy: Materials and Problems' in *American Casebook*, 7th edn (Eagan, West Academic Publishing, 2009) 34–35.

duty bearers (especially according to the external corporate governance approach as opposed to the internal one).[42]

The business partners of some companies, such as suppliers and subcontractors, or even direct subsidiaries, may be more autonomous than those of others, but any corporation or head firm has the ability to influence and orient their subsidiaries' and partners' operations: (i) by means of an internal corporate management system; and (ii) through an external transnational corporate governance infrastructure. In this chapter I generally argue that a GVC liability should be precisely the liability arising from the gaps in the external GVC organisation.

As I demonstrated in previous sections, business relationships play an important role in establishing the criteria for duties leading to liability. When determining the latter, one of the key notions here is influence – ie the influence of lead companies over their commercial partners. Here, the power of big firms to shape the core of relevant norms and, ultimately, laws, through business practices is especially relevant. 'The question in such cases is whether the practice concerned should be accepted as *legally effective* …' (emphasis added).[43]

B. Nature of Legally Effective Practices

There are several types of legally effective practices that create a relationship of influence between a lead firm and other actors down the chain, and they may be less obvious than the traditional ties between parents and their subsidiaries. Subcontracting is one of them.

When persons, including legal persons such as firms, contract out some part of their work to other persons they are subcontracting. If, during the execution of such delegation, subcontractors do not respect fundamental rights, local laws, health, safety, environmental and consumer regulation or other relevant rules and standards, they thus create societal harms. Here, there are several possible avenues via which to establish the first company's liability. The firm that initially subcontracted could be held liable for negligence in the pre-subcontracting phase due to a lack of due diligence in choosing its subcontractors, or in not properly controlling them so as to prevent resulting societal harms in the post-subcontracting phase.[44]

In delimiting legally-effective practices, one should look at: (i) subcontracting or buying from third suppliers and similar outsourcing, and harms arising thereof; and (ii) the results of the interactions of a firm with its subsidiaries. Under the relevant international framework, chiefly 'business and human rights' surveyed in

[42] See generally CA Williams and JM Conley, 'An Emerging Third Way – The Erosion of the Anglo-American Shareholder Value Construct' (2005) 38 *Cornell International Law Journal* 493.

[43] Muchlinski (n 1) 85.

[44] eg UNGPs (n 16) principle 19, commentary; OECD, *Guidelines For Multinational Enterprises*, the 2011 update, the latest so far, at http://mneguidelines.oecd.org/guidelines/, ch II.

Chapter 4, together such actions within a chain could be deemed as 'activities' of a 'business enterprise'.[45] In this framework, if an activity of a business enterprise – a lead firm – contributes or may contribute to causing harm, it is under the duty to take the necessary steps to stop or prevent its contribution.[46] 'Contributing' could mean an activity that causes, facilitates, or incentivises another entity to cause harm.[47] However, the OECD Guidelines seem to deal only with the final case, namely harms caused by a business enterprise through *its own actions*, including its activities in a GVC.[48] While there is no clear guidance on the criteria of separating a TNC's 'own actions' in a chain from those completed through a business relationship, it is presumed here that the actions of a firm's subsidiaries would fall under the above second category.

Conversely, under this international law framework, harms arising from subcontractors' or suppliers' activities are likely to be deemed as adverse societal impacts caused by entities with which a given company has a business relationship – that is, when that firm is *directly linked* to those commercial partners' production, services, or operations through its actions of subcontracting or buying from them.[49]

There are several limitations to the above international law avenues. Generally, it is unclear to what extent a failure to supervise its subsidiaries or intervene in the harmful conduct of commercial partners, such as subcontractors or suppliers, could amount to an adverse impact and hence represent grounds for a liability for negligence.

Second, some research argues that in the 'directly linked' situation, '[i]f the business enterprise has leverage to mitigate the adverse impact it should exercise this, as in the contribution scenario[;] [i]f it lacks leverage, it should try to increase its leverage'.[50] However, if a company has considerable leverage in a chain to mitigate, cease or prevent a wrongdoing by other entities, that would also prove its control over those entities. Under private law, this could lay the groundwork for a sufficiently considerable control, founding a retention of control and supervision of an undertaking, and, hence, also constitute grounds for private law liability if a dispute arises.

As another research puts it, '[t]his leads to a nigh schizophrenic conundrum: for liability-related reasons lead firms generally do not want to be seen as having control over their suppliers'.[51] However, if they abide by the above international

[45] United Nations Office of the High Commissioner for Human Rights (OHCHR), *The Corporate Responsibility to Respect Human Rights: An Interpretative Guide* (Geneva, United Nations, 2012) 15–19.

[46] Not to mention that, according to the same UNGP principle, if a business enterprise causes or may cause harm, it is under a duty to take the necessary steps to stop or prevent such harm: UNGPs (n 16) principle 19(b); OHCHR, *Guide* (n 45) 17–19.

[47] OECD Guidelines (n 44) ch II and commentary para 14.

[48] UNGPs (n 16) principle 13(a); OECD Guidelines (n 44) ch II and commentary para 17.

[49] UNGPs (n 16) principle 19, commentary; OECD Guidelines (n 44) ch II, A 12.

[50] N Bueno, 'The Swiss Federal Initiative on Responsible Business – From Responsibility to Liability' in LFH Enneking et al (eds), *Accountability and International Business Operations: Providing Justice for Corporate Violations of Human Rights and Environmental Standards* (London, Routledge, 2020) 5.

[51] Salminen (n 28) 429.

law framework, they must exercise such control to mitigate, cease, or prevent societal harms of their suppliers or other commercial partners within a chain. And lead firms are possibly not likely to openly exercise their control to prevent harms in these cases precisely because they wish to avoid private law liability.

At the end of the day, a lack of control asserted by the underlying contractual relationships reduces the chances of both public international law (the international business and human rights framework) and transnational private law (contract and tort) contributing to founding liability.

I therefore submit that the advanced criteria of differentiation between various types of corporate liability within GVCs should be: (i) actual and potential effects of the legally effective practices of a lead (or the biggest) company vis-à-vis other firms in a value chain; and (ii) whether such practices result in a relationship. In particular, such commercial, corporate and all the more contractual bonds described in the above sections, could be seen – and should be used – not as limits to corporate liability, but as workings that structure ongoing relationships in a GVC, thus also implying liability for the influencing company.

As established in previous chapters, black-letter corporate law (in Europe, company law) creates the organisational structure that allows a mere foreign direct liability to be established.[52] Some scholarship at the interface of company law and tort law looks at the question of whether other tort law principles, notably the principle of indirect liability, could apply independently of company law in some situations.[53] However, to date, the prospects of using tort to infer the indirect liability of parent or just lead companies for the wrongdoings of other firms in their value chain appear restricted in practice, since in all Rana Plaza cases, including the inconclusive *Auchan* litigation, the complaints based on indirect liability were dismissed on the grounds that the defendants owed the plaintiffs no duty of care, because the latter were not the defendant's workers.[54]

Major challenges to classical private – tort, and especially contract-centred – modes of determining and enforcing a GVC liability are hence the legal construction of the substance of legally effective practices and similar bonds.

In this section, I have drawn the approximate contours of a purely legal catalogue of legally effective bonds that arguably form influence over a value chain and can hence found a GVC liability. As is quite apparent from the above argument, doing so while equipped solely with classical tort and contract law tools appears an arduous feat.

[52] See generally V Ulfbeck and A Ehlers, 'Tort Law, Corporate Groups and Supply Chain Liability for Workers' Injuries: The Concept of Vicarious Liability' (2016) 13 *European Company Law* 167. See also Salminen (n 28).

[53] See generally J Spier (ed), *Unification of Tort Law: Liability for Damage Caused by Others* (The Hague, Kluwer Law International, 2003); European Group on Tort Law, *Principles of European Tort Law. Text and Commentary* 1st edn (Vienna, Springer, 2005); L Emneking, *Foreign Direct Liability and Beyond* (The Hague, Eleven International Publishing, 2012).

[54] See eg Chapter 5, section II and Chapter 7, section II.A.

A taxonomy of legally effective practices resulting into a relationship and thus founding CSL should go far beyond classical structures of equity ownership, privity and similar constructs. Since organisational forms of GVC production vary significantly, a taxonomy of this nature, I argue, could and should extend to contractual and commercial arrangements; planning and governance of a value chain; and overall regulation of a GVC through chain-wide standards.

III. Conceptual Prospects for Corporate Social Liability in Global Value Chains

A. Shorter-term Influence: Contractual and Commercial Arrangements

Since the mid-twentieth century, the growing popularity and influence of public international economic law (ie the post-war increase and expansion of international trade and, later, investment law through international treaties) also encouraged crucial developments in private transnational economic governance.[55] While public international law supported nation-states in their post-war recovery and overall industrialisation, parallel private transnational apparatuses started confining certain nations to the industrial and production peripheries.[56] Among those workings were, of course, the interests of western corporations promoting the global fragmentation of production and division of labour captured in the core-periphery dynamic.[57]

By progressively eliminating barriers to the free movement of goods, services and capital, PIEL has helped to create a dependency relationship between the industrial core and the periphery, which also gave impetus to a peculiar GVC production and trade governed by essentially private means, including private law.[58] Thanks to GVCs, the core's corporations started outsourcing less value-intense stages of their production, such as parts manufacturing, to the periphery.[59] Orthodox corporate and contract law, in turn, provided for the limitation of corporate liability for harms and other issues arising from transboundary production.[60] As discussed above, the limited direct liability construct is an obvious proof of

[55] See Chapter 2, especially section II.B on the impact of the heightened PIEL on the regulation and governance of transboundary production.

[56] AG Frank, 'The Development of Underdevelopment' (September 1966) *Monthly Review*, 17.

[57] JKM Ohnesorge, 'Developing Development Theory: Law and Development Orthodoxies and the Northeast Asian Experience' (2007) 28 *University of Pennsylvania Journal of International Economic Law* 219, 242.

[58] Chapter 2, section II.

[59] Ohnesorge (n 57) 241–44; T Dos Santos, 'The Structure of Dependence' in KT Fann and DC Hodges (eds), *Readings in US Imperialism* (Boston, Porter Sargent Publishers, 1971) 226–30.

[60] Ohnesorge (n 57) 247–49.

such 'minimalist' contractually-focused approaches to liability for outsourced production. There is another example from corporate law of an approach that not only maintains the status quo but also obstructs the establishment of a transnational liability. This is equity ownership, addressed in Chapter 5 (see, for example, the *Areva* case) and in this chapter.

Increasingly, the GVC production actors from the centre and the periphery were separated geographically, socially and legally through corporate and contractual channels, while remaining linked both commercially through GVC production, and economically and organisationally through international standards of production, such as the ISO standards.[61]

Logically, however, the more production is geographically and industrially dispersed, the more it needs effective legal and organisational control. Regarding the latter, earlier it was argued that, even if it decides to outsource the production to external suppliers at some point, a firm leading a value chain already explicitly exercises some elementary control.[62] Therefore, even in cases when contractual arrangements of geographically diffuse GVC operations are short-term ad hoc transactions, they represent a basic control of a value chain-wide production. When such transactions are repeated, this amounts to a more explicit governance of outsourced production. Through such repeated transactions, a relationship could be formed. Such external suppliers might thus become subcontractors, and the contractual relationship of a one-off exchange with them might grow into relational contracting. This type of planning and governance of subcontracting are, I argue, proof of an enhanced influence within a GVC.

B. Longer-term Influence: Planning and Governance of GVC Operations

When a contract 'involves not merely an exchange, but also a relationship, between the parties',[63] this is relational contracting. When contracting in this way triggers collaboration, trust, interdependence, and – eventually – planning, it could be argued that it creates governance. I suggest that GVCs should be seen as networks characterised by long- or at least medium-term relational agreements that often go beyond one-off contracting.

On the one hand, as highlighted above, it is not easy to empirically support a perception of GVCs as networks or as (platforms for) relations.[64] For instance, a

[61] See Chapters 6–9.

[62] See Salminen and Rajavuori (n 33) 8.

[63] MA Eisenberg, 'Relational Contract' in J Beatson and D Friedmann (eds), *Good Faith and Faith in Contract Law* (Oxford, Oxford University Press, 1995) 291, 296.

[64] Gary Gereffi and Miguel Korzeniewicz were the first to conceptualise global commodity chains as inter-firm networks connecting manufacturers, suppliers and subcontractors. See the discussion in Chapter 2, section IV above.

fraction of contracts for production in Rana Plaza were ad hoc, negotiated through brokers and eventually many brands and retailers did not know exactly whether Rana Plaza factories were producing for them.[65] On the other hand, today, research increasingly underlines the fact that the lead companies of GVCs are:

> engaged in the governance of a product or service, for example by owning a brand and related intellectual property rights, by designing the product or service, marketing it and making decisions over how different aspects of production are organized: in-house, within the corporate group, or by outsourcing to external suppliers.[66]

Or, in the words of the UKSC in the *Vedanta* case,

> [t]here is no limit to the models of management and control which may be put in place within a multinational group of companies. At one end, the parent may be no more than a passive investor in separate businesses carried out by its various direct and indirect subsidiaries. At the other extreme, the parent may carry out a thoroughgoing vertical reorganisation of the group's businesses so that they are, in management terms, carried on as if they were a single commercial undertaking, *with boundaries of legal personality and ownership within the group becoming irrelevant, until the onset of insolvency*, as happened within the Lehman Brothers group.[67] (emphasis added)

Here the UKSC answered in the positive the question whether an intervention involving planning and governance is tantamount to control over the particular damaging activity undertaken by the subsidiary and, if so, whether it would be enough to found liability. Moreover, the UKSC avoided offering a scale of levels of control high enough to found liability or classifying some relationships that would fall within – and others outside – a model underlying liability. After *Vedanta*, I could clearly see that influence, and thus control, and corporate liability based on such control go far beyond a parent-subsidiary relationship and extend to planning and governance of a business enterprise and even the whole value or supply chain.

Apart from the assumption of liability, which in *Vedanta* was based on public disclosures of corporate governance reports of the head company in its *supply* chain, in the context of *value* chains the other most typical examples of transactions involving an interdependence and trust beyond formal contractual exchanges, and ultimately resulting into a relationship, are employment and distributorship.[68] In terms of corporate liability in GVCs, these would be a liability for indirect suppliers and subcontractors.

In common law, establishing liability for subcontractors and indirect suppliers is not an easy task, as confirmed for example by the Rana Plaza cases *Rahaman*

[65] See Chapter 2, section VIII above.

[66] See Salminen and Rajavuori (n 33) 608.

[67] *Vedanta Resources plc and Another (Appellants) v Lungowe and Others (Respondents)* [2019] UKSC 20 para 51.

[68] For a more complete list of paradigmatic examples of relational contracts, see D Kimel, *From Promise to Contract. Towards a Liberal Theory of Contract* (Oxford, Hart Publishing, 2003) 81–82.

and *Das*. Furthermore, the current position taken by courts outside common law systems, and thus beyond the principles and tests of the English common law of negligence, does not shed much light either, as seen in the recent German *KiK* decision.[69]

A different avenue to establishing control of a GVC through relational contracting, and – eventually – governance, is buyer's control. This type of liability is arguably similar to foreign direct liability in that it is based on a lead purchasing firm's control of its value chain. Here buyers specifically intend to broaden control over outsourced production under modular and relational governance.[70] Currently, the most obvious example of a claim about a buyer's liability is the *Walmart* case. As seen in Chapter 5, however, both the district and the appeals court rejected the claim. Notably, in the two Rana Plaza judgments, the case arose out of situations that were factually different from the *Walmart* case, but at the end the defendants had a comparable fate. Note that Walmart was involved as a respondent in the *Rahaman* case.[71]

All in all, GVCs could be deemed a modern horizontal continuation of earlier vertical corporate integration.[72] Similarly to corporations, GVCs could thus be seen as single contracting networks linking various natural and legal persons who own, manage or work for them and, in so doing, the shared engagements of these actors are hence streamlined in joint projects alongside GVCs.[73]

C. Overall Influence: Regulation through Setting the Standards along GVCs

One of this chapter's opening enquiries was to consider to what extent 'influence' is 'control'. Throughout the whole chapter, the analysis has shown that there is not just one simple response, as the answer depends on the perspective from which one is approaching this question – whether it is dependency theory, value chain studies, private law, or business and human rights framework. In the course of the analysis in this chapter, I have detected various milestones to bringing evidence about: (i) the conduct of head firms located abroad; (ii) their influence over the acts of others; and (iii) their controlling role.

[69] *Mohamed Jabir et al v KiK Textilien und Non-Food GmbH*, Case No 7 O 95/15, discussed further in Chapter 5.

[70] See various types of GVC governance in Chapter 2, section IV.

[71] *Rahaman et al v JC Penney Corpn, Inc et al*, CA No N15C-07-174 MMJ (Del Super Ct May 4, 2016). Defendants included JC Penney Corporation, The Children's Place, and Wal-mart Stores Inc. The judgment is available at http://courts.delaware.gov/Opinions/Download.aspx?id=240380. See also L Kaye, 'US Court Dismisses Rana Plaza Lawsuit' (9 May 2015) Triple Pundit, http://www.triplepundit.com/2016/05/u-s-court-dismisses-rana-plaza-lawsuit/#.

[72] See Chapter 3.

[73] See Chapter 3, section II above and Chapter 7, section I below.

Establishing control thus appears to be critical in determining a lead company's liability but, at the same time, this is the most difficult condition to meet. As my analysis in the present chapter demonstrates, the term 'control' is multifaceted. Within the business and human rights framework, the notions of contribution,[74] leverage,[75] and a direct link[76] are crucial for determining a company's liability for harm caused by its subsidiaries, subcontractors or suppliers.

The general starting point for private law, however, is very different: if one firm controls the affairs of another, then the first company is liable for harms caused by the other to third parties, thus involving liability for the effects of negligent control.[77] We should bear in mind here that the sanctions anticipated by the two regimes are also not the same: so far, the international business and human rights framework, such as the UNGPs (not to mention the OECD Guidelines) does not contain any specific recommendations about legal sanctions or even corporate liability for relevant breaches. In contrast, private law liability for the contractual failures or else the general tort of negligence results in fines, restitution and other concrete legal sanctions. This discussion is outside the scope of this part and will be developed in Part IV of the book.

Control could also stem from the factual situation, and may hence result from an exercise of influence in a business relationship.[78] Scholarship has also argued that, in some circumstances, a corporation may have de facto control over another entity outside its own legal structure through the exercise of *economic* control.[79] That is to say, if a firm is the only buyer of a supplier, even if the latter in this case is not a direct subsidiary, a relationship of economic control and dependence fairly exists.[80] This example also feeds into a larger power play of the constructed links between large purchasing companies from the industrial centre and dependent firms from the periphery, described in section A above.

In terms of safety, sustainability and other international CSR standards that are streamlined by the first companies into GVCs, it is clear that value chain leading firms exercise de facto control (ie economic control) over actors further down the value chain. Notwithstanding some research that is of a different opinion,[81] I argue here that this de facto economic control (sometimes called modular or else trilateral governance, or private compliance[82]) could have various clearly legal consequences. I elaborate below.

[74] OECD, *Guidelines* (n 44) ch II, commentary, para 14; OHCHR, *Guide* (n 45) 19.
[75] UNGPs (n 16) principle 19, commentary.
[76] ibid; OECD, *Guidelines* (n 44) ch II, A 12; OHCHR, *Guide* (n 45) 56.
[77] Salminen (n 28) 9.
[78] Bueno (n 50) 15.
[79] ibid.
[80] ibid.
[81] See generally RM Locke, *The Promise and Limits of Private Power: Promoting Labor Standards in a Global Economy* (Cambridge, Cambridge University Press, 2013).
[82] See Salminen (n 28) 8.

As such, the questions of regulation *of* as well as *by* standards are central in understanding the way the upstream norm-givers – typically, lead GVC corporations – shape the functional division of labour and entry barriers along a value chain. In various GVCs, be they food production chains or auto-motive ones, key retailers or assemblers require standards certification of the rest of the chain, thus controlling and monitoring the production processes and quality systems of the suppliers.[83] Rarely will a lead firm of the chain resort to a supplier that does not openly produce goods according to specific standards, due to monitoring and quality control costs along the whole chain. As such, controlling corporations hold a special position in streamlining standards and product regulation across jurisdictions and creating solid, quasi-universal guidelines for worldwide detail and gross producers.[84] Such global standards-producing 'giants' as the ISO, naturally, provide the forum for this regulation.

On the one hand, value chain research suggests that access to advanced economies' markets has become increasingly dependent on participating in global production networks led and controlled by firms, and especially corporations from the Global North, following the standards, including environmental ones, that are 'ordered' or even set by those same corporations.[85] Other operators down the value chain are hence expected to prove compliance with standards by showing business efficiency and customer satisfaction, but also, and, indeed, increasingly, the sustainability of the production process and of their management.[86] Through setting management standards across their value chains, head firms thus interfere in the management of other business partners. Following the *Vedanta* logic, this would be enough to found supervision and control over particular damaging activities undertaken by the lower tier operators, and thus private law liability of a lead company.

Legal research, on the other hand, argues that 'for liability-related reasons lead firms generally do not want to be seen as having control over their suppliers', however:

> at the same time for reasons related to organizing production, such as guaranteeing compliance with product safety standards, value-chain-wide cost management, research and development, and maintaining an ethical image, they are interested in maintaining control over their value chains.[87]

Ultimately, despite contractual and corporate limits, a head firm could also handle a GVC almost as one whole and effectively govern it as a single entity.[88] In those

[83] See Chapter 2, sections IV, V and VIII.

[84] Chapter 2, section IV.

[85] On different accounts of the value chain studies, see Chapter 2, section III.B. This view is, however, contested. Quadros argues that evidence of adoption of quality standards and certification has not led to closer technical relationships between carmakers and local suppliers in Brazil. See generally R Quadros, 'Global Quality Standards, Chain Governance and the Technological Upgrading of Brazilian Auto-components Producers' (May 2002) *IDS Working Paper* 156 (Brighton, IDS-Sussex).

[86] See Chapter 2, section V.

[87] Salminen (n 28) 9.

[88] Salminen and Rajavuori (n 33) 608.

situations, we deal not only with enhanced influence over a value chain by that company, meaning its governance, but also regulation sometimes amounting to control of a GVC. Thus, in section B above I argued that when a series of GVC contractual transactions create a relationship triggering interdependence and/or cooperation and trust, this could be deemed relational contracting representing a chain-wide governance. Going one step further, I suggest that when such a relationship creates cooperation, trust and interdependence that could be seen as produced and reproduced social facts, and also leads to concrete behavioural imperatives and subjective perceptions such as norms and expectations, that is a GVC-wide *regulation*.

In practice, this could be demonstrated through, for instance, environmental standards or labelling easily imposed by a head firm on a whole given GVC. Such standards could form both product-related PPMs and non-product related PPMs.[89] From the perspective of value chain studies, all that the application of such environmental schemes needs here is that such schemes should be environmentally relevant, specific and verifiable. On the contract law front, however, a published or otherwise publicised label, standard, or code, such as an ISO 14000 series standard, may be seen as a promise to customers that they are buying products that are certainly ethically sound and environmentally friendly.[90]

More precisely, the trusting party may derive its legitimate expectations from the promises of its interaction partners, including eco-labelling, and from relevant corporate codes, customs and professional standards, and even advertisement.[91] Such a promise creates legitimate expectations that could be potentially defended in national courts under the principle of protection of trust in contract law.[92]

At a post-national level, EU law includes within the product conformity assessment the totality of the characteristics that constitute the value of a product.[93] This normally comprises the CSR-based corporate promises and all related corporate governance statements of sorts, including eco-labelling.[94] EU law thus allows for the retailers', the producer and/or producer's representatives' statements about both product-related PPMs and non-product-related PPMs to have a value of a legal statement.[95] The latter thus potentially forms not only a simple communication between the sellers and the buyers but also – and, indeed, especially – a contractual promise.

[89] See Chapter 3, section II.
[90] ibid.
[91] ibid.
[92] ibid.
[93] Directive of the European Parliament and of the Council 2011/83/EU of 25 October 2011 on consumer rights, amending Council Directive 93/13/EEC and Directive 1999/44/EC of the European Parliament and of the Council and repealing Council Directive 85/577/EEC and Directive 97/7/EC of the European Parliament and of the Council Text with EEA relevance [2011] OJ L 304/64.
[94] ibid, art 2(2)(d).
[95] Chapter 3, section II.

There are also avenues arising from tort law. Under the latter, minimum standards of care could result from CSR statements, and if so, their breach would involve tort liability.[96] These would be based on the measures recognised as necessary as well as common practices of producers, assemblers, etc.[97] Notably, here the corporate codes of self-governance by some companies could actually become a minimum threshold defined by the practice of a certain fraction of the community of peers and hence extend to those producers and other operators of production and retail who never expressly adhered to them. Here, we observe the workings of the tort law obligation of due diligence, requiring that damages must be foreseeable and thus avoidable.[98]

It could thus be said that every 'CSR minimum standard' arises from typical practices and measures taken to prevent damage that are usually applied and taken in the practice of a certain fraction of the community of producers, assemblers, etc in a given supply or value chain, or, speaking about national law, firms working in the same line of business or industry. A presumption of negligence could hence arise if an actor does not comply with these minimum standards.[99]

Last but not least, as outlined at the beginning of the chapter, both internal regulation of corporate behaviour (typical firm-wide CSR codes) and external chain-wide regulation (various industry-wide codes and standards) allocate rights and duties along the whole chain. In theory, these could be expedient tools for determining influence and control, and thus liability in contract and in tort.

In the *Das* case, for instance, the defendant, Loblaws, hired social auditor Bureau Veritas to carry out a 'basic social audit'.[100] According to the services contract between Loblaws and Bureau Veritas, the scope of the social audit was identical to the scope of Loblaws' CSR standards, ie a verification of the Rana Plaza factory's compliance with Loblaws' standards for its suppliers.[101] I argue that, based on my reasoning over the previous paragraphs, those buyer's standards for suppliers already represent a GVC-wide regulation and hence could found control for the purposes of establishing private law liability of the buyer. In addition, Loblaws, by requiring its suppliers to follow certain standards that it created for them, extended governance to these GVC actors. After the Rana Plaza collapse, Loblaws could thus have been held liable precisely for being negligent in practising GVC-wide governance.

Nevertheless, existing litigation to date has shown that domestic judges in various jurisdictions are not always ready to recognise CSR, sustainability and other

[96] C Glinski, 'Bridging the Gap: The Legal Potential of Private Regulation' in O Dilling et al (eds), *Responsible Business: Self-Governance and Law in Transnational Economic Transactions* (Oxford, Hart Publishing, 2008) 50.

[97] ibid.

[98] ibid.

[99] See eg *Ward v The Ritz Hotel (London)* [1992] PIQR 315.

[100] *Das v George Weston Ltd*, 2017 ONSC 4129, at 55.

[101] ibid.

typical corporate governance codes and standards as a basis that would be enough to found either liability in tort or in contract. The *Walmart* judges in both courts dismissed the alleged failure by the defendant to enforce its code of conduct and thus to respect local laws and specific standards. In the *KiK* case, judges denied a duty of care based on the safety standards and contractual terms and conditions related to safe work environment. In this framework, the *Vedanta* ruling stands out, as it recognises that the group-wide CSR policies that are published and publicly available may make a head firm

> incur the relevant responsibility to third parties if, in published materials, it holds itself out as exercising that degree of supervision and control of its subsidiaries, even if it does not in fact do so. In such circumstances its very omission may constitute the abdication of a responsibility which it has publicly undertaken.[102]

There are empirical examples of head firms who, without adjusting production deadlines and prices, have changed, for example, technical standards requirements – say, product characteristics – for suppliers, thus compelling them to breach legal standards, such as environmental or human rights norms, in order to deliver on time (or at all).[103] According to the above analysis and following the Vedanta line, this could fairly make part of a substantial contribution that causes, facilitates, or incentivises another entity to produce adverse societal impact.

To close this section on the three modes of legally effective practices and ensuing influence over a value chain, it is important to underline that there is no clear boundary between each of the modes. Indeed, the opposite is true; the one does not exclude the others, but rather the three approaches would in practice complement each other. The first (ad hoc contract and commercial agreements with foreign partners) and second (an explicit governance of transnational production through relational contracting) modes embed subcontracting and especially outsourcing to foreign suppliers deeply in the contractual arrangements used to govern GVC-wide production. Tort law avenues, in particular the general tort of negligence, also play an important role. This is especially true regarding the second – governance of GVCs through relational contracts – and third – private regulation of GVCs through chain-wide standards – modes of influence offered in this section.

Concluding Remarks on Part III

A broader conclusion of the above chapter, and of Part III of the book in general, is that, notwithstanding several normative and behavioural avenues, my analysis has demonstrated a few uncertainties for all parties involved. Those uncertainties concern concrete legal elements conditioning the establishment of CSL for the acts

[102] *Vedanta* (n 67) para 53.
[103] OHCHR, *Guide* (n 45) 19.

of others in a value chain. It hence seems to be up to both the legislature and the courts to clarify these legal conditions for realising corporate liability in GVCs. Here, the international business and human rights soft and hard law framework has a part to play, albeit a limited one, most probably as a 'compass' for future judicial interpretation. On the litigation front, however, and especially after the *Nevsun* ruling, international human rights gain momentum in the realisation of transnational CSL.

I would thus posit that a growing focus on transnational private governance and regulation, as well as ensuing liability based on contractual promises and duties of care, could incentivise lawyers, legislators, and above all adjudicators to come up with a somewhat general transnational duty founded in a CSL recipe of domestic tort and civil remedies and international business and human rights framework. I discuss these perspectives and their limits in the next and final part of this book.

PART IV

Pitfalls and the Future of Corporate Social Liability in Global Value Chains

In the final part of the book, I look at whether, and how, a systemic approach to CSL should or could be adapted and adopted. Ultimately, I look at how the theoretical considerations (norm as a behavioural imperative, norm as a social fact, norm as a subjective perception) tie into the development of corporate liability in GVCs.

Through an in-depth discussion of current and possible, as well as impossible, liability through judicialisation and legalisation in national systems and beyond, Chapters 7–8 mark a recent paradigm leap from nonbinding and unenforceable CSR to binding and enforceable CSL. Chapter 9 addresses more normative questions, ie 'what are the drivers of this regulatory move and a paradigm change' and 'is this new paradigm fairer than the old one'?

7

Liability through Judicialisation, Legalisation, and Alternative Dispute Settlement

I. General Direct Liability

In Chapter 6 I underlined liability for the acts of others, particularly subcontractors and suppliers, as one of the vectors of developing CSL. Another prospect for CSL is a direct liability for one's own – extraterritorial – actions (and, by extension, of one's subsidiaries, if such extension is applicable) and hence one's extraterritorial liability. From a traditional private law perspective, the natural starting point for both types of CSL (especially for third-party liability) is tort law, stretching from employer's primary liability vis-à-vis its workers[1] to vicarious liability in corporate structures and GVCs.[2] Notably, the latter also theoretically foresees avenues for foreign direct liability for subcontractors and thus the breaches at the intersection of tort and contract law.

As I mentioned earlier, one of the most predictable forms of direct liability would be the employers' primary liability based on their non-delegable duty of care.[3] In most western jurisdictions, under this rubric, a tort protection provided by statutes obliges the employer to supply its employees with adequate materials,[4] that is, safe 'equipment' in a quite broad sense.[5]

In this regard, the corresponding liabilities of employers in the Rana Plaza disaster would have fallen within the scope of the lead firms' direct duties to provide safe materials only if the first-world firms were recognised as direct employers

[1] See eg Chapter 3, section II above.

[2] V Ulfbeck and A Ehlers, 'Tort Law, Corporate Groups and Supply Chain Liability for Workers' Injuries: The Concept of Vicarious Liability' (2016) 13 *European Company Law* 167, 169–72.

[3] C Elliott and F Quinn, *Tort Law*, 7th edn (Essex, Pearson, 2009) 150–51; S Deakin et al, *Markesinis and Deakin's Tort Law*, 7th edn (Oxford, Oxford University Press, 2013) 543–44.

[4] See eg the UK Employers' Liability (Defective Equipment) Act 1969 (c 37).

[5] In the UK *Coltman* case, the House of Lords adopted a rather purposive interpretation of the Employers' Liability (Defective Equipment) Act 1969 by interpreting the term 'equipment' widely enough to include vessels in its ambit: see *Coltman v Bibby Tankers Ltd* [1988] AC 276. Later, in *Knowles*, the Court of Appeal took a similar path by holding that equipment also covered a flagstone on which the employee in question was working: *Knowles v Liverpool City Council* (1992) Times, 2 July, quoted in Deakin et al (n 3) 550 and fn 51.

of the third-world garment factory workers. The factual background of the Rana Plaza cases, however, suggests the opposite – namely, that the victims were the employees of the defendants' suppliers, and the applicable legal framework does not per se allow supplier workers to be likened to the buyers' own employees. And, ultimately, neither the US nor Canadian judges in the related Rana Plaza cases ruled that there could be a general duty of care to protect supplier workers from harm. In both cases, the judges preferred to give effect to the clear wording of statutes, while the Canadian tribunal mentioned – but still put aside any – overwhelming policy reasons to rule otherwise.[6]

At the same time, the employers' duty regarding a safe place of work, which could be based on professional standards, case law or legislation, is arguably another relevant avenue.[7] Additionally, in cases where workers have suffered injuries in the course of activities related to their employment but not clearly arising from the performance of their immediate duties under the employment contract, tribunals typically look at whether the complainant was acting 'in the course of his employment', thus applying the test of employers' vicarious liability.[8]

Another relevant rubric is vicarious liability of corporate groups and supply chain liability for harm to workers.[9] To date, however, the prospect of using tort to establish extraterritorial liability of lead companies for the wrongdoings of other firms in their value chain in practice appears restricted, as explicitly demonstrated by the decisions in the Rana Plaza cases. The *Nevsun* ruling may change the situation with direct liability of corporations in customary international law, but this prospect goes partially beyond national tort systems. I discuss those avenues in detail in various sections of the remainder of this part.

On the one hand, due to the abundance and increasing complexity of GVC structures, foreign direct liability sometimes intermingles with direct liability for one's actions. Various rulings discussed in Chapter 5, each in its own way, gather into a bigger picture to show that suing subsidiaries in their parent company's domestic legal system could substantiate foreign direct liability. On the other hand, even if that were possible, suing, for example, Eritrean subcontractors in Canada would probably have few practical results for realising CSL.

[6] For the doctrine of policy reasons in English tort law, see eg Elliott and Quinn (n 3) 16–17. See also the next section of this chapter.

[7] Regarding legislative framework, today art 153 of the TFEU, for example, gives the EU the authority to adopt directives in the field of safety and health at work. Based on that, the EU Framework Directive (1989/391/EEC) and further directives focusing on specific aspects of safety and health at work are the fundamentals of European health and safety legislation, thus transposed into national legal systems of all EU Member States. Regarding national case law, see eg *Wilson v Tyneside Window Cleaning Co* [1958] 2 QB 110. Regarding professional and technical standards, see eg ISO Standard 45001 'Occupational health and safety management systems – Requirements', providing a framework to improve employee safety, reduce workplace risks and create safer working conditions, https://www.iso.org/iso-45001-occupational-health-and-safety.html.

[8] Deakin et al (n 3) 551.

[9] See generally Ulfbeck and Ehlers (n 2).

Otherwise, as a result of the *Vendanta* and, to some extent, the *Nevsun* rulings, rich-country firms may distance themselves from poor-country subsidiaries or suppliers for fear of triggering a transnational duty of care.[10] Seen through a traditional (voluntarist) lens, the prospect of direct liability is likely to result in western TNCs displaying undesirable reluctance and even precaution regarding general dealings with poor countries. One of the most recent examples of such reluctance was the refusal of many US-based global buyers to sign the Accord on Fire and Building Safety in Bangladesh, which I address in detail later in this chapter. Within the rubric of next section, the question that needs to be considered is the following: if direct extraterritorial liability for a company's actions at home does not seem to represent a viable prospect for CSL, what are the other possibilities for a transnational liability through judicialisation?

II. A(n) (Im)Possibility of Judicial Assertiveness: A General Duty of Care for Global Value Chains

In Chapter 3, I showed how, in the evolving common law approach of establishing the duty of care through the two-tier, then three-tier and eventually 'three-plus'-tier tests, one of the crucial elements was the tier of foreseeability. The approach evolved precisely because a myriad of new relevant factual situations arose, and are constantly arising, especially due to ever-escalating technological progress. Hence, where a completely new factual situation occurred, often a duty of care would be established if there were sufficient 'policy reasons' to do so.[11]

The idea of policy reasons implies that 'judges take into account not just the legal framework, but also whether they *believe society would benefit* from the existence of a duty' (emphasis added).[12] Additionally, as early as the 1932 decision in *Donoghue v Stevenson*, Lord Atkin said that every person 'must […] reasonably foresee what would be likely to injure […] persons who are closely and directly affected by [one's] act'.[13] In spelling out the 'neighbour' principle, Lord Atkin was obviously not only referring to actual neighbours, that is, people living next door, but those who were directly and considerably affected by one's action according to what a reasonable person could have foreseen.[14]

Based on the above, I suggest that the upsurge in outsourced GVC production (which is due to the fact that the transborder GVC webs escape traditional forms of

[10] See eg A Yilmaz-Vastardis, 'Vedanta v Lungowe Symposium: Potential Implications of the UKSC's Decision for Supply Chain Relationships' *OpinioJuris* (23 April 2019) http://opiniojuris.org/2019/04/23/vedanta-v-lungowe-symposium-potential-implications-of-the-ukscs-decision-for-supply-chain-relationships/.

[11] Elliott and Quinn (n 3) 20.

[12] ibid.

[13] *Donoghue v Stevenson* [1932] AC 562, 280.

[14] ibid.

control of state institutions, including oversight and enforcement) could fairly be evidence of a new type of (global) circumstance. In these changed circumstances, lead GVC firms must foresee the situations in which their actions may directly and seriously affect third parties, such as supplier workers, local communities, the environment, etc – especially if such third parties are situated in the Global South. If they do not take such reasonable care, they should be held liable and sanctioned accordingly. This could hopefully inspire judges, especially in transnational contexts, to be more open to new policy reasons to rule on the existence of a duty that would benefit society at large.

My above assumption draws on the core theoretical model that I built in Chapter 1. Specifically, here I aim to infer some particular CSL norms from their context and look at the question in terms of actors, instruments, and practices. It will be recalled that the approach consists of distinguishing between the attributes that underlie the nature of norms – together these form the general delineation of the sociological concept of norms – and other attributes that are characteristic of certain groups of norms – in the present case, legal norms. The definition of a legal norm includes its essential attributes, common to all norms (behavioural imperatives, social facts, and subjective perceptions), as well as its additional attributes specific to legal norms.[15]

It is, therefore, crucial to specify and scrutinise additional norm attributes. The focus is on three clusters: (i) the cognitive context in which the norm is active; (ii) the systemic conditions that apply to the situation at hand; and (iii) the values associated with the imperative (ie an essential norm attribute, relating to an 'ought'). As a result, the analysis deconstructs norms, that is, their raison d'être, as well their key driving forces.[16]

In the context of this book, the currently predominant interpretative framework for the legal issues relevant for CSL does not seem to permit the formation of the legal norm of a general 'GVC duty of reasonable care'. This very *impossibility* of establishing that legal norm, I argue, *is* per se still the presently dominant *social norm* of CSL. This social norm is both informed by, and equally reproduces, the existing political, economic and governance approaches to GVCs (eg Chapter 2, sections II–IV); as well as traditional first-world private law constructs, and the conventional judicial approach to liability in GVCs (see Chapters 3 and 5). At these two levels, the main decision-makers are still dealing with corporations as if they were vertically integrated enterprises with separate legal personality, limited liability for harm beyond tier one of their production or supply chain, as well as other corollaries of black-letter corporate law and contract law.[17]

[15] See Chapter 1, section IV.B.

[16] H Hydén and M Svensson, 'The Concept of Norms in Sociology of Law' (2008) 53 *Scandinavian Studies in Law* 15, 24.

[17] See Chapter 3, sections I–II above. See in particular the landmark case of UK company law giving an orthodox view of separate legal personality: *Salomon v A Salomon & Co Ltd* [1897] AC 22.

However, the dramatic increase in GVC production and trade presents a different and novel set of circumstances. It represents a shift in the factual situations of horizontal relational arrangements between affiliated entities within the globalised network of the head corporations controlling them. Second, the dispersed GVC production makes it quasi-impossible to ground the liability of those head companies and enforce the law against them. Third, and crucially, corporate human rights, environmental and societal abuses in GVCs grow in number, degree and variety of harms. Thus, a new socially reproduced normative imperative ordering actors' behaviour through the actors' subjective perception of the social expectations surrounding their behaviour (a sort of incorporation of and reaction to socially produced normative imperatives) must also differ from that of the previous dealings with corporations as vertically integrated enterprises with limited liability. The key features of this new social norm, I argue, should be informed by horizontal relationships in GVC networks de facto controlled by their head companies. This would thus allow CSL to be realised through the creation of this – legal – norm of a general GVC duty of reasonable care.

The attributes of the norm belonging to a particular field (in this case, law) are the cognitive context, the systemic conditions, and the values associated with the CSL imperative. These three have also changed. More specifically, today claims about persisting human rights abuses, lack of safety at work, and the destruction of our planet that capitalism brings forth through GVC production have become mainstream. They thus make it necessary to move beyond the earlier reliance on legal constructs of limited liability and privity that traditional private ordering used to offer to deal with corporate liability, including in GVCs.

Applying such a model to real life, the adjudicators, according to their legal intuition, are expected to decide what relevant analogy in positive law could be applied to a particular case. As I said above, the current social norm regarding CSL posits that it is impossible to establish a general GVC duty of reasonable care. I suggest that the legal norms informing this interpretative space are privity of contract and separate corporate personality with limited liability. Liability based on contractual promises and the general transnational duty founded in a CSL recipe of contract, tort, and business and human rights law should thus replace the orthodox corporate and contract doctrines that limit the realisation of CSL. The doctrine of policy reasons could, I argue, help to apply these theoretical advances in practice.

In particular, a construct such as the imperative of policy reasons could influence the interpretation and application of positive law by affecting the choice of use – or non-use – of a particular analogy in positive law, the direction of generalisations on the basis of a particular material, and deduction of the specific inferences from the general principles. Such influence is likely to impact the course of the judicial reasoning and other practices of positive law. Such influence per se could thus be deemed a norm. Even if it places a more psychological weight on the development of positive law, according to the three-tier model of norms introduced in Chapter 1 above, it could still be considered a norm. Consequently, rulings framed in the policy reasons doctrine are likely to pre-empt charges of excessive judicial activism, thus providing judges with a way to demonstrate that they are ensuring compliance with current norms, including current social values, expectations, and needs, rather than engaging in policy-making.

In practice, a literal invocation of policy reasons in the context of GVCs has already taken place in the Rana Plaza cases. In these two related cases, *Rahaman* and *Das*, the issues regarding a duty of care concerned the defendant's duty to protect the plaintiffs from a foreseeable risk of harm caused by third parties, thus making it a question of a general GVC duty of care. In both cases, such a general duty of care was, however, denied by the judges.[18]

Particularly regarding the question of policy reasons in the formation of a GVC duty of care, in *Das* the court had actually looked at policy reasons to found such duty. The policy reasons that were invoked referred to new circumstances such as the need for:

> accountability by Canadian corporations as responsible corporate citizens [...] preventing [them] from exploiting the regulatory vacuum in developing countries, and [...] advancing the common law duty of care in a manner that reflects the globalized economy in which Canadian entities participate.[19]

Rather paradoxically though, the judge in the *Das* case, Perell, ultimately found that other 'policy' reasons outweighed the policy reasons for a general GVC duty of care, namely, 'the law's hesitancies to impose liability for nonfeasance and to impose a duty of care to protect the plaintiff from harm caused by a third party'.[20] Scholarship equally notes that the approach of establishing policy reasons began to be criticised as 'the apparent need to find such reasons was said to be holding back development of the law'.[21]

How then is it conceivable to form a general GVC duty of care by foreseeing actual or potential harms to, for instance, one's employees, and thus to establish a general duty to protect employees, including those working for indirect suppliers?[22] Both *Rahaman* and *Das* have shown the weaknesses of negligence

[18] *Rahaman et al v JC Penney Corpn, Inc et al*, CA No N15C-07-174 MMJ (Del Super Ct May 4, 2016) 27–28; *Das v George Weston Ltd*, 2017 ONSC 4129, 450.

[19] *Das*, ibid 451.

[20] ibid 452.

[21] Elliott and Quinn (n 3) 20. But see various reflections on policy reasons in tort law, particularly US product liability law. For example, in the framework of the market share liability doctrine in US product liability, scholarship has for a long time focused on policy reasons, such as: victim compensation as a goal of tort law, deterrence, and fairness to those that have been harmed. See JH Grundhauser, 'Case Note. The DES Manufacturer Identification Problem: A Florida Public Policy Approach' (1986) 40 *University of Miami Law Review* 857, 862 (addressing victim compensation); RM Russell, 'Note. The Causation Requirement: Guardian of Fairness or Obstacle to Justice – Making Sense of a Decade of DES Litigation' (1991) 25 *Suffolk University Law Review* 1071, 1102 (addressing fairness) and 1105 (addressing deterrence).

[22] See generally Ulfbeck and Ehlers (n 2).

claims where buyers demonstrated a little de jure control over suppliers aside from demanding elementary compliance and checking this through *outsourced* monitoring, the latter itself being 'minimalistic'.[23]

Notably, the *Das* judge Perell explained his decision by quoting the same passage from Lord Atkin's statement of the 'neighbour' principle in *Donoghue v Stevenson*.[24] Although Perell drew on the same precedent I did earlier in this subsection, he established basically the opposite to what I am suggesting here. According to Perell, no general duty of reasonable care could be placed on buyers to anticipate actual or potential harms to supplier workers, thus protecting them. Foreseeing actual or potential harms to, for instance, one's workers, and thus establishing a general duty to protect employees, whether those of subsidiaries or suppliers (or else, establishing a general duty of reasonable care placed on buyers) would be preferable in many cases, particularly if it were to take the form of strict liability.

In the *Das* case, an expert retained by the complainants noticed that Loblaws, in commissioning a social audit, had to acknowledge the deplorable record '[...] of garment factories in Bangladesh, which has a history of factory fires and collapses from poor structural design or construction', and that they should take this 'into account in defining the scope of the audit'.[25] This is a clear example of a general duty of reasonable care. However, the crystallisation of such a duty of care seems to take some time due in particular to a quite negative current attitude of many lawyers, scholars and practitioners alike, towards the formation of a general duty of reasonable care.[26]

The present lack of emphasis on, and, apparently also interest in, founding a general GVC duty of reasonable care and a strict private law liability through judicial channels exposes the practical obstacles to opening avenues for 'reasonable' judicial assertiveness.

Theoretically, there are at least two possible avenues for enhancing judicial assertiveness and thus enforcement of a general duty imposing transnational liability for offshore operations. One of them would be to incorporate into any GVC-relevant agreement (including supply contracts, subcontracting, etc) references to sustainability-oriented international instruments, global framework agreements, and transnational company agreements.[27] Another possibility is to insert the so-called sustainability clauses into any commercial contract with

[23] *Das* (n 18) 52, 54–57.

[24] *Das*, Reasons for Decision, 2.

[25] *Das* (n 18) 69.

[26] For a practitioner's opinion, see above (nn 19–20). For a scholarly opinion, see Elliott and Quinn (n 3) 20. But see C Terwindt et al, 'Supply Chain Liability: Pushing the Boundaries of the Common Law?' (2017) 8(3) *Journal of European Tort Law* 261.

[27] See eg E Kocher, 'Codes of Conduct and Framework Agreements on Social Minimum Standards – Private Regulation?' in O Dilling et al (eds), *Responsible Business: Self-governance and Law in Transnational Economic Transactions* (Oxford, Hart Publishing, 2008) 67, 69–72.

transnational reach.[28] The problem with the latter prospect is that with this kind of reference in private commercial agreements, the sustainability clauses themselves have to be sufficiently precise in order to be enforced, which is usually not the case.[29]

Regarding the former option of using references to various global instruments, the international or global framework agreements (IFAs/GFAs), sometimes taking form of transnational company agreements (TCAs) typically apply to all present and future companies fully consolidated within a corporate group's scope of consolidation and also to those in which the group has dominant influence.[30] Notably, Thyssenkrupp's recent IFA says that its suppliers must only be *informed in a suitable manner* about relevant fundamental principles.[31] Moreover, the group merely *encourages* its suppliers to consider these principles in their own company policy.[32] Lafarge's GFA represents a slightly stricter exception by saying that:

> any substantive harm to the health and safety of direct and indirect employees, the protection of the environment or basic human rights, which is not corrected after a warning, will result in the termination of relations with suppliers and subcontractors, subject to contractual obligations.[33]

Again, real-life examples break most of the promises on this path to enforcing a general GVC duty of care. Namely, there seems to be a considerable gap between the head firms' chain-wide ethical engagements and their actual management practices. This includes the disrespecting of fundamental rights in different sites of production, as was the case in the *Auchan* claim in France (although the *Samsung* litigation initiated under the Vigilance law is still ongoing and may have a different fate). Furthermore, recall that in the *Walmart* case the court concluded that language used by Walmart did not imply that the company had a duty to monitor suppliers, but merely that it reserved the right for Walmart to do so. Thus, as for IFAs and TCAs, one might expect that they would be interpreted in a way similar

[28] Generally, K Peterkova Mitkidis, 'Sustainability Clauses in International Supply Chain Contracts: Regulation, Enforceability and Effects of Ethical Requirements' (2014) *Nordic Journal of Commercial Law* 1; K Peterkova Mitkidis, *Sustainability Clauses in International Business Contracts* (The Hague, Eleven Publishing, 2015).

[29] ibid.

[30] See eg the GDF Suez's 'Global Agreement on Fundamental Rights, Social Dialogue and Sustainable Development' (2010): 'This agreement applies to all present and future GDF Suez companies fully consolidated within GDF Suez Group's scope of consolidation and those in which the Group has dominant influence'.

[31] Thyssenkrupp's International Framework Agreement (2016): 'Thyssenkrupp ensures that its suppliers shall be informed in a suitable manner about these fundamental principles. Thyssenkrupp encourages its suppliers to consider these principles in their own company policy'.

[32] ibid.

[33] Lafarge's Global Framework Agreement on Corporate Social Responsibility and International Industrial Relations (2013): 'Any serious breach of the legislation concerning the health and safety of direct and indirect employees, the protection of the environment or basic human rights, which is not corrected after a warning, will result in the termination of relations with the concerned enterprise, subject to contractual obligations'.

to the relevant *Walmart* judgment's interpretation because these agreements are drafted in a very general and soft manner.

To summarise the analysis in this chapter so far, theoretically, the formation of CSL through a general GVC duty of care is feasible through a kind of mix of contract law and tort law channels, notwithstanding the present status quo of most of the surveyed prevailing legal approaches, both doctrinal and judicial. Indeed, if one seeks to found a general duty of care in a particular national legal system, it would be possible to apply law of the selected jurisdiction through a reference in a contractual arrangement. Conversely, the avenue of founding CSL through (foreign) direct liability prioritises the usage of the general tort of negligence. And even in this case, some additional 'help' might be needed. In this regard, the *Nevsun* judges ruled that 'it was not plain and obvious' that Canadian courts cannot develop a civil remedy in domestic law for corporate violations of customary international law that is part of Canadian national law.[34] Moreover, this could be done either through the development of new torts or through a direct remedy for violations of customary international law.[35]

In domestic practice, however, it currently seems nigh on impossible to establish either a general direct liability or a general duty of reasonable care through domestic judicial channels alone. Apart from the use of general international law, discussed later in this chapter, the probable remaining options are: (i) a transfer of business relationships to selected jurisdictions through private contracts; (ii) a general legalisation of CSL through legislation creating statutory duties; or (iii) the creation of transnational governance contracts. The last of these – creation of a transnational CSL agreement or programme – could be precisely that middle ground between the intricate possibilities of relocation of business relationship to specific jurisdictions and the option of statutory establishment of CSL, which efficiency seems to be constrained at present because of its apparently limited enforceability. The question is whether such a transnational CSL programme should be a governance agreement applying to a series of one-off deals and contracts within a value chain, or rather a kind of a transnational contract directly linking the upstream and the downstream of GVCs. In the remainder of this chapter, I look at this and related questions.

Note that the prospect of creating a general 'GVC' duty of care as part of a recognisably new legal paradigm appears quite uncertain. Among the few things that are clear is that a stricter liability standard, placing a presumption of liability on lead firms with very limited exceptions, would be a very helpful development. This could be explained, on the one hand, by recent litigation trends, where, at least in some cases, a discussion of the possible role of contractual causes of action has taken place (eg in *KiK* and *Walmart*). On the other hand, there are a growing number of various initiatives and actual laws seeking to create a more general duty

[34] *Nevsun*, para 122.
[35] *Nevsun*, paras 127–28.

of care that would broadly require human rights due diligence throughout a lead company's value chain (eg French and Dutch due diligence laws).

In the remainder of this chapter, I analyse the pitfalls and future of such statutory developments (section III), as well as those of a potential transnational governance contract, a programme binding parties to accept as compulsory the submission of the disputes to international arbitration (section IV). Since there are avenues for international arbitration through judicialisation as an alternative to the formation of CSL, the respective likelihoods of international investment arbitration are analysed in turn (section V). Lastly, I briefly sketch some alternatives of realising CSL ex ante by extra-legal means (section VI).

III. Legalisation through Legislation: Liability Disciplines in Current French and Dutch Law

In Chapter 5 (see especially Table 5.1), I featured two instruments that, in my opinion, reached the third stage of CSL, namely, liability disciplines. They are: the 2017 French Vigilance law and the 2019 Dutch Child Labour Due Diligence Law. I focus in this subsection on these two examples of legalisation of CSL liability disciplines that have already materialised into legislation in force. Note that, apart from many policy statements and legislative processes in the EU Member States, those are also the two only adopted laws in the EU so far. On paper, these are legally binding and enforceable liability laws. Here, I scrutinise them in terms of actual scope, inclusiveness, enforceability, and overall efficiency.

The French Vigilance law, adopted on 21 February 2017 by the National Assembly, aims to increase societal responsibility within GVCs to the level of binding legal obligation. It requires large French companies and corporate groups to ensure that serious violations of human rights and fundamental freedoms, as well as serious environmental damage, do not occur in their value chains. To this end, the law requires the covered actors to make a vigilance plan preventing and detecting violations of these rights and freedoms both in France and abroad, committed by their subsidiaries, subcontractors and any suppliers with whom they maintain an established business relationship, to the extent that these activities are related to the relationship.[36]

On 23 March 2017, the law was partially censored by the French Constitutional Council in a corresponding decision, while the provisions validated by the Constitutional Council entered into force on 29 March 2017.[37]

[36] Loi n°2017-399 relative au devoir de vigilance des sociétés mères et des entreprises donneuses d'ordre, promulguée le 27 mars 2017, JORF n°0074 du 28 mars 2017, texte n° 1, Art 1.

[37] Ministry of Economy and Finance, France, DG Trésor, *Nouvelle loi sur le devoir de vigilance des sociétés mères et des entreprises donneuses d'ordre* (9 May 2017) https://www.tresor.economie.gouv.fr/Articles/2017/05/09/devoir-de-vigilance-des-societes-meres-et-des-entreprises-donneuses-d-ordre

The companies covered by the law must prepare and implement a vigilance plan, also 'consulting the stakeholders' during that process.[38] The plan should include 'reasonable due diligence measures' to identify risks and prevent 'serious violations of human rights and fundamental freedoms, and damages to human health and safety, and the environment'.[39] The law further specifies that the plan must include the following measures:

- risk-mapping for identification, analysis and prioritisation of risks;
- procedures for regularly assessing the situation of subsidiaries, subcontractors and suppliers with whom an established business relationship is maintained;
- appropriate actions to mitigate risks or prevent serious harm;
- an alert mechanism as well as a tool for collecting risk signals, drawn up in consultation with the representative trade unions in a given company; and
- a system for monitoring the implemented measures and evaluating their effectiveness.[40]

Entities subject to the law are typically joint-stock companies whose head office ('real seat' or 'effective seat' as per the corporate doctrine of *siège social effectif*) is established in France.[41] A company is subject to the law if, including the employees of its subsidiaries, it employs at least 5,000 employees in France or at least 10,000 employees worldwide.[42]

Failure to comply with the Vigilance law may result in fines of up to €10 million.[43] If the violation causes damage, the fine may be increased by up to three times, that is, up to €30 million.[44] Although the biggest fines are clearly identified, the exact conditions for imposing sanctions and the criteria for assessing the extent of damage – and hence the amount of the fine – remain ambiguous.

Unlike those fines due to the state, the fines due to harmed individuals under the torts rubric for reparation of damages caused by a violation of the law will not be imposed.[45] The paragraphs providing for the imposition of a civil fine were initially present in the Bill, but were censored by the Constitutional Council.[46] This repeal was based on the principle of legality of the offences and punishments stemming from article 8 of the 1789 Declaration of the Rights of Man and the Citizen (DDHC). The principle requires that a sanction with a clear character of punishment can only apply to offences that are defined in sufficiently clear and precise terms, which, according to the Council, is not the case for 'human rights'

[38] French Vigilance law, art 1.
[39] ibid.
[40] ibid.
[41] ibid.
[42] ibid.
[43] ibid.
[44] French Vigilance law, art 2.
[45] As per arts 1240 and 1241 of the French Civil Code.
[46] Decision 2017-750 DC of the Constitutional Council, 23 March 2017.

and 'fundamental freedoms', while the Council also sees the entities and activities covered by the law as too broad in scope.[47] Hence, it is not accurate to speak of a 'human rights due diligence' legislation in the case of this law.

Since in its final verdict the French legislator refers to extra-contractual civil liability based on fault, negligence or recklessness, it is therefore the general principles of articles 1240 and 1241 of the French Civil Code that apply.[48] As the key terms used by the law such as 'enforcement', 'sanctions', or 'risk assessment', for example, are unclear or completely undefined, the scope of different corporate duties seems to be vague. Indeed, the law and also the preparatory works[49] leave many questions unanswered, including:

- What risks must be covered and what risks could be excluded? How should the risks be classified? Although risk-mapping is to be done regularly, the analysis and classification will mainly depend on the business sectors and geographical areas of the activities of entities covered.[50] So, at the end of the day, it is about mapping only and not about risk classification per se.
- The law is also silent about the content of risk mitigation and prevention measures that are deemed 'appropriate'.
- The same is true for the term 'serious harm'. The mechanism for assessing the benchmark of gravity above which harm falls within the scope of the law is not specified. Which environmental damages must be avoided or otherwise sanctioned? For example, is damage due to CO_2 emissions prohibited? In that case, the covered entities buying extra CO_2 allowances under the EU Emission Trading Scheme[51] might arguably be found to be breaching the Vigilance law. And what is the benchmark for the seriousness of human rights and fundamental freedoms violations? Think of the Gulf countries or India, for example – should French companies stop, limit or sanction business with firms from countries that have a caste system or employ only men in many sectors of production and services?
- Do trade unions, environmental organisations and consumers fall within the scope of stakeholders covered by the law? In addition, is the consultation of these unidentified stakeholders optional or compulsory? Article 1 of the law is written in a way that seems to suggest that consultation is only a recommendation – thus, not even an obligation of conduct, let alone of result.

[47] ibid *considérant* 13.

[48] See eg A Aseeva, 'Développements récents en matière de la protection des droits de l'Homme et de l'environnement dans les chaines globales de valeur' in C Titi (ed), *Droits de l'homme et droit international économique* (Brussels, Bruylant, 2019) 51, 70.

[49] National Assembly, France, *Travaux préparatoires de la Loi n° 2017-399 du 27 mars 2017 relative au devoir de Vigilance des sociétés mères et des entreprises donneuses d'ordre* https://www.legifrance.gouv.fr/dossierlegislatif/JORFDOLE000030421923/.

[50] The risk-mapping definition is inspired by the definition in art 17 of the law Sapin 2. Loi n° 2016-1691 du 9 décembre 2016 relative à la transparence, à la lutte contre la corruption et à la modernisation de la vie économique, *JORF n° 0287 du 10 décembre 2016, texte n° 2.*

[51] See European Commission, 'EU Emissions Trading System (EU ETS)' https://ec.europa.eu/clima/policies/ets_en.

The Vigilance law, however, clarifies that direct suppliers as well as subcontractors (*sous-traitants*, ie suppliers of suppliers) are subject to the obligations of the vigilance plan.[52] More precisely, these are direct suppliers and subcontractors who have an 'established' business relationship with the covered entities.[53] The Constitutional Council has specified that the vigilance obligations only apply to the part of the activities of those suppliers and subcontractors that is covered by an established relationship with the concerned entity.[54] According to the French Commercial Code, a business relationship is deemed to be 'established' (*relation commerciale établie*) when it is of a monitored, stable and regular nature and where the parties can reasonably anticipate a certain continuity of the flow of business with a commercial partner.[55]

Regarding the formation of a GVC liability, such a narrow scope of legally effective bonds may not, in fact, cover the whole value chain. Instead of forming a general duty of care requiring the covered entities to intervene to protect others down the value chain (say, supplier employees) from a foreseeable risk of harm caused by third parties (say, suppliers) the law focuses only on subsidiaries within one corporate group, as well as first-tier suppliers and subcontractors.

The Vigilance law, therefore, seems to be innovative yet problematic due to potential gaps in its implementation somehow compelled by the French Constitutional Council. On the one hand, the law states that it imposes legal obligations on the entire value chain, thus involving a GVC liability. On the other hand, these obligations are relatively vague and indefinite. Furthermore, a GVC liability determination that is primarily based on an established business relationship is likely to considerably limit the scope of such liability, since it covers only first-tier relationships.

The Council of State is authorised by law to issue decrees clarifying issues of implementation of French legislation. In the case of the Vigilance law, such decrees could specify the procedures for realising the vigilance plans, as well as adding more particular measures to the list of those included in the vigilance plan. These decrees, defining the scope, application and enforcement of the GVC liability, would help to increase legal certainty.

So far, no decree has been issued, and French judges are likely to face a complicated task to solve the problems that will inevitably arise when interpreting and enforcing the law without much guidance from the legislator. *Samsung*, the very first litigation under the Vigilance law is still ongoing.[56] Hence, for the moment many interpretative questions of the law's possible scope, application and enforcement still lack clear answers.

[52] French Commercial Code, art L.233-16, *titre* II.
[53] ibid.
[54] Constitutional Council (n 46).
[55] French Commercial Code, art L.442-6-I-5.
[56] See the summary of the claim in Chapter 5, section II, above.

The Dutch Due diligence law was adopted in May 2019. Notably, several aspects of interpretation – especially implementation of the law – are still pending, subject to passing the instrument known as a General Administrative Order or GAO (*Algemene Maatregel van Bestuur or AMvB*).[57] The GAO for this law must be approved by both Chambers of the Dutch Parliament.[58] The law was supposed to enter into force on 1 January 2020 but, because the government first needed to elaborate the related GAOs, the law is expected to enter into force in 2022.[59] In comparison with the French Vigilance law, the Dutch Due diligence law arguably applies beyond first-tier relationships and potentially extends to the whole value chain.[60]

Several points of the Dutch law deserve attention in light of CSL and the above discussion on French law. First, as I outlined in section I of Chapter 5 above the Dutch law introduces a duty of care to prevent the supply of goods or services whose production involved child labour. This is a statutory duty to realise due diligence, which is owed to the society of the jurisdiction in question. It is thus different from the common law duty of care in tort law, owed only to harmed persons in question.

Second, the law applies to all operators selling or supplying goods or services to Dutch end-users, including companies registered outside the Netherlands (such companies are covered if they supply goods or services to the Dutch market at least twice a year).[61] With a view to performing due diligence, the covered firms must establish whether there is a risk or a reasonable presumption that a product or service involves child labour. If such a presumption exists, the companies must develop and implement an action plan.[62] The investigation must be based on sources that are 'reasonably knowable and consultable'.[63] Similar to most of the CSL legislation surveyed in Chapter 5, the law requires companies to produce a statement declaring that the operator has conducted due diligence.[64]

Notably, regarding the assessment, the law draws on the joint ILO and International Organisation of Employers' 'Child Labour Guidance for Business', the latter itself drawing on the UNGPs.[65] Where there is a reasonable presumption that child labour contributed to the product or service at hand, the firm should present an action plan in line with international guidelines – either the UNGPs or the OECD Guidelines – to cease that, and prevent any future, impact.[66]

[57] MVO Platform, 'Update: Frequently Asked Questions about the new Dutch Child Labour Due Diligence Law' (3 June 2019) https://www.mvoplatform.nl/en/frequently-asked-questions-about-the-new-dutch-child-labour-due-diligence-law/.

[58] ibid.

[59] ibid.

[60] ibid.

[61] Dutch due diligence law, art 4.1.

[62] ibid art 5.1.

[63] ibid art 5.2.

[64] ibid art 4.

[65] MVO Platform (n 57).

[66] ibid.

Third, disagreements arose during the enactment of the law, amidst claims that a binding law would jeopardise the existing Dutch governance model for addressing corporate human rights due diligence through the so-called agreements on responsible business conduct (*convenanten*) – a variation of TCAs discussed in the previous section (section II).[67] Such a sustainability agreement thus arguably represents the current social norm of human rights due diligence in the Netherlands. However, the law implicitly embraces those agreements, stipulating that, subject to the Dutch government's approval, and developed in cooperation with trade unions, employer associations, and NGOs, a joint action plan to detect and prevent the use of child labour in the production of goods and services of parties to those covenants may be enacted.[68] Therefore, in spite of the above concerns, the binding legislation – as a legal norm – would not weaken, but, on the contrary, re-confirm and strengthen those voluntary sustainability agreements arguably representing relevant Dutch social norm. In addition, based on the relevant presumptions in Chapters 3 and 6 that the promises made by companies in their corporate codes and similar voluntary pledges, could, under some circumstances, become promises binding their creators, the law is likely to transform those voluntary Dutch TCA initiatives into binding instruments.

There are, however, shortcomings regarding locus standi under this Dutch law and its enforcement. Namely, the parties that are directly concerned, such as victims or consumers, cannot directly sue a company. If they have concrete evidence of non-compliance, they must complain to the regulator (*toezichthouder*).[69] A dedicated regulator is tasked with publishing the corporate human rights due diligence statements in an online public registry.[70] The concerned parties can take a case to the regulator only if a company's reaction is 'inadequate' according to the applicants, or if the company ignored the complaint six months after filing it.[71] Note that the regulator cannot enforce the law pro-actively, as only complaints submitted by third parties may trigger enforcement.[72]

In cases of non-compliance, the law foresees sanctions that include regulatory fines and criminal penalties. If an operator fails to produce the required statement, investigate, or undertake an action plan, or if those actions are deemed inadequate, the regulator may first impose a symbolic fine of €4,100.[73] If a company is fined twice within five years, it becomes an economic offender under the Economic Offences Act,[74] and a further violation can lead to the imprisonment

[67] See eg https://www.rsm.nl/fileadmin/Images_NEW/Sites/Chair_IBHR/Publications/Van_Dam_-_Statutory_HRDD_duties_in_NL.pdf.
[68] Dutch due diligence law, art 5.4.
[69] ibid art 3.2–3.3.
[70] ibid art 4.5.
[71] ibid art 3.4.
[72] MVO Platform (n 57).
[73] Dutch due diligence law, arts 7.2 a and b.
[74] Economic Offences Act, 1950 (NL) https://wetten.overheid.nl/BWBR0002063/2018-07-25.

of the responsible director.[75] At the most extreme, on top of imprisonment, non-compliance can lead to fines of €750,000 or 10 per cent of the company's annual turnover.[76]

There remain a few concerns regarding the law, such as: which authority will perform the role of the regulator;[77] what exact requirements should the corporate action plan meet;[78] and whether some types of operators' firms, such as SMEs, will be exempted from the law.[79] Moreover, the law has very limited scope. In addition, companies do not seem to be required to guarantee the absence of child labour in their production and services, but only to state that they have done what they could. Last but not least, its alleged inclusivity is ambivalent, as in fact the victims and other concerned stakeholders such as NGOs have no possibility to directly enforce the law in courts, but can only do so through the regulator. The ultimate enforcement and effectiveness of the law will depend on how the Dutch government elaborates these elements in the relevant GAOs.

To summarise, both the French and Dutch laws establish legal obligations of due diligence for certain categories of companies. The advantage of both laws is that they establish a duty of care and lead to civil (the French law) and criminal (the Dutch law) liability for negligence in the case of corporate activity leading to a foreseeable harm inadequately addressed by the due diligence plan.

A notable example of a limitation of the French law is that we cannot speak about a GVC-wide liability of the head companies, as such liability is restricted to first-tier relationships. Nor would I call the French law human rights due diligence legislation, due to a peculiar French interpretation of the term 'human rights' for the purposes of the corporate liability under the torts rubric, discussed above. In the case of the Dutch law, there seem to be no such domestic law limits regarding the definition of human rights due diligence. In addition, the law is limited to child labour only, which makes its scope very narrow but unambiguous compared to the scope of the French law. In the Dutch case, however, it is unclear how the regulator will assess whether due diligence was sufficient or insufficient in situations where a complaint provides evidence of child labour. In addition, the French law can be directly enforced by both victims and third parties – something that the Dutch law does not allow. However, while under the Dutch law non-compliance becomes a national economic offence, the fines are due only to the state and, just as under the French law, no fines are paid to harmed individuals under the torts rubric for reparation of damages caused by the violation of the Dutch law.

All in all, it could thus be argued that under both laws, companies are somehow invited to set the standards of conduct for themselves, non-implementation of which could lead to a breach of legal obligations and possibly to liability. While the

[75] MVO Platform (n 57).
[76] ibid.
[77] Dutch due diligence law, art 1(d).
[78] ibid art 5.3.
[79] ibid art 6.

two pieces of legislation technically amount to the third and ultimate stage of CSL as delineated in this book – liability disciplines – their enforcement and effectiveness remain more than dubious. And if the highest national CSL disciplines that exist to date appear to be so limited, what, if any, way forward exists for CSL in GVCs? In the remainder of this chapter I seek to find such way(s), although most of the possible options have been exhausted in my preceding analysis.

IV. Transnational CSL Legalisation: Bangladesh Accord and Bangladesh Alliance

In Parts I (Chapter 2) and II (Chapter 3) above, I demonstrated how, at every important moment in the history of liability of corporations, especially those operating globally through GVCs, the western capital-exporting states – led by the US – managed to come up with a 'counter-policy instrument' to shield their FDI and its main vehicle – corporations – from any binding instrument and relating developments. This has happened from the misadventures of the nascent ITO and its draft Havana Charter, through the rise and fall of the NIEO, through the failure of the draft UNCTNC Code, through the creation of the OECD Guidelines, through the shifting focus of relevant multilateral efforts from the UN to the GATT, to the ultimate paradigm shift to private and voluntary corporate governance through CSR in the 1990s-early 2000s.

The 2013 Accord on Fire and Building Safety in Bangladesh (the Accord)[80] is no exception to those 'counter-strikes' on behalf of the global capitalism, although it is more successful than its normative predecessors mentioned above. It was signed on 15 May 2013 in the aftermath of the Rana Plaza building collapse. As a legally binding agreement, the Accord directly connects the typical upstream of a value chain – Global South workers – with its downstream, buyers from the Global North.[81] In this configuration, the Alliance for Bangladesh Worker Safety (the Alliance),[82] yet another non-binding CSR instrument, plays the role of the emblematic 'counter-policy instrument'. A number of US-incorporated global buyers have refused to join the Accord because of its enforceable contractual nature, which includes workers of TNCs' supply chains. This has also been called 'a contributory reason for the existence of two initiatives, the Accord and the Alliance, instead of just one'.[83] Below I scrutinise relevant aspects of these two transnational instruments and the barriers and prospects they represent for forming CSL.

[80] Accord on Fire and Building Safety in Bangladesh [Accord] (13 May 2013) https://bangladesh.wpengine.com/wp-content/uploads/2018/08/2013-Accord.pdf.

[81] ibid.

[82] Alliance for Bangladesh Worker Safety http://www.bangladeshworkersafety.org/who-we-are/about-the-alliance.

[83] J Salminen, 'The Accord on Fire and Building Safety in Bangladesh: A New Paradigm for Limiting Buyers' Liability in Global Supply Chains?' (2018) 66 *AJCL* 411, 416.

The Accord is a 'legally binding agreement between brands and trade unions designed to work towards a safe and healthy Bangladeshi Ready-Made Garment Industry'.[84] In terms of its scope, this agreement is thus significantly limited, covering only fire and building safety in the Bangladeshi garment industry. In terms of form, the Accord is an international legally binding contract, arguably directly enforceable.[85] Moreover, the Accord includes global and Bangladeshi trade unions, which means that employees of the head firms' suppliers are also included in the agreement and have not only the standing, but also some substantive rights, such as the right to refuse unsafe work conditions, for example.[86] Finally, it contains an obligation to end business relationships with any supplier breaching its undertakings under the Accord, as well as the standard disclosure and due diligence obligations of the buyers.[87] All the above obligations represent responsibility for production, services or operations, and hence make part of CSL ex post.

In addition, the Accord requires the buyers to pay suppliers prices taking into account possible repairs, renovations and the overall safe functioning of their factories, and binds suppliers to implementing repairs and renovations as determined in the inspections.[88] Such requirements represent obligations of (re)distribution leading to a CSL ex ante.

The Accord is thus an independent, binding, and directly enforceable agreement between the upstream employees' representatives from the Global South and the downstream first-world global buyers.

Initially intended to last five years, the Accord is now already in its second term, agreed in June 2017 (Transition Accord), extending the application of the programme until 2021.[89] The Transition Accord builds upon the existing provisions regarding most of substantive obligations of the Accord, but with some modifications, especially regarding procedural guarantees. For example, the arbitration clause of the Transition Accord has been significantly changed, thus also modifying the Accord's enforcement mechanism. Indeed, the 2013 Accord's arbitration *compromis* (a compromissory clause) designated the United Nations Commission on International Trade Law (UNCITRAL) Model Law on International Commercial Arbitration 1985 (with amendments as adopted in 2006) as the law governing the disputes.[90]

[84] ibid.

[85] Accord, art 5.

[86] ibid arts 1, 13–15, 16–18. See also Accord Signatories https://bangladeshaccord.org/signatories.

[87] ibid arts 13, 20–21.

[88] ibid arts 12, 21–23.

[89] 2018 Accord on Fire and Building Safety in Bangladesh: May 2018 [Transition Accord] (21 June 2017) https://bangladesh.wpengine.com/wp-content/uploads/2020/11/2018-Accord.pdf.

[90] In full, the 2013 Accord's *compromis* reads as follows: 'Any dispute between the parties to, and arising under, the terms of this Agreement shall first be presented to and decided by the [Steering Committee], which shall decide the dispute by majority vote of the [Steering Committee] within a maximum of 21 days of a petition being filed by one of the parties. Upon request of either party, the decision of the [Steering Committee] may be appealed to a final and binding arbitration process. Any arbitration award shall be enforceable in a court of law of the domicile of the signatory against whom

While there was no clear designation of either arbitration seat or rules involving the ambiguities as to the initiation of arbitration and the jurisdiction, these gaps in the 2013 Accord's *compromis* in theory represented an opportunity because the concerned parties were free to conclude an arbitration agreement.[91] Yet the latter avenue is built on an understanding, prevailing in both orthodox private law and international arbitration, that the parties concluding an arbitration agreement are equal – something which is not often the case in practice. This is definitely not true where the Accord links unequal parties, that is, the Global North buyers and the Global South supplier employees. At the same time, such choice of law was somewhat abstruse, as Roger Alford underlined that

> [i]f a party refuses to arbitrate, there will be no obvious court for the petitioner to file a motion to compel arbitration. Instead the arbitration proceedings are to be governed by the UNCITRAL Model Law on International Commercial Arbitration as a sort of free-floating 'anational' governing clause. I suppose that makes the UNCITRAL Model Law the chosen arbitration rules, but I've never seen the Model Law function in this fashion. If that's what the clause does, then any court where an action is brought can compel arbitration and the arbitral panel will be empowered to fill in most of the gaps, including determining the arbitration seat, the governing law, and the scope of its jurisdiction (See Articles 8, 16, 20, 28). Not ideal, but it may do the trick.[92]

The arbitration seat, the governing law, and the scope of the tribunal's jurisdiction in the two 2016 arbitration claims filed by the trade union parties to the 2013 Accord, UNI Global Union and IndustriALL Global Union, against unnamed fashion brands to the Permanent Court of Arbitration (PCA), were determined exactly pursuant the above methodology predicted by Alford.[93] More precisely, the parties chose The Hague as the seat of arbitration, and chose the 2010 UNCITRAL Arbitration Rules as the applicable law. Two years later, the dispute was settled ordering the brand, which cannot be named under the terms of the settlement, to pay US$ 2 million in compensation to more than 150 garment factories in Bangladesh, and another US$ 300,000 to the two global trade unions that initiated the arbitration.[94]

enforcement is sought and shall be subject to the Convention on the Recognition and Enforcement of Foreign Arbitral Awards (the 'New York Convention'), where applicable. The process for binding arbitration, including, but not limited to, the allocation of costs relating to any arbitration and the process for selection of the Arbitrator, shall be governed by the United Nations Commission on International Trade Law (UNCITRAL) Model Law on International Commercial Arbitration 1985 (with amendments as adopted in 2006)': Accord, art 5.

[91] See eg R Alford, Arbitrating Bangladesh Labor Rights (Part II) http://arbitrationblog.kluwerarbitration.com/2013/05/15/arbitrating-bangladesh-labor-rights-part-ii/.

[92] ibid.

[93] *IndustriALL Global Union & UNI Global Union v Certain Fashion Brands*, PCA Case No 2016-36 and PCA Case No 2016-37.

[94] ibid. See also D Rushe, 'Unions Reach $2.3m Settlement on Bangladesh Textile Factory Safety', *The Guardian* (22 January 2018) https://www.theguardian.com/business/2018/jan/22/bandgladesh-textile-factory-safety-unions-settlement.

Notably, by replacing the commitment to ad hoc arbitration with a pledge to institutional PCA arbitration under the UNCITRAL Arbitration Rules, with The Hague as the only possible seat of arbitration, the new *compromis* in the 2018 version of the Accord has limited any freedom of parties to the dispute to determine the arbitration seat, the governing law, and the jurisdictional scope.[95]

While research and the overall coverage of the new 2018 *compromis* seem almost uniformly optimistic, and see the changes in the original language of the Accord's arbitration clause as improvements,[96] a few critical remarks are in order. First and foremost, the degree of *righteousness* of arbitration as a mode of dispute resolution is directly correlated to the freedom *and* the power of each party to each dispute to determine the arbitration seat, the governing law, and the jurisdiction. Consequently, by committing the Accord's arbitration to only one institution under the determined seat and rules of arbitration, the 2018 Transition Accord jeopardises any previous potential of a redistribution of power in case of dispute in arguably asymmetrical relations between the parties to the Accord. As argued above, under the 2013 *compromis*, impartial ad hoc arbitral tribunals, and not the stronger parties to the Accord, were empowered to fill the gaps, including determining the applicable law, the seat and the jurisdiction of the tribunal in each dispute in an ad hoc manner. Under the 2018 *compromis*, however, those gaps seem to be filled once and for all by those parties to the Accord who have stronger bargaining power. Those are hardly third-world supplier employees.

Regarding the appropriateness of international commercial arbitration as a mode of dispute settlement between buyers and supplier employees more generally, a few other issues arise. To begin with, international commercial arbitration operates within the rubric of the so-called freedom of contract and the will of supposedly equal parties and an international enforcement framework.[97] Those elements distance both arbitral proceedings and enforcement from any oversight and legal safeguards embedded in national law that are intended to protect weaker parties, including employees. I scrutinise that problem and related normative issues of the Accord and of international arbitration more generally as a possible mode of dispute resolution between the first-world head firms and the third-world supplier workers in the more normative analysis in Chapter 9 below.

Coming back to the present discussion, unlike the Accord, which is an international contract between unions representing supplier workers and buyers, the Alliance for Bangladesh Worker Safety is a corporation, domiciled in Delaware

[95] Transition Accord, art 3.

[96] For an overview of the related doctrinal opinions and more general reporting, see generally E Vidak-Gojkovic et al, 'The Medium Is the Message: Establishing a System of Business and Human Rights Through Contract Law and Arbitration' (2018) 35(4) *Journal of International Arbitration* 379. The authors are themselves quite positive about that change. See ibid, 384–87.

[97] M Kerr, 'International Arbitration v. Litigation' (1980) 24 *JBL* 164, 165. Specifically about the parties' consent and the arbitration clauses, see eg JM Jacquet et al, *Droit du commerce international* (Paris, Dalloz, 2007) 751–60; MS Moses, *The Principles and Practice of International Commercial Arbitration* (Cambridge, Cambridge University Press, 2008) 17 and 202–19.

with US buyers as its members, thus excluding any possibility for a realistic representation of the supplier workers.[98] Just like the Accord, the Alliance is said to be a legally binding, five-year programme aimed at improving safety in Bangladeshi ready-made garment factories.[99] Moreover, like the Accord, it provides the possibility of resorting to international arbitration.[100] Unlike the Accord, the Alliance is not a contract, but a 'commitment'.[101] Consequently, the Alliance excludes employee participation and lacks any hard law enforcement on behalf of workers. It has been argued that 'the Alliance superficially resembles the Accord while omitting the Accord's most important substantive elements'.[102] The Alliance thus represents a typical west/US-sanctioned 'counter-policy instrument' aiming at shielding corporations from liability by opting for softer CSR approaches. In addition, the Alliance seems to have frozen since 2018.

The Accord may therefore be seen as a leap from the earlier voluntary self-regulation/CSR constructs discussed in Chapter 2 above, to a binding and enforceable form of CSL. In addition, its enforcement seems to work, thanks to a system of alternative dispute settlement of international arbitration. Some scholars believe that the interface of contract law and international arbitration offers not only a procedural venue of choice for transnational corporate liability disputes, but also an environment fostering both the evolution of related substantive rights and their enforcement and effective redress.[103] Since in this section I have already outlined the main related points of international commercial arbitration, in the following section I look at the relevant events at the interface of corporate liability in GVCs and international investment arbitration.

V. Alternative Dispute Resolution through International Investment Arbitration

GVCs provide for the splitting up of today's capitalistic production and trade processes, and then the outsourcing of different stages of this process to subsidiaries, subcontractors and indirect – beyond first-tier – suppliers. This is done on a global scale, as the GVC organisation dictates the choice of each outsourced task's location depending on the most optimal gains that the location might offer. In terms of corporate organisation, this fragmentation represents intra-firm trade – certainly in situations when the subsidiaries and suppliers (at least, the first-tier

[98] Salminen (n 83) 419.

[99] About the Alliance for Bangladesh Worker Safety, http://www.bangladeshworkersafety.org/who-we-are/about-the-alliance.

[100] Alliance, FAQ, 'Is the Alliance Legally Binding?' http://www.bangladeshworkersafety.org/who-we-are/faq.

[101] ibid.

[102] Salminen (n 83) 419.

[103] See generally Vidak-Gojkovic et al (n 96).

ones) delivering intermediate parts or products to a lead company of a compiling country are situated abroad.[104] In legal terms, the interface of the way GVCs are integrated with the intra-firm trade constitutes FDI.

Beyond relevant domestic private law constructs which I have by now scrutinised in meticulous detail, a particular crossing point of GVCs and FDI is of some interest for the present analysis. Globally, the GVC-FDI nexus is governed by the regime of international – or transnational, or foreign – investment law and arbitration (IILA). The dispute settlement in this regime is part of alternative dispute resolution (ADR), where arbitrators replace judges, and every arbitral tribunal is ad hoc and draws its jurisdiction on a case-by-case basis depending on the arbitration clause in each case. Arbitration agreements could be restricted to 'investment disputes [...] or to alleged violations of the substantive rights in the investment treaty'.[105] They are consistently included in bilateral and multilateral treaties providing the extent of the tribunal's jurisdiction.[106] It is important for the tribunal to assess whether a claimed investment is actually an 'investment' under the related treaty in order to establish its own mandate over a dispute.

A conventional approach to the private investors' international law obligations in IILA is characterised by the 'one-sided' nature of investment treaties as well as of their application and interpretation, providing foreign corporate investors with an asymmetrical right to quasi-judicial review of national regulatory action of host states,[107] including national regulation in the public interest. This approach partially results from a traditional idea of a very narrow jurisdiction of investment tribunals. Such an approach excludes from the jurisdictional scope of investment tribunals any 'extra-economic' considerations – namely, matters not directly related to the investment – such as human rights, the environment, and similar societal matters.[108]

An older generation of investment treaties, especially those concluded before the 2010s, clearly delimit themselves to apply only to breaches of those treaties' obligations, that is, breaches that are directly relevant for investments, thus potentially excluding any concern with CSL relevance.[109] The bulk of traditional IILA

[104] OECD, *Glossary of Statistical Terms*, 'Intra-firm Trade' https://stats.oecd.org/glossary/detail.asp?ID=7262.

[105] LE Peterson and KR Gray, 'International Human Rights in Bilateral Investment Treaties and Investment Treaty Arbitration', (2005) *IISD Research Paper for the Swiss Department of Foreign Affairs* 10.

[106] See Jacquet et al and Moses (both n 97).

[107] J Ostřanský, 'The Termination and Suspension of Bilateral Investment Treaties due to an Armed Conflict' (2015) 6 *Journal of International Dispute Settlement* 136.

[108] C Reiner and CH Schreuer, 'Human Rights and International Investment Arbitration' in PM Dupuy et al (eds), *Human Rights in International Investment Law* (Oxford, Oxford University Press, 2009) 82, 83.

[109] See eg the Energy Charter Treaty (ECT), art 26(1) and (2), which delimit the Treaty's applicability only to breaches of Part III, ie, to breaches of ECT obligations; the North American Free Trade Agreement (NAFTA) art 1116 delimits NAFTA's applicability to only breaches of Section A, ie, to breaches of NAFTA obligations.

scholarship, as well as a number of treaty models, actual treaties, and jurisprudence that could be qualified as 'old-generation', suggest a one-sided and categorical understanding of investment agreements in general, and specifically regarding societal concerns, both in terms of jurisdiction and applicable substantive law.[110]

These restrictions on disputes originating from the breach of a treaty obligation, coupled with the fact that these treaties contain no substantive standards relating to human rights, environmental protection and similar societal concerns, result in arbitral tribunals often declaring a lack of competence to rule on claims involving issues with CSL relevance.[111] In this regard, the ICSID decision in *Urbaser* represents something of a break from the traditional understanding of investment treaties and the jurisdiction they grant to tribunals concerning CSL-related issues.[112] In their ruling, the arbitrators dismissed the complainant company's objection regarding the asymmetric nature of investment treaties that, in the latter's view, prevented the host state from invoking any right based on the applicable treaty.[113]

The *Urbaser* arbitral award represents a modest yet critical shift relevant for establishing transnational corporate liability. First and foremost, the arbitrators stated that an investment dispute and a human rights claim were not mutually exclusive.[114] Second, they ruled that since corporations were the right-holders under international investment agreements, they were subjects of international law and thus also bound by obligations in international law, including international human rights obligations.[115] Last but not least, the tribunal underlined that CSR was 'a standard of crucial importance for companies operating in the field of international commerce'.[116]

To sum up, as demonstrated by the *Urbaser* decision, investment arbitrators do not necessarily need new treaty formulations of substantive societal obligations of investors to exercise a kind of judicial assertiveness to rule that TNCs along with states are subjects of international law, bearing international human

[110] Reiner and Schreuer (n 108) 82. Before the 2010s, the Model BITs of China (2003), France (2006), Germany (2005), the UK (2005) and the US (2004) were silent about human rights or clearer references to the environment, sustainable development, etc. See R Dolzer and C Schreuer, *Principles of International Investment Law* (Oxford, Oxford University Press, 2008) 352, 360, 368, 376 and 385. For the most illustrious mentions in case law, see eg *Compañia del Desarrollo de Santa Elena SA v Republic of Costa Rica*, ICSID Case No ARB/96/1, Award, 17 September 2000, paras 71–72.

[111] A Aseeva and KL Yip, 'Stakes and Prospects of the Right to Free, Prior & Informed Consent in "One Belt One Road" Projects in the context of Transnational Investment Law and Arbitration' in J Chaisse and J Górski (eds), *The Belt and Road Initiative. Law, Economics, and Politics* (Leiden, BRILL-Nijhoff, 2018) 523, 525.

[112] A Aseeva, '(Un)Sustainable Development(s) in International Economic Law: a Quest for Sustainability' (2018) 10(11) *Sustainability* 4022, 4030.

[113] The arbitral tribunal referred to the arbitration clause of the Spain-Argentina BIT, namely, art X (1); Aseeva ibid.

[114] *Urbaser SA and Consorcio de Aguas Bilbao Bizkaia, Bilbao Biskaia Ur Partzuergoa v The Argentine Republic*, Award, 8 December 2016, ICSID Case No ARB/07/26, para 1154.

[115] ibid paras 1155 and 1194.

[116] *Urbaser*, para 1195.

rights obligations owed to adversely affected third parties, among others. In cases of claims by employees, local population, civil society, or consumers, the appropriateness of international investment arbitration may still be far from obvious. This is because the means allowed by international arbitration, including party autonomy and the secrecy of proceedings, are likely to block otherwise available national public law and, for that matter, public policy remedies.

Beyond IILA, the use of international law in general, and particularly international human rights law, may be one possibility for weaker private parties. This could be done through a recognition of the TNC's home state international human rights obligation to provide an effective remedy and thus develop a civil remedy in domestic law for corporate violations of the customary international law that is part of the law of that state. This could be possible either through the development of new torts or through a direct remedy for violations of customary international law. I consider this avenue, especially in light of the 2020 *Nevsun* ruling in the different sections further in this part. In the remainder of this chapter I outline some other mechanisms, both domestic and transnational, for making CSL work for weaker private parties.

VI. Enforcing Corporate Social Liability ex ante

When hard law mechanisms do not work as expected, public and social quasi-judicial enforcement could fill those gaps. That is to say, apart from judicialisation and direct legalisation, an increasing and arguably efficient pressure on corporations could be exerted through relevant monitoring and reporting, as well as through market and social pressure. This line of reasoning also corresponds to the relevant claims of management and business ethics research, mentioned in Chapter 1, section IV.B, about various degrees of obligations of social responsiveness of corporations to market forces and legal constraints, as well as prevailing social norms, values, expectations, and needs.

Lack of legal enforceability does not mean lack of effective implementation. Specifically, one prospect for a CSL alternative to an adjudicatory enforcement of liability ex post could be a quasi-adjudicatory enforcement ex ante, such as monitoring. Monitoring mechanisms, involvement of local actors, representativeness of the signatory parties, etc could all be methods of CSL enforcement ex ante.

At a transnational level, as I have already partially demonstrated in the analysis of the Bangladesh Accord, there is a role to play for global trade union associations and local trade unions. For example, '[i]n two cases in Brazil, a local trade union in a highly organized auto plant invoked the GFA signed by the parent TNC in support of union officials at suppliers to the plant who had been fired'.[117]

[117] J Sydow et al, 'Implementation of Global Framework Agreements: Towards a Multi-organizational Practice Perspective' (2014) 20(4) *Transfer: European Review of Labour and Research* 489, 491.

Another prospect is the role of trade and commercial associations in at least three instances, namely in: (i) the creation of GVC-wide standard contracts; (ii) the mediation of potential and fledgling disputes, and also, to some extent (iii) a role in the enforcement of chain-wide standards, including CSR codes, IFAs/GFAs/TCAs, etc.

Lastly, and perhaps slightly more pragmatically – or at least effectively – CSL could be enforced through related activities of dedicated state agencies acting as quasi-enforcers. To wit, the French competition and consumer protection watchdog *Direction Générale de la Concurrence, de la Consommation et de la Répression des Fraudes* (DGCCRF) recently issued fines to such large retailers as Casino and Intermarché for abusive relationships with their suppliers,[118] while it took Amazon to court for similar practices.[119] It equally offers an alternative means of relevant conflict resolution, including mediation.[120]

A 'CSL' mediation is also possible at a transnational level. OECD National Contact Points (NCPs) offer ADR through mediation between the civil society, labour unions and other worker organisations, and the business community on any subject related to the implementation of the OECD Guidelines.[121] In situations where an individual, a community or an organisation consider that non-compliance with the OECD Guidelines has occurred, they can reach out to NCP for a dialogue aimed at helping the parties to discuss the conflict and reach a compromise.[122] In Canada, for example, a company acting in non-compliance or bad faith may lose the government's trade support at home and abroad and, if the corporation continues such behaviour, it may potentially lose project finance credit and other types of financing and overall support from Export Development Canada.[123]

The final point above, about financing the projects abroad, raises a more important avenue for CSL enhancement. Regarding a CSL enforcement ex ante, both state/institutional and private investors must carry out rigorous due diligence to avoid investing in companies that affect people and the environment through their business activities.[124] Then, public and institutional investors could threaten the firms with the withdrawal of money, and, in case of non-compliance, actually do so. For instance, regional or international banks who finance developmental

[118] DGCRRF, 'Sanctions' https://www.economie.gouv.fr/dgccrf/sanctions-protection-economique-des-consommateurs.

[119] ibid.

[120] DGCRRF, 'Resoudre un litige de consommation' https://www.economie.gouv.fr/dgccrf/consommation/Resoudre-un-litige-de-consommation.

[121] See Chapter 4, section II.B above.

[122] Global Affairs Canada, 'Canada's National Contact Point for the Organisation for Economic Co-operation and Development Guidelines for Multinational Enterprises' https://www.international.gc.ca/trade-agreements-accords-commerciaux/ncp-pcn/index.aspx?lang=eng.

[123] ibid.

[124] See eg Forum pour l'investissement responsable, 'Chaîne d'approvisionnement et investissement responsable' https://www.frenchsif.org/isr-esg/wp-content/uploads/Cahier_FIR-A2_ChaineApprovisionnement.pdf.

projects should withdraw their funding from societally unsustainable projects that they finance.

More precisely, the Investor Alliance for Human Rights invites all institutional investors to sign up to a statement entitled The Investor Case for Mandatory Human Rights Due Diligence. The statement calls on all governments to develop, implement, and enforce mandatory human rights due diligence (MHRDD) requirements for all companies headquartered or operating within their own jurisdictions or, where appropriate, to further strengthen these regulatory regimes where they already exist.[125] Private investors can use their leverage to ensure that portfolio companies do not engage in practices that damage individuals, communities and the environment through their cross-border activities.[126]

* * *

To summarise this chapter, I submit that private law regimes such as contract law and tort law should be reinforced by the models of relevant public oversight. Major challenges to private – tort, and especially contract-focused – modes of determining and enforcing liability are the legal construction of the contents of relevant legal relationships, the nature of relationships beyond privity, and the use of private ordering to limit liability materially and procedurally. Hence, effective regulation and public governance of GVCs, including monitoring and public-social oversight by civil society, global and local trade unions and commercial associations, state agencies, private and institutional investors and individual citizens, are necessary to complement the private law side of the subject matter.

[125] Business and Human Rights Resource Centre, 'Open for Sign-on: Statement on the Investor Case for Mandatory Human Rights Due Diligence' (25 November 2019) https://www.business-humanrights.org/en/latest-news/un-forum-2019-statements-session-content/#c199448.

[126] See eg Business and Human Rights Resource Centre, 'Advocacy through the Courts' (20 November 2019) https://www.business-humanrights.org/en/from-us/briefings/silencing-the-critics-how-big-polluters-try-to-paralyse-environmental-and-human-rights-advocacy-through-the-courts/.

8

The Reality and Prospects of European and International Law of Corporate Liability in Global Value Chains

I. European Law

In Chapter 4, I discussed the fact that there was not (yet) any EU-wide due diligence regulation. In 2020, the debate on such or similar pan-European instrument has intensified, so, we can expect the creation of such a general EU legislation in the coming years (see section A below). I then considered the major GVC due diligence instruments that exist to date in EU law. Two of them, the EU Timber Regulation and the EU Conflict Minerals Regulation are further analysed in this part of the chapter (in sections B and C, respectively). While in Part II of this book I merely described them, the analysis made in Part III, including different degrees of CSL disciplines as well as various modes of influence within GVCs, now allows me to assess those two regulations in light of the main questions of this book. The scrutiny of the gaps in the scope and effectiveness of the existing EU sectoral GVC regulations also informs the extent of the normativity and efficiency of any prospective EU-wide intersectoral due diligence regulation.

A. Towards EU-wide Due Diligence Regulation?

As mentioned, the EU already has sector-specific GVC regulations applying, among others, to illegal timber and conflict minerals. According to its commitments under the Paris Agreement, the EU has yet to enact rules applying to the interface of global deforestation with EU trade and consumer regulation.[1] More precisely, it must improve its forest governance, regulate land use as well as its

[1] The Independent Nationally Determined Contributions (INDCs) were created by the Ad Hoc Working Group on the Durban Platform for Enhanced Action (ADP) as a means to get voluntary contribution plans from countries for inclusion in a mandatory agreement at the Conferences of the Parties (COPs) 19 and 20, now make part of the Paris Agreement https://unfccc.int/process-and-meetings/the-paris-agreement/the-paris-agreement/nationally-determined-contributions-ndcs. See also European Parliament, 'Outcomes of COP 22 climate change conference,' (2016) http://www.europarl.europa.eu/RegData/etudes/ATAG/2016/593547/EPRS_ATA(2016)593547_EN.pdf.

imports of agricultural commodities, namely trade and consumption of so-called 'forest-risk commodities' such as soya, palm oil, beef, leather and cocoa.

On 29 April 2020, the European Justice Commissioner Didier Reynders stated that the Commission committed itself to creating an instrument on mandatory corporate environmental and human rights due diligence. He did not specify in any detail the concrete form of the rules, timeframe, possible dates of its introduction and enactment, etc.[2]

Before that statement, on 5 November 2019, the European Parliament's committees on international trade (INTA), human rights (DROI), and environment (ENVI) requested a new EU regulation to address global deforestation.[3] However, at the moment it is unclear whether that would be: (i) an EU-wide due diligence regulation applying to GVCs of all forest-risk commodities; (ii) a measure limiting market access for those commodities; or (iii) a label.[4]

If it were to be the last of these options, the introduction of an EU labelling scheme marking deforestation-free goods is likely to shift the burden of tackling the EU's forest footprint, and thus also the responsibility, from regulators and companies to consumers.[5] Such a measure would also mean that regulators agree to allow products causing deforestation and human rights abuses to continue to be available on the EU market. The adoption of a measure regulating market access for such products is highly unlikely, as the EU may find itself in breach of its WTO obligations, as well as those under the myriad of FTAs. In this light, a due diligence regulation applying to GVCs of forest-risk commodities could be seen as an optimal solution. In practice, however, European due diligence regulations in other sectors, such as timber and minerals, seem to have controversial scope and effects. In the remainder of this section I address the particular issues with those two regulations.

B. The EU Timber Regulation: A Questionable Effectiveness

From Chapter 4 we know that the EUTR carries mandatory due diligence obligations for operators in the timber sector,[6] as well as the obligation of traceability. The latter means that traders should be able to identify both ends of their business, that

[2] H Hautala, 'EU is Well Placed to Show Leadership with its Future Due Diligence Legislation' (27 May 2020) https://heidihautala.fi/en/eu-is-well-placed-to-show-leadership-with-its-future-due-diligence-legislation/.

[3] Renew Europe Group, 'EU must be United at the COP 25 in Madrid' https://reneweuropegroup.eu/en/news/1365-eu-must-be-united-at-the-cop-25-in-madrid/.

[4] Business and Human Rights Resource Centre, 'EU-wide Due Diligence Regulation' https://www.business-humanrights.org/en/latest-news/eu-parliament-committees-on-environment-trade-human-rights-affirm-support-for-eu-wide-due-diligence-regulation/.

[5] See the detailed discussion on the sustainability labelling schemes in Chapter 3, section II.A.i.

[6] Regulation (EU) No 995/2010 of the European Parliament and of the Council of 20 October 2010 laying down the obligations of operators who place timber and timber products on the market. Text with EEA relevance [2010] OJ L 295/23, art 4(2).

is, both the purchase and sales ends of each transaction they performed, as well as keep that information for at least five years and provide it to competent authorities upon request.[7] The most recent statistics show, however, that most global forestry companies producing wooden furniture or paper not only fail to protect their employees from various risks, including forced labour, but even fail to disclose the relevant human rights and environmental information and performance.[8]

Take, for example, the Russian Federation, one of the world's leading timber exporters and the EU's primary source of related imports.[9] Immediately before the creation of the EUTR, according to official data from the country's Federal Forestry Agency (*Рослесхоз* – Rosleskhoz), roughly a quarter of all timber harvested in Russia in 2010 was of illegal or at least questionable origin.[10]

Since the EUTR came in force, Russia has only increased its massive timber exports: in 2015, it exported EUTR-regulated products to 118 countries and territories, totalling 41.04 billion kg, of which 26.7 per cent was exported to the then-EU-28 by weight and 34 per cent by value.[11] Illegal logging remains a significant issue (estimated 20 per cent of logging nationwide in 2016 was illegal),[12] particularly in the country's Far East (an estimated 80 per cent of its Far East logging in 2013 was illegal), where, as investigations show, illegally harvested hardwoods are massively exported to China.[13]

The EU is Russia's primary timber importing partner, but it has high sustainability standards. For these reasons, Russian timber exports potentially face the strictest due diligence and related requirements in the EU. However, according to article 2 of the EUTR, one of the requirements for imported timber to be legal is to simply respect the relevant legal framework of its country of origin. Since the EUTR has been in force, all Russian operators who formally respect the applicable Russian legal framework,[14] and participate in relevant certification systems or at least in appropriate CSR schemes, are in theory exporting legally to the EU market. The most common certification systems in which the companies could participate are the related WWF systems and the Forest Stewardship Council (FSC). Wood carrying a FLEGT (EU Forest Law Enforcement, Governance and Trade Action Plan) licence, or a CITES (Convention on International Trade in

[7] Regulation 995/2010, art 5.

[8] Business and Human Rights Resource Centre https://www.business-humanrights.org/en/blog/largest-forestry-companies-are-failing-to-combat-forced-labour-in-their-supply-chains/.

[9] European Commission, DG Environment, *Russian Federation Country Overview to Aid Implementation of the EUTR* (2018), 3 http://ec.europa.eu/environment/forests/pdf/Country_overview_Russian_Federation_03_10_2018.pdf.

[10] Russian Federal Forestry Agency (*Рослесхоз* [Rosleskhoz]), *Claims* (2010) http://rosleshoz.gov.ru/statements/answers.

[11] United Nations Statistics Division, UN Comtrade Database (2017) https://comtrade.un.org/data/.

[12] European Commission (n 9) 3.

[13] EIA, *Liquidating the forests: hardwood flooring, organised crime and the World's last Siberian tigers.* EIA (2013) https://content.eia-global.org/posts/documents/000/000/609/original/EIA_Liquidating_the_Forests.pdf?1479504214.

[14] Regulation 995/2010, art 2(g).

Endangered Species of Wild Fauna and Flora) permit, is considered to comply with the EUTR.[15]

In practice, however, the situation is very different. First, Russia has been a member of CITES since 1992, actually succeeding as part of the former USSR, which had been party to CITES since 1976.[16] Thus, the condition to participate in relevant CSR or international certification schemes is formally met by virtually all Russian timber exporters, because all EUTR-covered Russian timber exporters are likely to have a valid CITES permit. Second, the current Russian 'law-on-the-books' is almost silent about the conservation of both biodiversity and nature in general[17] and does not seem to effectively tackle the particular problem of illegal logging.[18] Notably, only about two per cent of all Russian forests are situated in protected areas,[19] which means that the rest is not protected from logging by law, or at least is in a legislative grey area. Moreover, relevant Russian 'law-in-action' seems to drastically differ from the books. Indeed, while legislation is formally respected on paper, most illegal logging occurs through deliberate misuse of an actual issuance of permits, such as sanitary logging permits, or overharvesting relative to permits actually issued.[20] Therefore, even if the condition of EUTR article 2, stipulating that imported timber must respect its country of origin relevant legal framework, is formally met by Russian timber exporters, both Russia's relevant legal framework itself and the actual situation in its national logging sector are more than questionable.

The above analytical grid applied to Russian timber exports is likely also to reveal the actual illegality of timber 'legally' imported to the EU under the EUTR from other large third-country timber producers. For example, this could fairly be said to apply in the cases of Brazil and Peru.[21] Moreover, human rights violations take place not only outside, but also inside, the EU. A 2019 study showed that forestry workers, particularly migrant ones, in Estonia and the Czech Republic are

[15] European Commission, DG Environment, *EUTR: Frequently Asked Questions* http://ec.europa.eu/environment/eutr2013/faq/index_en.htm.

[16] Convention on International Trade in Endangered Species of Wild Fauna and Flora (CITES) https://www.cites.org/eng/cms/index.php/component/cp/country/RU.

[17] Notably, most Russian legislation on environment and ecology dates of the 1990s or at best early 2000s, except the intriguing Regional Law No 81 OZ 'On some issues of the status of the head of village' [2018]: FAO, *FAO LEX Database* http://www.fao.org/faolex/country-profiles/general-profile/en/?iso3=RUS.

[18] Rosleskhoz, *Legal and Regulatory Documents*, last update 17 January 2020, http://rosleshoz.gov.ru/documents/federal; NEPCon (Nature Economy and People Connected), *Timber Legality Risk Assessment: Russia, 2017* https://www.nepcon.org/sites/default/files/library/2017-06/TIMBER-Russia-Risk-Assessment.pdf; Forest Legality Initiative (FLI), Report *Russian Federation*, 2016 https://forestlegality.org/risk-tool/country/russian-federation.

[19] FAO, *Global Forest Resources Assessment 2015. Desk reference* (2015); UNEP-WCMC, *Protected Area Profile for the Russian Federation from the World Database of Protected Areas*, 2018 https://www.protectedplanet.net/country/RU.

[20] European Commission (n 9) 3.

[21] See eg US Department of Labor, '2018 List of Goods Produced by Child Labor or Forced Labor' https://www.dol.gov/sites/dolgov/files/ILAB/ListofGoods.pdf, 14.

subject to forced labour through debt bondage schemes, forcing them to work to pay off debt to their employers.[22]

On the company front, a 2019 study of 39 of the largest publicly listed firms in the paper and forestry and wooden furniture retail sectors, including several European companies, revealed that most of them are failing to protect their employees from forced labour. Disclosure-wise, the study showed that while 59 per cent of the surveyed firms follow a supplier code of conduct including the ILO core labour standards such as the right to freedom of association, only 8 per cent (three out of 39 surveyed companies) include provisions prohibiting worker-paid recruitment fees.[23] This may, however, trap migrant workers into debt bondage as explained above. Regarding due diligence, only 8 per cent of the survey's participants actually do assess forced labour risks in different tiers of their value chains.[24] In terms of liability, or at least of remedy, only 5 per cent of firms have a mechanism for lodging a complaint and/or reporting violations of their supplier code of conduct, thus revealing an enormous underreporting of actual violations.[25] None of the 39 survey participants said that they had engaged with labour unions in their value chains.[26] Both timber GVCs and their current regulation are thus characterised by low levels of actual company liability, remedies, due diligence, and even of the disclosure performance.

The specialists working with forestry, the *KnowTheChain* project, say that:

> [t]he world's forestry sector has a systemic problem of forced labour, and right now companies show a lack of action to address this appalling abuse. Responsible investors have a role to play in ensuring the people carrying out logging or producing pulp, paper or wooden furniture are safe from forced labour and exploitation. […] Forestry investors [may] drive meaningful change in this sector, avoid risk, and protect workers from forced labour and abuse.[27]

Note that institutional investment in forestry has multiplied ten-fold in less than 20 years, from an estimated US$ 10–15 billion in the early 2000s to over US$ 100 billion in 2019.[28]

These empirical examples show that the main EUTR due diligence obligations of timber operators, specifically those requiring them to verify the legality of timber imports (articles 4(1) and 5 EUTR) either by themselves or through relevant

[22] US Department of State, 'Trafficking in Persons Report' (June 2019) https://www.state.gov/wp-content/uploads/2019/06/2019-Trafficking-in-Persons-Report.pdf, 171 and 190.

[23] Business and Human Rights Resource Centre, the *KnowTheChain* project, https://media.business-humanrights.org/media/documents/files/KTC_Forestry_appendix.pdf.

[24] ibid.

[25] ibid.

[26] ibid.

[27] Business and Human Rights Resource Centre, 'Largest forestry companies are failing to combat forced labour in their supply chains' https://www.business-humanrights.org/en/blog/largest-forestry-companies-are-failing-to-combat-forced-labour-in-their-supply-chains/.

[28] Business and Human Rights Resource Centre (n 23).

certification schemes,[29] and through relevant legal frameworks of the timber's country of origin (article 2(g) EUTR) seem to have limited actual effectiveness.

C. The EU Conflict Minerals Regulation: Questionable Scope and Application

The EUCMR lays down mineral supply chain due diligence obligations for EU importers of the four 'conflict' minerals, ie tin, tantalum, tungsten, and gold originating from conflict-affected and risk areas, if the imports exceed the threshold, which is to be amended every three years after 1 January 2021. According to the Regulation, such importers have a duty to comply with the due diligence obligations, particularly to carry out internal and external risk management in their mineral supply chain, and to report annually on current due diligence practices and policies for responsible sourcing. The EUCMR generally emphasises compliance and not sanctions. The relevant Member States' authorities are empowered to inspect compliance with due diligence obligations through the ex-post checks and determine responsibility in case of infringement. National tort laws of negligence and tortious liability hence theoretically apply also to violations that constitute unlawful acts towards third parties. Yet the application of liability in tort will depend on each jurisdiction.

In France, for instance, the final version of the Vigilance law, adopted after the revisions and due opinion of the French Constitutional Council, excludes the paragraphs providing for the imposition of fines for a tort of negligence due to harmed individuals.[30] As outlined in Chapter 7, section III, the basis of this decision is the French principle of legality of the offences and punishments stemming from article 8 of the DDHC, requiring that a sanction having the character of a punishment can repress only violations defined in sufficiently accurate and exact terms.[31] In this context, it is also not clear whether the appropriate penalties, such as fines for liability in tort, will apply in France under the EUCMR either. Indeed, if the French Constitutional Council maintains that the terms 'human rights' and 'fundamental freedoms', as well as the scope of the actors and activities covered by the Vigilance plans, are terms that are not sufficiently clear and precise for the French civil law to apply to related violations, the implementation of the EUCMR can expect a similar fate in France.

Regarding the scope of the application of the EUCMR, while its jurisdictional scope is rather restricted (ie it only applies to four minerals), the potential geographic scope of the regulation is global. Unlike the Dodd-Frank Act, which

[29] Regulation 995/2010, arts 4(1) and 5.

[30] See Chapter 7, section III.

[31] France, Constitutional Council, *La décision n° 2017-750 DC du Conseil constitutionnel* du 23 mars 2017, considérant n°13.

applies only to the Democratic Republic of the Congo and nine neighbouring countries, the EUCMR covers commodities and products from mining operations in conflict or high-risk areas around the world. Such areas include those in a situation of armed conflict or fragile post-conflict areas, and ones characterised by weak and/or non-existent governance and security, such as a failed state, and by routine and systematic violations of international law, including human rights abuses.[32]

In other words, operators from all countries that export to the EU, whether they export raw materials or metals produced from these four minerals, potentially fall within the scope of the regulation's due diligence regime.[33] The absence of a positive list of areas covered, however, creates a risk of inconsistency as well as of irregular compliance. More precisely, the question of whether a region is a conflict area or a high-risk one requires an evaluation that can sometimes produce quite ambivalent results.[34]

Businesses that are covered by the Regulation will, therefore, face the risk of breaches even in cases when they are unable to determine with certainty whether a particular region with which they work is one of the areas covered by the EUCMR. Two devices have been designed within the EU to mitigate these risks. First, the Commission has been tasked with introducing guidelines for economic operators, to create certainty and coherence between the practices of economic operators, in particular small- and medium-sized enterprises (SMEs), around the world.[35] These guidelines should explain the best way to determine and apply the criteria for identifying conflict and high-risk areas under the Regulation.[36]

Furthermore, the Commission was tasked with compiling a list of conflict-affected and high-risk areas, based on expert analysis.[37] More precisely, the EUCMR's relevant provisions say that this list must be updated regularly and companies operating in covered areas which are not on the list must also comply with the due diligence requirements.[38] Thus, the list helps but will not eliminate the risks of uncertainty, irregularity and breaches of all kinds. For if a region is on the list of conflict and high-risk areas, a company will probably be inclined to treat

[32] Regulation 2017/821, art 2(f).

[33] European Commission, DG Trade, *Combatting Conflict Minerals* (7 March 2019) http://ec.europa.eu/trade/policy/in-focus/conflict-minerals-regulation/index_en.htm.

[34] This is especially the case of intra-state armed conflicts, where the border between armed conflict, violence and a high-risk situation is not so clear-cut and easily defined, especially in terms of international law.

[35] European Commission (n 33).

[36] Regulation 2017/821, art 14(1).

[37] ibid art 14(2). For details, see also the Commission Recommendation (EU) 2018/1149 of 10 August 2018 on non-binding guidelines for the identification of conflict-affected and high-risk areas and other supply chain risks under Regulation (EU) 2017/821 of the European Parliament and of the Council, C/2018/5367 [2018] OJ L 208/94, point 11.

[38] A Aseeva 'Développements récents en matière de la protection des droits de l'Homme et de l'environnement dans les chaines globales de valeur' in C Titi (ed), *Droits de l'homme et droit international économique* (Brussels, Bruylant, 2019) 76.

it as such, even if its assessment suggests otherwise. If a region is not on the list, a company could either avoid the region or make its own assessment. In any case, the companies importing into the EU the minerals and products covered by the EUCMR will have to apply a kind of precautionary principle. This means that, in case of insufficient information, operations in an ambiguous area will rather be altogether avoided. The positive effects of such excessive precaution on European as well as global trade do not appear to be clear cut.[39]

Additionally, the EUCMR directly addresses EU-based companies operating in the value chains of industries that use the four covered minerals in their production. These industries primarily include the electronics, aerospace, automotive and communications sectors.[40] Companies in these sectors potentially use minerals within the scope of the regulation to produce such goods as computers, smartphones, cars and aircraft. According to the Commission's estimations, the EUCMR will apply directly to European importers, ie between 600 and 1 000 companies, and will indirectly concern more than 500 smelters and refineries of the four minerals, whether or not they are located on the territory of the EU.[41]

Similar to the French Vigilance law and the EUTR, the EUCMR stipulates that EU importers of the covered minerals must establish a pre-verification programme for the entire chain and keep a paper-trail of documents to demonstrate compliance with the obligations imposed by the Regulation, including the results of third-party independent audits. Companies exercising due diligence must check *à la source* because in this way they can ensure outright that they are not contributing to the funding of a conflict or other high-risk practices covered by the EUCMR.[42]

The EUCMR requires importers to follow the OECD due diligence guidance for GVCs of conflict minerals,[43] which sets out five due diligence steps:

(i) establish sound business management systems;
(ii) identify and assess the risks associated with the supply chain;
(iii) design and implement a strategy to respond to identified risks;
(iv) perform an independent third-party audit of the due diligence in the supply chain; and
(v) publish annually a report on the exercise of the due diligence in the supply chain.[44]

The covered operators must also set up a chain of custody or a system of traceability of their supply chain, including a detailed description of the covered minerals with their trade name and type; the name and address of covered suppliers to whom the EU importer has addressed himself; the country of origin of the covered minerals; the quantities, volume or weight, of extracted minerals, including the

[39] ibid.
[40] ibid 77.
[41] European Commission (n 33).
[42] Regulation 2017/821, art 5(1) pts (a) and (b); *Commission Recommendation (EU) 2018/1149*.
[43] See Chapter 4, section II.B.
[44] Regulation 2017/821, art 4.

date of extraction, etc.[45] In short, compliance with the EUCMR will require a great deal of information, documents and verification from the Member States, and also, especially, from the concerned companies.

In practice, however, chances are high that the volume and diversity of the data needed to comply with the EUCMR may involve such significant extra costs for the covered operators that they might then pass them on to the customers down the value chain, or – more likely in the mining sector – to the workers, most of whom are in the Global South, for example by reducing their wages, social benefits or similar elements of a labour package.

Quite similarly to the French Vigilance law, the EUCMR covers EU-based operators working with minerals and processed products thereof whose annual import volumes exceed certain defined thresholds.[46] However, notably, most of the covered operators – typically, the smelters and refineries – at the upstream of the relevant minerals value chains, are not based in the EU, for the simple reason that the deposits of those minerals and hence the upstream operation facilities are situated outside the EU. The importers of the concerned minerals and related metals are also bound by the EUCMR. However, contrary to the Dodd-Frank Act, the downstream users of the covered minerals operating beyond the metals phase, including EU importers of finished products containing those minerals, do not appear to be bound by the regulation.[47]

All in all, the EUCMR particularly addresses the operators at the downstream of relevant value chains – such as the value chains of electronics, aerospace, automotive and communications sectors – and thus, mostly companies from the Global North. At the same time, it generally exempts the operators at the upstream of related production who are typically situated in the Global South. Therefore, a number of EU firms may be adversely encouraged by the regulation to simply strategically relocate outside the EU any stages of production that strictly fall within the EUCMR scope yet are possibly movable – in particular, the processing of products that still fall within the metals phase. In addition, in post-Brexit Europe, those EU companies that would decide to strategically relocate outside the EU in the EUCMR context, may now simply relocate to the UK if no relevant legislation restricting such relocation is introduced.

To summarise section I, both the EUTR and the EUCMR apply to industries whose end products – printer paper, smartphones, computers, furniture, cars – are necessary for a 'normal' everyday life in the first world, but whose extraction and processing of raw materials presents a threat to the third world people and environment. Both industries bear a very high risk of illegal labour and harmful environmental practices, including forced labour, illegal logging, and the like. The above regulations, however, seem to work as a 'therapeutic disclosure' for companies that continue the high-risk operations. In terms of CSL disciplines, both the

[45] ibid.

[46] See Regulation 2017/821, Annex I.

[47] European Commission (n 33).

EUTR and the EUCMR are compliance-based instruments and go no further than step two of CSL – ie due diligence disciplines.

The question arises whether investors in companies who produce smartphones and computers, paper and timber products, should (or indeed could) try to influence those rich-country final producers to adopt and follow new and better business practices. This would probably trigger the hardening effects of CSL through influencing the social processes, which would likely be a new type of CSL and of law- and norm-making that I partially addressed in Chapter 7 and discuss in further chapters of this book. Regarding a more traditional – 'legalistic' – means, at the international level, lawyers from all over the world are working hard to create the binding language of liability for a prospective international treaty on business and human rights. I analyse the results of those efforts to date and their likely future developments in the section below.

II. International Business and Human Rights Framework: Guiding or Binding the Global Business?

In Chapter 4, I introduced the two main sets of international initiatives that until recently framed the business and human rights approach in international law. The UNGPs represent the first global effort to achieve corporate liability under voluntary guidelines, while the OECD Guidelines for TNCs represent allegedly more detailed and concrete relevant actions. My analysis suggested that neither appeared efficient, because of the limits of the scope and substance of the instruments. For example, the main subjects of both initiatives are states. Moreover, the UNGPs, in their principle 2, lower the extraterritorial duty of states to protect human rights, especially their duty to oversee and influence the corporations they are in a position to persuade.

Those, and other problems highlighted in Chapter 4, have triggered a process of negotiating an international treaty on the issue of business and human rights, the TBHR.[48] In this section I therefore delve into the most recent developments regarding the binding norms of corporate liability in GVCs based on human rights due diligence in international law.

The first draft of the TBHR, the so-called zero draft, was released in 2018,[49] and a revised version was published on 16 July 2019.[50] At the time of writing, the

[48] UN Human Rights Council, *Resolution 26/9 Elaboration of an international legally binding instrument on transnational corporations and other business enterprises with respect to human rights* (A/HRC/RES/26/9), 14 July 2014.

[49] Open-Ended Intergovernmental Working Group on Transnational Corporations and Other Business Enterprises With Respect to Human Rights (IGWG), *Zero draft of a legally binding instrument to regulate, in international human rights law, the activities of transnational corporations and other business enterprises* [Zero draft] (16 June 2018) https://www.ohchr.org/Documents/HRBodies/HRCouncil/WGTransCorp/Session3/DraftLBI.pdf.

[50] IGWG, *Revised draft of a legally binding instrument to regulate, in international human rights law, the activities of transnational corporations and other business enterprises* [Revised draft] (16 July 2019)

revised draft forms the basis for negotiations at the textual level, as of the fifth session (14–18 October 2019) of the Open-ended Intergovernmental Working Group (OEIGWG) mandated by the UN Human Rights Council.[51] The aspects of the revised draft that are relevant for this analysis comprise the scope of the proposed treaty and the procedural questions (see section A below), as well as its implementation, including controversial due diligence and liability-related matters (see section B below).

A. The TBHR Revised Draft: A Procedural and Substantive Outlook

The scope of the proposed TBHR embraces all corporations, namely 'all business enterprises', and not just TNCs, while still focusing on operations with a transborder reach.[52] Whereas this expansion is seen as significant by some commentators,[53] article 3(1) of the revised draft limits the scope by including 'except as stated otherwise' and 'substantial effect', which constitutes an unnecessary limitation to liability that is indispensable in confronting the TBHR's bottlenecks.[54]

The revised draft also looks at the consistency of the future treaty with PIEL, and especially international trade and investment agreements. Yet it seems that the draft aims to keep the status quo regarding relevant international treaties, as it calls for the states parties to:

> agree that any bilateral or multilateral agreements, including regional or sub-regional agreements, on issues relevant to this (Legally Binding Instrument) and its protocols, shall be compatible and shall be interpreted in accordance with their obligations under this (Legally Binding Instrument) and its protocols.[55]

However, given that a growing number of international trade and investment treaties, including regional and sub-regional ones, provide for the promotion of responsible business conduct,[56] more consideration could have been given to the

https://www.ohchr.org/Documents/HRBodies/HRCouncil/WGTransCorp/OEIGWG_RevisedDraft_LBI.pdf.

[51] UN Human Rights Council, the Open ended Intergovernmental Working Group [OEIGWG] https://www.ohchr.org/en/hrbodies/hrc/wgtranscorp/pages/igwgontnc.aspx.

[52] TBHR, Revised draft (n 50) art 3.

[53] N Bernaz, 'Clearer, Stronger, Better? – Unpacking the 2019 Draft Business and Human Rights Treaty' (19 July 2019), *Rights as Usual* http://rightsasusual.com/?p=1339; M Mullen, 'Keeping Perspective – Article 30 Commentary on the Revised Draft of the Proposed BHR Treaty', *Business & Human Rights Resource Centre* https://www.business-humanrights.org/en/blog/keeping-perspective-article-30-commentary-on-the-revised-draft-of-the-proposed-bhr-treaty/.

[54] Mullen, ibid.

[55] Revised draft (n 50) art 12(6).

[56] See eg Agreement Between Canada and the Federal Republic of Senegal for the Promotion and Protection of Investments (Canada-Senegal BIT) (signed 27 November 2014, entered into force 5 August 2016), art 16; Agreement Between the Government of Canada and the Government of the Republic of Benin for the Promotion and Reciprocal Protection of Investments (Canada-Benin BIT)

responsibility of states parties to ensure human rights are respected by those who benefit from such agreements – typically, industries and corporate investors.

This idea also reflects the zero draft's article 13(6), saying that states should ensure that they maintain 'human rights in the context of business activities by parties benefiting from such agreements'.[57] A national democratic oversight may be created through inserting in the prospective TBHR a requirement to subject trade and investment treaties to specific vetting and approval procedures by dedicated national bodies.[58] An extreme option would be to make the prospective treaty *lex specialis*, and trade and investment agreements *legi generali*, for example by stipulating in the text of the TBHR a superiority of the latter's obligations over the obligations under trade and investment treaties. This was, in a way, already provided in the zero draft's article 13 but was dropped in the revised draft.[59]

Article 16(2) of the revised draft contains an optional compromissory clause: states parties may choose to 'accept [...] as compulsory' the 'submission of the dispute to the [ICJ]' or 'arbitration in accordance with the procedure and organization mutually agreed by both state parties'. An internal critique is that, since the *compromis* is optional, it obviously weakens the dispute settlement system of the prospective treaty. Nadia Bernaz is more optimistic: she notes that such an opt-in 'mechanism is different from that of existing UN human rights treaties which either include a general compromissory clause (CERD), or a compromissory clause with the possibility to opt out (CEDAW, CAT, ICPRAMW, and ICPPED)'.[60]

A more external and normative problem of the revised dispute settlement clause is the outsourcing per se of the human rights due diligence dispute resolution to such an ADR as international arbitration. While the international arbitral (both commercial and investment) institutional framework may be well equipped to provide an effective alternative to state courts for settling conflicts between commercial parties or between a corporate investor and a state (though the latter postulate is debatable), it does not seem fit to carry out public law adjudicatory

(signed 9 January 2013, entered into force 12 May 2014), art 16; the Republic of Côte d'Ivoire Foreign Investment Code, Ordinance No 2018 646 of 1 August 2018, eg art 48, available in French http://www.tourisme.gouv.ci/uploads/Ordonnance-2018-646-du-01-08-2018code-investissement.pdf.pdf.

[57] Zero draft (n 49) art 13(6).

[58] By mobilising the efforts of national and regional parliaments, stakeholders can affect the negotiation of trade and investment agreements. In Belgium, for example, the regions have jurisdiction over international agreements negotiated at federal level. In such a way, in 2016 Wallonia used the veto for a megaregional agreement, CETA, that its country was about to sign, thus stalling the whole process within the Council of the European Union.

[59] Zero draft (n 49) art 13(6)–(7) reads as follows: 'States Parties agree that any future trade and investment agreements they negotiate, whether amongst themselves or with third parties, shall not contain any provisions that conflict with the implementation of this Convention and shall ensure upholding human rights in the context of business activities by parties benefiting from such agreements. States Parties agree that all existing and future trade and investment agreements shall be interpreted in a way that is least restrictive on their ability to respect and ensure their obligations under this Convention, notwithstanding other conflicting rules of conflict resolution arising from customary international law or from existing trade and investment agreements'.

[60] Bernaz (n 53).

functions in relation to human rights abuses. I discuss the (in)adequacy and (un)fairness as well as the key reasons why international arbitration is currently preferred – and why it should not be – to protect weaker parties such as workers, local communities, indigenous peoples, or the environment, in the normative analysis in Chapter 9.

B. The TBHR Revised Draft: Controversial Due Diligence and Liability Provisions

Regarding the liability disciplines of the revised draft posited in article 6, the obligations require states parties to ensure 'that their domestic law provides for a comprehensive and adequate system of legal liability for human rights violations or abuses in the context of business activities, including those of transnational character'.[61]

The mentions of 'domestic law' and 'comprehensive and adequate system' surely provide for a broad host of measures leading to CSL, ranging from criminal to administrative to civil liability. Regarding civil liability, however, it is unclear which degree exactly – if any – of CSL (transparency, due diligence or strict liability disciplines) article 6 of the revised draft provides and whether we are talking about statutory liability only, or about the common law tort of negligence as well. The above matters are likely to be clarified only when the actual treaty – if it is adopted – is at the execution stage, and will be decided, among others, by a monitoring body that is being created under the prospective TBHR.[62]

Notably, article 6(7) of the revised draft obliges states to ensure that their domestic legislation provides for civil, administrative, or criminal liability of legal persons for the offences that include the *jus cogens* violations as well as extrajudicial execution, forced labour, forced eviction, sexual and gender-based violence, and similar human rights abuses. Moreover, it requires states parties to equally sanction the participation or complicity in related criminal offences. However, the scope of the latter rubric is limited to 'offences as defined by their domestic law'.

On the one hand, given that many jurisdictions, such as Russia, for instance, do not adopt criminal liability in their legal systems for business enterprises as legal entities, article 6(7) surely adds value to the prospective treaty. On the other hand, the requirement that domestic legislation should provide for civil liability for the breaches of *jus cogens* by companies seems to echo the accusations that the Canadian corporation Nevsun faced in the *Nevsun* litigation. An intricacy, which seems to be even more important than in the case of civil liability in the abovementioned article 6(1), lies in the detail that the prospective civil liability for *jus cogens* violations in the *Nevsun* case relates to the common law tort of negligence,

[61] Revised draft (n 50) art 6(1).
[62] Revised draft (n 50) art 15.

the development of new torts or through a direct remedy for violations of customary international law, and not to a statutory duty of care.

Yet article 6(7) of the draft treaty provides for the domestic *legislation* only, thus introducing a needless restraint to the potentially broad range of situations in which corporations could be held liable under the rubric of transnational duty of care – especially given that the relevant common law avenues already exist in real life, eg in the *Nevsun* litigation. The final treaty wording of this provision should read not 'legislation' but 'domestic law' of states parties providing for civil, administrative or criminal liability of legal persons for the jus cogens and related offences enumerated in article 6(7), thus fully and explicitly extending its scope to the common law. Otherwise, it could be problematic for claims for damages arising out of alleged breaches of customary international law under TBHR article 6(7) to found a civil proceeding based on the common law tort of negligence.

As Doug Cassel notes in this regard, 'civil liability for complicity is also consistent with the requirement that states establish a "comprehensive and adequate system of legal liability" (article 6.1 [of the draft TBHR])'.[63]

Another important but highly debatable point is that article 6(6) stipulates liability of a firm for harm caused by other firms (no matter the location), but only when the first company controls or supervises the activities that caused harm. This provision is further limited by the reference to a 'contractual relationship' between the two companies, thus falling completely into the realm of privity. Obviously, as for example in the case of the French Vigilance law, the liability of the head company is clearly limited to the harms caused by direct subsidiaries and first-tier suppliers.

Article 5 of the revised draft is on human rights due diligence. It binds states to take the measures necessary to ensure that all corporations conduct human rights due diligence. The requirements that states should impose upon businesses are quite typical for due diligence disciplines and do not differ much from those in recent legislation surveyed in Parts II and III of this book: ie situating risk areas, planning accordingly, monitoring impact, reporting to the designated authorities and/or openly publishing on the related developments and performance.

Strikingly, however, unlike the French or the Dutch due diligence laws, the current TBHR draft article 5 is missing any obligation (that states parties should place on corporations, that is) to present a concrete due diligence plan or similar strategy. Moreover, there is no mention of liability in draft article 5 that would require states parties to adopt effective, dissuasive and proportionate sanctions against business enterprises that fail to comply with the provision.

The next controversial point of draft article 5 is that, on the one hand, it recognises the 'ILO 190 Convention concerning the elimination of violence and

[63] D Cassel, 'Five ways the new draft treaty on business and human rights can be strengthened' *Business & Human Rights Resource Centre* (9 September 2019) https://www.business-humanrights.org/en/blog/five-ways-the-new-draft-treaty-on-business-and-human-rights-can-be-strengthened/.

harassment in the world of work' and that '[c]onsultations with indigenous peoples will be undertaken in accordance with the internationally agreed standards of free, prior and informed consultations, as applicable'.[64] On the other hand, however, the term 'consultation' is a catch, especially in the context of corporate liability. Namely, *consent*, not consultation, is crucial in terms of procedural rights enabling both whole communities and individual citizens to defend their rights in the context of cross-border business, such as local participation in the decision-making.

As I have argued elsewhere, under the ILO 169 Convention and other relevant international and national law, the free, prior and informed consultation (FPICON) requirement could at best imply obligations of conduct.[65] At worst, that might mean a mere whitewashing of the entities who, no matter what, seek to develop a project on ancestral land of indigenous peoples (as was the case in the *Choc* litigation) or of the rural farming communities entirely relying on the local environment as means of subsistence (as in the *Vedanta* case). This is because it is easier to circumvent the requirement of negotiating in good faith in dealing with the obligation of consultation rather than that of consent. Thus, the prevention of human rights abuses will probably be more efficient through the incorporation into the draft TBHR of the obligation of free, prior and informed consent (FPIC) rather than FPICON.

Experts' comments on the TBHR expressing resentment that indigenous peoples' rights have now also been mentioned in the draft, but that the text refers to '*consultation* instead of *consent*, watering down international standards' thus only confirm my above insights regarding the inclusion of FPIC, and not (or, at least, not only) FPICON, going beyond the realm of corporate due diligence and extending to indigenous peoples' rights.[66]

Another shortcoming of draft article 5 relates to the same limitation of its scope as discussed above in draft article 6. Namely, due diligence should be exercised regarding actual or potential human rights violations or abuses that may arise from corporations' own business activities, or from their 'contractual relationships'.[67] Notably, this is a step backwards even compared to the UNGPs, as the latter oblige corporations to strive to prevent or mitigate negative impacts to which they are directly linked by their 'business relationships'.[68] A business relationship

[64] ILO Convention concerning Indigenous and Tribal Peoples in Independent Countries (adopted in Geneva during 76th ILC session held 27 June 1989, entered into force 5 September 1991) C169 (ILO C169); The United Nations Declaration on the Rights of Indigenous Peoples (UNDRIP), adopted by the United Nations General Assembly (UNGA), UNGA Res 61/295 (13 September 2007). For a critical comparison of consultation and consent obligations, see generally A Aseeva and KL Yip, 'When Yes means Yes: Free, Prior & Informed Consent in "One Belt One Road" projects in the framework of transnational investment law and arbitration' (2017) 14(3) *Transnational Dispute Management* 13.

[65] Aseeva and Yip (n 64) 19.

[66] G Quijano, 'A new draft Business and Human Rights treaty and a promising direction of travel' *Business & Human Rights Resource Centre* https://www.business-humanrights.org/en/blog/a-new-draft-business-and-human-rights-treaty-and-a-promising-direction-of-travel/.

[67] Revised draft (n 50) art 5(2).

[68] UNGP, principles 13 and 17.

may include not only contractual ties, but also links with 'business partners, entities in its value chain, and any other non-State or State entity directly linked to its business operations, products or services'.[69]

More specifically, the UNGPs, through Principle 17, extend the responsibilities of due diligence beyond the adverse impacts of a corporation's own activities. Explicitly, they also include those 'which may be directly linked to its operations, product or services by its business relationships'. Commentators assert that 'the "directly linked" element is critical, the nature of the business relationship less so'.[70] I disagree, recalling that, for example, the scope of liability under the French Vigilance law is limited to established business relationships, the latter being defined by article L. 442-6-I-5 of French Commercial Code as being first-tier relationships only. So, the *nature* of a business relationship, often defined by national commercial law, is not so insignificant. In the implementation of the TBHR this could be of crucial importance. Seen in this light, limiting the TBHR's scope of corporate due diligence to contractual relationships – ie basically to the first-tier – paradoxically seems quite coherent, even with examples of the highest CSL discipline – liability – let alone the inferior CSL disciplines as defined in this book.

Last but not least, Gabriela Quijano posits that '[d]epending on how "contractual" is to be interpreted under the treaty, this could also leave subsidiaries out of the scope of a *parent* company's due diligence duties' (emphasis added).[71] Here, however, I doubt that the mention of 'contractual' in the common law of negligence will leave subsidiaries outside the scope of parent company's liability. Indeed, in the *Vedanta* case, for example, judges confirmed that the liability of parent companies in relation to the activities of their subsidiaries is not, in itself, a distinct category of negligence. Notably, draft article 5(2b) foresees liability for a 'failure to prevent' harm by certain third parties, thus potentially extending the liability for acts of others, but of only 'certain' others – namely, those linked to the first firm by a contractual relationship. Or, in other words, all animals are equal but some animals are more equal than others. This may thus be a positive development, but also a very confusing one.

To conclude, the revised draft TBHR is likely to cover only the second mode of influence of GVCs introduced in Chapter 5 above, namely, relational contracting (mode 2) – and only if the planning and governance of GVC operations are recognised as contractual links in the sense of the prospective TBHR. However, neither the first mode of influence, that is, ad hoc contract and commercial agreements with foreign partners, nor (and even less so) the third mode, ie private regulation of GVCs through chain-wide standards, seem to be covered by the potential binding treaty.

[69] UNGP, principles 13, Commentary.
[70] Quijano (n 66).
[71] ibid.

Furthermore, the current draft TBHR's potential for corporate liability for non-compliance with human rights due diligence is likely to be diminished. This potential is jeopardised by almost exactly the same shortcomings that lessen the prospects of CSL based on a general GVC duty of care and an overall transnational liability in private law, discussed in Chapters 5–7. This is first and foremost due to the scope of corporate due diligence, which is limited in the draft TBHR to contractual relationships, ie to the first tier only. Alas, this seems to be quite coherent with the examples of the actual relevance of the highest degree of CSL disciplines (liability), as demonstrated by the French and EU examples in Chapter 7, section III and Chapter 8, section I.

9

On the Gap-filling Corporate Social Liability (and its Gaps)

So far, in the fourth and last part of the book, I have sought to map the emerging system of CSL, its pitfalls and opportunities, including: (i) the 'hardening' – CSL – effects, primarily through transnational private contracting and regulation creating both de jure legal norms and de facto legal effects; (ii) the boom of recognition of private parties as subjects of international law; (iii) the growing use of international arbitration as an alternative venue for CSL disputes; (iv) the emergence of other alternative dispute resolution means of CSL disputes; as well as (v) the apparent gaps in the above transformations, including questions of scope, enforcement and, especially, effectiveness.

The developments outlined in Chapters 7 and 8 keep unfolding at different speeds and with varying degrees of accomplishment. It is therefore reasonable to ask at what moment will a tipping point be reached and a noticeably new system of law can be inaugurated? Is a new legal paradigm – a paradigm imbued by interests that are equally public and private – any closer to being reality? And if so, to what extent is the nascent law of CSL inclusive and fair, and, therefore, desirable? In this final chapter I depart from a critically descriptive approach and pursue more normative enquiries about the emerging law of CSL.

I. The Pitfalls of International Arbitration for Realising Transnational CSL

In Chapter 7, sections IV–V and Chapter 8, section II, I outlined a growing trend to submit the CSL dispute resolution to international arbitration. Indeed, the 2018 (Transition) Bangladesh Accord's only dispute settlement option is institutional PCA arbitration under the UNCITRAL Arbitration Rules. The revised draft TBHR offers an opt-in mechanism, but one of the two dispute resolution options is international arbitration (the other being the submission of disputes to the ICJ).

The Transition Bangladesh Accord's new *compromis* committing to international arbitration, is generally applauded by scholarship.[1] Some scholars submit

[1] See generally the state-of-the-art in E Vidak-Gojkovic et al, 'The Medium Is the Message: Establishing a System of Business and Human Rights Through Contract Law and Arbitration' (2018) 35(4)

that, regarding human rights due diligence, international arbitration as a procedural mechanism is available to a wide range of non-corporate third parties who freely accede to the agreement, including labour unions and NGOs arguably due to 'the unique nature of the arbitration proceedings, which stand on the crossroads of public and private interests'.[2] Those third parties, it is assumed, would also have the procedural right to arbitrate the business and human rights issues against contracting parties who breached their undertakings.[3] Such an expansion of the scope of potential applicants is generally seen as a positive development and as having significant implications for future arbitrations.[4] This is in part on account of an allegedly 'expanded pool of potential arbitration claimants', since the Accord 'made it more likely for that diverse interests would be addressed' – for example, through claims brought by the NGO signatories,[5] as was the case in the two PCA arbitrations under the Accord discussed in Chapter 7, section IV above.

Notably, in 2018 the former ICJ Judge Bruno Simma gathered in The Hague an informal group of international lawyers, practitioners and scholars alike, called the Drafting Team of The Hague Rules on Business and Human Rights. Quite unambiguously, the team aimed to create 'an international private judicial dispute resolution avenue available to parties involved in business and human rights issues as claimants and defendants, thereby contributing to filling the judicial remedy gap in the UN Guiding Principles on Business and Human Rights'.[6] In December 2019 the group proposed 'The Hague Rules on Business and Human Rights' – a set of arbitral rules that could be allegedly used by adversely affected third parties harmed by the transnational corporate activities. Within this 'hermeneutical' group of lawyers, the boundaries between those engaged in theorising the process of elaboration of such rules, those who have actually been taking an active part in it, and those who would have more 'work' as arbitrators in the prospective claims now expected to be massively filed in The Hague are not at all clear cut. At the same time, this project seems to be in line with the overall politics of the installation of international arbitration in a host of key routes for deciding transnational CSL disputes, fuelled by the Transition Bangladesh Accord and related dynamics.

Journal of International Arbitration 379. For a critique of the arbitration avenues in the Transitional Accord, see J Salminen, 'The Accord on Fire and Building Safety in Bangladesh: A New Paradigm for Limiting Buyers' Liability in Global Supply Chains?' (2018) 66 *AJCL* 411, 444–49.

[2] Vidak-Gojkovic et al (n 1) 387.

[3] ibid.

[4] ibid. In this regard, more generally, see also Center for International Legal Cooperation (CILC), 'The Hague Rules on Business and Human Rights' (12 December 2019) https://www.cilc.nl/project/the-hague-rules-on-business-and-human-rights-arbitration/. 'This project was initiated by the Business and Human Rights Arbitration Working Group, a private group of international practicing lawyers and academics, aimed to create an international private judicial dispute resolution avenue available to parties involved in business and human rights issues as claimants and defendants, thereby contributing to filling the judicial remedy gap in the UN Guiding Principles on Business and Human Rights'.

[5] Vidak-Gojkovic et al (n 1).

[6] CILC (n 4).

A few criticisms of the above are in order. First and foremost, international arbitration, both investment and commercial, is hardly a 'public law' matter. It is either an entirely private dispute settlement, such as traditional commercial arbitration resolving disputes between private parties, or an allegedly (public) *international* law matter, if we are speaking about international investment arbitration.[7] While Judge Simma and his companions from The Hague Drafting team stress the judicial remedy gaps in the UNGPs, both commercial and investment arbitration have their own structural and institutional gaps that make quite obvious their inadequacy as actual public law adjudicatory fora[8] – and particularly so in disputes involving unequal parties such as poor-country workers or local populations acting against TNCs.

Second, and consequently, there are a host of normative considerations to bear in mind, not least the doubtful virtues of outsourcing human rights due diligence and a broader CSL dispute settlement to post-national ADR mechanisms, such as international arbitration. For one thing, in various contexts with CSL relevance, such as claims by employees, including supplier employees, local communities, indigenous peoples, civil society, consumers, and the like, the evenhandedness of international arbitration is far from guaranteed.[9] In addition, international arbitration distorts and re-shapes the legal framework in which agreements are interpreted. Indeed, as I outlined in Chapter 7, section IV, based on the norms of party autonomy and privity, international arbitration provides parties with the means to bypass national substantive law and procedural safeguards through the arbitration *compromis*. Moreover, and especially in investment arbitration, the framework balances states' right to regulate with private parties' contractual and property rights.[10] The asymmetrical structure of arbitration clauses can go so far as permitting private investors to use arbitration to seek a quasi-constitutional review of national public policy and regulatory action.[11]

Each state determines what is considered public policy in its jurisdiction. That is, national public policy varies greatly regarding the non-arbitrability of some specific types of claims, such as real estate, criminal cases, or, more relevantly for this book, labour and consumer-business disputes.[12] The specific

[7] See generally M Sornarajah, *The International Law on Foreign Investment*, 4th edn (Cambridge, Cambridge University Press, 2015); N Andrews, *Arbitration and Contract Law: Common Law Perspectives* (Cham, Springer International Publishing, 2016) 66.

[8] See generally D Schneiderman, *Constitutionalizing Economic Globalization. Investment Rules and Democracy's Promise* (Cambridge, Cambridge University Press, 2008).

[9] GB Born, *International Commercial Arbitration*, 2nd edn (The Hague, Wolters Kluwer, 2013) 942–44.

[10] A Aseeva and KL Yip, 'Stakes and Prospects of the Right to Free, Prior & Informed Consent in "One Belt One Road" Projects in the Framework of Transnational Investment Law and Arbitration' in J Chaisse and J Górski (eds), *The Belt and Road Initiative. Law, Economics, and Politics* (Leiden, BRILL-Nijhoff, 2018) 523, 524.

[11] ibid.

[12] GB Born, *International Arbitration: Law and Practice*, 2nd edn (The Hague, Wolters Kluwer, 2016) 87.

limits for contractual agreements to arbitrate selected types of disputes draw on public rights and fundamental freedoms and make the latter exclusively subject to each state's right to hear disputes of what it considers high public priority and not to give effect to the possibility of such arbitration.[13] For example, in Russia the legislator excludes certain categories of disputes from the scope of arbitration, while national courts invoke the doctrine to protect state interests in commercial disputes.

Arbitration-friendly jurisdictions, on the contrary, reduce their lists of non-arbitrable matters to a minimum. Hong Kong allows arbitration of disputes over enforceability, infringements and other aspects of IP rights.[14] Labour disputes can be generally submitted to arbitration in the US.[15] Consumer disputes are recognised as arbitrable in the UK.[16] In the EU, however, most jurisdictions generally take a contrary position in maintaining or even expanding the list of non-arbitrable matters in domestic legislation on arbitration.[17]

A different array of normative questions concerns the intersection of state public policy and the freedom and autonomy of parties to a contract to conclude the compromissory agreements they deem appropriate. Such an interface is not likely to seriously affect the enforcement of the prospective TBHR, given that its dispute settlement is an opt-in mechanism and arbitration is only one of the two options. However, those problems could have an impact on transnational contract-like agreements such as the Accord.[18]

Last but not least, as mentioned previously, contracts between the rich-country buyers and the poor-country supplier workers are likely to be asymmetrical agreements, even when the employees are represented by unions, as in the case of the Accord. In this regard, it has been asserted in the literature that 'the Accord might [...] liken supplier employees to the buyer's own employees so that both would fall under public-policy-related employee protection schemes'.[19]

While I agree with the above assertion, my concern here is somewhat different: the mentioned asymmetry exposes a more fundamental lack of equality, reciprocity and autonomy of the parties to the arbitration agreement, thus casting serious doubts on the legitimacy and even the validity of the arbitration clause of the Bangladesh Accord.

If the Accord is something of a 'last bastion' for a concrete realisation of transnational CSL in GVCs, what, then, is the way forward – particularly, for weaker private parties adversely affected by the GVC-related operations?

[13] GB Born and P Rutledge, *International Civil Litigation in United States Courts*, 6th edn (The Hague, Wolters Kluwer, 2018) 1177; Andrews (n 7) 66.

[14] Hong Kong Arbitration Ordinance (Cap 609), s 103D.

[15] *Directv, Inc v Imburgia*, 136 S Ct 463.

[16] UK Arbitration Act 1996 (c 89).

[17] Born (n 9) 1008–20.

[18] See generally Salminen (n 1).

[19] ibid 441.

II. The Limits and Opportunities of the Interface of Domestic Private Law with Public International Law

The revised draft TBHR limits the scope of both human rights due diligence and liability of a corporation to merely its contractual relationships, in articles 5(2) and 6(6), respectively. Thus, both due diligence and the liability of the head company are limited to the obligations regarding, and harms caused by, its direct subsidiaries and first-tier suppliers only. After all, from a black-letter contract law perspective, a contract only binds the parties to it.[20]

In Chapter 5, I presented several cases with CSL relevance where a contractual relationship, amongst others, was at stake to determine a transnational liability: eg *Walmart*, *Rahaman*, *Das*, *Arica*, and *KiK*. This relationship could not be regulated ex ante through a mechanism related to an international agreement. Indeed, while a treaty such as the prospective TBHR could potentially embrace – and thus concern – a wide range of actors, including corporations, their subsidiaries and suppliers, as well as the employees thereof, neither companies nor their employees can be directly bound by such or similar international treaty.

However, an interface of customary international law and domestic private law, particularly tort law, may offer some avenues for realising CSL. Especially after the paradigmatic *Nevsun* ruling, the prospects for weaker private parties to sue corporations in their home states under international law become brighter. The SCC stated that it was obvious that Canadian courts can develop a civil remedy in domestic law for corporate violations of customary international law, the latter being part of Canadian domestic law. Moreover, this could be done either through the development of new torts or through a direct remedy for violations of customary international law.[21]

Certainly, this ruling has opened the floodgates for lawsuits to be brought in Canadian courts for corporate violations of fundamental rights against Canadian extractive corporations operating transnationally.[22] While *Nevsun* is a seminal judgment in terms of opening Canadian courts to these types of claims, it may also be persuasive in other common law jurisdictions. In that regard it has the potential to take the international community to where the US Supreme Court's *Kiobel* ruling hoped to take it a few years ago.

Regarding more generally international human rights obligations of corporations, in the famous *Urbaser* counterclaim, the investment tribunal held that, while the norms of customary international law provide for a duty to perform for certain rights, *jus cogens* norms lay down a universal obligation of 'the international community of states in its entirety' to abstain from committing certain acts.[23]

[20] See discussions on classical contract law theories and their repercussions for CSL in Chapter 3, section II and Chapter 6, sections I.C, II.B and III.A.

[21] See Chapter 5, section II.

[22] ibid.

[23] Vienna Convention on the Law of Treaties (VCLT), 23 May 1969, entered into force on 27 January 1980, UNTS 1155, 331, art 53.

In *Urbaser*, the human right to water was determined as an obligation to perform, implying a state obligation to provide its population with water.[24] The arbitrators ruled that the situation would have been different in a case where an obligation to abstain, such as a prohibition on committing acts that violate human rights, was at stake. Such an obligation can be of immediate application, not only to states, but equally to individuals and other private parties.[25] This assertion, it is argued, extended beyond human rights norms framed as customary international law, to those human rights framed as prohibitions – *jus cogens*.[26] While in *Urbaser* the adjudicators did not specify which norms bound foreign investors, in *Nevsun* the judges were quite clear that these prohibitions could apply to foreign private companies.

Although not in contradiction with the *Urbaser* tribunal's reasoning, in *Nevsun* the SCC went far beyond it regarding the obligations of corporations under international law. It concluded that there was no reason for customary international law (with no distinction between positive and negative obligations) to not apply directly to corporations for violations of obligatory, definable and universal norms of international law.[27] It is even argued that, had the *Urbaser* tribunal followed the *Nevsun* interpretation, the investor would have clearly been in violation of its duty to perform – a positive obligation to ensure citizens' international human right to water: the *Nevsun* logic would make it a direct obligation under international law instead of a mere contractual obligation.[28]

To summarise this section, the interface of international law and relevant domestic law can be used to found and control CSL by substantive and procedural means. The challenges and opportunities of that interface show how different actors and society at large today deal with the conflicts of jurisdictions and clashes of norms. They underline the importance, and, indeed, ways of going beyond a plain, unitary boundary of modern law to capture the relations of different legalities in the global CSL drift. The law that arises out of diversity that those failures and successes offer differs institutionally and formally from the 'model' modern law. It seems to constitute a more diverse and pluralistic system that better integrates strategic litigation, aspirations for local participation and legal representation, as well as concrete sustainability considerations – in sum, a less hierarchical and unequal, more horizontally applicable, and definitely more inclusive law. This nascent 'CSL' law is obviously not without uncertainties and flaws. I outline those in the next and final section of this chapter.

[24] *Urbaser SA and Consorcio de Aguas Bilbao Bizkaia, Bilbao Biskaia Ur Partzuergoa v The Argentine Republic* [*Urbaser*]; Award, 8 December 2016, ICSID Case No ARB/07/26, para 1208.

[25] *Urbaser*, ibid para 1210.

[26] E Guntrip, 'Urbaser v Argentina: The Origins of a Host State Human Rights Counterclaim in ICSID Arbitration?', *EJIL: Talk!* (10 February 2017) https://www.ejiltalk.org/urbaser-v-argentina-the-origins-of-a-host-state-human-rights-counterclaim-in-icsid-arbitration/.

[27] *Nevsun Resources Ltd v Araya*, 2020 SCC 5 [*Nevsun*] para 113.

[28] SS Aatreya, '"Private" Breaches of International Law: Lessons from Domestic Courts for International Investment Law' *OpinioJuris* (4 March 2020) http://opiniojuris.org/2020/03/04/private-breaches-of-international-law-lessons-from-domestic-courts-for-international-investment-law/.

III. Whither Corporate Social Liability?

In this final part of the book, I have so far looked at the various possibilities, as well as the downsides, challenges and advantages, of forming a heightened corporate liability in GVCs. On the one hand, 'internal', inherently legalistic, options of transferring business relationships to selected jurisdictions through private contracts and of general legalisation of CSL through enacting national binding laws appeared as tricky routes with quite a limited usefulness for the purposes of realising CSL (Chapter 7, sections I–III). An alternative to those was a creation of transnational governance contracts directly linking the upstream and the downstream of GVCs. On the other hand, an 'external' behavioural approach, delving into subjective perception and overall social context, was likely to complement the overly legalistic CSL approaches of judicialisation and alternative dispute settlement (Chapter 7, sections II and IV–VI), and an enhanced legalisation of CSL in national, EU and international law (Chapter 7, section III and Chapter 8, sections I–II).

The Bangladesh Accord was expected to be one such 'highway exit' for both internal legalistic and external contextual and behavioural avenues. While it is a transnational binding contract with a compulsory dispute resolution, the Accord seeks to affect non-signatories and compels outsiders to use the information to influence signatories, thus also impacting on the behaviour of lead GVC firms. Through influencing the head corporations, the above could have arguably changed behavioural patterns throughout the entire chain. So far, in Chapters 7 and especially 8, however, I exposed not only the opportunities but also the limits of the Accord as a model of transnational GVC governance contracts.

A direct liability, including foreign direct liability, that was much hoped to emerge with a 'new', re-imagined (more sustainable, fair and inclusive) transnational contract law,[29] unexpectedly came from a different side. I say 'unexpectedly' because since the 2000s, and surely since early 2010s – in particular, the *Kiobel* litigation[30] – the whole international community, and especially lawyers, scholars and practitioners alike, working with transnational corporate liability, business and human rights, and related issues[31] have been anticipating the creation of

[29] See various works of Jaakko Salminen cited in this book, eg J Salminen, (1) 'The Accord on Fire and Building Safety in Bangladesh: A New Paradigm for Limiting Buyers' Liability in Global Supply Chains?' (2018) 66 *AJCL* 411; (2) 'From Product Liability to Production Liability: Modelling a Response to the Liability Deficit of Global Value Chains on Historical Transformations of Production' (2019) 23 *Competition and Change* 420.

[30] See Chapter 5, section II.

[31] This body of work is voluminous. To quote just a few, see eg P Simons, 'International Law's Invisible Hand and the Future of Corporate Accountability for Violations of Human Rights' (2012) 3(1) *Journal of Human Rights and the Environment*; H Muir Watt, (1) 'Les enjeux de l'affaire Kiobel: le chaînon manquant dans la mise en oeuvre de la responsabilité des entreprises multinationales en droit international public et privé' [2010-2012] *Travaux du Comité Français de Droit International Privé* (Paris, LGDJ, 2013) 233; (2) 'L'Alien Tort Statute devant la Cour suprême des États-Unis, territorialité, diplomatie judiciaire, ou économie politique ?' (2013) *Revue critique de droit international privé* 595.

extraterritorial tort liability of corporations for serious fundamental rights, environmental and related abuses. Foreign direct liability of corporations was in fact much expected. However, until 2020, the fate of such lawsuits against corporations elsewhere, in the common and civil law courts alike, was the same: a 'not guilty' verdict.[32] Therefore, in 2020 the long-awaited *Nevsun* judgment took us where the ruling in *Kiobel* was hoped to take us in 2013.

In the introductory chapter, I submitted that governance and the very construct of GVCs are beyond easy categorisation, especially in legal terms: they are neither essentially global nor local, neither innately public nor private.[33] The underlying nature and driving forces of GVCs materialise specifically from a point which is at the crossroads between practices, actors, social classes, political institutions, and legal rules that at the outset have little in common. A type of liability arising out of a domestic court's decision on a lawsuit ultimately claiming a private right to civil remedies in national law for violations of customary international law by a transnational corporation seems to accurately capture the above GVC dynamics.

In *Nevsun*, the SCC ruled that it was obvious that Canadian courts can develop a civil remedy in domestic law for corporate violations of customary international law that is part of Canada legal system.[34] According to the SCC, at least two solutions are possible: either a direct remedy for violations of customary international law or the development of new torts.[35] Now, the case has been sent back to the British Columbia Supreme Court, which will have to rule in September 2021 whether Nevsun has breached customary international law and if so, how such harm should be remedied.[36]

Apart from opening the door for more cases to be brought in Canadian courts – and, possibly, other common law jurisdictions – for violations of human rights and similar breaches against corporations operating transnationally, the *Nevsun* judgment plainly adds to the debate around the horizontal application of international law, particularly corporate obligations under customary international law. The latter is among the ground rules of international law, ie primary sources of international law as per ICJ Statute article 38(1)(b). In a nutshell, customary international law is identified through two cumulative factors: (i) a well-established general practice of states regarding the subject matter of a norm in question; and (ii) a general acceptance by states of a norm as law (*opinio juris*).[37] The second element also differentiates a custom from simple habit or usage.[38]

[32] See various cases in Chapter 5, section II.

[33] See Chapter 1, section II.A.

[34] *Nevsun* (n 27) para 122.

[35] ibid paras 127–128.

[36] *Nevsun* (n 27) para 131.

[37] International Law Commission (ILC), 'Draft conclusions on identification of customary international law adopted in first reading' in *ILC Report at its Seventieth Session*, UN Doc A/73/10 (2018), conclusion 10.

[38] ibid, conclusion 9, para 2.

Coming back to the CSL discussion in the particular context of the *Nevsun* ruling, I argue that, if more states recognise new torts based on customary international law or direct liability in customary international law, it may contribute to state practice and *opinio juris* on this issue. In the specific *Nevsun* case, the court had not explicitly mentioned anything relating to the debate on whether there was a clear customary international law obligation to conduct a human rights due diligence, and even less so concretely in GVCs. Neither did the SCC say anything that would expressly contribute to an *opinio juris* that such a due diligence, or any other degree of CSL disciplines as per this book, were required. If, however, the *Nevsun* ruling activates the already existing relevant decisions of domestic courts (*Shell, Vedanta*), supports the ongoing CSL lawsuits (*Choc, Samsung*) and triggers new ones, I suggest that that would arguably create the necessary amount of evidence to show that CSL is accepted as law, through the element of rulings of national courts.[39]

If my above assertion about the nascent 'CSL' law becoming part of international law reveals itself to be too optimistic, at least the *Nevsun* line would make it much more difficult for states and corporations to contest the idea that the latter have international 'CSL' obligations. Here, however, an important reservation is in order: whether international law may provide obligations for corporations in domestic law is a factor for each jurisdiction to consider on its own.

Another avenue for CSL, apparently less legalistic, though not less feasible, would be to appeal to the impact on corporate behaviour through subjective perceptions and overall social context.[40] Peterkova Mitkidis, for instance, argues that '[u]sing the form of a binding commitment, even though the undertaking may not be legally enforceable, is a signal of its seriousness towards suppliers'.[41] In this sense, drawing on the model that I built in Chapter 1, we could use a socio-legal imperative that governs actors' legal behaviour (through the use of binding language – binding laws and courts' rulings alike), which may change the actors' perceptions of the social expectations surrounding their own behaviour (ie a sort of incorporation of and reaction to socially reproduced normative imperatives) – in our case, imperatives of CSL.

Such an integration of the norm into an individual actor's value system may thus lead to a subsequent endorsement of, and obedience to, such norm even without the enforcement of any publicly-driven sanction against an actor (as per Bourdieu and Durkheim).[42] Hence, a process of internalisation of a norm would take place because an actor could not deviate from it without experiencing guilt or shame – or simply out of something of a cost-benefit analysis of what is socially the

[39] ibid, conclusion 10, para 2.

[40] See Chapter 1, section IV.B.

[41] K Peterkova Mitkidis, 'Sustainability Clauses in International Supply Chain Contracts: Regulation, Enforceability and Effects of Ethical Requirements' (2014) *Nordic Journal of Commercial Law* 1, 25.

[42] See Chapter 1, section III.B.

most optimal thing to do in order to enhance and/or not to damage its image. For the head firms of GVCs who compete on value, a successful brand management and reputation are key components in market competition.[43]

A general outcome of the above is that making a statement through a treaty, a law, a private agreement, and even more so through court decisions may all impact on social norms and behaviour relevant for realising CSL. For instance, an increased hard law character of a commitment through the use of binding language, and especially the usage of concrete formal sanctions and/or an obligation of result might have a deterrent effect, thus somehow enforcing a CSL-related law or a contractual clause ex ante. The acceptance could extend beyond the parties to a supply agreement within a GVC, to third parties.

'... [T]urning a promise into a contract means that the promise is to be believed, accepted and relied upon'.[44] On the other side of the spectrum lie international voluntary guidelines and other international soft law instruments relevant for CSL, such as various OECD guidelines, the UNGPs, etc. Domestic cultural and social norms can be very strong and thus hard to change through international law. However, judges may rely on international soft law both in situations involving applicable (mostly national) CSL laws and international law (in the *Nevsun* type of claims). Notwithstanding their very limited direct effectiveness,[45] such international soft law instruments could positively affect the interpretation and application of national/ regional CSL hard law, by affecting the direction of generalisations made by judges on the basis of a particular material. This, in turn, could influence the course of judicial reasoning in cases with CSL relevance.

Of course, to avoid actual unenforceability, such firm and loud statements should not be made in a national and regional, public and social vacuum. As already suggested elsewhere in this book, it is not only typical powers such as the state legislative, executive and judiciary that should join forces to enhance corporate liability. State watchdogs, labour unions, trade and commercial associations, NGOs, consumers, shareholders and financial institutions should all be actively involved at various stages to make corporate liability truly *social*.

To conclude, CSL oscillates between social and economic, material and individual, public and private, global and local, external and internal. It is not only a connection between the corporation as an organisational form of platforms for contracts,[46] on the one hand, and GVCs as networks of horizontal contractual arrangements between affiliated entities within the transnational organisation of corporations, on the other.[47] CSL is also, and especially, a conductor between an external broad socio-ecological perspective on GVCs, seeing them as a sweeping

[43] See discussions in Chapter 6.

[44] D Rousseau, *Psychological Contracts in Organizations: Understanding Written and Unwritten Agreements* (SAGE Publishing, 1995) 18.

[45] See Chapters 4 and 8.

[46] See Chapter 1, section IV.A.

[47] See Chapter 1, section II.A.

makeover of international economic relations transforming the global capitalism,[48] and an internal narrow legalistic approach to liability in GVCs.[49]

From a broad external perspective, it is also crucial to stress that the causes of all socio-ecological disasters and legal actions analysed in this book, from armed conflicts and atrocities within and across the Global South, through discrimination and violence against indigenous peoples in both North and South, to pollution, destruction of the environment, and global climate crisis, lie in the idiosyncratic methods of GVC production and trade as the latest contemporary form of global capitalism.[50] The geoeconomics of such capitalism underlies and explains a fundamental change in the global political economy, where corporations, cities, countries, and regions alike now compete on value.[51]

Therefore, CSL must act as not only a conductor between public and private, international and national law, but also as a bond between now and then: it must operate far beyond the internal legal rubrics of foreign direct liability, or any kind of direct liability, to show that we need to transform the global political economy and society. In particular, corporations must not only be held directly liable for their violations, including violations of universal norms of international law. My claim here is that corporations must also have positive obligations to ensure, among others, local populations' fundamental rights, such as rights to water, a clean environment, minimum decent standards of living and the like. This claim brings us back to questions about what the corporation was initially conceived for – namely, for social use. This might be beyond the arguably 'technical' (tool)box of many lawyers. Instead of box-ticking, lawyers should look for a systemic solution to our problems that may simply lie outside (the box of) contemporary capitalism, including the institutions of contract, modern business corporations, and GVCs.

[48] See Part I above in its entirety.
[49] See the whole of Parts II and III above.
[50] See Chapter 1, section II.A.
[51] See various discussions in Chapter 2.

Conclusion: Where Do We Stand and Is There a Way Forward?

This book has shown that GVCs exist in their current (a)legal form for particular historical reasons related to the global spread of post-colonial corporate capitalism (Chapter 2). The value chain form of production and trade has marked a shift from vertically integrated companies to horizontal contractual arrangements between affiliated entities within the global(ised) network of the corporation (Chapter 2). Dispersing transnationally, GVC production and trade serve not only the purpose of lowering factor costs and thus maximising shareholders' profits. In addition to the norms of separate legal personality and limited liability that are already lowering corporations' exposure to law enforcement action, dispersed GVC operations make it almost impossible to enforce the law against the GVC dominant firms through more traditional channels of private law (Chapters 5–7).

As a response to these regulatory and governance gaps, attempts to create multilateral hard and global soft regulatory instruments (Chapter 2) do not represent a success story. These attempts include the OECD relevant guidelines, the UNGPs, and the revised draft TBHR (Chapters 4 and 8). CSR equally falls short of making corporations responsible for the societal harms in their GVCs (Chapter 2). The schemes navigating under the banner of 'CSR' have important limits: they are voluntary schemes with no enforcement mechanisms. Some avenues exist for enforcing them through domestic law. Contract law may see publicised CSR statements or any such corporate pledges of self-regulation as a promise to consumers that they are acquiring ethically-sound and environmentally-friendly products (Chapter 3). A promise, in turn, creates legitimate expectations: the trusting party may derive such expectations from the promises of the producers, including labelling, corporate codes, and even advertising. The potential of these avenues to become reality much depends on the willingness of those who rule on the related disputes to overcome judicial formalism in contract law and litigation.

National law may also intervene, through a statutory duty of due diligence (Chapter 7), thus making it an obligation owed to society at large; failure to fulfil this duty would involve strict liability. Dutch due diligence law, for example, creates a minimum legal standard for sustainability agreements (*convenants*) – voluntary initiatives linking companies in the Netherlands with suppliers and their labour unions, as well as with civil society. The law is likely to turn the *convenants* into instruments binding those companies.

Nevertheless, throughout this book, my analysis has revealed particular difficulties in enforcing virtually all of the surveyed instruments, including the highest CSL disciplines of liability found in the national law of some first-world jurisdictions. At present, those shortcomings are partially explained by the reluctance of national judges in CSL-related litigation with a transnational context to think outside the box, even without any excess of judicial activism (Chapters 5–7). Moreover, all the enacted domestic hard laws that have been surveyed in this book have several deficiencies. Serious gaps in the actual application of almost all these laws, including in enforcement and effectiveness, thus cast doubt on how genuine are the intentions of the respective legislatures of those allegedly advanced democracies to make corporations liable for GVC harms. Therefore, though most CSR and international hard and soft instruments, as well as regional and national binding laws, seem to tick the right social boxes, they are merely strengthening societal perception of enhanced corporate responsibility, and are ultimately whitewashing global GVC capitalism, notwithstanding the genuineness of intent of many involved.

Besides, both the taxonomy of GVCs (Chapter 2) and most existing legal literature on and approaches to the interface of private law with GVC governance, including transnational governance contracts (Chapters 4–8), appear insensitive to the broader external socio-ecological effects of GVC production and trade.

As a result, the current attitude of most lawyers about CSL in GVCs disregards such socio-ecological questions as global and local equality and distributive justice, and instead remains internal and too square, focusing on an essentially legalistic approach to CSL. And even within this internal, legalistic, conception, the quest for corporate liability through its enhanced judicialisation, including strategic litigation and legalisation at national and regional levels (Chapters 5–7), as well as international arbitration and the international business and human rights treaty endeavours (Chapters 7–9), seems to create value for – and legitimise – the lead chain firms and, consequently, GVC capitalism. Slowly some exceptions are beginning to emerge: the most recent domestic rulings of common law courts – the 2019 UK *Vedanta* judgment and the 2020 Canadian *Nevsun* decision – challenge a general status quo of realising CSL through judicialisation thanks to foreign direct corporate liability. Note that both rulings, while being directly relevant for realising transnational CSL as defined in this book, concern a mining supply chain.

In Chapter 9 I sketched the present state of play and likely future developments of foreign direct CSL. In particular, the immediate and future outcomes of the *Nevsun* ruling create possibilities for a shift from the current legal epitome of the global political economy – supply chains and more contemporary GVCs. Beyond the likelihoods of foreign direct liability, which are promising yet internal and inherently legalistic prospects, an external normative claim ensuing from my analysis is that we ('we' the lawyers, and 'we' the people) need radically different perspectives and practices of organisation of corporations, economy and society.

At the very beginning of this book, I argued that, due to the distinctive – ie chain – organisation of contemporary business enterprises, the head firms of chains are virtually exempt from any liability because of the 'economically dependent – legally independent' relationship between core corporations and their controlled or economically dependent entities from the global periphery. More concretely, I claimed that 'we' as lawyers needed to find the way(s) to demonstrate legal dependence and, hence, legally effective relationships between head companies and their economically dependent entities, thus paving the way for transnational CSL. Furthermore, globally, 'we' as a society need to reduce to a minimum such economic dependence on chains – which is far too excessive – through ensuring a level playing field economically and socially. I address the two sets of conclusions and recommendations related to each claim in turn.

I. Where Do We Stand?

In this book, I explored the legal doctrines, statutes and case law relevant to corporate liability in GVCs, not only in a comparative perspective, but also in their ideological, social, economic and political contexts. In addition to critically engaging with the key applicable doctrines and approaches, I sought to explain the ideology behind them and assess the degree to which they may serve further interests – beyond those of the parties to an international treaty, a private contract, or a corporate charter – including those of society at large.

If it was traditionally accepted by the orthodoxy that classic contract law doctrines promote both free trade and fair competition, things are not so certain in today's global capitalist economy, shaped by the transboundary networks of production and distribution – GVCs. The aim of this book was to broaden appreciation and understanding of the subject matter, by comparing and then linking the relevant big ideas in international economic law and corporate law, contract and tort theories, and a more recent business and human rights approach, and exploring how they relate to actual practices, behaviour, and standards collectively held and shared by the key actors across GVCs.

In Part I above, I revealed that, since the 1950s, the post-war ontological model was the embedded liberalism with alleged conceptions of regulatory and sovereign equality, and a general underlying idea of post-war recovery. However, since the late 1970s, liberal ontology was gradually replaced by neoliberalism. De-regulation was the accompanying conception of neoliberalism, aimed at radically heightening the market freedom of individual market actors by helping them to comprehend and navigate the global web of norms and institutions, in order to realise their transboundary business ends. Since the 1970s, de-regulation, optimisation of conditions for model market citizens to realise their private ends both locally and globally, and the overall market efficiency as an encompassing metaphor, have become the watchwords of the day.

Since the mid-twentieth century, the growing popularity and influence of public international economic law, namely the dramatic post-war increase and expansion of international trade, and, later, investment law through international treaties, also encouraged crucial developments in private transnational economic governance. While public international law supported nation-states in their post-war recovery and overall industrialisation, parallel private international – or rather transnational – workings have consigned certain nations to the industrial and production periphery. These mechanisms, of course, include the interests of corporations promoting the global fragmentation of production and division of labour captured in the core-periphery dynamic.

Consequently, by progressively eliminating barriers to the free movement of goods, services and capital, PIEL has helped to create a relationship of dependency between the industrial core and the periphery, which also gave impetus to an idiosyncratic GVC production, governed by essentially private means, including private law. Thanks to GVCs, the core's corporations started outsourcing less value-intense stages of their production, such as parts manufacturing, to the periphery. GVC production actors from the global centre and the periphery were increasingly separated both geographically and socially, while linked commercially through GVC production and trade, as well as organisationally – through international standards of production, such as the ISO standards. As demonstrated in Part II of the book, orthodox corporate and contract law, in turn, provided for separating the core entities from their periphery partners, thus limiting corporate liability for harms and other issues arising from transboundary production and trade. For example, a limited direct liability construct is but one of countless proofs of such 'minimalist' contractually-focused approaches to business liability for outsourced production.

Since the 2000s, the gaps in realisation of corporate liability in GVCs have triggered a wave of national legislation extending to production outsourced to other jurisdictions, and of lawsuits concerning human rights violations, violence in the workplace and other labour-, health-, and environment-related abuses, aiming to harden head corporations' responsibilities for harm occurring in their chains of production and distribution. In Part III, I evaluated these two strands of national developments with CSL relevance.

However, the social debates on modern slavery and climate change have lasted for more than 30 years and go far beyond environmental degradation, violence in the workplace or labour law. Such debates are rooted in an older architecture facilitating de-regulation, capital markets, financialisation of companies and public services, market competition and its incentives, both positive and negative, for corporate managers. Those resulted in the formation of a social norm that the board and corporate managers, and, by extension, *corporations* hold responsibilities principally towards shareholders.[1] These developments have transformed global production and distribution processes, and hence also work processes, by increasing the work rhythm and introducing quantified objectives, permanent reporting, relentless reorganisations, and, ultimately, *outsourcing* in all its forms. This type of corporate management intensified the work and emptied it of its

[1] eg, B Sjåfjell and M Taylor, 'Clash of Norms: Shareholder Primacy vs Sustainable Corporate Purpose' (2019) 13(3) *International and Comparative Corporate Law Journal* 40, 52.

meaning by reducing it to a quantitative indicator – value. The violence at the Bisha Mine of Nevsun was not generated by monsters or aliens, but by managers trying to best accomplish *the* mission of creating value for the shareholders, as explained in Parts II and III above.

II. The Way Forward

In Chapter 1, specifically at section III.A, I argued that CSL must be not only about corporate liability for the effects of GVC production, services, and operations (ex post), but also about corporate responsibility of (re)distribution (rather ex ante), such as caring about the environment, health and safety at work, training of workers, and such like. The borderline between responsibilities ex post and responsibilities ex ante is obviously not so clear cut, as a firm can be held liable ex post for a manifest failure to provide safety at a workplace. My aim here is, however, not to discuss the differences and similarities of these two strands, but rather to propose CSL as both an obligation of distribution (see section A below) and a responsibility for the effects of GVC production, services, and operations (see section B below), although the two intermingle extensively.

A. CSL as an Obligation of Distribution

In Chapter 3 above I cited some management scholarship, which stated that in the nineteenth-century US – the birthplace of corporations as we know them today – a charter of incorporation was a favour bestowed only on those businesses that were socially useful – an approach abandoned after the US Civil War, thus making charters nearly impossible to revoke. Corporations hence began to dominate the US and global economy, and such concentrated economic power was drawn into the hands of a few, raising up a corporate ruling class with almost limitless power.[2]

Today, the prohibition of those plainly pathogenic corporate management methods of such a corporate ruling class that aim at increasing value for shareholders at any price is a major concern in terms of workplace health and safety. On normative level, this means *making corporations socially useful again*. Rome wasn't built in a day, so I suggest that a good start would be to begin by departing from outsourcing and any other practices solely aimed at creating value for the corporation's shareholders, and making a systemic shift to a corporation's duty to care about health and safety at the workplace and *around*, including the environment. On a practical level, the above corporate management methods may be mitigated

[2] A Carroll, 'A History of Corporate Social Responsibility: Concepts and Practices' in A Crane et al (eds), *The Oxford Handbook of Corporate Social Responsibility* (Oxford, Oxford University Press, 2008) 23.

through a top-down approach, for example, through state dissuasive sanctions or even bans. At the same time, a bottom-up approach must prevent harmful practices in poorer countries – the upstream of GVCs – by creating and enforcing rights and freedoms of employees and their representatives *throughout* the GVCs, and not only by strengthening the legislation on GVC risk prevention and a 'therapeutic' disclosure at the downstream of GVCs, ie in the first-world states.

Notably, the corporate limited liability and the shareholder primacy norms endanger not only the periphery workers, but also the indigenous peoples, local communities, the environment, and, indeed, the whole planet. These challenges call for structural changes. Several structural reforms appear necessary to better sanction – but also, and above all, to prevent – corporate violence against people, the environment, and the planet.

First, the use of subcontracting should be limited or, speaking about risky sites, banned altogether. As I have shown in different chapters in Parts I and III of this book, the use of subcontracting, temporary workers and precarious workers is a structural strategy for large corporations to produce, accumulate and exchange value. This strategy allows them to transfer risk management and dangerous work to other companies, at low cost, by imposing on them drastic conditions of time and cost, incompatible with the prevention of professional and environmental risks. To avoid this, it is necessary to make the head buyers responsible for the application of their home country labour and environmental law throughout the whole chain of subcontracting which depends on them. For example, for employees of suppliers and subcontractors declared unfit due to occupational diseases or industrial accidents, the obligation of reclassification which is imposed within French corporations (article L1226 -2) must be extended to the final buyer.[3]

Regarding more substantial environmental risks, my analysis of transnational litigation involving recent environmental disasters from Chapter 5 onwards has demonstrated the insufficiency of the obligations of disclosure and due diligence between the first-world ordering corporations and their third-world subcontractors. We now may face the necessity of prohibiting outsourcing in all its manifestations, such as subcontracting and temporary work, in hazardous sectors: mining, waste management, etc.

The work of local labour unions must also be strengthened by granting them the right to organise labour inspections and guaranteeing the independence of such inspections. In particular, the right granted to the agents of labour inspectorates to suspend labour activities on the basis of certain limited physical risks should

[3] '[L]obligation de reclassement est réputée satisfaite lorsque l'employeur a proposé un emploi, dans les conditions prévues à l'article L. 1226-2 [ou à l'article L. 1226-10 pour l'inaptitude professionnelle], en prenant en compte l'avis et les indications du médecin du travail', arts L. 1226-2 and L. 1226-10, French Labour Code. Notably, prior to 2017, employers had to consult the employees' representatives only when an incapacity was found after a period of suspension of the worker's employment contract following an industrial accident or occupational disease. Since 2017, French labour law has aligned the procedure of incapacity of non-professional origin with that of professional origin.

be extended to all situations where a serious danger to the health of workers, local communities or to the environment is found. Independent labour inspections need substantial staff, both quantitatively – in terms of number of its members, and qualitatively – in terms of their skills and expertise. Both their independence and prerogatives must be strong and guaranteed.

B. CSL as a Legal Responsibility for the Effects of Production, Services, and Operations

Drawing on the results of my analysis in several sections of this book,[4] *scope-wise*, the emerging legislative CSL framework that I propose here should cover a dominant influencer over transactions in a GVC and its controlled and economically dependent entities for adverse societal impacts of their activities within the GVC, including production, services, and any other operations.

As I argued in the introduction (see Chapter 1, section II.A), regarding the *duties* and *obligations*, the covered entities must be: (i) held liable for any above negative impacts; and (ii) obliged to prevent them. The main obligations thus include both obligations of conduct and obligations of result. These obligations must apply to lead companies' GVCs and all their business relationships, including any entities they own or control at home and abroad (ie both subsidiaries and economically dependent entities). I elaborate on each set of obligations below.

In Chapter 4, sections I and II and Chapter 5, section I, I classified the CSL disciplines into four categories according to the degree of their normative force: (0) CSR; (1) mandatory disclosure, including transparency and monitoring; (2) mandatory due diligence, including both human rights and environmental due diligence; and (3) liability, properly so called.

Regarding CSR and transparency obligations, the covered entities must first of all respect the relevant international legal framework in all their activities covered by the proposed legislative model. They must also monitor and ensure that such a framework is respected throughout the whole GVC. 'Relevant international legal framework' encompasses international law, including customary international law, international human rights law, international sustainability and CSR standards, including UNGPs and various OECD guidelines, and other such standards.

Regarding due diligence obligations, the covered entities must first of all ensure adequate and continuous monitoring, identification, and assessment of real and potential harm due to their relevant activities (production, services, and other operations) throughout the GVC. More specifically, drawing on my analysis in Chapter 5, section I and Chapter 6, section III, in particular the project of the Swiss Popular Initiative, the UNGPs, and the OECD Guidelines, the covered entities

[4] See particularly Chapter 4, sections I–II, Chapter 5, section I, Chapter 6, sections I–III, Chapter 7, sections I–IV and Chapter 8, sections I–II.

must identify risks affecting human rights and the environment, and take measures to prevent the potential and imminent, or cease current, internationally-recognised human rights and environmental abuses, and other such negative societal impacts. They must also report publicly about the measures taken, as well as their effectiveness, and continuously evaluate and improve the effectiveness of their due diligence. In addition, drawing on my analysis of all existing due diligence and liability disciplines, including the newest French and Dutch due diligence laws, covered entities must guarantee the absence of child labour and forced labour in their production, services, and operations. The covered entities must present concrete due diligence plans or similar strategies in a regular and timely manner.

In addition, according to my analysis of the draft TBHR in Chapter 8, section II, the covered entities must have a duty to undertake relevant consultations and obtain consents. More precisely, according to relevant ILO Conventions and other international standards, the consultations with indigenous peoples and local communities must be undertaken in accordance with the internationally agreed standards of free, prior and informed consultation (FPICON) and consent (FPIC), as applicable. Furthermore, relevant consent, not consultation, must ensure procedural rights that enable both whole communities and individual citizens to defend their rights in the context of the covered activities, such as local participation in the decision-making. More concretely, the covered entities must directly consult and obtain FPIC from impacted and potentially impacted indigenous peoples, local communities, and other similar stakeholders in an adequate and timely manner, and respect their opinions and requirements expressed through both FPICON and FPIC before defining and proceeding with the due diligence plan and related measures.

Regarding liability, GVC head corporations must be held liable for harm arising out of adverse societal impacts caused or contributed to by them or their controlled or economically dependent entities. According to my analysis in Chapter 6, section III, as per UNGP principle 19, commentary, and OECD Guidelines, ch II, A 12, GVC head corporations must be held liable for harm arising from subcontractors' or suppliers' activities deemed to be adverse societal impacts caused by entities with which a given company has a business relationship – that is, when that firm *sufficiently relates* to those commercial partners' production, services, or operations through *legally effective business practices*, unless they act with due care and take all reasonable measures to prevent harm.

Note, however, that the above international business and human rights framework uses the term 'is directly linked' instead of the term 'sufficiently relates' that I use. My proposal, I argue, is better suited to the purpose of founding the CSL. First, entities may not be directly linked, yet may still be economically very dependent, which is precisely the case with first-world final buyers and various third-world suppliers within GVC production and trade. Second, I therefore submit that the advanced criteria for founding CSL within GVCs should be: (i) actual and potential effects of legally effective practices (eg repeated business transactions, value chain-wide standard-setting) of a lead (or the biggest) company vis-à-vis other firms in a value chain; and (ii) whether such practices result in a relationship. What I mean is that, for instance, when a business transaction in a GVC is repeated, a relationship is formed. And hence, an external supplier becomes a subcontractor, and the contractual relationship that commenced as a one-off exchange grows into relational contracting. Another example is when external GVC-wide regulation (various industry-wide codes and standards) allocates rights and duties along the whole chain. Such types of planning and governance are, I argue, proof of an enhanced influence through a relationship of dependence within a GVC (see the various arguments in Chapter 6, section III above), and should thus be seen as legally relevant.

Regarding the *burden of proof* and *evidence*, there should be a presumption of liability of head entities of GVCs. Drawing on both recent litigation trends analysed in Chapter 5, section II above, where – at least in some cases – a discussion of the possible role of contractual causes of action has taken place (eg in *KiK* and *Walmart*), and on a growing legislative process seeking to create a more general duty of care that would broadly require human rights due diligence throughout a first company's value chain (eg French and Dutch due diligence laws), the presumption of liability should be on the parent company or similar head undertaking. Moreover, the burden of proving that the relationship between the main entity and other entities involved in the harm is legally ineffective or otherwise irrelevant must be on the main entity.

In terms of *enforcement*, following my analysis,[5] it must be up to individual states to ensure that their legal systems provide for civil, administrative, and criminal liability of legal persons for the *offences as defined by their law and practice*, including international law and *jus cogens* violations as well as extrajudicial execution, forced labour, forced eviction, sexual and gender-based violence, and similar human rights abuses. Drawing particularly on my conclusions in Chapter 7, section III on the strengths and weaknesses of the French and Dutch CSL laws, it is clear that states must not only choose competent enforcement authorities but also – and indeed especially – guarantee that members of civil society and the public may claim liability for breaches by the covered entities directly before the national judiciary.

Based on my analysis of relevant litigation in Chapter 5, section II and Chapter 7, sections I–III, especially the *Garcia*, *Vedanta*, and *Choc* cases, in terms of appropriate *judicial forum*, the most significant or otherwise substantial relationship with a particular jurisdiction should be determined primarily according to where the plaintiffs could reasonably obtain fair trial process and substantive justice. The time limitation considerations should be reasonable and in any case sufficient for a transnational CSL litigation.

[5] In Chapter 5, sections I–II, Chapter 7, sections I–III and Chapter 8, section II.

III. Final Concluding Remarks

This book reveals how GVCs, initially an organisational construct of modern capitalistic production and distribution, materialised into a legal construct of contemporary global capitalism. However, GVCs are not appropriate for the realisation of CSL for cross-border production and trade; quite the opposite – at present the construct exacerbates corporate impunity for harms accruing along value chain commerce.

In most of this book, I examined contexts and then various options for demonstrating and proving legally effective relationships between a head GVC corporation and its controlled or economically dependent entities. That was necessary in order to understand ('why'), describe ('what'), and ultimately realise ('how') CSL. The exact aim of that exercise was to find a substantial legal link through a dependence created through GVC production and trade – a dependence that is first of all economic. Proving such a legal link based on a substantial economically-driven dependence is, I argue, helpful for founding CSL, thus fulfilling the short- and even medium-term objectives of anyone fighting for transnational corporate liability in GVCs. In other words, that is an answer to the main question of this book from an internal – lawyers' – perspective. From the external perspective of our society as a whole, a longer-term objective should not – or at least not only – be to found CSL based on substantial economic dependence of the global production periphery on the global centre, but to get rid of this excess of economic dependence, inequality, and of the very 'centre-periphery' World system that exists today.

Post-colonial GVC capitalism seems to (still) currently dominate most 'law on the books', 'law in action', and 'law in minds' that yield CSL disciplines. Part of the problem is, of course, the minimalist and quite retrograde constructs of applicable corporate and contract law still prevailing in 2021 in the majority of world jurisdictions. Apart from a few interpretational exceptions from domestic common law courts, these constructs prevent more progressive corporate and contract approaches – as well as national tort law and international human rights rules – from applying to cases of corporate abuses abroad in order to ground the lead firms' GVC liability. One of the explanations may be that today's relevant key social norm actually draws on the shareholder model of corporation: ie today, corporations' first and foremost responsibility is the creation of value for its shareholders. However, the above accounts do not seem to be the primary reasons for the present impossibility of realising CSL in GVCs. Of course, given that since the Second World War, corporations have been among the most powerful actors in national and international relevant law-making, one explanation may be that corporations continue lobbying, or otherwise influencing, much of such law-making processes. Those laws, in turn, arguably continue to help corporations to pass undetected under the radar of any legal liability and remain clear, while creating value for shareholders by any means available.

Yet, the flipside of the almost impossibility of realising CSL and today's domination of the shareholder model is, I suggest, no less than the recent rise of nationalism and populism elsewhere in the first world. Paradoxically, the recent surge in national regulation on GVC production surveyed in this book seems to fit neatly into the pattern of growing nationalist and populist sentiments in the West. What I mean is that those regulatory and legislative developments may in reality aim to uphold the competitiveness of national industrial enterprises on the global market.

In this pattern of shielding, maintaining, and improving national industry competitiveness, the collateral reasons of the recent rise of western populism are, absurdly, the constant and continuing deterioration of first-world working conditions due to a growing relocation of most of the core's working class jobs to the GVC periphery. On the one hand, the worsening of the western working conditions results into election of nationalist and populist governments. On the other hand, it induces the austerity policies imposed on the working class and the backlashing protests, social unrest, and violence that we witness today in many western democracies.

A systemic response to contemporary GVC capitalism violence in both the first and the third world should thus go beyond any legal or even legal-political solutions. When, in order to stay competitive, various national industries outsource less value intense stages of production – and, increasingly, of services – to the lower-waged GVC periphery and semi-periphery, the GVC centre's citizen-consumer must think about the social costs of lost jobs at home and degrading treatment of both people and environment in that GVC periphery, rather than about the economic benefits of the fast design apparel, cheap Global South food products, or (quasi-)free supermarket plastic bags. Cooperatives must become the principal form of state enterprise. Domestic corporations must ensure full employment at home. Workers elsewhere must be well represented and empowered, both directly and through strong institutionalised labour unions. It is probable that, at present, capitalism cannot be eliminated, but it must be domesticated – by, among other things, rolling back the boundaries of the globalised market, and ensuring a level playing field economically and socially.

BIBLIOGRAPHY

UK Governments

UK Office for National Statistics, 'Ownership of UK quoted shares: 2018', 14 January 2020.

Report of the Committee on the Financial Aspects of Corporate Governance (Cadbury Report), Committee on the Financial Aspects of Corporate Governance 1992 (UK).

European Union

European Commission, Non-Financial Reporting.

—— Environment: New timber regulation comes into force (Press release of 1 March 2013).

—— DG Environment, EUTR: Frequently Asked Questions.

—— DG Environment, Russian Federation Country Overview to Aid Implementation of the EUTR (2018).

—— DG Trade, Combatting Conflict Minerals (7 March 2019).

—— EU Emissions Trading System (EU ETS).

European Parliament, Outcomes of COP 22 climate change conference (2016).

International Organisations

CITES, Convention on International Trade in Endangered Species of Wild Fauna and Flora.

Codex Alimentarius 'Codex Alimentarius Commission'.

EIA, *Liquidating the Forests: Hardwood Flooring, Organised Crime and the World's Last Siberian Tigers* (2013).

FAO, *FAO LEX Database.*

—— *Global Forest Resources Assessment 2015. Desk reference* (2015).

—— Henson, S, and Humphrey, J, 'The Impacts of Private Food Safety Standards on the Food Chain and on Public Standard-setting Processes' FAO/ WHO Report (2009).

—— *Standard Material Transfer Agreement* (2004).

—— *Food Safety and Quality as Affected by Organic Farming* (22nd FAO Regional Conference for Europe, Porto, 24–28 July, 2000).

International Institute for Sustainable Development (IISD), *Global Green Standards, ISO 14000 and Sustainable Development*, Report (1996).

—— *ISO Social Responsibility Standardization*, Report (2004a).

—— *Issue Briefing Note: Stakeholder Engagement, ISO and Corporate Social Responsibility*, Report (2004b).

OECD, Activity F of the programme of work 2005–2006 *The Impacts of Private Voluntary Standards on Market Access*, 'Interaction of public and private standards in the food chain', Document AGR/CA/APM(2006)21/FINAL, 5–6.

—— *Glossary of Statistical Terms*, 'Intra-firm Trade'.
OIE, Wolff, C, and Scannell, M, 'Implication of Private Standards in International Trade of Animals and Animal Products' (2008) in *Proceedings of OIE 76th General Session of the Informal Committee.*
UN, 'Bases of discussion drawn up in 1929 by the Preparatory Committee of the Conference for the Codification of International Law (The Hague, 1930), in FV Garcia-Amador, Special Rapporteur on State responsibility, Extract from *the Yearbook of the International Law Commission*, vol II, A/CN.4/96, Annex B, 1956. E-United Nations Treaty Collection.
—— 'Questionnaire No 4 adopted by the League of Nations Committee of Experts for the progressive codification of international law, On 'Responsibility of States for damage done in their territories to the person or property of foreigners', in 'Report on International Responsibility' in FV Garcia-Amador, Special Rapporteur on State responsibility, Extract from *the Yearbook of the International Law Commission*, vol II, A/CN.4/96, Annex A, 1956. E-United Nations Treaty Collection.
—— UN Global Compact.
—— United Nations Statistics Division, UN Comtrade Database (2017).
UNCTAD, World Investment Report 1994: *Transnational Corporations, Employment and the Workforce.*
—— World Investment Report 1996: *Investment, Trade and International Policy Arrangements.*
—— World Investment Report 2002: *Transnational Corporations and Export Competitiveness.*
—— World Investment Report 2009: *Transnational Corporations, Agricultural Production and Development.*
—— World Investment Report 2011: *Non-Equity Modes of International Production and Development.*
UNEP-WCMC, *Protected Area Profile for the Russian Federation from the World Database of Protected Areas*, 2018.
World Bank, Global Value Chain Development Report 2019 *Technological Innovation, Supply Chain Trade and Workers in a Globalized World* (2019).
—— 'Doing Business Index'.
—— 'World Development Report 1996: From Plan to Market' (1996).
WTO, 'Communication from Bangladesh (on behalf of the LDC Group), Botswana, China, Cuba, Egypt, India, Indonesia, Kenya, Malaysia, Nigeria, Philippines, Tanzania, Uganda, Venezuela, Zambia and Zimbabwe' (2003), WT/GC/W/514 and Corr.1; WT/MIN(03)/W/4 (2003) (a Ministerial document that the WT/GC/W/514, (2003) became after having been formally reissued, with correction).
—— Committee on Sanitary and Phytosanitary Measures 'Effects of SPS-Related Private Standards' Descriptive Report – Note by the Secretariat, WTO Doc No WTO G/SPS/GEN/932 10.
—— Working Group on the Relationship between Trade and Investment 'Communication from China, Cuba, India, Kenya, Pakistan and Zimbabwe, "Investors' and Home Governments' Obligations"' WTO Doc WT/WGTI/W/152 (19 November 2002).
—— Working Group on the Relationship between Trade and Investment 'Communication from the European Community and its Member States, "Where are We on Foreign Investors' Behaviour?"' WTO Doc WT/WGTI/W/81 (20 September 1999).

Foreign Governments

Canada, Global Affairs Canada, 'Canada's National Contact Point for the Organisation for Economic Co-operation and Development Guidelines for Multinational Enterprises'.
France, 'La société est gérée dans son intérêt social et en prenant en considération les enjeux sociaux et environnementaux de son activité' *La proposition du gouvernement* (2018).
France, Ministry of Economy and Finance, Government Shareholdings Agency, 'The French State as Shareholder' (2012).
France, Ministry of Economy and Finance, DG Trésor, *Nouvelle loi sur le devoir de vigilance des sociétés mères et des entreprises donneuses d'ordre* (9 May 2017).
Russian Federation, Rosleskhoz, *Legal and Regulatory Documents*, last update 17 January 2020.

Russian Federation, Russian Federal Forestry Agency (*Рослесхоз* [Rosleskhoz]), *Claims* (2010).
Swedish Government, 'Swedish Seal Label'.
US Board of Governors of the Federal Reserve System, 'Financial Accounts of the United States. Flow of Funds, Balance Sheets, and Integrated Macroeconomic Accounts' Third Quarter 2019, Release of 12 December 2019.
US Customs and Border Protection, 'Basic Importing and Exporting' (4 March 2020) https://www.cbp.gov/trade/basic-import-export.
US Department of Labor, '2018 List of Goods Produced by Child Labor or Forced Labor'.
US Department of State (June 2019), 'Trafficking in Persons Report'.
US Department of State. Proposals for expansion of world trade and employment (Washington, Pub 2411, Commercial Policy Series 79, 1945).

Books

Agarwala, AN and Singh, SP (eds), *The Economics of Underdevelopment* (Bombay, Oxford University Press, Indian Branch, 1958).
Andrews, N, *Arbitration and Contract Law: Common Law Perspectives* (Cham, Springer International Publishing, 2016).
Baars, G, *The Corporation, Law and Capitalism: A Radical Perspective on the Role of Law in the Global Political Economy* (Boston, BRILL-Nijhoff, 2019).
Baars, G and Spicer, A (eds), *The Corporation, A Critical, Multi-Disciplinary Handbook* (Cambridge, Cambridge University Press, 2017).
Bainbridge, SM, *Corporate Governance After the Scandals and the Financial Crisis* (Oxford, Oxford University Press, 2012).
Basile, ME et al (eds), *Lex Mercatoria and Legal Pluralism: A Late Thirteenth Century Treaties and Its Aftermath* (Cambridge, Ames Foundation, 1998).
Baudouin, JL, *Les obligations* (Cowansville, Yvon Blais, 1989).
Bauman, JD, *Corporations, Law and Policy: Materials and Problems*, American Casebook, 7th edn (Eagan, West Academic Publishing, 2009).
Becker, HR, *Outsiders: Studies in Sociology of Deviance* (New York, The Free Press, 1963).
Beckers, A, *Enforcing Corporate Social Responsibility Codes: on Global Self-regulation and National Private Law* (Oxford, Hart Publishing, 2015).
Berger, KP, *The Creeping Codification of the New Lex Mercatoria*, 2nd edn (Zuidpoolsingel, Kluwer Law International, 2010).
Berle, A and Means, GC, *Modern Corporation and Private Property* (New York, Harcourt, Brace & World, 1968).
Bernaz, N, *Business and Human Rights. History, Law and Policy – Bridging the Accountability Gap* (Abingdon-on-Thames, Routledge, 2017).
Born, GB, *International Commercial Arbitration*, 2nd edn (The Hague, Wolters Kluwer, 2013).
—— *International Arbitration: Law and Practice*, 2nd edn (The Hague, Wolters Kluwer, 2016).
Born, GB and Rutledge, P, *International Civil Litigation in United States Courts*, 6th edn (The Hague, Wolters Kluwer, 2018).
Bourdieu, P, *Distinction: A Social Critique of the Judgment of Taste*, R Nice tr (Harvard, Harvard University Press, 1984).
Braithwaite, J, *Regulatory Capitalism. How it Works, Ideas for Making it Work Better* (Cheltenham, Edward Elgar, 2008).
Braithwaite, J, and Drahos, P, *Global Business Regulation* (Cambridge, Cambridge University Press, 2000).
Chayes, A and Chayes, AH, *The New Sovereignty: Compliance with International Regulatory Agreements* (Cambridge, Harvard University Press, 1995).

Coase, RH, *The Firm, the Market, and the Law* (Chicago, University of Chicago Press, 1990).
Cogolati, S and Wouters, J, (eds), *The Commons and a New Global Governance* (Cheltenham, Edward Elgar Publishing, 2018).
Cotterrell, R, *The Sociology of Law: An Introduction*, 2nd edn (Oxford, Butterworths, 1992).
—— *Émile Durkheim: Law in a Moral Domain* (Redwood, Stanford University Press, 1999).
Cremona, M, Hilpold, P, Lavranos, N, Staiger Schneider, S, and Ziegler, AR (eds), *Reflections on the Constitutionalisation of International Economic Law: Liber Amicorum for Ernst-Ulrich Petersmann* (Leiden, Martinus Nijhoff Publishers, 2014).
Dales, DH, *Pollution, Property & Prices: An Essay in Policy-making and Economics* (Northampton, Edward Edgar Publishing, 2002).
Deakin, S, Johnston, A and B Markesinis, *Markesinis and Deakin's Tort Law*, 7th edn (Oxford, Oxford University Press, 2013).
Deva, S and Bilchitz, D (eds), *Human Rights Obligations of Business: Beyond the Corporate Responsibility to Respect?* (Cambridge, Cambridge University Press, 2013).
Dolzer, R and Schreuer, C, *Principles of International Investment Law* (Oxford, Oxford University Press, 2008).
Dunoff JL, and Trachtman, JP (eds), *Ruling the World? Constitutionalism, International Law, and Global Governance* (Cambridge, Cambridge University Press, 2009).
Durkheim, E, *The Division of Labor in Society* (New York, Free Press, 1947).
—— *Les Formes élémentaires de la vie religieuse. Le système totémique en Australie* (Paris, Presses Universitaires de France, 1979).
—— *The Rules of Sociological Method and Selected Texts on Sociology and its Method* (London, Macmillan Publishers, 1982).
—— *Les règles de la méthode sociologique* (Paris, Flammarion, 1988).
Easterbrook, F and Fischel, D, *The Economic Structure of Corporate Law* (Cambridge, Harvard University Press, 1996).
Eichengreen, B, *The European Economy since 1945: Coordinated Capitalism and Beyond*, The Princeton Economic History of the Western World (Princeton, Princeton University Press, 2006).
Elliott, C and Quinn, F, *Tort Law*, 7th edn (Essex, Pearson, 2009).
Emneking, L, *Foreign Direct Liability and Beyond* (The Hague, Eleven International Publishing, 2012).
European Group on Tort Law, *Principles of European Tort Law. Text and Commentary* 1st ed. (Vienna, Springer, 2005).
Fallers, LA, *Law without Precedent* (Chicago, University of Chicago Press, 1969).
Fisher, R, *Improving Compliance with International Law* (Charlottesville, University Press of Virginia, 1981).
Friedman, LM, *The Legal System: A Social Science Perspective* (New York, Russel Sage Foundation, 1975).
Friedman, W, *The Changing Structure of International Law* (London, Stevens and Sons, 1964).
Gereffi, G and Korzeniewicz, M (eds), *Commodity Chains and Global Capitalism* (Westport, Connecticut, Praeger, 1994).
Gurvitch, G, *L'expérience juridique et la philosophie pluraliste du droit* (Paris, Pédone, 1935).
—— *Sociology of Law* (New Jersey, Transaction Publishers, 2001).
Hale, T, Held, D and Young, K, *Gridlock. Why global cooperation fails when we need it most* (Cambridge, Polity Press, 2013).
Hall, PA and Soskice, D (eds), *Varieties of Capitalism: The Institutional Foundations of Comparative Advantage* (Oxford, Oxford University Press, 2001).
Hannoun, C, *Le devoir de vigilance des sociétés mères et entreprises donneuses d'ordre après la loi du 27 mars 2017* (Paris, Dalloz, 2017).
Hayek, FA, *The Road to Serfdom* (Chicago, University of Chicago Press, 1944).
Hilty, R and Henning-Bodewig, F (eds), *Corporate Social Responsibility – Verbindliche Standards des Wettbewerbsrechts?* (Cham, Springer, 2014).
Horsey, K and Rackley, E, *Tort Law* (Oxford, Oxford University Press, 2009).

Hurst, JW, *The Legitimacy of the Business Corporation in the Law of the United States 1780–1970* (Charlottesville, The University Press of Virginia, 1970).
Ibbetson, DJ, *An Historical Introduction to the Law of Obligations* (Oxford, Oxford University Press, 1999).
Jacquet, JM, Delebecque, P and Corneloup, S, *Droit du commerce international* (Paris, Dalloz, 2007).
Kagan, RA, *Adversarial Legalism: The American Way of Law* (Cambridge, Harvard University Press, 2003).
Karavias, M, *Corporate Obligations under International Law* (Oxford, Oxford University Press, 2013).
Kassis, A, *Théorie Générale des usages du commerce: Droit comparé, contrats et arbitrage internationaux, lex mercatoria* (Paris, Librarie Générale de droit et de jurisprudence, 1984).
Kelsen, H, *General Theory of Law and State* (New York, Russell & Russell, 1961).
—— *The Pure Theory of Law*, M Knight tr (Berkeley, University of California Press, 1967).
Kimel, D, *From Promise to Contract. Towards a Liberal Theory of Contract* (Oxford, Hart Publishing, 2003).
Kolb, R, *Lessons from the Financial Crisis: Causes, Consequences, and Our Economic Future* (Hoboken, New Jersey, Wiley, 2010).
Kraakman, R, Armour, J, Davies, P, Enriques, L, Hansmann, H, Hertig, G, Hopt, K, Kanda, H and Rock, E, *The Anatomy of Corporate Law: A Comparative and Functional Approach*, 2nd edn (Oxford, Oxford University Press, 2009).
Leczykiewicz, D and Weatherill, S (eds), *The Images of the Consumer in EU Law: Legislation, Free Movement and Competition Law* (Oxford, Hart Publishing, 2016).
Lessig, L, *Code and Other Laws of Cyberspace* (New York, Basic Books, 1999).
Locke, RM, *The Promise and Limits of Private Power: Promoting Labor Standards in a Global Economy* (Cambridge, Cambridge University Press, 2013).
Lustig, D, *Veiled Power: International Law and the Private Business Corporation, 1886–1981* (Oxford, Oxford University Press, 2020).
McBarnet, D, Voiculescu, A and Campbell, T (eds), *The New Corporate Accountability. Corporate Social Responsibility and the Law* (Cambridge, Cambridge University Press, 2007).
Mańko, R, Cercel, CS and Sulikowski, A (eds), *Law and Critique in Central Europe: Questioning the Past, Resisting the Present* (Oxford, Counterpress, 2016).
Mattei, U, *Comparative Law and Economics* (Michigan, University of Michigan Press, 1998).
Ménard, CM and Shirley, MM (eds), *Handbook of New Institutional Economics* (New York, Springer, 2005).
Milhaupt, C and Pistor, K, *Law and Capitalism: What Corporate Crises Reveal about Legal Systems and Economic Development around the World* (Chicago, University of Chicago Press, 2008).
Morck, RK (ed), *A History of Corporate Governance around the World: Family Business Groups to Professional Managers*, National Bureau of Economic Research Conference Report (Chicago, Chicago University Press, 2005).
Morgan, J, *Contract Law Minimalism. A Formalist Restatement of Commercial Contract Law* (Cambridge, Cambridge University Press, 2013).
Moses, MS, *The Principles and Practice of International Commercial Arbitration* (Cambridge, Cambridge University Press, 2008).
Muchlinski, PT, *Multinational Enterprises and the Law*, 2nd edn (Oxford, Oxford University Press, 2007).
Newcombe, A and Paradell, L, *Law and Practice of Investment Treaties, Standards of Treatment* (Alphen aan den Rijn, Kluwer Law International, 2009).
Nolan, J and Baumann-Pauly, D (eds), *Business and Human Rights: From Principles to Practice* (Abingdon-on-Thames, Routledge, 2016).
Paiement, P, *Transnational Sustainability Laws* (Cambridge, Cambridge University Press, 2017).
Peterkova Mitkidis, K, *Sustainability Clauses in International Business Contracts* (The Hague, Eleven Publishing, 2015).
Petrazycki, LI, *Teoriya Prava i Gosudarstva v Svyazi s Teoriei Nravstvennosti* [Theory of Law and State in Connection with the Theory of Morality] (Moscow, Urait, 2018).
Porter, TM, *Trust in Numbers: The Pursuit of Objectivity in Science and Public Life* (Princeton, Princeton University Press, 1995).

Prahalad, CK and Doz, YL, *The Multinational Mission: Balancing Local Demands and Global Vision* (New York, Free Press, 1987).
Roe, MJ, *Strong Managers, Weak Owners: The Political Roots of American Corporate Finance* (Princeton, Princeton University Press, 1994).
Rousseau, D, *Psychological Contracts in Organizations: Understanding Written and Unwritten Agreements* (SAGE Publishing, 1995).
Rühmkorf, A, *Corporate Social Responsibility, Private Law and Global Supply Chains* (Cheltenham, Edward Elgar, 2015).
Salmon, A, *Les nouveaux empires: Fin de la démocratie?* (Paris, CNRS, 2011).
Schepel, H, *The Constitution of Private Governance: Product Standards in the Regulation of Integrated Markets* (Oxford, Hart Publishing, 2005).
Schneiderman, D, *Constitutionalizing Economic Globalization. Investment Rules and Democracy's Promise,* (Cambridge, Cambridge University Press, 2008).
Siems, M, *Comparative Law*, 2nd edn (Cambridge, Cambridge University Press, 2018).
Slaughter, AM, *A New World Order* (Princeton, Princeton University Press, 2004).
Soederberg, S, *Corporate Power and Ownership in Contemporary Capitalism* (Abingdon-on-Thames, Routledge, 2009).
Sornarajah, M, *The Pursuit of Nationalized Property* (Leiden, Martinus Nijhoff Publishers, 1986).
—— *The International Law on Foreign Investment* (Cambridge, Cambridge University Press, 4th edn, 2015).
Spier, J (ed), *Unification of Tort Law: Liability for Damage Caused by Others* (The Hague, Kluwer Law International, 2003).
Tamanaha, B, *A General Jurisprudence of Law and Society* (Oxford, Oxford University Press, 2001).
Timasheff, NS, *Law and Morality by Leon Petrazicki* (Cambridge, Harvard University Press, 1955).
Timoshina, EV (ed), *Petrazycki, Teoriya i Politika Prava. Izbrannie Trudi* [Petrazycki, Theory and Politics of Law] (Saint Petersburg, University Publishing Consortium Juridical Book, 2011).
Trevino, LK and Nelson, KA, *Managing Business Ethics* (New York, John Wiley & Sons, 2010).
Twining, WL, *Globalisation & Legal Theory* (Cambridge, Cambridge University Press, 2000).
Ulfbeck, V, Andhov, A and Mitkidis, K (eds), *Corporate Social Responsibility in Supply Chains: Contract and Tort - Interplay and Overlap* (Abingdon-on-Thames, Routledge, 2019).
VanGrasstek, C, *The History and Future of the World Trade Organization* (Geneva, WTO Publications, 2013).
Vogel, D, *Trading Up. Consumer and Environmental Regulation in a Global Economy* (Cambridge, Harvard University Press, 1995).
Vytopil, L, *Contractual Control in the Supply Chain. On Corporate Social Responsibility, Codes of Conduct and (Avoiding) Liability* (The Hague, Eleven International Publishing, 2015).
Wallerstein, I, *Historical Capitalism* (London, Verso, 1983).
Weber, M, *The Protestant Ethic and the Spirit of Capitalism* (London, Routledge, 1992).
Williamson, O, *The Economic Institutions of Capitalism* (New York, Free Press, 1985).
Zweigert, K and Kötz, H, *An Introduction to Comparative Law*, 3rd edn (Oxford, Oxford University Press, 1998).

Chapters in Edited Volumes

Arcuri, A, 'The TBT Agreement and Private Standards' in T Epps and MJ Trebilcock (eds), *Research Handbook on the WTO and Technical Barriers to Trade* (Northampton, Edward Edgar, 2013).
Aseeva, A, 'Global Trade Governance and Informal Voluntary Standards: The Socio-Normative Analysis of Legitimacy of the ISO' in A Tutumlu and G Gungor (eds), *Multilateralism in Global Governance: Formal and Informal Institutions* (Oxford, Peter Lang, 2016).
Aseeva, A, 'Développements récents en matière de la protection des droits de l'Homme et de l'environnement dans les chaines globales de valeur', in C Titi (ed), *Droits de l'homme et droit international économique* (Brussels, Bruylant, 2019).

Aseeva, A, 'Intergenerational Climate Justice' in T Cottier et al (eds), *Intergenerational Equity: Environmental and Cultural Concerns* (Boston, BRILL-Nihjoff, 2019).

Aseeva, A and KL Yip, 'Stakes and Prospects of the Right to Free, Prior & Informed Consent in 'One Belt One Road' Projects in the Context of Transnational Investment Law and Arbitration' in J Chaisse and J Górski (eds), *The Belt and Road Initiative. Law, Economics, and Politics* (Leiden, BRILL-Nijhoff Classics in International Law series, 2018).

Banakar, R, 'Who Needs the Classics? – On the Relevance of Classical Legal Sociology for the Study of Current Social and Legal Problems' in O Hammerslev and MR Madsen (eds), *Retssociologi* (Copenhagen, Hans Reitzels Forlag, 2012).

Bauman JD, 'Corporations, Law and Policy: Materials and Problems' in *American Casebook*, 7th edn (Eagan, West Academic Publishing, 2009).

Blanpain, R, 'Multinational Enterprises and Codes of Conduct, The OECD Guidelines for MNEs in Perspective' in R Blanplain (ed), *Comparative Labour Law and Industrial Relations in Industrialized Market Economies* (Alphen aan den Rijn, Kluwer Law International, 2004).

Boisson de Chazournes, L, 'Standards, régulation internationale et organisations internationales', in B Frydman and A Van Waeyenberge (eds), *Gouverner par les standards et les indicateurs: de Hume aux* rankings, (Brussels, Bruylant, 2014).

Bueno, N, 'The Swiss Popular Initiative on Responsible Business. From Responsibility to Liability' in LFH Enneking, I Giesen, FGH Kristen, L Roorda, CMJ Ryngaert, ALM Schaap (eds), *Accountability and International Business Operations: Providing Justice for Corporate Violations of Human Rights and Environmental Standards* (Abingdon-on-Thames, Routledge, 2020).

Cardwell, M, and Smith, F, 'Contemporary Problems of Climate change and the TBT Agreement: Moving Beyond Eco-labelling" in T Epps and MJ Treblicock (eds), *Research Handbook on the WTO and Technical Barriers to Trade* (Northampton, Edward Edgar, 2013).

Carroll, A, 'A History of Corporate Social Responsibility: Concepts and Practices' in A Crane, D Matten, A McWilliams, J Moon and DS Siegel (eds), *The Oxford Handbook of Corporate Social Responsibility* (Oxford, Oxford University Press, 2008).

Dos Santos, T, 'The Structure of Dependence' in KT Fann and DC Hodges (eds), *Readings in U.S. Imperialism* (Boston, Porter Sargent Publishers, 1971).

Eisenberg, MA, 'Relational Contract', in J Beatson and D Friedmann (eds), *Good Faith and Faith in Contract Law* (Oxford, Oxford University Press, 1995).

Foster, JW, 'The role of Non-Governmental Organisations and social movements in developing countries' in JJ Kirton and MJ Trebilcock (ed), *Hard Choices, Soft Law. Voluntary Standards in Global Trade, Environment and Social Governance* (Aldergate, Ashgate Publishing Limited, 2004).

Gereffi, G, and Korzeniewicz, M, 'Global Production Systems and Third World Development' in B Stallings (ed) *Global Change, Regional Response: The New International Context of Development* (Cambridge: Cambridge University Press, 1995).

Glinski, C, 'Bridging the Gap: the Legal Potential of Private Regulation' in O Dilling, M Herberg and G Winter, *Responsible Business: Self-governance and Law in Transnational Economic Transactions* (Oxford, Hart Publishing, 2008).

Goldman, B, 'The Applicable Law: General Principles of Law – the Lex Mercatoria' in JDM Lew (ed), *Contemporary Problems in International Arbitration* (London, The Eastern Press, 1987).

Gwendolyn, A, 'The Global Sullivan Principles' in N Cohen (ed), *Green Business: An A-to-Z Guide*, vol 5 (Thousand Oaks, Sage Publications, 2011).

Henson, S and Humphrey, J, 'Private Standards in Global Agri-food Chains' in A Marx, M Maertens, J Swinnen and J Wouters (eds.), *Private Standards and Global Governance. Economic, Legal, and Political Perspectives* (Northampton, Edward Elgar Publishing, 2012).

Herberg, M, 'Global Legal Pluralism and Interlegality. Environmental Self-Regulation in Multinational Enterprises as Global Law-Making' in O Dilling, M Herberg and G Winter (eds), *Responsible Business: Self-Governance and Law in Transnational Economic Transactions* (Oxford, Hart Publishing, 2008).

Howse, R, 'Consumer Labelling on Trial at the WTO: Misunderstanding the Behavioural Law and Economics of Consumer Information' in M Cremona, P Hilpold, N Lavranos, S Staiger Schneider, and AR Ziegler (eds), *Reflections on the Constitutionalisation of International Economic Law: Liber Amicorum for Ernst-Ulrich Petersmann* (Leiden, Martinus Nijhoff Publishers, 2014).

Hydén, H, 'Looking at the world through the lenses of norms' in K Papendorf, S Machura and K Andenaes (eds), *Understanding Law in Society, Developments in Socio-legal Studies* (Münster, LIT Verlag, 2011).

Jenks, W, 'Multinational Entities and the Law of Nations' in W Friedman (ed), *Transnational Law in a Changing Society. Essays in Honor of Philip C. Jessup* (New York, Columbia University Press, 1972).

Kennedy, D, 'Law-and-Economics from the Perspective of Critical Legal Studies' in P Newman (ed), *The New Palgrave Dictionary of Economics and the Law* (London, Palgrave Macmillan UK, 1998).

—— 'Legal Formalism' in N J Smelser and P B Baltes (eds), *Encyclopaedia of the Social and Behavioural Sciences*, vol 13 (Amsterdam, Elsevier, 2001).

Kocher, E, 'Codes of Conduct and Framework Agreements on Social Minimum Standards – Private Regulation?' in O Dilling, M Herberg and G Winter (eds), *Responsible Business: Self-governance and Law in Transnational Economic Transactions* (Oxford, Hart Publishing, 2008).

Kreitner, K, 'Multiplicity in Contract Remedies', in N Cohen and E McKendrick (eds), *Comparative Remedies for Breach of Contract* (Oxford, Hart Publishing, 2005).

Lagoutte, S, 'The UN Guiding Principles on Business and Human Rights. A Confusing 'Smart Mix' of Soft and Hard International Human Rights Law' in S Lagoutte and JC Gammeltoft-Hansen (eds), *Tracing the Roles of Soft Law in Human Rights* (Oxford, Oxford University Press, 2016).

Marx, A, Maertens, M, Swinnen, J and Wouters, J, 'Introduction: Private Standards and Global Governance in A Marx, M Maertens, J Swinnen and J Wouters (eds), *Private Standards and Global Governance. Economic, Legal, and Political Perspectives* (Northampton, Edward Elgar Publishing, 2012).

Mertens, HJ, 'Lex Mercatoria: A Self-appying Beyond National Law?', in G Teubner (ed), *Global Law Without a State* (London, Dartmouth Publishing Co Ltd, 1997).

Muchlinski, PT, 'Global Bukowina' Examined: Viewing the Multinational Enterprise as a Transnational Law- making Community' in G Teubner (ed), *Global Law Without a State* (London, Dartmouth Publishing Co Ltd, 1997).

Muir Watt, H, 'Les enjeux de l'affaire Kiobel: le chaînon manquant dans la mise en oeuvre de la responsabilité des entreprises multinationales en droit international public et privé' [2010–2012] *Travaux du Comité Français de Droit International Privé* (Paris, LGDJ, 2013).

Newton, S, 'The Dialectics of Law and Development' in DM Trubek and A Santos (eds), *The New Law and Economic Development: a Critical Appraisal* (Oxford, Hart Publishing, 2006).

Reardon, T, Stamoulis, K, Balisacan, A, Cruz, ME, Berdegue, J and Banks, B, 'Rural Nonfarm Income in Developing Countries' in *The State of Food and Agriculture* (Rome, United Nations Food and Agriculture Organization, 1998).

Reiner, C and Schreuer, CH, 'Human Rights and International Investment Arbitration', in PM Dupuy, EU Petersmann and F Francioni (eds) *Human Rights in International Investment Law* (Oxford, Oxford University Press, 2009).

Riffard, JF, 'La mutation de la norme: l'avènement d'un droit nivelé? Ou retour sur quelques aspects de l'unification et la globalisation des droits' in N Martial-Braz, JF Riffard and M Béhar-Touchais (eds), *Les mutations de la norme* (Paris, Economica, 2011).

Robé, JP, 'Multinational Enterprises: the Constitution of a Pluralistic Legal Order' in G Teubner (ed), *Global Law without a State* (London, Dartmouth Publishing Co, 1997).

Ruiz Fabri, H, 'Regulating Trade, Investment and Money' in J Crawford and M Koskenniemi (ed), *The Cambridge Companion to International Law* (Cambridge, Cambridge University Press, 2012).

Stanton, GH, 'Food Safety-related Private Standards: The WTO Perspective' in A Marx, M Maertens, J Swinnen and J Wouters (eds), *Private Standards and Global Governance. Economic, Legal, and Political Perspectives* (Northampton, Edward Elgar Publishing, 2012).

Stone, K, 'Globalization and the Middle Class' in G de Burca, C Kilpatrick and J Scott (eds), *Critical Legal Perspectives on Global Governance* (Oxford, Hart Publishing, 2013).

Svensson, M, 'Norms in Law and Society: Towards a Definition of the Socio-Legal Concept of Norms' in M Baier (ed), *Social and Legal Norms* (London, Ashgate Publishing, 2013).

Svensson, M, Larsson, S and de Kaminski, M, 'The Research Bay – Studying the global file sharing community' in B Gallagher and D Halbert (eds), *IP in Context: Law and Society Perspectives on Intellectual Property* (Cambridge, Cambridge University Press, 2013).

Teubner, G, '"Global Bukowina": Legal Pluralism in World Society' in G Teubner (ed), *Global Law without a State* (London, Dartmouth Publishing Co, 1997).

Thomsen, S, 'Convergence of Corporate Governance during the Stock Market Bubble: Towards Anglo-American or European Standards?' in A Grandori (ed), *Corporate Governance and Firm Organization: Microfoundations and Structural Forms* (Oxford, Oxford University Press, 2004).

Van Waarden, F, 'Governing Global Commons: The Public-Private Protection of Fish and Forests', in Marx, M Maertens, J Swinnen and J Wouters (eds), *Private Standards and Global Governance. Economic, Legal, and Political Perspectives* (Northampton, Edward Elgar Publishing, 2012).

Verbruggen, P, 'Private Regulatory Standards in Commercial Contracts: Questions of Compliance' in R Brownsword, R van Gestel and H Micklitz (eds), *Contract and Regulation: A Handbook on New Methods of Law Making in Private Law* (Cheltenham, Edward Elgar, 2017).

Wouters, J, Marx, A, and Hachez, N, 'Private Standards, Global Governance and International Trade: The Case of Global Food Safety Governance' in A Marx, M Maertens, J Swinnen and J Wouters, J (eds), *Private Standards and Global Governance. Economic, Legal, and Political Perspectives* (Northampton, Edward Elgar Publishing, 2012).

Articles

Abbott KW, and Snidal, D, 'Strengthening International Regulation through Transnational New Governance: Overcoming the Orchestration Deficit' (2009) 42 *Vanderbilt Journal of Transnational Law* 501.

Amsler, C, Bartlett, R and Bolton, C, 'Thoughts of Some British Economists on Early Limited Liability and Corporate Legislation' (1981) 13(4) *History of Political Economy* 774.

Arrighi G, and Drangel, J, 'The Stratification of the World-economy' (1986) 10 *Review* 9.

Aseeva, A, '(Un)Sustainable Development(s) in International Economic Law: a Quest for Sustainability' (2018) 10(11) *Sustainability* 4022.

Bainbridge, SM, 'Director Primacy in Corporate Takeovers: Preliminary Reflections' (2002) 55 *Stanford Law Review* 791.

Bair, J, 'Global Capitalism and Commodity Chains: Looking Back, Going Forward' (2005) 9 *Competition and Change* 153.

Bilchitz, D, 'The Necessity for a Business and Human Rights Treaty' (2016) 1(2) *Business and Human Rights Journal* 203.

Boisson de Chazournes, L, Casini, L, and Kingsbury, B (eds), 'Symposium on Global Administrative Law in the Operations of International Organizations' (2009) 6 *International Organizations Law Review* 315.

Bonnitcha, J and McCorquodale, R, 'The Concept of 'Due Diligence' in the UN Guiding Principles on Business and Human Rights' (2017) 28 *European Journal of International Law* 899.

Braithwaite, J, et al, 'Can Regulation and Governance Make a Difference?' (2007) 1 *Regulation & Governance* 1.

Calabresi, G, 'Some Thoughts on Risk Distribution and the Law of Torts' (1961) 70 *Yale Law Journal* 499.

Carlin, W and Mayer, C, 'Finance, Investment and Growth' (2003) 69 *Journal of Financial Economics* 191.

Cass, DZ, 'The 'Constitutionalization' of International Trade Law: Judicial Norm-Generation as the Engine of Constitutional Development in International Trade' (2001) 12 *European Journal of International Law* 39.

Cassese, S, 'Administrative Law Without the State? The Challenge of Global Regulation' (2005) 37 *NYU Journal of International Law and Politics* 663.

—— 'Global Standards for National Administrative Procedure' (2005) 68 *Law and Contemporary Problems* 109.

Cernic, LJ, 'Corporate Responsibility for Human Rights: A Critical Analysis of the OECD Guidelines for Multinational Enterprises' (2008) 3 *Hanse Law Review.*

Chayes, A and Chayes, AH, 'On Compliance' (1993) 47 *International Organization* 175.

Coase, RH, 'The Nature of the Firm' (1937) 4 *Economica* 386.

—— 'The Problem of Social Cost' (1960) *Journal of Law and Economics* 3.

—— 'The New Institutional Economics' (1998) 88 *American Economic Review* 72.

Coffee Jr, JC, 'The Rise of Dispersed Ownership: The Roles of Law and the State in the Separation of Ownership and Control' (2001) 111 *Yale Law Journal* 1.

Colvin, E, 'The Sociology of Secondary Rules' (1978) 28 *University of Toronto Law Journal* 196.

Cotterrell, R, 'Rethinking 'Embeddedness': Law, Economy, Community' (2013) 40 *Journal of Law and Society* 49.

—— 'Spectres of Transnationalism: Changing Terrains of Sociology of Law' (2009) 36 *Journal of Law and Society* 481.

—— 'What is Transnational Law?' (2012) 37 *Law & Social Inquiry* 500.

Danielsen, D, 'Economic Approaches To Global Regulation: Expanding The International Law And Economics Paradigm' (2011) 10 *Journal of International Business & Law* 28.

De Hoon, MW and Mak, V, 'Consumer Empowerment Strategies – A Rights-Oriented Approach versus a Needs-Oriented Approach' (2011) 19 *Zeitschrift für Europäisches Privatrecht* 518.

De Schutter, O, 'Towards a New Treaty on Business and Human Rights' (2016) 1 *Business and Human Rights Journal* 41.

Delbard, O, 'CSR legislation in France and the European regulatory paradox: An analysis of EU CSR policy and sustainability reporting practice' (2008) 8 *Corporate Governance International Journal of Business in Society* 397.

Deva, S, 'Guiding Principles on Business and Human Rights: Implications for Companies' (2012) 9(2) *European Company Law* 101.

Dunoff, JL, 'Why Constitutionalism Now? Text, Context and the Historical Contingency of Ideas' (2005) 1 *Journal of International Law & International Relations* 191.

Edelman, LB, Fuller, SR, and Mara-Drita, I, 'Diversity Rhetoric and the Managerialization of Law' (2001) 106 *American Journal of Sociology* 1589.

Eisenberg, A, 'Actual and virtual specific performance' (2005) 93 *California Law Review* 975, 998.

Esty, DC, 'Good Governance at the Supranational Scale: Globalizing Administrative Law' (2006) 115 *Yale Law Journal* 1490.

Fischer-Lescano, A and Teubner, G 'Regime Collisions: The Vain Search for Legal Unity in the Fragmentation of Global Law' (2004) 25 *Michigan Journal of International* Law 999.

Frank, AG, 'The Development of Underdevelopment' (September 1966) *Monthly Review* 17.

—— 'The Sociology of Development and the Underdevelopment of Sociology' (1967) *Catalyst* 20.

French, PA, 'The Corporation as a Moral Person' (1979) 16(3) *American Philosophical Quarterly* 207.

Friedman, LM, 'Is there a Modern Legal Culture?' (1994) 7 *Ratio Juris* 117.

Gereffi, G, 'Global Value Chains and International Competition' (2011) 56 *The Antitrust Bulletin* 37.

—— 'A Global Value Chain Perspective on Industrial Policy and Development in Emerging Markets' (2014) 24 *Duke Journal of Comparative and International Law* 433.

Gereffi, G, Humphrey, J, and Sturgeon, T, 'The Governance of Global Value Chains' (2005) 12 *Review of International Political Economy* 78.

Grundhauser, JH, 'Case Note. The DES Manufacturer Identification Problem: A Florida Public Policy Approach' (1986) 40 *University of Miami Law Review* 857.

Guzman, AT, 'A Compliance-Based Theory of International Law' (2002) 90 *California Law Review* 1826.

Hallberg, L and Pöpke, T, 'Liability for damages due to export of toxic waste: final ruling' (2019) *International Law Office.*

Hansmann, H and Kraakman, R, 'The Essential Role of Organizational Law' (2000) 110 *Yale Law Journal* 387.

—— 'The End of History for Corporate Law' (2001) 89 *Georgetown Law Journal* 439.
Harlow, C, 'Global Administrative Law: The Quest for Principles and Values' (2006) 17(1) *European Journal of International Law* 187.
Harlow, C and Rawlings, R, 'Promoting accountability in multilevel governance: A network approach' (2007) 13 *European Law Journal* 542.
Henson, S and Northern, J, 'Economic Determinants of Food Safety Controls in the Supply of Retailer Own Branded Products in the UK' (1998) 14 *Agribusiness* 113.
Holderness, CG, 'The Myth of Diffuse Ownership in the United States' (2009) 22 *The Review of Financial Studies* 1377.
Holmes, OW, 'The Path of the Law' (1897) 10 *Harvard Law Review* 457.
Holvoet, B, and Muys, B, 'Sustainable Forest Management Worldwide: a Comparative Assessment of Standards' (2004) 6 *International Forestry Review* 99.
Hopkins, T and Wallerstein, I, 'Patterns of development of the modern world-system' (1977) 1 *Review* 111.
—— 'Commodity Chains in the World Economy Prior to 1800' (1986) 10 *Review* 157.
Hughes, J, 'What Value Creation Will Look Like in the Future' *Harvard Business Review* (17 May 2013).
Humphrey, J and Schmitz, H, 'Governance in Global Value Chains' (2001) 32 *IDS Bulletin*.
Hydén, H and Svensson, M, 'The Concept of Norms in Sociology of Law' (2008) 53 *Scandinavian Studies in Law* 15.
Jacoby, SM, 'Corporate Governance in Comparative Perspective: Prospects for Convergence' (2001) *SSRN Electronic Journal*.
Kahan, M and Rock, EB, 'Hedge Funds in Corporate Governance and Corporate Control' (2007) 155 *University of Pennsylvania Law Review* 1021.
Kerr, M, 'International Arbitration v. Litigation' (1980) 24 *JBL* 164.
Kingsbury, B, Krisch, N and Stewart, RB, 'The Emergence of Global Administrative Law' (2005) 68 *Law & Contemporary Problems* 15.
Koskenniemi M and Leino, P, 'Fragmentation of International Law? Postmodern Anxieties' (2002) 15 *Leiden Journal of International Law* 553.
Krisch, N and Kingsbury, B, 'Introduction: Global Governance and Global Administrative Law in the International Legal Order' (2006) 17 *European Journal of International Law* 1.
La Porta, R, de Silanes, FL and Shleifer, A, 'Corporate Ownership Around the World' (1998) 54 *Journal of Finance* 471.
Lockwood, JE, and Schmeisser, WC, 'Restrictive Business Practices in International Trade' (1946) 11 *Law and Contemporary Problems* 663.
Gray, CW, 'In Search of Owners: Privatization and Corporate Governance in Transition Economies' (1996) *World Bank Research Observer* 179.
Long, C, 'After Rana Plaza' *Jacobin* (16 June 2014).
Macneil, IR, 'The Many Futures of Contract' (1974) 47 *Southern California Law Review* 691.
Maniruzzaman, AFM, 'State Contracts in Contemporary International law: Monist versus Dualist Controversies' (2001) 12 *European Journal of International Law* 309.
Markesinis, B, 'An Expanding Tort Law–The Price of a Rigid Contract Law' (1987) 103 *Law Quarterly Review* 354.
Muir Watt, H, 'L'Alien Tort Statute devant la Cour suprême des États-Unis, territorialité, diplomatie judiciaire, ou économie politique ?' (2013) *Revue critique de droit international privé* 595.
Nemeth, JN and Smith, DA, 'International Trade and World-System Structure: A Multiple Network Analysis' (1985) 8 *Review (Fernand Braudel Center) Quantitative Studies of the World-System* 517.
Nonet, Ph, 'For Jurisprudential Sociology' (1976) 10 *Law & Society Review* 525.
O'Connor, M, 'Labor's Role in the American Corporate Governance Structure' (2000) 22 *Comparative Labor Law & Policy Journal* 97.
Ohnesorge, JKM, 'Developing Development Theory: Law and Development Orthodoxies and the Northeast Asian Experience' (2007) 28 *University of Pennsylvania Journal of International Economic Law* 219.
Ostřanský, J, 'The Termination and Suspension of Bilateral Investment Treaties due to an Armed Conflict' (2015) 6 *Journal of International Dispute Settlement* 136.

Payne, J, 'Private Equity and Its Regulation in Europe' (2011) 12(4) *European Business Organization Law Review* 559.
Peterkova Mitkidis, K, 'Sustainability Clauses in International Supply Chain Contracts: Regulation, Enforceability and Effects of Ethical Requirements' (2014) *Nordic Journal of Commercial Law* 1.
Pietrobelli, C, and Rabellotti, R, 'Global Value Chains Meet Innovation Systems: Are There Learning Opportunities for Developing Countries?' (2011) 39 *World Development* 1261.
Prebisch, R, 'Le développement économique de l'Amérique latine et ses principaux problèmes' (1962) New-York: United Nations, reprinted in *Economic Bulletin for Latin America* (7 February 1962) 1.
Riviere, A, 'The Future of Hedge Fund Regulation: A Comparative Approach: United States, United Kingdom, France, Italy, and Germany' (2011) 10 *Richmond Journal of Global Law & Business* 263.
Rott, P and Ulfbeck, V, 'Supply Chain Liability of Multinational Corporations?' (2015) 23(3) *European Review of Private Law* 415.
Ruggie, JG and Sherman, JF III, 'The Concept of 'Due Diligence' in the UN Guiding Principles on Business and Human Rights: Reply to Professors Bonnitcha and Mccorquodale' (2017) 28 *European Journal of International Law* 921.
Russell, RM, 'Note. The Causation Requirement: Guardian of Fairness or Obstacle to Justice?-Making Sense of a Decade of DES Litigation' (1991) 25 *Suffolk University Law Review* 1071.
Sako, M and Helper, S, 'Determinants of Trust in Supplier Relations: Evidence from the Automotive Industry in Japan and the United States' (1998) 34 *Journal of Economic Behavior and Organization* 387.
Salminen, J, 'The Accord on Fire and Building Safety in Bangladesh: A New Paradigm for Limiting Buyers' Liability in Global Supply Chains?' (2018) 66 *AJCL* 411.
—— 'From Product Liability to Production Liability: Modelling a Response to the Liability Deficit of Global Value Chains on Historical Transformations of Production' (2019) 23 *Competition and Change* 420.
Salminen, J and Rajavuori, M, 'Transnational sustainability laws and the regulation of global value chains: Comparison and a framework for analysis' (2020) 26(5) *Maastricht Journal of European and Comparative Law* 602.
Schneiderman, D, 'Constitutional Approaches To Privatization: An Inquiry Into The Magnitude Of Neo- Liberal Constitutionalism' (2001) 63 *Law and Contemporary Problems* 83.
Sethi, SP, 'Dimensions of Corporate Social Performance: An Analytic Framework' (1975) 17 *California Management Review* 58.
Simons, P, 'International Law's Invisible Hand and the Future of Corporate Accountability for Violations of Human Rights' (2012) 3(1) *Journal of Human Rights and the Environment* 5.
Sjåfjell, B and Taylor, M, 'Clash of Norms: Shareholder Primacy vs. Sustainable Corporate Purpose' (2019) 13(3) *International and Comparative Corporate Law Journal* 40.
Slaughter, AM, and Burke-White, W, 'An International Constitutional Moment' (2002) 43 *Harvard International Law Journal* 1.
Stumpff Morrison, A, 'Case Law, Systematic Law, and a Very Modest Suggestion' (2013) 35(2) *Statute Law Review* 159.
Svensson, M and Larsson, S, 'Intellectual Property Law Compliance in Europe: Illegal File Sharing and the Role of Social Norms' (2012) 14 *New Media Society* 1147.
Swire, P, 'Safe Harbors and a Proposal to Improve the Community Reinvestment Act' (1993) 79 *Virginia Law Review* 349.
Sydow, J, Fichter, M, Helfen, M, Sayim, KZ and Stevis, D, 'Implementation of Global Framework Agreements: Towards a Multi-organizational Practice Perspective' (2014) 20(4) *Transfer: European Review of Labour and Research* 489.
Tenbrunsel, AE, Smith-Crowe, K and Umphress, EE, 'Building Houses on Rocks: The Role of the Ethical Infrastructure in Organizations' (2003) 16(3) *Social Justice Research* 285.
Terwindt, C, Leader, S, Yilmaz-Vastardis, A and Wright, J, 'Supply chain liability: Pushing the boundaries of the common law?' (2017) 8(3) *Journal of European Tort Law* 261.
Thomsen, S, 'Should Private Equity Be Regulated?' (2009) 10(1) *European Business Organization Law Review* 97.
Twining, WL, 'A Post-Westphalian Conception of Law' (2003) 37 *Law and Society Review* 199.

—— 'Diffusion of Law: a Global Perspective' (2004) 49 *Journal of Legal Pluralism* 1.
—— 'Social Science and Diffusion of Law' (2005) 32 *Journal of Law & Society* 203.
—— 'Legal Pluralism and Normative Pluralism: A Global Perspective' (2010) 20 *Duke Journal of Comparative and International Law* 472.
Ulfbeck, V and Ehlers, A, 'Tort Law, Corporate Groups and Supply Chain Liability for Workers' Injuries: The Concept of Vicarious Liability' (2016) 13 *European Company Law* 167.
Van Dam, C, 'Tort Law and Human Rights: Brothers in Arms on the Role of Tort Law in the Area of Business and Human Rights' (201) 2 *Journal of European Tort Law* 221.
Vidak-Gojkovic, E, Blair, C et al, 'The Medium Is the Message: Establishing a System of Business and Human Rights Through Contract Law and Arbitration' 35(4) *Journal of International Arbitration* 2018.
Vogel, D, 'The Private Regulation of Global Corporate Conduct. Achievements and Limitations' (2010) 49 *Business & Society* 77.
Von Bogdandy, A, Goldmann, M, and Dann, Ph, 'Developing the Publicness of Public International Law: Towards a Legal Framework for Global Governance Activities' (2008) 9 *German Law Journal*, 1375.
Wallerstein, I, 'The Rise and Future Demise of the World Capitalist System: Concepts for Comparative Analysis' (1974) 16 *Comparative Studies in Society and History* 387.
Williams, CA and Conley, JM, 'An Emerging Third Way – The Erosion of the Anglo-American Shareholder Value Construct' (2005) 38 *Cornell International Law Journal* 493.
Wojcik, D, 'Change in the German Model of Corporate Governance: Evidence from Blockholdings 1997–2001' (2003) 35 *Environment and Planning A: Economy and Space* 1431.
Wolff, RD, 'Economic Development and Rana Plaza' *Monthly Review* (16 May 2013).
Zumbansen, P, 'Transnational Leal Pluralism' (2010) 1 *Transnational Legal Theory* 141.

Research and Working Papers

Aerni, P, 'Do Private Standards Encourage or Hinder Innovation?' (2013) 18 *NCCR Trade Working Paper*.
Banakar, R, 'The Sociology of Law: From Industrialisation to Globalisation' (2011) *University of Westminster School of Law Research Paper* No 11-03, 2011.
Becker, T, 'The Economics of Food Quality Standards' *Workshop paper presented to Second Interdisciplinary Workshop on Standardisation Research Hamburg* (24–27 May 1999).
Cernic, LJ, 'The 2011 Update of the OECD Guidelines for Multinational Enterprises' (2012) 16 *American Society of International Law Insights*.
Davis, KE, Kingsbury, B and Engle Merry, S, 'Indicators as a Technology of Global Governance' (2010) *NYU IILJ Working Paper* 2010/2 (Global Administrative Law Series).
De Schutter, O, 'Transnational Corporations and Human Rights' (2005) *Global Law Working Paper* 01/05.
Frydman, B, 'Prendre les standards et les indicateurs au sérieux' (2013) 4 *Working Papers du Centre Perelman de Philosophie du Droit*.
Hatto, P, for the European Commission, 'Standards and Standardisation. A Practical Guide for Researchers' (2010).
KPMG International Cooperative, *The KPMG Survey of Corporate Responsibility Reporting 2017* (2017).
Kudryavtsev, A, 'Private Standardization and International Trade in Goods: Any WTO Law Implications for Domestic Regulation?' *Society of International Economic Law Working Paper* (2012).
Peterson, LE and Gray, KR, 'International Human Rights in Bilateral Investment Treaties and Investment Treaty Arbitration', (2005) *IISD Research Paper for the Swiss Department of Foreign Affairs*.
Quadros, R, 'Global Quality Standards, Chain Governance and the Technological Upgrading of Brazilian Auto-components producers' (May 2002) *IDS Working Paper* 156 Brighton: IDS-Sussex.
Stanton, GH, 'Private (Commercial) Standards and the SPS Agreement' (24 September 2007) *Remarks at The Round Table on The Role of Standards in International Food Trade*, The Cosmos Club, Washington, D.C.

Strange, S, 'What theory? The theory in Mad Money' (1998) *CSGR Working Paper* No 18/98.
Ulfbeck, V, 'Vicarious Liability in Groups of Companies and in Supply Chains – Is Competition Law Leading the Way?' (December 5, 2019) *CEVIA Working Paper Series*, Issue 4.
University of Amsterdam and KPMG Global Sustainability Services, *KPMG International Survey of Corporate Responsibility Reporting 2005* (2005).
Yates, Y and Murphy, CN, 'Coordinating International Standards: The Formation of the ISO' (2007) *MIT Sloan Research Paper* No4638-07.

Newspapers and Blogs

Aatreya, SS, '"Private" Breaches of International Law: Lessons from Domestic Courts for International Investment Law' *OpinioJuris* (4 March 2020).
Alford, R, Arbitrating Bangladesh Labor Rights (Part II).
Amnesty International, R Ying and T Morlier, 'Entreprises: L'histoire d'une loi contre les violations des droits humains' (2017) *Amnesty France.*
Bernaz, N, 'Clearer, Stronger, Better? – Unpacking the 2019 Draft Business and Human Rights Treaty' (19 July 2019), *Rights as Usual.*
Burk, J, 'Rana Plaza: one year on from the Bangladesh factory disaster' *The Guardian* (19 April 2014).
Business & Human Rights Resource Centre, 'Samsung Lawsuit'.
—— 'Advocacy through the Courts'.
—— 'EU-wide Due Diligence Regulation'.
—— 'Open for Sign-on: Statement on the Investor Case for Mandatory Human Rights Due Diligence'.
—— 'Largest forestry companies are failing to combat forced labour in their supply chains'.
—— the *KnowTheChain* project.
Cassel, D, 'Five ways the new draft treaty on business and human rights can be strengthened' *Business & Human Rights Resource Centre* (9 September 2019).
Center for International Legal Cooperation (CILC), 'The Hague Rules on Business and Human Rights' (12 December 2019).
Forest Legality Initiative (FLI), Report *Russian Federation*, 2016.
Guntrip, E, 'Urbaser v Argentina: The Origins of a Host State Human Rights Counterclaim in ICSID Arbitration?', *EJIL: Talk!* (10 February 2017).
Hautala, H, 'EU is Well Placed to Show Leadership with its Future Due Diligence Legislation', personal blog (27 May 2020).
Jarry, E and Rosemain, M, 'Plainte contre Samsung en France pour pratiques trompeuses' Reuters (2018).
Kaye, L, 'U.S. Court Dismisses Rana Plaza Lawsuit' (9 May 2015) TRIPLE PUNDIT.
Le Figaro, 'Areva gagne contre un salarié au Niger' (25 October 2013).
Locke, RM, 'Private efforts to improve global working conditions have failed' *Boston Review* (21 May 2013).
Mollah, S, and Bin Habib, W, 'It crumbles like a pack of cards' *The Daily Star* (25 April 2013).
Mullen, M, 'Keeping Perspective – Article 30 Commentary on the Revised Draft of the Proposed BHR Treaty', *Business & Human Rights Resource Centre.*
MVO Platform, 'Update: Frequently Asked Questions about the new Dutch Child Labour Due Diligence Law' (3 June 2019).
NEPCon (Nature Economy and People Connected), *Timber Legality Risk Assessment: Russia, 2017.*
Nowak, L, Poell, J, Hood, P and Jennett, JH, 'Supply chain liability under the law of negligence: What does Jabir and Others v KiK Textilien und Non-Food GmbH mean for European companies with supply chains in the sub-continent and other common law countries?' HLR Regulation (2018).
—— 'Jabir and others v. KiK Textilien und Non-Food GmbH Dortmund court dismisses lawsuit' HLR Regulation (2019).
Poole, J and Millan Lombrana, L, 'Nevsun Finds a White Knight in Zijin With $1.41 Billion Deal', *Bloomberg* (5 September 2018).

Quijano, G, 'A new draft Business and Human Rights treaty and a promising direction of travel' *Business & Human Rights Resource Centre.*
Renew Europe Group, 'EU must be United at the COP 25 in Madrid' *Renew Europe Group.*
Rushe, D, 'Unions Reach $2.3m Settlement on Bangladesh Textile Factory Safety', *The Guardian* (22 January 2018).
Swoffer, K, 'GFSI and the Relationship with Codex' (2009) *Presentation made at CIES international Food Safety Conference*, Paris.
Van Calster, G, 'Jabir and others v. KiK Textilien und Non-Food GmbH. German court kicks supply chain CSR litigation into the long grass. Questions on Statutes of limitation under Rome II left out in the open' *GAVC Law* (2019).
Yilmaz-Vastardis, A, 'Vedanta v. Lungowe Symposium: Potential Implications of the UKSC's Decision for Supply Chain Relationships' *OpinioJuris* (23 April 2019).

Miscellaneous

About the Alliance for Bangladesh Worker Safety.
Alliance for Bangladesh Worker Safety, 'Who we are'.
Alliance, FAQ, 'Is the Alliance Legally Binding?'.
Blue Angel, 'Products'.
Carbontrust, 'Carbon Trust'.
DGCRRF, 'Resoudre un litige de consommation'.
—— 'Sanctions'.
Fair Trade, 'Fair Trade'.
Fair Trade, 'History of Fair Trade'.
Forum pour l'investissement responsable, 'Chaîne d'approvisionnement et investissement responsable'.
FSC, 'FSC'.
GAA Alliance, 'Best Aquaculture Practice'.
GDF Suez's 'Global Agreement on Fundamental Rights, Social Dialogue and Sustainable Development' (2010).
GLOBAL G.A.P, 'About Us'.
Global Social Compliance Program, 'GSC'.
International Food Standard, 'Certification'.
ISEAL, 'About us'.
ISEAL, 'Our work'.
ISO, 'ISO 14000'.
—— 'ISO 14020: 2000'.
—— 'ISO 26000'.
—— 'Report to ISO COPOLCO on Desirability and Feasibility of ISO CSR Standards' (2002).
——'What is Conformity Assessment?'.
Label Rouge, 'Label Rouge'.
Lafarge's Global Framework Agreement on Corporate Social Responsibility and International Industrial Relations (2013).
Marks & Spencer, 'Marks & Spencer Carbon Labelling Scheme'.
MSC, 'MSC'.
Nordic Ecolabel, 'Nordic Ecolabel'.
Safe Quality Food, 'Services'.
Tesco, 'Tesco Nature's Choice'.
Thyssenkrupp's International Framework Agreement (2016).

INDEX

Lightning Source UK Ltd.
Milton Keynes UK
UKHW021318101121
393710UK00003B/76

9 781509 930579